GOVERNING CITIES IN A GLOBAL ERA

URBAN INNOVATION, COMPETITION, AND DEMOCRATIC REFORM

Edited by

Robin Hambleton and Jill Simone Gross

First published in 2007 by
PALGRAVE MACMILLAN™
175 Fifth Avenue, New York, N.Y. 10010 and
Houndmills, Basingstoke, Hampshire, England RG21 6XS.
Companies and representatives throughout the world.

PALGRAVE MACMILLAN is the global academic imprint of the Palgrave Macmillan
division of St. Martin's Press, LLC and of Palgrave Macmillan Ltd. Macmillan® is a
registered trademark in the United States, United Kingdom and other countries.
Palgrave is a registered trademark in the European Union and other countries.

ISBN-13: 978-0-230-60230-4   (paper back)
ISBN-10: 0-230-60230-4   (paper back)
ISBN-13: 978-1-4039-7573-7   (hard cover)
ISBN-10: 1-4039-7573-6   (hard cover)

Library of Congress Cataloging-in-Publication Data

Governing cities in a global era: urban innovation, competition, and democratic
reform / edited by Robin Hambleton and Jill Simone Gross.
    p. cm.
  Includes bibliographical references and index.
  ISBN 1-4039-7573-6 (hardcover: alk. paper) — ISBN 0-230-60230-4 (pbk.: alk. paper)
1. Municipal government. 2. Globalization—Political aspects. I. Hambleton, Robin.
II. Gross, Jill Simone.
  JS78.G74 2007
  320.8'5—dc22

2007013463

A catalogue record for this book is available from the British Library.

Design by Macmillan India Ltd.

First edition: December 2007

10 9 8 7 6 5 4 3 2 1

Printed in the United States of America.

Transferred to Digital Printing in 2009

PRAISE FOR GOVERNING CITIES IN A GLOBAL ERA

"By examining the experiences of very different metropolitan areas in different parts of the world, Hambleton and Gross lead us in an exploration of the most relevant issues concerning urban governance in a time of rapid globalization. The case study illustrations and theoretical reflections demonstrate how important it now is to engage in cross-national learning, not just to understand urban phenomena but also to create the capacity to govern effectively in modern times."
—Professor Sandro Balducci, Head of the Department of Architecture and Planning, Milan Polytechnic

"What is local in a global era? Is it a region, a megaregion, or a system of cities? These are the issues of governance that Hambleton and Gross tackle with insight, breadth, and depth. This book provides an important contribution that will be of interest to all concerned about the future of cities."
—Edward J. Blakely, Professor of Urban Planning and Policy, University of Sydney, Australia, and Executive Director Recovery, City of New Orleans

"The authors reveal opportunities for local actors to pilot their city through troubled waters—sometimes strategically using the strong winds blown by globalization and urbanization. This book is important as it shows that social change can be influenced by political decisions taken at the local level. Moreover, it also makes clear that such political decisions follow a particular logic specific to each city, not of cities in general or a certain type of cities, such as the 'European city.'"
—Hubert Heinelt, Professor of Public Policy, Public Administration and Urban Studies, Institute of Political Science, Darmstadt University of Technology

"This book provides invaluable insights on the changing dynamics of global city development. The various chapters provide many helpful suggestions for city leaders on how to respond to the major urban challenges we now face. The Chinese experience is valuable for examining and sharing."
—Dr. Baoxing Qiu, Deputy Minister, Ministry of Construction, China

"This ambitious book on cities aims to achieve truly international coverage of the challenges posed by globalization, demographic change, social diversity, economic competition, growing inequality, and contemporary governance reforms. Academics, policy makers, and opinion formers from around the world will find much to interest, disturb, and inspire them in this book."

—Carole Rakodi, Professor in the Department of International Development, School of Public Policy, University of Birmingham

"Cities have become the strategic spaces where global forces shape current events, often in unexpected ways. Hambleton and Gross have brought together a diverse and international group of authors to provide us with one of the best books on the challenges of governing cities in a global era."

—Saskia Sassen, author of *Territory, Authority, Rights* (2006)

"Hambleton and Gross have brought us a big book with a grand sweep. The editors and authors of this volume breathe new life into globalization and the city's response to it. This important collection is the product of an international cast of authors who not only cover a lot of ground but do it with aplomb and incisiveness. Scholars and policy makers would do well to discover its lessons."

—Hank Savitch, Brown and Williamson Distinguished Research Professor, School of Urban and Public Affairs, University of Louisville

"Mayors, city managers, city planners, and community organizers would do well to study this book closely. It covers major issues—such as the need to provide efficiency and democracy, as well as legitimacy and participation—and discusses in realistic terms the stress on city governance. I expect it to be an important book for more than a decade and to spawn debates farther into the future."

—Dick Simpson, Professor and Department Head, Department of Political Science, University of Illinois at Chicago

"Hambleton and Gross offer us a rich array of theoretical and empirical contributions that help us to approach contemporary urbanization as intertwined global, national, and local processes in which universality and singularity come necessarily together."

—Carlos B. Vainer, Professor, Institute of Urban and Regional Planning and Research, Federal University of Rio de Janeiro

"In this timely contribution Hambleton and Gross provide a well-composed analysis of the challenges now confronting all stakeholders in cities that aspire to be world class. They focus on the key theme of urban governance and, by comparing cities in different continents, they provide insights that are attuned to different institutional contexts. It is inspirational reading but, more than that, it offers practical ideas on how to improve urban governance in a global era."

—Zhiqiang Wu, Dean and Professor of Urban Planning, College of Architecture and Urban Planning, Tongji University, Chief Planner of 2010 World EXPO Shanghai

"This book opens an interesting discussion about urban governance that concerns not only cities of the northern hemisphere but also those in the southern regions of the world. Furthermore, Hambleton and Gross introduce a wide variety of cases that challenge us to adopt a more critical attitude to the globalization process and to consider new vocations that could be developed to improve the quality of life in cities, given current international pressures."

—Sergio Zermeño, Researcher, Social Research Institute, National Autonomous University of Mexico

CONTENTS

LIST OF TABLES

LIST OF FIGURES

ACKNOWLEDGMENTS

The inspiration for this book was provided by conversations at the City Futures International Conference organized by the College of Urban Planning and Public Affairs (CUPPA) at the University of Illinois at Chicago and held in Chicago in July 2004. The conference, which was sponsored by the U.S.-based Urban Affairs Association (UAA) and the European Urban Research Association (EURA), attracted over 250 participants from 36 countries. Some 160 papers were presented and 11 of the chapters in this volume started out as papers to the conference.

At the outset, then, we express our thanks to the UAA and the EURA for supporting this conference and to all the participants who attended and contributed their thoughts.

As editors we would like to thank all the 18 authors who have contributed so much to this book. We were delighted that all the authors we approached readily accepted our invitation. If we include ourselves as editors, this book represents a collective endeavor involving 20 authors from 11 countries. It has been a real pleasure working with such a diverse group. We thank all our authors who have responded with goodwill and tolerance to our editorial interventions, and we hope that they feel the outcome is worthwhile.

On behalf of all the authors we wish to thank the support staff and librarians in universities across the world who make a book like this possible.

As editors our greatest debt is to the research assistants who worked for Robin Hambleton in the Dean's Office at CUPPA in 2005–2007. Glenda Garelli, ChaNell Marshall, Jennifer Martin, Ada Varshavsky, and Karla Walter did an absolutely tremendous job in transforming the 16 papers into a first-class manuscript for submission to the publishers. Hard work, professionalism, tact, diplomacy—you name it, they could do it! Robin would also like to thank his assistant, Michael Clark, who helped to organize the City Futures International Conference and who has helped with the book. Special thanks to Michael Clark, Glenda Garelli and Evelyn Yang for their excellant work on the index.

Jill would like to offer thanks to Roosevelt House Policy Center at Hunter College, City University of New York, for its support to her research on Chapter 6. And she offers a very special thank-you to Mike Marks, who has been a great support to her all along the way.

Robin would like to thank Pam, Jake, and Beth for all their advice and support.

We offer thanks to the Terra Foundation for American Art for permission to reproduce the marvelous painting by Charles Demuth—*Welcome to Our City,* 1921—which graces the cover of this book.

Lastly, we want to say that we have enjoyed collaborating on this book, and we hope you enjoy reading it.

Robin Hambleton, Chicago
Jill Simone Gross, New York

Notes on the Contributors

John J. Betancur is Associate Professor of Urban Planning and Policy in the College of Urban Planning and Public Affairs (CUPPA) at the University of Illinois at Chicago (UIC), United States. Before this, he worked at the UIC's Center for Urban Economic Development, assisting community organizations and city governments in economic development projects. He has been an Associate Professor at Universidad Pontificia Bolivariana in Medellín, Colombia, and continues collaborating with various universities in Latin America.

Janice Bockmeyer is Associate Professor of Government at John Jay College of Criminal Justice, City University of New York (CUNY), United States, and has taught urban politics at Brooklyn College, CUNY, USA, and at the Freie Universität Berlin, Germany. Her current research is on immigrant nonprofit organizations and political incorporation in German cities.

Jonathan S. Davies is Senior Lecturer in Public Policy at the University of Warwick, United Kingdom. His research in urban politics and public policy has been instrumental in his developing critique of the political fashion for governance through urban partnerships and networks.

Jill Simone Gross is an Associate Professor of Political Science in the Department of Urban Affairs and Planning at Hunter College, CUNY, United States, and has taught at Barnard College, Columbia University, New York University, and Queens College and Brooklyn College, CUNY. She teaches and conducts research in comparative urban politics and development in Western European and North American cities, with an emphasis on issues of equity and inclusion.

Robin Hambleton is Professor of City Leadership in the Faculty of Environment and Technology at the University of the West of England, Bristol, and Director of Urban Answers, a private UK-based company. He was Dean of the College of Urban Planning and Public Affairs (CUPPA) at the University of Illinois at Chicago until 2007. He now holds Emeritus Professorships in Urban Planning and Policy and in Public Administration at CUPPA, and a Visiting Professorship in City Planning in the College of Architecture and Urban Planning at Tongji University, Shanghai, China.

Dennis R. Judd is a Professor in the Department of Political Science and Fellow of the Great Cities Institute at the UIC. He is currently collaborating on a book on urban power in St. Louis and a study of the recurring theme of the ideal city in Chicago.

Sinead Kelly is a Temporary Lecturer in the Department of Geography at the National University of Ireland, Maynooth, and is currently engaged in her doctoral research in the Department of Geography, Trinity College, Dublin, Ireland. She is a Director of the Forum for Irish Urban Studies and has worked on community-based research projects in Dublin's Liberties and O'Devaney Gardens.

Daniel Kübler is an Assistant Professor in the Department of Political Science of the University of Zurich, Switzerland. From December 2004 to April 2005, he was a visiting researcher at the City Futures Research Centre of the University of New South Wales, Sydney, Australia.

John Nalbandian chairs the Department of Public Administration at the University of Kansas, United States, known for its emphasis on city management and urban policy. In addition to his academic position, from 1991 to 1999, he served on the Lawrence, Kansas, city commission, including two one-year terms as the city's mayor.

Michael Punch is a Lecturer in the School of Sociology at University College Dublin and a Research Fellow at the Centre for Urban and Regional Studies at Trinity College, Dublin, Ireland. He is Secretary of Tenants First in Dublin and has also worked with many other community-voluntary groups on action-research projects.

Bill Randolph is Professor and Director of the City Futures Research Centre at the Faculty of the Built Environment, University of New South Wales, Sydney, Australia. He is currently undertaking research on several fronts into the outcomes of metropolitan planning proposals in Sydney and other Australian cities.

Declan Redmond is a Lecturer in the School of Geography, Planning and Environmental Policy at University College Dublin, Ireland. He is the Programme Director of the professional masters' degrees in planning and Deputy Head of School. Until recently he was on the board of a not-for-profit housing association in Dublin.

Manfred Röber is Professor of Public Management at the University of Applied Sciences for Technology and Economics in Berlin, Germany. He has a number of research projects to his credit and has written several books and papers in refereed journals on various aspects of public sector modernization.

Eckhard Schröter is Professor of Public Administration in the Department of Public Management and Governance at Zeppelin University in Friedrichshafen, Germany. Before joining Zeppelin University, he taught at the Humboldt-University, Berlin, Germany, and the University of California at Berkeley, United States.

James M. Smith is a PhD student in the Department of Political Science at the UIC.

Richard E. Stren is an Emeritus Professor of Political Science at the University of Toronto, Canada, and former director of the university's Centre for Urban and Community Studies. He has worked extensively as a consultant and researcher in cities of the developing world, most particularly in Africa. He is a former fellow of the Woodrow Wilson International Center for Scholars, Washington, D.C., and was cochair of the Panel on Urban Population Dynamics of the National Academy of Science, Washington, D.C.

Pawel Swianiewicz is a Professor in the Faculty of Geography and Regional Studies at Warsaw University, Poland. He is also President of the European Urban Research Association.

Takashi Tsukamoto is an Assistant Professor in the Department of Political Science at the University of North Carolina at Greensboro, United States. He graduated from the University of Louisville in December 2005 with a PhD in Urban and Public Affairs.

Ronald K. Vogel is Professor of Political Science and Director of the PhD program in Urban and Public Affairs at the University of Louisville, Kentucky, United States. He chairs the Comparative Urban Politics group in the American Political Science Association.

Tingwei Zhang is Associate Professor of Urban Planning and Policy at CUPPA. He is currently the Chair of the International Association for China Planning and serves as a member of the National Planning Expert Committee of the Chinese Ministry of Construction. He was Deputy Director of the Department of City Planning in Tongji University, Shanghai, and Deputy Director of the China National Training Center for Planning Directors before he came to the United States.

"Anxiety for the future time, disposeth . . . [us] to enquire into the causes of things: because the knowledge of them, maketh . . . [us] better able to order the present to [our] best advantage."

Thomas Hobbes (1651), The Leviathan,
Part 1, Chapter 11

CHAPTER 1

GLOBAL TRENDS, DIVERSITY, AND LOCAL DEMOCRACY

JILL SIMONE GROSS AND ROBIN HAMBLETON

The world is changing very rapidly. As a result, new challenges now present themselves to those in leadership positions in the public, private, and nonprofit sectors—particularly those who exercise civic leadership. In our view, these challenges create remarkable, new opportunities for bold and imaginative city leadership. But, in a dynamic, fast-moving environment, it is also the case that these dramatic changes magnify the risks of error.

Skeptics will say that every generation believes it is living through tumultuous change. Cities have always faced tough challenges. What's new? We take the view that there are two overarching reasons why the current dynamics of change present unprecedented challenges for those concerned with the governance of cities. These reasons can be summarized in two words: globalization and urbanization.

GLOBALIZATION AND URBANIZATION: THE TWIN CHALLENGES FOR CIVIC LEADERS

The economic, political, social, environmental, and cultural changes implied by the term "globalization" are truly startling. Hutton and Giddens bring together a collection of essays on the contours of contemporary capitalism that give weight to this issue, claiming that "it is the interaction of extraordinary technological innovation combined with the world-wide reach driven by global capitalism that give today's change its particular complexion. It has now a speed, inevitability and force that it has not had before" (2000, p. vii). Other studies in more recent years support this interpretation (Hutton 2002; Friedman 2005). At the same time, while global pressures may appear to be uniform, domestic responses vary as civic leaders seek competitive advantage within this evolving global system.

In his somewhat breathless but intriguing analysis, Friedman (2005) takes the view that the world has now been "flattened." Horizontal connectivity aided by computers, e-mail, networks, teleconferencing, and dynamic new software means that " . . . it is now possible for more people than ever to collaborate in real time with more other people on more different kinds of work from more different corners of the planet and on a more equal footing than at any previous time in the history of the world . . ." (Friedman 2005, p. 8). Friedman argues, then, that globalization manifests itself in somewhat universal terms—economic restructuring; new divisions of labor; increased mobility of people, ideas, and goods; new networks of communication; and rapid technological advancement.

We take the view, however, that the world is *not* "flat," as Friedman contends. Rather, along with other social scientists, we take the view that global forces map onto an *uneven* terrain of politics and power, and that this unevenness remains even in an era of hyperconnectivity. As many urban scholars have demonstrated, globalization produces "new centers and margins," as cities seek to position themselves as "strategic nodes" for investment and production within the "space" of global economic "flows" (Castells 1989, 1996; Sassen 2002). In this analysis, those occupying strategic nodes within the global system are advantaged. They become magnets for people, investment, resources, and power. Cities outside these flows are disadvantaged and can spiral into decline. It follows, therefore, that the world is far from "flat." Rather, there are peaks and troughs in the landscape of economic advantage—some cities and city regions are far better placed to take up the opportunities presented by globalization than others.

But global dynamics are more complex than a landscape of peaks and troughs implies. As well as sharp variations in economic vibrancy among cities (and city regions), remarkable shifts are taking place *within* cities. As Smith observes, the urban world is far from orderly; rather, the city is " . . . a fluid site of contested social relations of meaning and power" (2001, p. 67). Smith is reminding us that between cities and within cities, there are some who are connected to beneficial global flows and others who are marginalized. Thus, even in the advantaged cities with spectacular levels of inward investment, the gaps between the wealthy and the poor are continuing to widen. How these uneven dynamics are understood and managed become central challenges for the way we govern cities. We will revisit this theme of connectivity and globalization shortly. But what of the second major change driver: urbanization?

The evidence suggests that urbanization trends are just as startling as globalization trends. Indeed, the two are heavily interlinked. It is a mistake, however, to allow talk of globalization to obscure the importance of urbanization per se. Given the remarkable and inexorable movement of people into cities and towns in the modern era, urbanization needs to sit alongside globalization as a key driver of societal change. More people now live in urban areas than in the entire history of the world. More than that, it is now the case that the urban population outnumbers the rural.

Demographers argue about the details of this remarkable spatial shift but the United Nations (UN) website gives us the gist. In 2005 most of the 6.5 billion people on the planet lived in rural areas—roughly 3.3 billion. In 2007, the year this book was published, the urban population of the world is set to overtake the rural. As with globalization, urbanization also reflects some regional variation— according to the World Bank, Western Europe and the United States are currently the most urbanized parts of the world at 77 percent, though Latin America is just a step away with some 75 percent of the population living in urban areas. In the Middle East and northern Africa, 59 percent of the population is urban, followed by 35 percent in east Asia and the Pacific, and 34 percent in sub-Saharan Africa (World Bank 2002). The UN projects that the global urban population will grow by leaps and bounds—but the pace of growth will vary by region. We will shortly revisit these urbanization projections and their implications for governance.

At the outset, however, we want to stress that we believe that these two forces—globalization and urbanization—mean that we do, indeed, live in a period when city leadership, defined broadly, faces unprecedented challenges. How leaders and communities respond to these challenges and/or seek to redefine them is of enormous importance for the well-being of billions of people.

ALTERNATIVE CITY FUTURES

In 2004 we organized, with others, an international conference on "City Futures." Held in Chicago, this event, which brought together over 250 policy makers and scholars from 36 countries, set out to share urban experiences from across the world and to examine the impact of global forces on cities and city regions.[1] In setting the scene for the conference, Hambleton outlined two different visions for the future of cities.[2] The alarming scenario envisaged globalization threatening local jobs, widening social divisions, and leading to social disintegration. On the basis of this interpretation, the city becomes a balkanized world with consumers living isolated lives in separate fortified enclaves. The rich get richer and the poor get poorer. Political tensions draw forth the erosion of civil liberties as governments struggle to manage the "ungovernable" city.

The more optimistic scenario suggested that global awareness would grow rapidly. Transnational migrants would continue to refresh the culture, economic vitality, and politics of increasingly lively urban areas. In many cities, tolerance between different ethno-religious groups would improve, as diverse communities came to understand each other and work out ways of living together. Local democracy would be revitalized, the public realm would be expanded, and cities would reestablish themselves as centers of culture and civilized living.

As a device for provoking fresh thinking and forward-looking debate, the scenarios deliberately highlighted the possibility of very different urban futures. Authors were encouraged to examine trends, evaluate experience, and draw lessons for policy. The response from participants was fascinating and rewarding—many of the papers offered not just good analysis but also positive suggestions on how to address current challenges. Almost all the chapters in this volume are updated and revised versions of papers given at the City Futures International Conference. In various ways contributors examine the way different cities in different contexts are responding to the challenges of globalization and urbanization. They explore concepts that may help us better understand the dynamics of urban change and, hopefully, assist in shaping ways of improving the quality of urban life at a time when conflict appears to be growing in many societies and cities.

Before we outline the case for giving more attention to diversity in the multicultural city and to the role of governments in governing cities and city regions, it is necessary first to say a little more about our two major themes.

GLOBALIZATION AND THE MODERN CITY

It is not just the rapid growth in urban areas that provides compelling evidence about the importance of cities and city regions in the world economy—it is the dramatic change in their economic function. A word of caution is needed—urban economies are not all the same. The prosperity of the citizens of Mumbai will, for example, rest on a different social and economic base from, say, that of the citizens of London or New York. Having said that, the global shift to the "knowledge economy" puts selected cities and city regions at the heart of national economic revival in most countries in the world.

There are various reasons for this. As Atkinson (2004) observes, most traded goods are, in order of value, cars, oil, computer parts, clothes, and semiconductors. "In other words, the basis of trade has shifted from what economists call comparative advantage (e.g. coffee does not grow very well in the US; but it does in Latin America) to factors of competitive advantage (the Japanese have figured out better than Americans how to make high-quality cars at a reasonable price)" (Atkinson 2004, p. 111). Natural resources still matter, but less than they used to. In addition, many cities and city regions (although not all) benefit enormously from being linked to global circuits of power and information (Castells 1989, 1996; Sassen 2002).

Some authors argue that cities cannot do much more than compete for inward investment. Tiebout (1956) pointed to this over 50 years ago, when he suggested that people and industry choose their locations based upon a simple cost-benefit ratio of goods and services available. Peterson (1981) later suggested that owing to local resource deficits and the need to maintain their competitive position, cities had become dependent on higher levels of government and private investment for survival. Thus, in his view, local policy is heavily constrained—in effect local leaders can do little in the face of wider economic forces. Urban dependency, on this analysis, increases as the world becomes increasingly global. Labor and capital are mobile, people follow jobs, and industry opts to move to more distant locations where the cost of land and labor is lower.

Others argue, however, that urban-dependency theories overstate the power of international and national actors and understate the power and influence of local leaders and activists. For example, Savitch and Kantor, in their cross-national comparative research on urban development, point out that city leaders can, in fact, bargain with business and that "cities with strong popular control systems exercise greater influence over capital investment and influence the course of economic development decisions" (Savitch and Kantor 2002, p. 45).

Other urban scholars support this view, and some even suggest that cities now have elevated importance in the global world (Jessop 1999; Denters and Rose 2005a). Various scholars have argued for the development of a more sophisticated view of the importance of "place"—for example, Abu-Lughod (1999) emphasizes the uniqueness that some localities derive from local history, culture, geography, and politics. Goetz and Clark (1993) in their analysis of "New Localism" suggest that it is the power of local leaders that is preeminent in explaining urban success. So, even if globalization is seen as a mainly "economic" phenomenon, the evidence suggests that it is wrong to think of global capital being insensitive to place.

Of course, "globalization" is *not* just an economic phenomenon—it has social, political, cultural, and environmental dimensions. Globalization enhances mobility and connectivity among people and can, as a result, enhance the local quality of life. In many urban centers we find the physical manifestation of these processes, as people with differing social, economic, religious, and sexual orientations live in close proximity with one another. In turn, cities become not simply economic hubs, but sociocultural and political hubs. How the differing needs of local stakeholders are met and how conflicts and cleavages are managed become critical components of urban success. As Body-Gendrot (2000) comments, " . . . the market does not favor social cohesiveness but generates tensions; it reinforces economic polarizations and inequalities in cities and the re-composition of space unveils power conflicts" (p. 227).

While all the authors in this collection agree that globalization is a key force shaping cities today, they also agree that globalization does not impact all cities in a uniform way. We follow Smith (2001) in trying " . . . to capture the notion of the city as a crossroads of social relations constituted by the interactions of local, national, and transnational actors and the networks through which they operate" (p. 184). The various chapters explore the nuances of urbanization and globalization and the differential experiences of cities in different continents.

OUR URBAN FUTURE

Reference was made earlier to the fact that we now live in a predominantly urban world. In fact, the world is urbanizing at a remarkable rate. Figure 1.1 shows how the overall population of the world is set to climb from 6.5 billion in 2005 to 8.2 billion in 2030. By then 5 billion people (or 61 percent of the world population) will live in urban areas. This is a staggering increase of 1.7 billion in the world urban population in a comparatively short span of time. Consider the fact that London has a population of 7 million at present. An increase of 1.7 billion is, then, equivalent to adding 250 cities the size of London to the global urban landscape in just 25 years. In 1950 there were 86 cities in the world with a population of more than 1 million; today there are 400, and by 2015 the UN predicts that there will be over 550.

This urban population growth is spectacular. From a public policy and a city planning point of view, it is just as important to record that this growth is mainly happening in areas that have *not* seen much in the way of urbanization in the past. As Davis (2006) points out, most of this surging urban expansion will occur in the developing countries. He notes, correctly, that the scale and velocity of third world urbanization dwarfs even that of Victorian Europe. For example, China, as discussed further by Zhang in Chapter 8, is urbanizing at a speed unprecedented in human history. It "added more city-dwellers in the 1980s than did all of Europe (including Russia) in the entire nineteenth century!" (Davis 2006, p. 2).

Table 1.1 lists the ten biggest megacities in 1950 and as projected for 2015. It shows that 60 years ago many of the really big cities in the world were in Europe or North America. Not anymore. True, the growth rate of some specific cities in the third world may falter

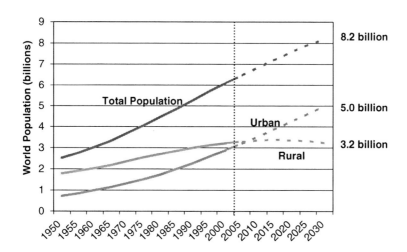

Figure 1.1   World population growth.

Source: United Nations World Urbanization Prospects, http://esa.un.org/unup/.

Table 1.1   Top ten megacities: 1950 and 2015

1950 (population, millions)		2015 (population, millions)	
1 New York	12.3	1 Tokyo	36.2
2 London	8.7	2 Mumbai	22.6
3 Tokyo	6.9	3 Delhi	20.9
4 Paris	5.4	4 Mexico City	20.6
5 Moscow	5.4	5 São Paulo	20.0
6 Shanghai	5.3	6 New York	19.7
7 Rhine-Ruhr North	5.2	7 Dhaka	17.9
8 Buenos Aires	5.0	8 Jakarta	17.5
9 Chicago	4.9	9 Lagos	17.0
10 Calcutta	4.4	10 Calcutta	16.8

Source: United Nations World Urbanization Prospects, http://esa.un.org/unup/.

as they encounter formidable air pollution and congestion problems. For example, as Davis (2006) points out, Mexico City, widely predicted to achieve a population of 25 million in the 1990s, experienced a slowdown in growth such that its population is now in the region of 19–20 million. However, the overall pattern of massive global urban expansion is unmistakable. Most of the new city dwellers in the coming period will be in the third world, and here the leadership challenge centers on supporting and managing these massive populations. Interestingly, the growth of cities in Europe and North America has slowed, and the resident population is aging, producing different challenges for city leaders.

As mentioned earlier, urban economies are not all the same, and it is clear that the size of a city's population does not necessarily provide a reliable indicator of its economic strength. Indeed, the whole thrust of the analysis put forward by Davis (2006) in his thought-provoking book, *Planet of Slums,* is to suggest that even the gloomy scenario for the future of cities outlined earlier is too optimistic for many cities in the third world. He marshals evidence from the cities of the South to argue that massive plant closures and deindustrialization have knocked the bottom out of the urban economy in cities such as Mumbai, Buenos Aires, and Sao Paulo. Neuwirth (2005), in *Shadow Cities,* estimates that one in six people, globally, are squatters: "Every day, close to two hundred thousand people leave their ancestral homes in the rural areas and move to cities. . . . The overwhelming majority . . . are simply people who came to the city, needed a place to live that they or their families could afford" (p. 9). A consequence is that much of the twenty-first-century urban world squats in squalor, surrounded by pollution, excrement, and decay. As explored further by Stren in Chapter 5 and Betancur in Chapter 9, the urban economy of many third world cities is shaped by the activities of informal and little-understood networks embedded in poor communities in the shantytowns and favelas. This environment of tension and distress raises formidable challenges for activists and leaders striving to improve approaches to urban government.

In contrast to the challenges of a burgeoning urban population, many of the cities of the wealthy West have experienced population decline. Most shrinking cities in the last 50 years have been in Western industrial countries, especially the United States (59), Britain (27), Germany (26), and Italy (23).[3] Older industrial cities such as Cleveland and Baltimore in the United States and Liverpool and Manchester in the United Kingdom have never really recovered from the period of deindustrialization, when jobs and population moved to suburban and exurban areas. In areas such as these, we find new initiatives to "bring people back to the city." This approach is commonplace in, for example, the U.S. context; and various studies have documented this trend (Gratz and Mintz 1998; Grogan and Proscio 2000; Gross, J.S. 2005) and some city mayors have contributed to this literature (Norquist 1998). Indeed, there is a growing recognition among city leaders that key players in the modern "knowledge economy"—sometimes referred to as the "creative class" (Florida 2002)—are vital to any serious hopes of urban renaissance. These talented and creative people, such as scientists, engineers, professors, artists, designers, architects, writers, think-tank researchers, editors, and inventors, as well as people in allied sectors, such as high-tech industries, financial services, and business management, have strong views about where they want to live.

While it is unwise to generalize too freely, people in the "creative class" appear to be attracted to areas that can offer, according to Florida (2002), a certain kind of lifestyle, including good cultural facilities, a lively nightlife, rich social interactions, a diversity of people (including gay and transsexual people), strong spatial identity, and a high-quality environment. Going by this analysis, successful cities will need to give much more attention to creating the right "people climate" rather than believing that sorting out the "business climate" is the key to economic health.

In relation to urbanization we can say immediately that the challenges facing urban leaders in different cities and continents vary dramatically. Shaping and managing high-speed urban growth is a high priority for city leaders in, for example, many cities in China and India. In many Western cities urban growth also presents a major challenge. We can surmise that in all countries there is at least some interest in bringing about what Americans call "smart growth"—that is, environmentally sustainable urban development. In many Western cities leaders and planners also need to refresh their thinking on how to attract citizens back into the city.

In relation to planning to conserve and protect the environment, European cities are ahead of those in other continents. As Newman and Thornley observe in their comparative analysis of city planning, "Europe displays an environmental priority through both policy at the European scale and in the enthusiastic take-up of environmental planning in most cities" (2005, p. 271). But there is no room for complacency. The environmental challenges facing all city leaders are formidable. Interestingly, while rapid urbanization creates significant stresses and strains in many cities, it is also the case that, with proper planning, dense urban living can help reduce the ecological impact of human habitations on the planet (Mau 2004). This is because a city with a higher population density requires fewer transportation facilities, fewer sewer and power lines, and fewer roads, and again, if designed properly, can be more energy efficient. Urbanization need not—indeed, should not —create an unpleasant, unsustainable environment. But livable cities require strong approaches to city planning and urban design.

EMBRACING THE MULTICULTURAL CITY

The earlier discussion of globalization and the modern city noted that urbanization and globalization are producing cities that are now much more multicultural than they have been in the past. In member countries of the Organisation for Economic Cooperation and Development (OECD), for example, there was a 7 percent increase in foreign-born population over the past decade (Mayr 2003). In addition, as Stren points out in Chapter 5, cities in the developing world are also becoming more multicultural, although patterns vary. In Latin American and African cities, growth is most commonly due to regional shifts. In Mexico City, for example, only 0.42 percent of the population is foreign born—the majority of new arrivals are from surrounding rural areas (Benton-Short et al. 2004). In Africa, tribal warfare in the countryside in some countries has forced migration to urban areas. In receiving cities, or immigrant gateway cities, such as Toronto in Canada, over 40 percent of city residents are foreign born, with the largest concentration of immigrants coming from China. It is not simply the number of immigrants but the diversity and origin of new arrivals that produce nuances at the local level—as immigrants bring with them their own unique cultural heritage that shapes their expectations and actions. As one analyst comments:

> International migration today touches the lives of more people and looms larger in the politics and economics of more states than ever before . . . One of the most urgent challenges most societies face in the years ahead is identifying a set of coherent responses to one of international migration's most important dimensions: its effect on receiving societies' cities and their residents—natives and immigrants.
>
> (Papademetriou 2001, p. 98)

There is little disagreement with the view that many cities today are experiencing a period of "hyper diversity" (Benton-Short et al. 2004). This theme runs through many of the chapters in this book and is given explicit attention by Gross in Chapter 6 and by Bockmeyer in Chapter 13.

Popular hypermobility has, of course, multiple dimensions. In cities in sub-Saharan Africa, for example, the most educated are immigrating, while the poor are migrating. Here, cities struggle to provide services for a growing population in the absence of resources and capacity. In other parts of the world, in postindustrial receiving cities such as Paris and London, the tensions differ. As competition for jobs grows more intense, these cities must respond to the diverse needs of asylum seekers and economic migrants if the new arrivals are not to be pushed to the margins of society. In cities such as Copenhagen and Oslo, where diversity is a more recent phenomenon, the challenges of responding to cultural and religious difference have moved to the center of the agenda for urban planners and policy makers.

Diversity can bring great vibrancy to the urban society so long as new groups are integrated—socially, politically, and economically. Indeed, the global city can be defined by the intermixing of cultures and ideas. Developing and adopting policies that head off conflict between insiders and outsiders is a challenge. Many of the chapters presented in this volume remind us that innovation in particular cities, and specific neighborhoods within cities, can break new ground in building multicultural understanding and cross-cultural collaboration. In the modern multicultural city the interests of new stakeholders must be acknowledged and their needs addressed. Recent urban riots on the outskirts of Paris are an illustration of the potential costs that can arise when governments fail to be responsive to local demographic changes and legitimate social needs. The variable geography of the multicultural city also requires city leaders to develop geographically sensitive policies. In the United States, for example, immigrants tend to settle in the inner city, while in much of Europe immigrant communities are more likely to be found on the periphery of the city—a geographical pattern that results from local housing and urban renewal policies. The goal of nurturing communities in a sensitive way is a theme in numerous chapters.

PUTTING THE GOVERNMENT BACK INTO GOVERNING

While all cities face common challenges as a result of the pressures created by globalization and urbanization, we have stressed that local responses can and should vary. Cities are pushed and pulled in many directions by powerful and fast-moving international currents of change, but how they respond is a function of local history, culture, politics, economics, geography, and planning. The macrotrends we have discussed in this chapter have physical manifestations in cities and their surrounding city regions. Those contributing to this collection are focused on these manifestations—all chapters examine, in various ways, the concrete side of globalization and urbanization. We have suggested that globalization can be discussed in somewhat universal terms—economic restructuring, new divisions of labor, and so on. But cities and local communities are not helpless victims in a global flow of events.

The authors of this book share the view that city leaders and citizens can, with adequate support, respond to these various challenges in a creative way. But for progress to be made, there will need to be some rethinking of the currently fashionable view—in some academic and policy circles—that "government" should give way to "governance." We define government as the democratically accountable institutions of the state operating in the locality—providing services, acting as channels for the representation of local interests, and generating a secure environment for residents, businesses, and visitors alike. Governance, in contrast, refers to the informal decision-making processes that have been dominating local policy arenas in many countries for the past two decades. According to Rhodes, "governance" refers to the "self-organizing, inter-organizational networks" that define and implement public policy (Rhodes 1996, p. 660). Pierre describes governance as "the processes and mechanisms through which significant and resource-full actors coordinate their actions and resources in pursuit of collectively defined objectives" (Pierre 2005, p. 452).

During the 1980s, when many national governments began to disinvest in cities owing to self-imposed resource constraints, governance emerged as a means by which cities could continue to maintain public services through partnerships with actors from the private and nonprofit sectors. The governance concept gained in importance and now has many advocates in both developed and developing countries. But the interest in building new forms of partnership between stakeholders at the local level has, in some countries at least, come to be questioned. Critics argue that governance is less a creative process for solving societal problems than a mechanism for allowing the state to abdicate its responsibilities for providing social care and support. We take the view that, while it is important to critique both "government" and "governance," there is a danger of a sterile discourse developing between two rival camps: those who favor a strong role for government and those who favor a weak role for it. We believe that the task of governing cities requires both strong government and imaginative collaboration among diverse stakeholders.

This book focuses on *governing* cities in a global era because governing sits at the junction between government and governance. Local governments play a crucial role as leaders, as regulators, as integrators, and as conduits for the conversion of ideas into policy. Governance is at the center of local capacity building—bringing private and nonprofit partners squarely into the policy and service arena in partnerships that can foster dialogue between local stakeholders and deliver innovative solutions to societal needs. But governance in the absence of strong government can lead to urban breakdown. This is because government—the elected, democratically accountable local state— is the only body that can ensure that different interests are fairly brought to the table and that decisions and actions clearly serve the broader public interest. A focus on governing spotlights the instrumental side of power in the city—to formulate policy, to generate resources, and to implement and provide services and infrastructure to meet the needs of *all* who live in the city.

In this volume we argue that governing the city in this global, urbanizing era is, therefore, not a trade-off between government and governance. All of the authors in this collection contribute to the idea that effective governance requires good government, and that good government requires effective governance.

OUTLINE OF THE BOOK

We have argued that globalization and urbanization are the twin drivers of social and economic change in the twenty-first century—and they are changing people's lives for both good and ill. New opportunities are opening up for many people in those cities and city regions that are well positioned in relation to the global expansion of the "knowledge economy" and innovation within the private sector. Transnational migrants continue to refresh the culture, economic vitality, and politics of increasingly lively urban areas in many parts of the world. But globalization is also creating new class divisions in society, with fabulous wealth at the top and grinding poverty at the bottom. New ethnic and religious tensions now present themselves in many cities with the risk that the social city—the polis—could fragment into a balkanized world of antagonistic enclaves working against one another to the detriment of the quality of life of all who live in the city. The key questions addressed in this book are:

- What are the implications of globalization for urban government and governance?
- How are cities and metropolitan areas responding to these unprecedented economic, social, environmental, and political changes?
- What are the implications for those who must lead and manage increasingly complex multicultural cities and city regions?

These three related questions are addressed through the three-part structure of this international, comparative book. By drawing on experience in six continents, authors from across the world throw new light on the interplay between global forces that drive homogenization and urban innovation that projects the value of geographical place and local identity. At the beginning of each part of the book, we provide an overview of the following chapters in the belief that this can make the book more accessible to readers and more useful for teaching purposes. Here we offer a concise overview of each part.

In Part I, the authors analyze the macro, or global, pressures on urban governments and governance. In Chapter 2, Tsukamoto and Vogel consider whether world cities are converging or diverging in the approaches they take to globalization. In Chapter 3, Röber and Schröter explore the way global forces are reshaping the government arrangements in several big cities in Europe. In Chapter 4, Punch, Redmond, and Kelly, by drawing on the notion of uneven development, expose the interplay between the global and the local in Dublin, Ireland. In Chapter 5, Stren takes us on a wide-ranging tour of cities in the developing world, pointing to the daunting challenges they face in a world of uneven development. These four chapters identify important themes that are examined in more detail in subsequent chapters.

In Part II of this collection, we move away from the macro and down to the micro level, seeking to explore innovations in urban government. Authors in Part II report on the practical experiences of cities in different regions of the world—examining progress with reforms as well as the obstacles to constructive innovation. They consider what cities are doing and what they are not doing and, in varying ways, point to ideas for the improvement of urban policy and practice. In Chapter 6, Gross examines local government reforms designed to enhance democracy and, by extension, create more responsive local policy arenas in cities in Canada and Western Europe. Swianiewicz takes us to Central and Eastern Europe in Chapter 7, to unearth insights on the way local government is changing to take on new challenges in a part of the world where there have been bold efforts to revitalize local democracy.

In Chapter 8, Zhang puts the spotlight on the changes taking place in the government of Shanghai and uses this analysis to argue that economic change in China at large is the key driver in bringing about change in the institutional form of local government. In Chapter 9, Betancur provides us with a perspective from a very different part of the world. He offers a detailed review of the history of the political economy of Medellín, Columbia, and concludes that informal and, to some extent, unruly forces are critical in shaping the local quality of life. He notes that the existence of strong, informal institutions in most cities in Latin America now poses formidable challenges for the governing process. Kübler and Randolph explore, in Chapter 10, the evolution of metropolitan governance in Australia. Following an examination of urban and regional restructuring in Sydney, they conclude that stronger action at the higher levels of government is needed if planning is to respond effectively to the needs of the metropolitan area as a whole. Judd and Smith wrap up this part of the book with their discussion of the growth of quasi-public authorities (or quangos) in Chapter 11. They argue that globalization has led to a rapid expansion of largely unaccountable special-purpose authorities operating beyond the reach of adequate public scrutiny. Their analysis suggests that the surge in the power of quasi-public authorities, established to serve the agenda of private interests and global capital rather than the needs of citizens, amounts to a revolution in the landscape of local political institutions. Their chapter heralds themes relating to local democracy that are given more detailed attention in subsequent chapters.

Part III offers five chapters examining leadership, partnership, and the democratic challenge. In many cities across different continents, there appears to be a decline in the strength of locally accountable democratic institutions. This is a worrying trend because, without strong democratic structures, wise political leadership, and healthy citizen participation, cities will inevitably move toward the disaster scenario we outlined earlier in this chapter. Self-interested behavior can be expected to gain momentum, the local polity will fragment, and the collective good will suffer seriously. Authors in Part III argue that it is essential to enhance the quality of city government and governance if cities are not to become mere sites for economic exploitation by stakeholders who have no real interest in the welfare of the local population.

In Chapter 12, Hambleton offers an analysis of the changing nature of both city management and local leadership and explores the new leadership agenda now opening up in cities across the world. He offers a robust critique of "new public management" and sets out the case for "new city management"—an approach that requires politicians and their appointed officers to work energetically with citizens to bring about democratic renewal as well as public service transformation. In Chapter 13, Bockmeyer puts the experience of immigrants at the center of the stage. Following an examination of recent innovations with neighborhood management in Germany, she concludes that the effective engagement of immigrants in decisions relating to community revitalization remains worryingly weak. In Chapter 14, Nalbandian echoes and extends themes introduced by Hambleton when he argues that local government professionals can play a vital role in bridging the gaps between administrative modernization and citizen engagement. He suggests that officers, by working more effectively with politicians and citizens, can play a key role in furthering public values and creating paths for civic discovery. Davies adopts a radical position in Chapter 15, where he argues that civic partnerships, contrary to the rhetoric that surrounds such formations, may actually work against the interests of local communities rather than empower them. Following an analysis of recent practice in the United Kingdom, he concludes that local people may be better off stepping away from formal partnership arenas that limit their political options and opting instead for organized campaigning and political resistance.

In our concluding chapter, Chapter 16, we revisit themes introduced in this opening chapter. In the light of the evidence presented in this volume, we address, once again, the key challenges facing civic leaders and local communities in an era of rapid social, economic, and political change. We contend that the neoliberal agenda for cities—involving the ascendancy of private interests over the public interest—is damaging the quality of life in cities in just about all continents. More importantly, we suggest that this is not an inevitable trend. Strong, good-quality government, working in a collaborative way with citizens and local stakeholders can shape urban futures more than is commonly realized. However, for this to happen, we need to move our thinking and practice beyond governance to governing.

NOTES

1. The International Conference on City Futures was organized by the College of Urban Planning and Public Affairs (CUPPA) at the University of Illinois at Chicago, with the support of the European Urban Research Association and the Urban Affairs Association. Over 160 papers were presented in three international tracks: (1) Comparative urban analysis, (2) Comparative urban planning, and (3) Comparative city governance. Most of the papers are available on the college web site— www.uic.edu/cuppa/cityfutures—together with a paper summarizing insights from international experience for U.S. public policy for cities (Hambleton 2006).

2. These two scenarios for alternative city futures were set out in the Call for Papers for the conference issued in 2003.

3. Information available at www.shrinkingcities.com.

GLOBAL PRESSURES ON URBAN GOVERNANCE

INTRODUCTION TO PART I

What are the global pressures shaping the way we govern our cities in the twenty-first century? How are these forces influencing approaches to urban governance in different settings? Are cities diverging or converging in the way they are responding to these global trends? It can be claimed that comparisons between cities operating within highly developed, developing, and underdeveloped regions of the world are unlikely to be fruitful. The local or regional differences, so the argument goes, are simply too great to allow for meaningful lesson drawing. We take the view that careful comparison of cities in different continents is actually worthwhile. Juxtaposition of different experiences enables the reader to see that, despite regional differences, there are numerous compelling *similarities* in the challenges now confronting city leaders and urban managers in very different contexts—managing urban growth, striving to find governmental legitimacy in the face of population shifts, promoting sustainable urban development, managing and creating infrastructure in resource-poor localities, attracting inward investment in a highly competitive environment, and, most broadly, working to place one's city at an advantageous position in relation to the fast-moving international flows of information, finance, and public perception.

By examining the changes taking place in particular cities, we can also draw insights from the *differences* we encounter in different countries. For example, the balance of power between localities and higher levels of government varies significantly as does the balance of power among civil society, state, and the private sector. These different power structures shape the way national and local leaders respond to the global pressures. The evidence suggests that some societies are adopting approaches that rely heavily on the elected governments—national, state, and local—to take a decisive lead. In other societies more reliance is being placed on approaches that seek to promote collaboration in improved patterns of city and regional governance—with the role of government being less to the fore.

In Chapter 2, Tsukamoto and Vogel consider whether the real-world experience of "world cities" matches up to what global theorists have proposed. Based on a comparison of the 20 most globalized "world cities," they argue that the globalization theory fails to offer a satisfactory explanation of what is happening. Contrary to the theory that globalization leads to political decentralization, they find that, in almost half of these globalized cities, power is actually centralizing. In several countries higher levels of government, whether national or state/province level, are intervening in a significant way in an attempt to shape urban fortunes.

In Chapter 3, Röber and Schröder highlight the significance of different administrative and political cultures but suggest that there are trends that transcend national borders. For these authors, the forces of globalization appear to be leading to the adoption of two-tier models of urban governance—at least in large cities. In their examination of big city government in Berlin, London, and Paris, they sketch the emergence of a strategic-level upper tier of government operating alongside a lower tier delivering welfare services.

In Chapter 4, Punch, Redmond, and Kelly explore the dynamics of one city—Dublin. They show how "global" forces encounter "life place" forces in the city and how this creates major frictions in local politics. As a way of framing these dynamics, they posit a "global-local nexus"—a theoretical framework that should be useful to other urban scholars.

In Chapter 5, Stren explores the governance of cities in Latin America, Africa, and Asia. His analysis shows that cities in these regions are growing much more rapidly than in the developed world. While the pace of urban growth is very different, the broad challenges faced by city leaders, managers, and communities are familiar. The chief difference is that most of these cities are very poor indeed—they are starved of public resources to tackle the formidable problems arising from urbanization and globalization.

Chapters 2, 3, and 4 suggest that, in varying ways, both government and private sector actors are the dominant forces shaping the modern city. Chapter 5 suggests that the situation in developing countries is somewhat different. In the face of both public and private sector neglect, the informal sector plays a crucial role. In summary, the authors in Part I suggest that, in the West European and North American context, global forces require an energetic response on the part of the state. Government needs to be strong in shaping urban development if cities are not to become mere sites for economic exploitation by private sector actors. In the less developed world it is civil society that needs to be strengthened, partly to hold the state accountable and partly to act as an effective counterforce to global capital.

CHAPTER 2

Rethinking Globalization— The Impact of Central Governments on World Cities

Takashi Tsukamoto and Ronald K. Vogel

Globalization and Cities

The "world city" and "global city" theses have emerged as central paradigms in urban studies. Indeed, a wave of new textbooks in sociology, political science, and geography have been oriented around these ideas (Sassen 1994; Short and Kim 1999; Abrahamson 2004). The general argument is that advanced telecommunications, global financial markets, and transnational corporations have led to a global division of labor and the rise of global or world cities as the strategic nodes in a global economic network (Smith and Feagin 1987; Knox 1995; Harrigan and Vogel 2003, pp. 154–5). Globalization determines the city's place in the new hierarchy of cities. Researchers have suggested that the rise of world cities marks a new international order characterized in part by the declining relevance of nation-states (Friedmann 1986; King 1990; Ross and Trachte 1990; Knox 1995; Sassen 2001a; Taylor 2004). In the new order, world cities are interdependent, yet they also compete with one another through a hierarchically structured network of cities (Friedmann and Wolff 1982; Friedmann 1986; Knox 1995; Sassen 2001a).

Friedmann's world city hypothesis (1986) conceptualizes "world cities" as a network of headquarter functions to theorize urban changes under advanced capitalism. Sassen (2004) defines the "global city" as an analytical construct that illuminates the urban consequences of denationalized economic systems. Sassen (2001a) distinguishes global cities from world cities, arguing,

> The difference between the classic concept of the world city and the global city model is one of level of generality and historical specificity. The world city concept has had a certain kind of timelessness attached to it where the global city model marks a specific socio-spatial historical phase. A key differentiating element between Friedmann and Goetz's formulation

and mine is my emphasis on the 'production' of the global economic system. It is not simply a matter of global coordination but one of the production of global control capacities.

(p. 349)

Today, the terms "global city" and "world city" tend to be used synonymously or in tandem, as researchers discuss "the globalized world city" (Hall 2004, p. 1).

Research on globalization and cities has been criticized on a number of grounds (e.g., Ward 1995; White 1998; Hill and Kim 2000; Smith 2001; Hill and Fujita 2003). Critics contend that the thesis embraces an "economistic" logic where macroeconomic structure determines urban development patterns while it neglects the role of governments at all scales. Political actors and their context-specific interactions are given little importance (Saito 2003). The contention between those writing on globalization and cities and their critics intensifies when the causal relationships between governments and global or world cities are discussed. The opinions are divided over: (1) the degree to which the central governments are instrumental to the making of world cities and (2) the degree to which world cities are free from the control of nation-states under the global economy (White 1998; Sassen 1998; Hill and Kim 2000 and 2001; Sassen 2001b; Friedmann 2001).

The latter point is an uncertainty in research on global or world cities. Scholars do problematize political territoriality in the local-national relationship but their answers are rather ambivalent (Friedmann and Wolff 1982; Sassen 2001a). There is widespread consensus that nation-states are declining in relevance. For example, Pickvance and Preteceille (1991) indicate that in an era of globalization, local governments become more mobilized, while the central governments devolve their responsibilities. Jessop (1993) argues that advanced capitalism and the global economy "hollow out" nation-states, giving more power to supra- and subnational political bodies. Taylor (1994) suggests that the world city network transcends the effectiveness of nation-states as an economic growth machine. Keating, Loughlin, and Deschouwer (2003) say globalization encourages reterritorialization of subnational regions as socially constructed, self-organized economic institutions. In his most recent work, Taylor (2004) says that "this is a book that promotes a city-centric view of the world and is written, in part, to counter the state-centric view of the world that emanates from most macro-level social science" (p. 27). However, do the world cities compete and win against other cities or nation-states in the global economy? Are the world cities and nation-states in a zero-sum power relationship? If not, what kind of interrelations do these two potentially conflicting scales maintain between them? These points are underdeveloped in the literature on globalization and cities.

One of the corollaries of these disagreements and questions surrounding the global city and world city theses are the need for greater synthesis of existing empirical research. Hence, in this chapter, we review the empirical evidence, drawing upon the work of others regarding the ways in which the global economy and the global or world cities interact and the degrees to which governments are involved in the interactions to provide some answers to these questions. Consequently, we hope we will be in a better position to understand the processes by which the global economy shapes urban development and leads to territorial rescaling or changes in local/regional governance in world cities.

GLOBALIZATION AND POLITICAL DECENTRALIZATION

In this section, we consider more carefully "political decentralization" and its relationship to globalization. There is a worldwide trend toward political decentralization (Dillinger 1994). Many link the drive toward decentralization in large measure to globalization (see Jun and Wright 1996). Garrett and Rodden (2001) say that "the decentralization of authority to state and local governments and the international integration of markets are widely perceived as two defining trends of the contemporary era" (p. 1). Fosler (1996), president of the National Academy of Public Administration, writes, "*De*centralization has become a watchword, if not the touchstone, from which new forms of governance are proposed, pursued, and assessed" (p. ix). A United Nations' report identifies decentralization as an important trend apparent in most nations (United Nations Centre for Human Settlements 2001, p. 59).

How might globalization drive decentralization? Jun and Wright (1996) explain that globalization is lessening the dominance of the national government and leading to "new, complex, and decentralized systems of networks that are radically different from the old centralized systems of governance" (pp. 3–4). Globalization thus leads to greater local initiative in local economic development, including "working with foreign business enterprises" as well as cultural exchange programs (such as sister cities) (Jun and Wright 1996, p. 4).

They further explain:

> Linkages of local (subnational) and national actions to global changes require institutional changes that take into account the decentralization of intergovernmental relations. In a centralized system of governance, the national government may not be very responsive to the needs and ideas of subnational governments. It is necessary to reform governing structures and processes in order to allow more autonomy at the local level so that local administrators can learn to become effective in solving local problems and active in promoting international activities. Centralized governments, in general, respond slowly not only to domestic but also to international problems.
>
> (Jun and Wright 1996, p. 4)

Scholars usually distinguish political decentralization from administrative decentralization. Under political decentralization, significant powers, functions, and resources are transferred to subnational governments so that they may "exercise discretion and decision making authority with a substantial measure of autonomy" (Jun and Wright 1996, p. 4). Administrative decentralization involves organizational decentralization without a delegation of power, transfer of resources, or authority. Rather, for administrative convenience, some activities and decisions are carried out by subordinate units but these are subject to review and veto from above. An important distinction is that where political decentralization occurs, "polyarchy and bargaining" characterize decision making (Jun and Wright 1996, p. 5).

Similarly, Stren (2003a) explains that "by decentralization we mean the transfer of significant powers and functions, along with fiscal responsibility to carry out these powers and functions, from the national to the local level of government" (p. 1). He continues:

> For this transfer to be meaningful, Philip Mawhood argues, the decentralized local body should have its own budget, a separate legal existence, and the authority to allocate substantial resources on a range of different functions, the decisions being made by representatives of the local people (Mawhood 1983, pp. 9–10). In federal states, decentralization may involve both the transfer of powers and functions from the national to the state or provincial level, as well as the transfer of powers and functions from the state or provincial level to the local. In both unitary and federal systems, the essential point is that local authorities (however they are defined) are strengthened.
>
> (Stren 2003, pp. 1–2)

Why is decentralization associated with globalization? First, the global economy is associated with "delocalised cities," which require new governance arrangements (Savitch 2002). Second, in response to globalization, nation-states have "devolved responsibilities that they had traditionally assigned to lower levels of government" (United Nations Centre for Human Settlements 2001, p. 234). Political institutions and the intergovernmental system are restructured in response to external pressure under globalization. Savitch (1998) explains that localities need to develop greater "institutional capacity" in light of globalization and increased competition in the world economy. He argues that "local democratic institutions and administrative systems will have to accommodate pressures for reform (greater responsibility, efficiency, and accountability)" (p. 255). To gain a "competitive advantage," local public officials must find ways to "offer goods and services more cheaply," "lower the costs of doing business," overcome fiscal limits, and adapt to the new urban culture and values (Savitch 1998, p. 256). Savitch indicates that local administrative systems that are smaller and more flexible will do better in this environment, especially those that develop many ties to other institutions at all levels. This provides more "mutual awareness and a sense of interdependence" so that, for example, a local municipality has greater strategic reach, a broader vision, and more resources to effectively compete in the competitive world economy (p. 260). He refers to this as "institutional thickness." In this context, real devolution enhances the likelihood of greater local institutional thickness, and there is, therefore, a greater chance that these connected communities will do well. Thus, nation-states should promote devolution if they seek to enhance the competitiveness of their cities.

Although globalization implies decentralization, there is still a strong role for the nation-state in urban policy. Savitch and Kantor (2003) point out that national governments still (1) provide the regulatory framework for employment, minimum wages, and benefits; (2) support regional development efforts; (3) underwrite and promote redevelopment and revitalization; and (4) help equalize resources across cities and regions. Indeed, Garrett and Rodden (2001) suggest that national governments probably continue to play a greater role than we may have realized. In exploring whether globalization causes decentralization, they examine "the balance of taxing and spending between central and local governments" and find surprisingly that "international market integration has been associated with fiscal centralization, rather than decentralization" (Garrett and Rodden 2001, p. 2). They suggest that "fiscal stabilization and inter-regional risk-sharing require a pooling of economic resources at the center." In addition, it is possible that "in order to mobilize votes for free trade in democracies, it may be necessary for the regions that benefit from free trade to send redistributive transfers to those that stand to loose" (Garrett and Rodden 2001, p. 3).

So we see that scholars of globalization as well as those who study intergovernmental relations and urban governance suggest a link between globalization and political decentralization (see also Borja and Castells 1997; Knox 1997; Keating 2001; Hambleton, Savitch, and Stewart 2002). However, we must acknowledge that the relationship between globalization and decentralization is more implied than demonstrated and may be tenuous. It is plausible that the global economy reduces local autonomy. If cities are limited or dependent (as suggested by Peterson 1981; Kantor 1988), then they must focus on development policy and shy away from redistribution. If the global economy is merely the rhetoric that rationalizes the agenda of corporate capital, then decentralization is the language that fools communities into believing they made these choices democratically. Finally, we must recognize that political decentralization may be a function of other forces rather than globalization. Stren (2003a) finds that political decentralization initiatives in the developing world have been "endogenous in origin" in most places (p. 11). Politics, not the global economy, may spur decentralization. We explore this relationship in the remainder of this chapter.

RESEARCH QUESTIONS AND FOUR PERSPECTIVES ON WORLD CITIES

We focus on two research questions. First, *what drives world city formation—politics or markets?* Second, *what forces promote political decentralization in world cities?* For example, is the global economy reducing central government control of the global world city? Is the central government bolstering local authority, or are local (city/urban) governments exercising greater local initiative? These research questions lead to two sets of alternative hypotheses (see table 2.1):

As a combination, the patterns of the answers to these two sets of hypotheses produce four positions, which correspond to four existing perspectives in the scholarly literature on world cities and globalization:

- The world city system perspective
- The state glocalization perspective
- The nested interaction perspective
- The new localism perspective

Table 2.2 summarizes the four perspectives highlighting the forces behind the formation of world cities and movement toward greater political decentralization. However, researchers of the world city thesis and globalization, including those referred to in this chapter, may not clearly fit into these four perspectives, which represent ideal types.

THE WORLD CITY SYSTEM PERSPECTIVE

The "world city system perspective" builds on the holistic approach of the world system theory (Smith and Timberlake 1995). It outlines the process by which globalization produces world cities and the consequences of the global economy on the internal organization of the city. Global market growth, actions of transnational corporations, and global

Table 2.1   Alternative hypotheses on world cities

Source of World City Formation		
Hypothesis 1		**Hypothesis 2**
The global market system (globalization) creates world cities	or	Political agency (politics) is the primary factor in the creation of world cities

Source of Political Decentralization		
Hypothesis 3		**Hypothesis 4**
The global market system (through the world cities) undermines the control of nation-states	or	Local political demands and initiatives lead to political decentralization (political cultures and processes)

Table 2.2   Four perspectives of the "world cities" and globalization literature

Source of decentralization	Source of World City formation	
	Global Economy	Government/politics
Global economy	**1. World city system** • Advanced market economy creates networks of strategic cities around the globe • The network of world cities in the global economy undermines the control of nation-states over cities	**3. Nested interaction** • Various sociopolitical scales interact, responding to the global economy to shape world cities • The global economic forces filter through various political scales, weakening the national scale
Government/ politics	**2. State glocalization** • The global economy promotes competitive cities to world cities • National/international decision makers implement neoliberal devolutionary policies	**4. New localism** • Local elites take strategic actions for economic growth • Local communities use their economic conditions to enhance autonomy

Note: The top bullet-point row of each box describes the source of world city formation and the bottom row, the source of decentralization.

financing produce world cities, which serve as strategic command nodes and advanced service-production sites (Friedmann 1986; Sassen 2001a). The world cities function as a system that is hierarchically structured. They converge in their economic structures and social characteristics (Friedmann 1986; Sassen 2001a). The networking of world cities reduces the political and economic controls that nation-states hold over their cities (Sassen 1998).

The tenets of the "world city system perspective" are widely held in the scholarly literature. For instance, Jessop (1993) describes how globalization "hollows out" nation-states; Ross and Trachte (1990) and Knox (1995) discuss how transnational corporations dilute national controls and identities; and Taylor (1995) outlines how the world city system shifts power from nation-states to local polities. Sassen (2001a) does warn that the global scale does not necessarily diminish the national scale in a zero-sum fashion. However, while acknowledging that nation-states continue to exercise political territorial control over global cities, she emphasizes the vulnerability of the national political scales to the system of world cities. Sassen (2001a, p. 347) explains: "Globalization is not simply something that is exogenous. It comes partly from the inside of national corporate structures and elites, a dynamic I conceive of as a process of incipient de-nationalization."

THE STATE GLOCALIZATION PERSPECTIVE

The "world city system thesis" and the "state glocalization perspective" both point to the global economy as the source of world city formation. However, for state glocalization theorists, world cities are not just an artifact of the world economy. Rather, nation-states act deliberately to create world cities *and* the global economy—thus, glocalization: a combination of globalization and localization in political economy. Nation-states seek to develop global or world cities to ensure their countries compete effectively in that global economy. National and international elites promote international trade alongside neoliberal and devolutionary policies to ensure continued economic growth (Swyngedouw 1997; Brenner 1999). Competition for development and growth by cities ensures a good business climate as well as the placement of a well-developed physical infrastructure and high-quality public services. Shifting responsibility for economic development down to cities or city-regions is the new neoliberal strategy embraced by the World Bank alongside the United Nations Centre for Human Settlements (HABITAT). Thus, global or world cities are disciplined by the free market system.

Hence, the global economic scale and the emergence of a world city system are the consequence of international neoliberal policies. The international division of labor is advanced through supranational organizations such as the International Monetary Fund, the World Trade Organization, and the World Bank, while global capitalism manages economic growth through cities (Smith 2001). Under the global market integration, the neoliberalism policies include market liberalization, privatization, devolution, and dismantling of the welfare state (Pickvance and Preteceille 1991). International and national political elites promote the global economic scale, which constructs the strategic sites of the economic system into world cities (Smith 2001). In effect, this perspective explains deliberate political intentions to allow the global market to produce the world cities. Local urban managers in these cities are more effective in promoting economic development than central bureaucrats. Brenner (1999, p. 439) explains:

> This dynamic of state re-scaling has emerged . . . to enable new forms of capital mobility on supranational [scale] to promote the global competitiveness of major sub-national growth poles and to enforce the de- and revalorisation of capital within declining cities and regions.

THE NESTED INTERACTION PERSPECTIVE

The "nested interaction perspective" starts with the recognition that the global economic system is profoundly impacting cities. Moreover, global or world cities are sociopolitically defined places that have limited authority and operate within a state and national legal-political system. Thus, world cities' local business and public officials operate at multiple scales, sometimes cooperating and sometimes fighting to pursue their varying political and economic interests in alliance with officials at other levels. Moreover, nongovernmental or private officials (such as trade associations, labor groups, and interest groups) also operate at multiple scales. All of these bodies exist in a nested form from global to local, and conditions of cities are always configured through the interrelations between these nested social scales (Hill and Fujita 2003).

Hence, geographically specific factors, including political structures, social cultures, and historic backgrounds, create world cities through interactions with market forces in a path-dependent fashion (Abu-Lughod 1999). In this view, nation-states are considered most influential for cities among various institutional scales. For example, the Japanese and Korean governments developed Tokyo and Seoul, respectively, into world cities as the engines of national developmental policies (Hill and Kim 2000), and the French government nurtured Paris as its cultural champion (White 1998). However, this does not mean that lower-level scales are powerless. On the contrary, Saito (2003) and Fujita (2003) show in the case of Tokyo that cities can have political independence and resist their central governments even under a strong unitary state system. Indeed, the "nested interaction" model accepts the declining influences of nation-states relative to international and subnational forces and the enhanced position of local governments under the global economy (Hill and Fujita 2003). What this model insists is its claim that the global market forces cannot affect local conditions in a direct and uniform fashion without being filtered through the influences of intermediary political scales, notably the nation-states. In other words, world cities are not converging in their development patterns:

> [Because] cities are nested in diverse national and regional configurations, the implications of globalisation for urban life cannot be deduced from any structural or market deterministic logic.
>
> (Hill and Fujita 2003, p. 212)

THE NEW LOCALISM PERSPECTIVE

The "new localism" view is based on grounded observations of local political actions finding that local elites' strategic actions and political choices are crucial for their cities' fortunes under the global economy. Local government is an active agent and broker for urban development, connecting local interests and macroenvironmental opportunities via strategic interventions (Clarke and Gaile 1998). Under globalization, localities assert themselves as the politically, socially, economically, and culturally autonomous units of space as opposed to nation-states (Taylor 1996).

The focal point is the strategic actions taken by local actors to produce world cities. For example, the city (i.e., the local state) can grow by investing in crucial public infrastructure (Erie 2002). Alternatively, city-regions can strengthen economic capacities through regional networking to take advantage of economic agglomeration effects (Savitch and Vogel 1996; Scott et al. 2001). Cities are capable of exerting themselves in the global economy as active players because they are the locations where actual value-adding activities take place though place-based human capital and knowledge accumulation (Amin and Thrift 1994; Clarke and Gaile 1998). Local actors engage in local state building when they identify themselves in the global scale, leading to economic autonomy (Keating, Loughlin, and Deschouwer 2003). But can cities really play in the global economy? Beauregard (1995, pp. 242–3) is optimistic about the cities and their capabilities in the global economy because:

> The global is the organization of many local actors on a broader geographical canvas, and that without local places the global cannot exist. Global actors hardly begin at the global scale . . . Rather, they work together outwards from the local, at least initially.

THE STUDY

If there is a relationship between globalization and political decentralization, this should be apparent in world cities, which have certainly been among the most globalized. This approach follows Eckstein's (1975) notions regarding testing a theory under the most favorable conditions (for example, "most likely" or "least likely" fit). Beaverstock, Smith, and Taylor (1999) provide a widely accepted operationalization of world cities (see table 2.3). We selected the 20 highest-ranked cities (10 Alpha and 10 Beta cities) in their roster of world cities to investigate the relationship between globalization and decentralization. We aim to provide a synthesis of the qualitative work on these 20 cities and then assess whether the theories of globalization adequately account for the empirical findings.

Much of theoretical work on globalization and cities in the field is informed by case studies research. Noblit and Hare (1988) developed the metaethnographic approach to synthesize findings drawn from thick case studies. The method involves coding cases for basic concepts, theories, and findings, focusing on common or divergent findings and insights and retaining the context of the individual case settings. We drew upon this

Table 2.3   The GaWC inventory of world cities

A.	Alpha world cities

12: London, Paris, New York, Tokyo
10: Chicago, Frankfurt, Hong Kong, Los Angeles, Milan, Singapore

B.	Beta world cities

9: San Francisco, Sydney, Toronto, Zurich
8: Brussels, Madrid, Mexico City, São Paulo
7: Moscow, Seoul

C.	Gamma world cities

6: Amsterdam, Boston, Caracas, Dallas, Dusseldorf, Geneva, Houston, Jakarta,
5: Johannesburg, Melbourne, Osaka, Prague, Santiago, Taipei, Washington
4: Bangkok, Beijing, Rome, Stockholm, Warsaw
     Atlanta, Barcelona, Berlin, Buenos Aires, Budapest, Copenhagen, Hamburg, Istanbul,
     Kuala Lumpur, Manila, Miami, Minneapolis, Montreal, Munich, Shanghai

Definitions: World-cityness values were produced by scoring 3 for prime center status, 2 for major center status, and 1 for minor center status. Cities are ordered in terms of world-cityness with values ranging from 1 to 12.
Source: GaWC inventory of world cities by Beaverstock and Taylor (1999, p. 56).

approach to synthesize key studies we identified on the 20 cities. We coded select studies in each of the 20 cities for the "metaphors" of interest related to globalization and decentralization.

In coding the cases, we focus on two research questions. First, what are the factors behind the development of global or world cities? Is the answer "global economic forces" (including functions, issues, incidences, and policy actions that are directly related to or resulting from the advancement of capitalistic global market)? Or, is the answer "government action or politics" (such as political actions, institutions, characteristics, conditions, culture, and power structures that are more or less indigenous to the locales)?

Second, is there evidence of political decentralization, and what was behind this decentralization? For example, does the case indicate that the global economy undermined the territorial control of the nation-state over the city? Was political decentralization initiated or extended in order to enhance the city's economic competitiveness? Did the city acquire greater local autonomy through the functioning of the global market system? On the other hand, is political decentralization more directly a function of local social movements or political ideology? As the discussion of globalization and political decentralization indicated, there are theoretical reasons why globalization might lead to greater centralization, and we include this possibility in our analysis.

We summarized the governance condition of each city in a snapshot description together with the evaluations as to what factor made it a world city, what process pushes it toward decentralization, and, finally, whether the city is currently more centralized or decentralized than in the past (see table 2.4).

FINDINGS AND ANALYSIS

IS THE GLOBAL ECONOMY THE FORCE BEHIND THE "WORLD CITIES"?

Here we ask what was the primary factor in the formation of leading world cities? Table 2.5 summarizes for the reader the information on world city formation found in table 2.4—Snapshots. Examining the 20 most-globalized cities as reported in Beaverstock,

Table 2.4   Snapshot of world city governance and cause/consequence evaluation

Snapshot of conditions of world cities	Political trend	Source of decentralization/ centralization	Source of world city formation
LONDON The neoliberal policies of the 1980s created the foundation for the world city, London. The Greater London Authority (GLA) was installed as a part of national strategy as well as democratization process in the 1990s. The central government tries to steer London to compete in the global economy while the GLA has acquired political power backed by the economic importance of the city.	Decentralized	Government/ politics	Global economy
PARIS The central state has built Paris, but the approach to its planning is changing. Intergovernmental relations are shifting from top-down to center-local cooperation to create local competitiveness under the global economy. Yet, the competition also motivates the central government strongly involved in Paris' development and planning.	(remains) Centralized	Global economy	Government/ politics
NEW YORK The city thrives in the economic globalization. Its world city status continues to rely on the global market system and the private sector under the American federal system. The neoliberal ideology since the 1980s mandates the city engages in growth policies under new federalism, although its fiscal dependence on the state government has increased.	(remains) Decentralized	Government/ politics	Global economy
TOKYO Tokyo has earned its world city status through developmental state policies. Decentralization gathers pace as a national policy, while Tokyo and the central government have increased interdependence to compete in the global economy. Tokyo has gained political clout vis-à-vis the central government owing to its economic might.	Decentralized	Global economy	Government/ politics
CHICAGO The American federal system and its neoliberal ideology since the 1980s determine the parameter within which Chicago implements urban development policies. Chicago had to experience a drastic industrial restructuring under globalization while it enjoys a world city status through headquarter functions and the Mercantile Exchange of Chicago.	(remains) Decentralized	Government/ politics	Global economy

City			
FRANKFURT Structurally, Germany has highly decentralized local governments. However, functionally, national and state interests heavily weighed in on Frankfurt through the party system to make it a German world city. Locally, the private sector has been active for regional development for competitiveness and political autonomy.	Decentralized	Global economy	Government/ politics
HONG KONG As the financial center of the Pearl River Delta Urban Region, Hong Kong's economy has converted to an advanced service economy under the global economy while maintaining political independence. Its expanded economic power provides the source of political strength.	Decentralized	Global economy	Global economy
LOS ANGELES Its public corporations were the backbones of Los Angeles' industrialization, which still constitutes a large sector of the city's economic basis. The public sector has also played an important role to redevelop the downtown business district that accommodates the advanced business-service operations. State policy, in addition to the federal system, conditions the city's political status.	(remains) Decentralized	Government/ politics	Government/ politics
MILAN Politics is instrumental for Milan's current economic status. The city relies on the central government to finance development via the strong party system. The central government has passed several new laws to encourage regionalism in recent years. Central/local linkage through the party system remains the persistent political culture.	(remains) Centralized	Government/ politics	Government/ politics
SINGAPORE Leadership and planning of the Singapore government have made this city-state a world city, transforming it from an offshore industrial economy to an advanced services economy. State control increased to steer the economy during/after the Asian economic crisis of the late 1990s.	(remains) Centralized	Global economy	Government/ politics
SAN FRANCISCO The city has grown on economic individualism under the American federalism. Regional and global competitions force the city to maintain growth politics. San Francisco's position as the American financial center of the west was a result of such efforts put up by the coalition of the city government leaders and business elites.	(remains) Decentralized	Government/ politics	Government/ politics
SYDNEY Sydney became a world city once Australia embraced the global economy. The state of New South Wales pushed through urban development projects in Sydney to compete under the global economy despite the objections raised by the Sydney City Council.	(remains) Centralized	Global economy	Global economy

(Continued)

Table 2.4   (Continued)

Snapshot of conditions of world cities	Political trend	Source of decentralization/ centralization	Source of world city formation
TORONTO The provincial government has been instrumental for Toronto's economic growth. In the late 1990s, the province government forced amalgamation of the city of Toronto, the Toronto metro government, and its five other suburban municipalities to create a conservative majority in the metropolitan area for better business environment and competitiveness.	Centralized	Global economy	Government/politics
ZURICH Zurich became a global financial center after international financial liberalization in the 1980s. Growth pressure from the new service economy conflicted with the city's planning policies in the early 1990s, culminating in the Canton of Zurich overriding the city's land use law to allow easier urban development with free enterprise zoning.	Centralized	Global economy	Global economy
BRUSSELS Brussels grew along with the European Union (EU). The laissez-faire attitude toward economic and land use planning changed the city into a world city as the importance and capacity of the EU headquarters expanded. Fragmentation along ethnic identities characterizes the city's political scene. The city is also divided between business leaders with global interests and those with parochial local interests.	Decentralized	Government/Politics	Government/Politics
MADRID Joining the European Community has prompted the growth of Madrid, with international investments coming in during the latter 1980s. Democratization process since the late 1970s has decentralized Spain's government system. The Community of Madrid, a province including the Madrid metropolitan area, has gained planning authorities during this democratization period.	Decentralized	Government/politics	Global economy
MEXICO CITY Under the General Agreement on Tariffs and Trade and the North American Free Trade Agreement, Mexico City has become a world city. Citizen actions and democratization implemented by the central government in the same periods increased local government power. However, globalization allows the president to retain strong control over Mexico City through economic policies.	(remains) Centralized	Global economy	Global economy

SAO PAULO

Neoliberal restructuring allowed São Paulo to develop into a world city during the 1990s. However, it also undermined the competitiveness of its industrial sector. The municipalities of the São Paulo metropolitan region face fiscal problems as the regional industries decline. Under competitive pressure, the central city and suburbs confront over economic development policies.

| (remains) Decentralized | Government/ politics | Global economy |

MOSCOW

Moscow has become a world city after adopting free market economy. Its mayor pushes forward urban development projects. Despite the general movement toward decentralization and democratization, recentralization of municipal governments is taking place in recent years to implement economic reforms and to pursue global market economy.

| (remains) Centralized | Global economy | Global economy |

SEOUL

Central government's focused efforts produced the world city Seoul. The democratization movement in the 1990s and criticism by city leaders resulted in increased autonomy in Seoul. But the importance of Seoul for South Korea has become even stronger as the global economy strengthened, making the state's relinquishing of the control over the city very difficult.

| (remains) Centralized | Global economy | Government/ politics |

Sources:

London   Fainstein 2001; MacLeod and Goodwin 1999; Newman and Thornley 1997; Pimlot and Rao 2002; Sanford 2002; Thornley 2003; Zimmerman 2003
Paris   Lefevre 2003; Levine 1994; Newman and Thornley 1996; Savitch and Kantor 2002
New York   Abu-Lughod 1999; Fainstein 2001; Kincaid 1999; O'Cleireacain 1997; Savitch and Kantor 2002
Tokyo   Kamo 2000; Muramatsu et al. 2001; Toki 2003; Vogel 2000; Yahagi 2002
Chicago   Abu-Lughod 1999; Hamilton 2002; Kincaid 1999; Rast 1999; Simpson 2004
Frankfurt   Freund 2003; Keil and Lieser 1992; Keil and Ronneberger 1994; Keil and Ronneberger 2000; Sellers 2002
Hong Kong   Cullinane 2003; Jessop and Sum 2000; Lin 1999; Ng and Tang 1999; Sir 2001; Smart 2002; Yeung 2000a; Yeung 2000b
Los Angeles   Abu-Lughod 1999; Erie 2002; Keil 1998; Kincaid 1999; Scott 2002; Walker 1996
Milan   Agnew, Shin and Bettoni 2002; Berselli 2001; Foot 2001; Gualini 2003; Savitch and Kantor 2002b
Singapore   Grunsven 2000; Yeoh and Chang 2001; Yeung 2000a; Yue 2001
San Francisco Deleon 1992; Godfrey 1997; Hartman 2002; Kincaid 1999; Walker 1996
Sydney   Badcock 2000; Murphy and Wu 2001; Searle 2002; Searle and Bounds 1999; Short et al. 2000
Toronto   Keil 2000; Savitch and Kantor 2002; Wolfson and Frisken 2000
Zurich   Church 2000; Hirz, Schmid and Wolff 1994; Hofer 2004; Linder and Vatter 2001
Brussels   Albrechts 2001; Baeten 2001; Kesteloot 2000; Swyngedouw and Beaten 2001
Madrid   Aja 2001; Ezquiaga et al. 2000; Maldonado 2003; Resina 2001
Mexico City   Davis 2002; Montero 2001b; Parnreiter 2002; Ward 1998
São Paulo   Bruna 2000; Graham and Jacobi 2002; Montero 2001a and 2001b; Rodriguez-Pose and Tomaney 1999; Santos 1996; Schiffer 2002
Moscow   Alden, Crow, and Beigulenko 1998; Colton 1995; Gel'man 2003; Gritsai 1997; Pagonis and Thornley 2000; Saunders 2001
Seoul   Kim and Choe 1997; Kim 1999 and 2000

Table 2.5   Breakdown of world cities by political trend, source of decentralization/centralization, and source of formation

Political trend	Source of decentralization/ centralization	Source of world city formation		
		Global economy	Government/politics	
Decentralized	Global economy	World cities system Hong Kong$^\alpha$ (1)	Nested interaction Tokyo$^\alpha$, Frankfurt$^\alpha$ (2)	3
	Government/ politics	State glocalization London$^\alpha$, New York$^\alpha$, Chicago$^\alpha$, Madrid$^\beta$, São Paulo$^\beta$ (5)	New localism Los Angeles$^\alpha$, San Francisco$^\beta$, Brussels$^\beta$ (3)	8
	Subtotal	6	5	11
Centralized	Global economy	Sydney$^\beta$, Zurich$^\beta$, Mexico City$^\beta$, Moscow$^\beta$ (4)	Paris$^\alpha$, Singapore$^\alpha$, Toronto$^\beta$, Seoul$^\beta$ (4)	8
	Government/ politics		Milan$^\alpha$ (1)	1
	Subtotal	4	5	9
	Grand total	10	10	20

Note: Cities marked with superscript "α" are "Alpha" world cities and those with "β," "Beta" world cities.

Smith, and Taylor (1999), our analysis indicates half are on the list because of global economic forces; the other half are on the list because of politics (see table 2.5, the two columns under the heading "Source of world city formation"). Although there is evidence that global market forces are important factors in the formation of half of the world cities, the role of politics at the central or the local level was equally important in the other half of the cases. Although there would be no "world cities" if there was no global economy, half of the most globalized cities based upon the roster of world cities are on the roster because of government and politics.

DOES GLOBALIZATION LEAD TO POLITICAL DECENTRALIZATION?

The literature on globalization and political decentralization suggests that globalization is strongly associated with political decentralization. With this in mind, we examined a set of global world cities to explore the relationship between the global economy and political decentralization. Specifically, we looked at the 20 most-globalized cities in a highly regarded ranking to consider whether there was evidence that significant decentralization was under way or had occurred in the recent past. Surprisingly, we find that decentralization is *not* the overwhelming trend as expected. Rather, there was clear evidence of decentralization processes in just over half the cases (11 out of 20; see table 2.5, shaded section). This is contrary to what our theoretical perspectives on globalization implied. Recall that we are examining cities that have been identified as the most globalized. Thus, the finding that almost half the cities in the analysis remained centralized or were moving in the direction of centralization points out a major deficit in globalization theory and world city perspectives.

WORLD CITY PERSPECTIVES

Table 2.5 also brings the analysis back to the four perspectives of the world cities and globalization literature. We find that the four main perspectives on globalization adequately explain world city formation and political decentralization in only 11 of our 20 world cities (see shaded section of table 2.5). That is, political centralization was almost as likely in the most globalized cities as political decentralization.

Focusing on the 11 places that were politically decentralized, only the case of Hong Kong corresponded with the descriptions the "world city system perspective." Hong Kong became a world city through competitive advantages offered by the global economy. Globalization also was the mechanism that enhanced its political autonomy, even if somewhat muted by the transfer back to the People's Republic of China.

London, New York, Chicago, Madrid, and São Paulo fit the *state glocalization* perspective. These cities owe their world city position to the globalized economy. The indigenous political conditions keep New York, Chicago, and Madrid decentralized. New York, of course, was already a global city but its advantages were multiplied as global financial trade accelerated. Economic globalization afforded Chicago new opportunities even as deindustrialization undermined its economic position. U.S. cities are noted for a high degree of political decentralization, and the advent of new federalism has required cities to be even more self-sufficient under the direction of a new breed of mayors (Savitch and Vogel 2005). In Madrid, democratization and new national policies favoring regional autonomy promote a high degree of political decentralization. At the same time, Madrid has benefited enormously from foreign direct investment upon joining the European Community. São Paulo's star has risen as a world city associated with global market forces as Brazil reduced economic regulations and integrated into the global economy. The transition to democracy and strong local activism promoted political decentralization.

Political decentralization in London requires more explanation. In the 1980s, the Thatcher administration embraced a market strategy alongside elimination of the Greater London Council, which had served as a center of Labour opposition to her Conservative policies of cutting back on the state welfare system. The reestablishment of a Greater London Authority is primarily a function of Blair's New Labour policies, which includes recognizing London as a global city that secures Britain's continued economic health. The absence of a metropolitan city of London was viewed as an impediment to the nation's economic security. Although state action is directly responsible for re-creating a metropolitan or regional capacity to act, it is motivated by the need to be responsive and proactive in regard to the global market system rather than primarily a concern over enhancing local democracy.

The "nested interaction" model describes Frankfurt and Tokyo. Frankfurt gained its original development thrusts from political actions (central-local political cooperation) and is now consolidating political independence through its economic strength, even posing a threat to London's primacy in Europe. In the case of Tokyo, the development state deliberately promoted Tokyo's world city status through infrastructure policies, national investment, and regulatory policies at the conclusion of the war. Now, concern over Japan's weak economic performance has motivated the government to promote decentralization. Tokyo enjoys greater autonomy than other large cities or prefecture governments in the Japanese system because of the revenues it raises from the large corporations that are located there. Thus, the global economy is a major source of political decentralization.

The "new localism" model matches with the experiences of Los Angeles, San Francisco, and Brussels. Their rise to world city status was a function of state action or politics, whether at the national level, supraregional level—the European Union (Brussels), or local level—local elite leadership (Los Angeles, San Francisco). In all of these cases, however, political decentralization was acquired through a strong institutional framework for governance at the city level, including significant resources, discretion, or autonomy provided in constitutions, customs, or a strong economy.

DOES GLOBALIZATION LEAD TO A HOLLOWING OUT OF THE NATION-STATE?

Perhaps of greater interest are the findings that greater political centralization was occurring in nine of the most globalized cities in the world, although the globalization literature suggested decentralization. Importantly, of the nine centralized cities, eight were centralized because the global economy stimulated their central governments to intervene for development (see table 2.5, lower portion). Given this, it would seem that the major perspectives on globalization and world cities and their relation to political decentralization are in need of modification. It bears repeating that in these eight cases, we find the central governments taking a leading role in their cities' development policies to enhance competitiveness because of the global or world economy.

We found that state action or politics was as important as economic globalization in the formation of the world cities. We also found that economic globalization can only partially explain political decentralization in the world cities. Globalization appears to spur higher-level governments, whether nation-states or provincial governments, to intervene in the policymaking of the world cities for political centralization. Decentralization movements are apparent in a number of world cities. In the cases we reviewed, politics was more likely than economic globalization to be the primary factor. Of the 11 decentralized cities, eight are so based upon political and governmental causes (see table 2.5, shaded portion).

The four perspectives on globalization and world cities are still wanting in describing what is taking place in the world cities under the global economy when arrayed against the actual experiences of the most globalized world cities. Much greater attention must be given to the role of the state in world city policies, even in the new localism perspectives. Central governments have a strong interest in promoting their world cities as the integration of the global economy intensifies. Hollowing out of nation-states is not apparent in the world cities in this review. Selective intervention in local governments may be an important part of strategic policies for central governments to compete in the global marketplace. This may be especially true for the Beta world cities in comparison to the Alpha cities. Six of the eight globalization-motivated centralized cities are Beta world cities. No Beta cities are decentralized due to the global economy.

CONCLUSIONS

In this chapter, we reviewed existing theories of globalization and their effects on the most globalized cities as well as the relationship between globalization and political decentralization. We find that globalization is exerting some pressures toward political decentralization. However, globalization is almost as likely to lead to greater political centralization as decentralization. This is counterintuitive, given conventional wisdom implicit, if not explicit, in the literature on globalization and political decentralization. Although it is true that globalization has spurred political decentralization in a number of world cities, globalization also appears to be encouraging higher-level governments, whether nation-states or states/provinces, to intervene in the policymaking of the world cities in favor of centralization.

It looks as though the world cities are functioning as the direct economic agents of the central governments in several countries despite the prevailing neoliberalism in the world economy. Our analysis highlights the role of higher-level governments and, especially, the nation-state in reordering intergovernmental relations and selectively changing geographic scales (such as reterritorializing the world cities while deterritorializing other areas). None of the four perspectives on world cities and globalization appears superior, and they miss important aspects of what is taking place in the world cities under the globalized economy when arrayed against our findings. Their common shortcoming is neglecting the direct involvement of central governments, which are now reinserting themselves in the world cities as a reaction to intensified global competition. As a result, the literature on globalization and cities, including the world city thesis, implies a decentralizing trend from higher governments, while our review suggests an almost equal association with centralization. Globalization and world city theories need to be modified to better correspond with the likelihood of central governments' direct and strategic involvement in world city policies and development. This also suggests that a more dynamic theory of globalization and cities is needed. The theories of globalization and world cities are probably more complementary than contradictory. This is probably the challenge and agenda that we take from the present analysis.

CHAPTER 3

Governing the Capital—Comparing Institutional Reform in Berlin, London, and Paris

Manfred Röber and Eckhard Schröter

BIG CITY GOVERNMENT: GLOBAL CHALLENGES AND INSTITUTIONAL CAPACITY

The inherent tensions between centralizing and decentralizing trends in big city government have been a recurrent issue of the local government literature. Arguably, these tensions are as old as the phenomenon of large cities that are home to millions of people and serve as centers of gravity for national and increasingly international functions in politics, culture, and the economy. On the one hand, many public services and competencies could be centralized easily because of the manageable territorial size of these cities. On the other hand, the sheer size of their population (and, in particular, the population density) requires more decentralized modes of service delivery and politico-administrative responsibilities (Barlow 1993). Far-reaching changes taking place in big European cities seem to indicate that traditional forms of hierarchical and bureaucratic political control have reached their limits and are now in retreat. At the same time it has become quite obvious (especially in London between 1986 and 2000) that all modes of horizontal self-coordination have severe disadvantages—as long as they do not operate in the shadow of hierarchical decision-making procedures as "ultima ratio." Against this background there are some indicators that politico-administrative arrangements in big cities converge toward two-tier-systems that take vertical and horizontal coordination problems in agglomerations into account and that might be able to reconcile potential conflicts between central and decentralized control mechanisms (see also Barlow 1993).

In the European context we can identify three ideal-typical models of two-tier-systems as represented by the cities of Berlin, London, and Paris. All three cities represent major and fairly distinct European administrative cultures that have been coining their own political and administrative models and reform profiles. In that respect, Berlin, London, and Paris can be treated as "most dissimilar cases" that mark important points of reference with regard to institutional variance, which makes it possible to raise and answer the question on convergent trends of political and administrative structures with some prospect of succeeding. In all three cities there is an intense ongoing debate about the precarious relation between centralized and decentralized control and steering mechanisms. This debate gives the impression that global economic challenges exert an enormous pressure on political decision makers to streamline their institutional arrangements according to global trends ("convergence thesis"). At the same time several scholars never tire of emphasizing country-specific features and trajectories and path-dependencies ("persisting divergence thesis"). In our contribution to this debate, we first briefly sketch the theoretical backdrop of those contrasting perspectives before examining the history and politics of institutional change in the three European capitals. In doing so, we go well beyond the current focus on "globalization" and seek to shed some light on the impact of earlier "megatrends" such as industrialization and suburbanization on big city government.

TOWARD "CONVERGENCE" OR "PERSISTING DIVERGENCE" IN BIG CITY GOVERNMENT?

The assertion of global convergence is theoretically underpinned by contributions of Neoinstitutional Economics, which assumes that more efficient institutional arrangements will, over time, replace less efficient ones. From this point of view, the genesis of institutions is a matter of finding (economically) optimal arrangements (Coase 1937; Ross 1973; Williamson 1981 and 1985; Barzel 1989; Horn 1995). That means the decisive criterion for designing politico-administrative institutions is (rationality based) efficiency. The "convergence thesis" also gets support from statements by representatives of the New Political Economy and from contributions to the Economic Theory of Bureaucracy that present top civil servants and politicians as actors driven by cost-benefit calculations (Dunleavy 1991). And further support comes from sociological variants of the New Institutionalism, which stresses the importance of diffusion and learning across countries in order to explain the widespread proliferation of administrative reform models. This position is strongly influenced by DiMaggio's and Powell's (1983) research work on institutional isomorphism.

It can come as no surprise that the "convergence thesis" has been questioned from other theoretical viewpoints. Representatives of the "Historical Institutionalism," particularly, have been criticizing the ostensible quasi-automatic processes of economic adjustment. In sharp contrast they emphasize the importance of case- and country-specific features and trajectories that reflect national and regional styles of administration ("persisting divergence thesis"). The starting point of their reflections is the assumption that when an institution has been already founded the path of its further development is predetermined (although not completely) and can only be changed or redefined under certain circumstances (critical junctures or critical institutional events) and with high costs (in financial as well as in social terms). According to this type of institutional theory, it is extremely important to look for turning points and key decisions in institutional genesis, which help to understand the functioning of institutions and the reasons of the present reform debates. Representatives of this approach also emphasize the power of ideas for path dependencies (Krasner 1984; Hall 1986; Immergut 1992; Steinmo, Thelen, and Longstreth 1992). Besides structural characteristics, ideas and images of institutional arrangements restrict possible and acceptable changes; but they provide a set of under-standings and organizational blueprints for certain problem areas. Therefore the choice of alternative institutional options is limited to a "reform corridor" that, normally, only allows incremental changes (March and Olson 1983; Tolbert and Zucker 1996). Following these theoretical considerations, one cannot necessarily expect a cross-national and cross-cultural convergence of politico-administrative institutions (built on purposefully designed reform programs) but a multitude of distinctive models that are shaped by patterns of different political and administrative cultures.

MAKING SENSE OF INSTITUTIONAL VARIETY

The genealogy of the institutional architecture of our three European capitals shows that each city started this century-long trajectory from a distinct position on the decentralization-centralization scale, which has left its decisive marks on the contemporary design of each city's political and administrative structure. And yet, the discernible patterns of institutional developments in Berlin, London, and Paris render, at the same time, fur-ther support for the hypothesis that the predominant model of big city government in Europe has gravitated over time toward a more centrist position on the decentralization spectrum. (This trend is presumed to be a result of a series of convergent institutional shift.) As a matter of fact, the institutional trajectories of all three cities—despite the still existing and significant differences in their structural layouts—appear to be relatively in sync with one another as measured by the timing, sequence, and content of major waves of reform activity.

THE RISE OF BIG CITY GOVERNMENT IN THE ERA OF INDUSTRIALIZATION AND URBANIZATION

Toward the end of the nineteenth century, the local government systems for the metro-politan areas of London and, albeit to a much lesser extent, of Berlin were mainly char-acterized by a relatively high degree of political and administrative fragmentation, with a multitude of small-scale authorities, oftentimes with geographically and functionally overlapping jurisdictions. The city of Paris, however, had been governed since the early eighteenth century in the strictly centralist and hierarchical fashion of the Napoleonic state and local government reform (Glum 1920; Hauck Walsh 1968; Debofle et al. 1979). Apart from short interludes in the revolutionary years of 1848 and 1870–71, since 1795 the city of Paris had never been—unlike local government in the rest of the country (Mabileau 1996)—represented by its own head of city government until the reform law of 1975 came into effect. Instead, the capital city was held in the tight grip of the pre-fect of the Seine *Departement,* who was, in his functions as representative of the state and head of the *departement* administration, concurrently the "mayor'" of Paris and kept a stern watch on all city affairs. The jurisdiction of a special state-appointed police prefect over security and order underscores in this phase once more the state endeavor to keep the metropolis Paris—as the center of gravity of the nation's economic and political power and simultaneously a potential hotbed of political and social unrest—in the firm grasp of political and administrative supervision. The then-existing twenty arrondisse-ments (without elected councils) were administered by mayors (*maires*) and a number of councillors (*adjoints*) who were appointed by the French central government.

In London and Berlin the reorganization of city governments placed particularly high emphasis on increasing the administrative capacity of local authorities, thus adding a distinctly centralizing, if not bureaucratic, flavor to the management of urban affairs. In part, this was achieved by establishing larger administrative units with more systematically delineated areas of responsibility and, eventually, by introducing a multipurpose authority for the whole built-up area of the metropolis.

In an early major move toward consolidating the city's government structure, the Metropolitan Board of Works was established in 1855 as London's first citywide self-government. The board of works represented some thirty-nine local authorities and was successively entrusted with a multitude of public tasks ranging from the fire service, building control, and health services to housing, poor law, and technical infrastructure development such as sewerage, bridges, tunnels, and tramways. While this new organizational approach enhanced London's administrative capacity, the rampant industrialization and urbanization of Victorian England—hand in hand with slow but steady developments toward more democratically controlled local governments in the United Kingdom—called for further political and administrative integration of the city's local government structure. Intriguingly, however, this reform pressure did not result in the creation of a new consolidated municipal government—as in the case of Berlin—but in the establishment of the London County Council (LCC), thus creating in 1888 an upper level of citywide administration while safeguarding the politically autonomous status of the lower-tier administrations as full-fledged local authorities (O'Leary 1987a; Sharpe 1995). The Local Government Act of 1888 created a new administrative county out of a group of parishes, vestries, and other subdivisions, with the directly elected LCC as major decision-making body.

The discussion concerning questions of the government of the Greater Berlin area, which are still instructive for the present administrative-political debate, set in at the end of the nineteenth century. Toward the solution of problems arising from rapid industrialization and urbanization reaching beyond the old city borders in this densely populated conurbation, a single-purpose agency (Zweckverband)—jointly organized by the then city of Berlin and a number of neighboring local authorities—was established in 1911. The agency's task was to regulate public transportation, to determine zoning plans, and to organize the acquisition and preservation of larger undeveloped spaces (e.g., forests, parks, meadows, lakes, playgrounds, sports facilities). Despite some successes it was quickly clear that entertained hopes of finding an effective and long-lasting administrative structure for the built-up area had not been fulfilled (Engeli 1986, p. 38). At the end of the First World War, discussion of an institutional architecture that took account of the demands of the conurbation flared quickly again. In contradistinction to the London situation, the discussion in Berlin ran along lines of a unified city government, which was achieved in 1920 with the Greater-Berlin Act legislated by the Prussian State Assembly. This piece of legislation can still be viewed as the basis of the present-day Berlin administrative model (for historical development compare Röber 2002 and Zivier 1998). It comprised a compromise reached between the varied political camps that took account of the fears of the bourgeois parties of a social-democratic dominance in a unified body as well as the hopes of the worker parties attached to a consequent incorporation. At the same time a comprehensive territorial reorganization was subsequently bound with the Greater-Berlin Act, which mainly affected the great number of incorporated rural communities and introduced twenty new districts as the second tier of the city government.

This rather centralizing tilt in big city government was compelled by a set of new challenges to the traditional forms of local management that proved increasingly inadequate in times of galloping industrialization and urbanization. This major stage in societal and economic development, which had already been under way in England since the early nineteenth century when it finally made its inroads in Germany and France during the second half of that century, was most closely associated with a completely new (Tayloristic) model of organizing the production process that rendered time-honored craftsmanship and artisan production techniques largely obsolete. The standardization of work processes and production techniques, the systematic use of new, capital-intensive technologies, and the establishment of large bureaucratic apparatuses in private and public institutions became hallmarks of the new era. While these features allowed for the mass production of consumer goods and provision of standardized mass services, they also brought about the advent of joint stock companies as the most important players in the new market.

As a consequence of industrialization, the rural population flocked in large parts to the urban centers, which experienced dramatic growth rates and were ill-equipped to accommodate the needs of the new arrivals. Increased urbanization went alongside the separation of working and living places, which—in combination with the breakup of the traditional family structure—resulted in a number of new social problems of an unprecedented magnitude in terms of both their qualitative and their quantitative dimensions. On top of that, the use of new technologies in the production process, as well as the logistical and infrastructure problems caused by the vast growth of the major cities, created an increased need for public oversight and control of hazardous goods, food safety, health and sanitary services, sewerage systems, and mass public transportation. At the same time the surge in the technical and logistical complexity of most production processes and infrastructure needs called for an equivalent increase in professional skills and formal qualifications that required higher standards of schooling. This tendency, in turn, propelled—particularly in countries such as France and Germany—the development (mainly under state control) of educational and vocational training systems with highly regulated standards and formal exams.

Against this background, it became only too obvious that traditionally fragmented and small-scale local authorities were overwhelmed by the new functions and public tasks they had to take on as a corollary of the underlying social and economic changes. While the newly established single-purpose agencies serving a larger metropolitan area were a helpful first step in developing and improving certain infrastructure networks for a transition period, in the long run the quest for political representation and increased administrative capacity at the citywide level could not be denied. This shift toward some form of consolidated administration for the whole of the built-up area of the metropolis can also be seen as a move to counterbalance the increasingly powerful industrial corporations and to establish functionally equivalent ways of organizing administrative tasks. Just as Taylorism in regard to industrial management seeks to exploit the efficiency gains from standardized production processes, so aims the principle of bureaucratic organization—as ideal-typically described by Max Weber—at the highest measure of calculability and reliability of organizational performance. The creation of a citywide administration for a larger conurbation, while maintaining a lower-tier local government, also sparked off an ongoing debate over the pros and cons of having a two-tier system of government that seems to dominate the administrative reform agenda in our sample cities—particularly London and Berlin—to the present day.

CAPITALS AND THEIR REGIONS: SUBURBANIZATION AND THE POSTWAR "PLANNING MOOD"

The administrative and political structure, as it emerged around the turn of the century in London and—with a little time lag—also in Berlin, had proven to be relatively impervious for a long span of time to a series of attempts to rearrange allocation of competencies and responsibilities. Of course, this also holds true for the city of Paris; however, there seem to be very different factors at work. Most significantly, the shape of Parisian city government had been effectively molded by the centralist tendencies of the French unitary state. On the one hand, this political dependency on state actors curtailed the city administration's room for maneuvre vis-à-vis the central government. On the other hand, it also flows from this that the French capital city could rely on strongly developed state institutions to assist the local authorities in coping with the new social and economic challenges in the wake of urbanization and to provide the necessary resources for tackling the new problems.

The economic and social changes in the aftermath of the Second World War provided fertile ground for a new round of major metropolitan reform activities to flourish. For obvious geopolitical reasons, the then divided city of Berlin—overshadowed by the East-West confrontation as it was—proved to be the odd one out in our sample group and was, at least partly, sidetracked from the mainstream of institutional and spatial developments in European big city government. In London and Paris, however, in the course of the 1950s and early 1960s, the debates over administrative reform had been receiving increasingly high currency with a view to creating even larger and more effective authorities for the whole of the still vastly growing metropolitan regions. These debates were also well embedded and nurtured by more far-reaching conceptual and political discourses that placed high emphasis on comprehensive and supposedly rational planning mechanisms as a means to control and fine-tune long-term economic and social developments. To be sure, this "planning enthusiasm" was also embraced by a wide range of other local, regional, and national governments; certainly, it was no stranger to the policy-makers in the city-state of (West) Berlin.

This proactive and planning-oriented policy approach owed much of its theoretical legitimacy to J. M. Keynes's economic theory, which appeared to provide the toolkit for governments to safeguard not only continued economic growth but also the benefits of having a full-fledged system of welfare-state services. In fact, the unprecedented growth rates allowed for constantly raising living standards and increasing supplies of consumer goods for wider strata of society. In particular, the upsurge in private transport accelerated the growth of suburban sprawl, which reached its peak in the 1960s and brought a host of new challenges for land-use planners in its wake.

This trend toward suburbanization mainly resulted, for the core cities of the metropolitan regions, in dramatic losses in the size of the middle-class population as well as in an outward movement of many service businesses and manufacturing industries (Lichtenberger 1976). It follows from this that the budgetary situation of many core cities was beginning to deteriorate rapidly with an ever-widening gap between the revenue and expenditure sides of the budget. While tax income from businesses and the upper-income or property tax brackets was decreasing, the core cities continued to fulfill their wider functions as providers of many—and often cost-intensive—services and infrastructure networks for the whole of the surrounding regions, if not beyond. Not surprisingly, transaction costs of intergovernmental cooperation and bargaining processes were escalating. At the same time, the central areas of the built-up regions also had to shoulder extra social costs as a consequence of the intensified processes of social segregation and polarization. It goes without saying that this growing disparity between inner-city and suburban areas also left its mark on the problem perception and political response patterns of local representatives.

Policy-makers in Berlin, London, and Paris responded to these challenges in a remarkably similar way, although each individual reform program had a distinct local and country-specific flavor to it. Conceptually driven and inspired by a widely shared belief system that had high hopes in the steering capacity of politico-administrative institutions and a lot of (with hindsight, largely unjustified) trust in the feasibility and appropriateness of long-term "social engineering," they sought to expand the planning powers and problem-solving capacities of regional and local authorities. The continuing enlargement of the built-up areas of the London and Paris regions well beyond the boundaries of the existing city government structures propelled planners and lawmakers into action directed at the creation of large-scale authorities.

Against this background, the era of the Greater London Council (GLC)—which was to last for twenty years—was ushered in by an act of parliament in 1965. This administrative construct showed all indications of a political compromise. Whereas its boundaries were set far beyond the limits of what used to be the LCC (now known as "inner London"), so as to include "outer London," other significant parts of the Outer Metropolitan Area still lay outside its jurisdiction, mainly owing to fierce resistance from local authorities against their incorporation into the new London-wide arrangements. In addition, the government plan for the metropolitan administration deviated from the original master plan in that it created new inner-city boroughs of almost twice the size as proposed by a royal commission (Herbert Commission). As a consequence, the now strengthened thirty-two London boroughs (plus the city of London)—with some of the largest and richest localities among them—acted as natural rivals of the upper-tier administration. Moreover, the emerging disparities between inner-city boroughs and outer-London boroughs led to political tensions and social cleavages within the GLC limits that were unheard of during the era of the more homogeneous LCC. On top of that, the GLC found itself in the uncomfortable position of suffering from a lack of some of the strategic and executive competencies to fulfill its planning and steering function—as originally envisaged by the reform protagonists (the London Government Act of 1965, as a matter of fact, fell short of what the Herbert Commission had originally envisaged). At the same time it was accused of being a monstrous bureaucratic apparatus. In the long run the GLC was not robust enough to stand the inherent tensions of its institutional architecture and the increasing partisan attacks launched mainly from the Conservative government under Margaret Thatcher's leadership (O'Leary 1987b). When the Conservative majority in the House of Commons abolished the GLC in 1986 (Young and Grayson 1988), this left a one-tier polycentric administrative structure for fourteen years relying on thirty-three boroughs (as full-fledged local authorities) and ministries of the national government that reserved some direct competences and responsibilities for themselves. A number of single-purpose agencies operating citywide as well as ad hoc boards and committees completed the new landscape of London's government structure. According to general lines of institutional development, this decision can be qualified as a relapse into the model of an extensive decentralized administrative structure.

The countrywide efforts toward a stronger decentralization of the national political and administrative systems brought with itself a reassessment of the Parisian situation. This development led in 1964 initially to the reorganization of the traditional *Seine departements* (*Seine, Seine et Marne, Seine et Oise*), whereby the *Ville de Paris*—which had the municipal-legal character of a city, but which was practically nothing other than an administrative district—was awarded the status of a *departement*. In the redrawing of *departement* borders, party-political points of view played a not insignificant role, for, in this way, a bourgeois majority in the French capital was assured. The newly created eight *departements* in the Parisian conurbation (including the *Ville de Paris*) were moreover united in *La Region Parisienne* and constituted the focal point of the *Ile de France,* the region introduced in 1971, which henceforth represented one of twenty-one such regions countrywide at this newly founded level of administration. In this mesh of local and regional administrations (consisting of 1,300 communes and eight *departements* in the *Ile de France*), the now more independent city of Paris, with 2.1 million residents (and thereby approximately a quarter of the population of the entire *Ile de France*), remains the central actor in relations with the neighboring administrative units and those of the region. The elevated role of the city of Paris is expressed, for example, in the fact that the prefect of the *departement* of Paris holds, ex officio, the position of regional prefect for the *Ile de France.* From a city- and regional-planning perspective, the three inner *departements* directly adjacent to the *Ville de Paris* form the "small crown" (*petite couronne*), which functionally and settlement-wise can be equated with the outmost ring of London city boroughs (the eighteen "outer boroughs"). In contrast, the four outlying *departements* form the "large crown" (*grande couronne*), the equivalent of the "Outer Metropolitan Area" in the London situation.

Consequently, the substantial recasting of metropolitan government structures during the 1960s and early 1970s in London and Paris with the establishment of the GLC and the introduction of the *Ile de France* showed a striking family resemblance in both the spirit and the political practice of the reform measures. Nevertheless, a closer look at the underlying rationales of the new institutional fabrics also reveals significant differences in policy content that reflect the well-established paths of institutional development in each city. While reform policies in London took great care to safeguard the political status of London boroughs as independent local authorities by applying the deeply entrenched organizing principle of a decentralized two-tier system of metropolitan government to a larger area, French reformers were more concerned with changes to the nationwide planning system (by introducing a new regional level) and concurrent shifts toward less hierarchically structured relations between state, regional, and local authorities. In a similar vein, the national decentralization program gave a boost to the democratic legitimacy and accountability of local and regional authorities in the Parisian conurbation.

Intriguingly, decision-making processes in both cities had been informed and heavily influenced by party-political considerations, chiefly with a view to establishing or maintaining structural majorities for the respective right-of-center party. Again, party-political tactics and gerrymandering in Paris and London followed a different logic. Whereas the then Gaullist elite of the French state tried to defend the national capital with its predominantly bourgeois inner-city neighborhoods as a bastion of conservative voters, British Conservatives in the executive and legislative branches of national government were aiming at a stable majority for their own party in the new London-wide council by adding more residential and affluent suburban boroughs to the traditionally socialist-leaning constituencies of the inner-London boroughs.

While Berlin's institutional development during that period of time should be best treated as an exceptional case owing to the city's precarious geopolitical status, we can still observe a number of important currents and trends that fit neatly into the mosaic of findings laid out above. In line with the international drive toward comprehensive planning approaches, Berlin's state administration developed its own complex system of inter- and intradepartmental planning units and procedures designed as a means to cope with pressing social and economic problems. This concept was underpinned by the notion of integrated program budgeting and worked on the assumption that larger planning units would be necessary to reach its full effect. Not only did this planning-oriented policy work to the disadvantage of lower-level authorities, it also served—among other reasons—for many years as a further justification for the infamously inflated public sector of the city-state of Berlin.

CAPITAL CITIES IN THE INTERNATIONAL MARKET PLACE: INCREASED GLOBALIZATION

In stark contrast to the "planning era" of the 1960s, the models and instruments of comprehensive, planning-oriented, and potentially interventionist socioeconomic policies have come under severe pressure by critics who question the wisdom of relying on monolithic bureaucratic institutions as well as their rather uniform and standardized range of services and delivery modes. In the 1970s more and more people treated comprehensive state activities with increasing skepticism due to sociocultural changes toward postmaterialistic values in middle-class strata of European societies. Berlin, for example, has responded to those developments by introducing modes of direct citizen participation in policy issues. In Paris, the linchpin of institutional reform was the establishment of a mayor's office for the city of Paris in 1975, the occupant of which first in 1977 was decided by indirect elections through the elected members of the Paris city council for a term of six years (Townshend 1984). At the same time the politics of decentralization rather changed the status of the arrondissements as well. Until 1982 the district mayors were appointed by the president of the republic at the proposal of the minister of the interior; additionally, there were until then no directly elected representations of the districts. Since the reorganization, the arrondissement mayors are much more anchored in local democracy by means of election by the *conseils d'arrondissments.*

In the 1980s the protagonists of the "neoliberal" revolution put every public sector institution under the suspicion of being grossly ineffective and, even more important from their point of view, hopelessly inefficient. This sea change in the perception of bureaucracy as the problem rather than the solution, however, was not only induced by a swing of the party-political pendulum toward the New Right, but was also facilitated and reinforced by substantial changes of the political and economic environment in which public institutions operate. These changes are usually encapsulated in the concept of globalization. Despite the often indiscriminate usage of the term, however, there appears to be widespread agreement that the accelerated speed of data exchange and transactions, the upturn of the service sector at the expense of the manufacturing industries, as well as the multinational organization of production processes are among the major attributes of the current phase of globalization. It has also been shown that a relatively small group of selected cities serve as home bases for many multinational headquarters (Friedman 1986, p. 322; Sassen 2001a, p. 122) with important ramifications for the local and regional economies of those "global cities."

These unleashed forces of globalization are crucial drivers in the intensified competition between regions and even more so between big cities (Lever and Turok 1999; Porter 2002). For the public sector, the pressure has been such that "preferred clients," most notably large business corporations, can claim "special treatment" by way of lowered transaction costs offered by "one-shop" agencies at the central level and project managers who navigate clients through the process of multilevel and interdepartmental decision-making processes. At the same time, however, big city governments are also being confronted by the spread of less secure employment situations and the widening gap between "winners" and "losers" of the socioeconomic changes associated with globalization. Both developments are potential sources of social and political tensions rooted in the increasingly polarized social structure of the urban population as well as the sociodemographic segregation of city dwellers (Sassen 2001a; see also King 1990 and Simmie 1994 for the case of London).

Against this background, it did not come as a surprise that the reform of regional government for London in 2000 (re)introduced a citywide administration in the form of the Greater London Authority consisting of a directly elected mayor and an assembly with 25 members (HMSO 1998; Schröter 1998; Ross 2001; Pimlott and Rao 2002; Travers 2004). In line with the agency concept, a set of hived-off executive agencies is attached to these political institutions, which, as self-standing administrative units, take over mostly executive but partly also planning responsibilities in the areas of local public transportation, economic advancement, and regional development, as well as public security and "law and order" (police, fire, and civil defense). They are accountable vis-à-vis the mayor's office. This institutional arrangement, reminiscent of a holding company, breaks in dramatic fashion with the British local government tradition (compare various local government traditions in Wollmann 1999 and 2000) and leans more strongly on a quasi-presidential model.

By the same token, the city of Paris appears to be approaching a more two-tier system of government from the other end of the spectrum by strengthening, however very cautiously, the arrondissements—particularly in view of local social and cultural measures (as such count the local youth, social, cultural, and sport facilities as part of the so-called *les équipements de proximité*). Additionally, there have also been efforts to strengthen local democracy in the arrondissements through the establishment of consultative organs at the *quartiers* level (*les conseils de quartiers*). In all likelihood, the most recent amendments to the French Constitution in regard to the devolution of additional competences to lower levels of government—including an explicit statement of the principle of subsidiarity and direct references to the strengthening of local democracy and financial autonomy of regional and municipal administrations—may provide a further impetus for further decentralization measures (see Crevel and Wagner 2003, p. 59).

Turning finally to the case of Berlin, the watershed of reunification of the city, with its dramatic political, economic, and financial challenges, marked the start of a renewed reform and modernization phase. A first reform package—rooted in the dominant cutback strategy in the public sector—joined varied measures toward managerial modernization of Berlin's public bureaucracies in the mid-1990s. A second reform package at the end of the 1990s, with changes to political institutions and decision-making processes (polity and process reform), served the goal of (re)balancing the relationship between upper and lower tiers of city government according to new global challenges. Additionally, the redrawing of district boundaries (territorial reform) and the downshifting of administrative competencies in favor of the districts (functional reform) were central to this second reform wave (compare Röber and Schröter 2002).

CONCLUSIONS

All in all, the empirical findings lend some support to our hypothesis that during the past century the institutional genealogy of big city government in our sample has been shaped by secular trends transcending national boundaries. Clearly, the currently highlighted tide of economic and cultural globalization is not the first wave of reform forces that have swept nationally and locally established institutions, nor have earlier pressures for change been less effective in influencing the architecture of big city government. Over the past decades, these megatrends have apparently worked toward a moderate convergence of the institutional fabric of European capitals—although the changes they have brought have largely remained within the confines of predetermined reform corridors that were established in early, formative phases of the institutional genesis in each of our three sample cities.

The precise nature and magnitude of future consequences of global competition for big city governments still remain to be seen. At the current level of our analysis, however, we seem to be on fairly safe ground to suggest that concepts for political and administrative reform have to strike a delicate balance between centralizing and decentralizing strategies; blueprints for institutional redesign that rely exclusively on either the "decentralization" or the "centralization" trump card will be ill-equipped to adequately deal with current and future challenges emanating from globalization and Europeanization. It follows from this that a two-tier system with a citywide administration, while maintaining a lower tier of local authorities, can serve as a role model for larger conurbations— not only for our three European capitals in particular, but for big cities in general. While this organizational model, as we have shown before, has been with us—in a number of variations—since the early days of urbanization and industrialization, the increased pressure from international economic competition as well as the dynamics of the developed welfare state seem to have added a specific flavor to this principle of municipal organization. Judging from more recent trends in administrative reform, upper-tier levels of government appear to have gotten "leaner" in that they reserve for themselves strategic planning functions and have assumed direct responsibility for nationally and internationally visible cultural events and economic projects, whereas delivery functions and welfare services have migrated to lower-level authorities.

CHAPTER 4

Uneven Development, City Governance, and Urban Change— Unpacking the Global-Local Nexus in Dublin's Inner City

MICHAEL PUNCH, DECLAN REDMOND, AND SINEAD KELLY

INTRODUCTION

The city can be read as the nexus of global change and daily life—a site of contestation in the flux of economic imperatives, urban policymaking, and local needs and values. Just as importantly, the key general processes at work—economic restructuring, flows of capital through the built environment, and the like—have proceeded most unevenly, as reflected in local problems of job loss, displacement, poverty, and a whole range of attendant urban struggles and social tensions. In particular, the processes of uneven development and globalization in the city have generated new and complex patterns of growth and inequality, raising important analytical and policy challenges. For example, recent years have seen the realignment of the state and the evolution of new forms of urban governance under conditions of flexible production, international competition, mobile investment, the restructuring of global commodity chains, and emergent consumption trends and lifestyle changes. All of these issues are relevant across different regions worldwide and at different points on the global urban hierarchy (from so-called world cities to "ordinary" cities), and thus remain the subject of important theoretical and political debates. Specifically, we are faced with conceptual and empirical questions about the processes and contradictions of this current period of flux, as well as practical questions about how societies and states should most effectively deal with the resultant social tensions and economic challenges.

Dublin City, Ireland, offers an important and instructive case study of these complex global-local processes owing both to its position geographically and to its recent efforts to deal with a period of rapid economic and social change. Dublin can be seen as an "ordinary" city in global terms, one that functions as a gateway on the edge of the European Union, while, at the same time, it is in a central position nationally (as a dominant and capital city). Moreover, the city has undergone rapid and intense transformation over recent decades, generating considerable economic opportunities but also deepening patterns of inequality and conflict. Notable trends include the erosion of the traditional economic base, the emergence of new commercial and financial spaces, the large-scale construction of private apartments and enclaves for middle/upper income households, and the adoption of an increasingly flexible approach to urban policy by the local state. The inexorable logic of these trends has led to the exclusion of local populations from access to both jobs and housing and the emergence and continuation of an inner-city crisis.

This chapter first explores some critical theoretical readings of uneven development, city governance, and the global-local nexus to provide a framework for the discussion. It then offers an empirical exploration of the recent reorientation of urban planning systems in Dublin under conditions of entrepreneurial governance. Particular emphasis is given to the resultant pressures in a number of working-class locales, drawing from recorded experiences and unfolding resistances that have emerged at the grassroots level. These local experiences are more broadly instructive, providing insight into the progress and contradictions of urban social change in the city under conditions of global economic pressure, the neoliberal realignment of urban governance, and deepening social and spatial inequalities.

A NOTE ON SOURCES AND METHODS

In the main, this chapter is based on primary data (interview material, documents, participant observation) from various research studies that the authors have undertaken since the late 1990s, as well as a number of ongoing action-oriented projects. This work revolves around a common, if broad, theme about the changing relationship between capital, the state, and the grass roots in the city, examining in particular the socioeconomic and political impacts of economic development processes and public polices on disadvantaged urban communities and the emergence of bottom-up responses and resistances. While set within the established parameters of academic discourse, some of the more recent research has also involved active engagement in community research programmes and oppositional movements to neoliberal urban policies, reflective of a move toward more activist and action-oriented research (Ward 2005). More specifically, this chapter draws on the work of Punch (2000, 2001, 2002a, 2002b, 2005), who has undertaken extensive qualitative research on uneven development and grassroots organizations in Dublin. It also draws from Redmond's (2001, 2002) explorations of the issue of tenant empowerment on social-housing estates and his analysis of the relationship between the local state and tenant movements. A more recent action-related research has involved all three authors in a community research project that is examining the issue of urban regeneration and exclusion in an inner area of Dublin (Punch et al. 2003a, 2003b, 2003c). The recent work of Kelly (2004) (see also Kelly and MacLaran 2004), examining gentrification and community change in inner Dublin, is also employed in this chapter.

THEORETICAL CONTEXT: UNEVEN DEVELOPMENT AND LOCALITY

This section constructs a theoretical framework in order to contextualize the detailed explorations of a changing city entered into later. The simultaneous processes of globalization and localisation have been important themes in recent work in critical social and spatial theory, raising many complex problems. These include, for instance, concerns with local "rootedness" and identity, the global mobility of capital, the (uneven) power geometry of time-space compression, the upward and downward shifts in power presaged through the "glocalization" of political economy, the global restructuring of capitalism and Fordist/post-Fordist regimes of accumulation, and the implications of all these processes across different social and spatial locations (see, for instance, Harvey 1989a; Massey 1995; Amin 1994; Bauman 1998; Beck 2000; Swyngeduow 2000; Perrons 2004).

The problematic of inequality and uneven development is central to many of these critical readings of the global and the local, with regard to questions of both culture and political economy. For example, taking a lead from Bauman's (1998) work on translocal cultures and lifeworlds, Beck (2000, p. 55, emphasis in the original) argues that globalization and localization are not simply two moments or dimensions of a single phenomenon, but " . . . driving forces and expressions of a new *polarization and stratification of the world population into globalized rich and localized poor.*" In a recent formulation, Eagleton makes a similar point, which has considerable resonance for the empirical and experiential analysis presented in later sections of this chapter:

> The problem at the moment is that the rich have mobility while the poor have locality. Or rather, the poor have locality until the rich get their hands on it. The rich are global and the poor are local—though just as poverty is a global fact, so the rich are coming to appreciate the benefits of locality. It is not hard to imagine affluent communities of the future protected by watchtowers, searchlights and machine-guns, while the poor scavenge for food in the wasteland below.
>
> (2003, pp. 21–2)

In a related vein, political-economy explorations of the global-local nexus frequently emphasize the mode of integration/disintegration of different places/social groups within the broader structure of capitalism through processes of uneven development (see, for example, Smith 1984; Massey 1995; Harvey 1996, 2000). This dialectical approach involves a reading of the dynamic restructuring of economic space and the general processes and forces generating change, while also allowing for the specificity of place (Massey 1993). It brings to the fore the central facts of economic power and the spatial organization of social relations, reflected in class, gender, and ethnic divisions as well as regional, urban, and local differences and variations. Importantly, these general and local dimensions of society and space are not seen as static or fixed (as, for example, a received or "finished" urban system), but as dynamic and contradictory, constantly unfolding and subject to change or, at times, violent disruption.

For Smith (1984, 1996), these uneven patterns and rhythms of sociospatial change are underpinned by a simultaneous process—the equalization and differentiation of levels and conditions of development. General processes such as capital accumulation (reflected in the uneven spatial and temporal patterns of investment and disinvestment) impact more or less everywhere (equalization), but the outcomes vary dramatically across a diverse existing landscape of resources, earlier rounds of investment, and sociocultural characteristics (for instance, levels and traditions of labor organization, the role and strength of civil society, "local" trade skills, etc.). This emphasizes the important point that it is not just a matter of the general (or global) acting on the local, but a complex dialectical tension between particular places (at whatever scale—regional, urban, local) and the broader structures and processes of economy and society. As Massey notes, "The point is that there are real relations with real content, economic, political, cultural, between any local place and the wider world in which it is set" (1993, p. 66). And this is a two-way street—the global and the local are mutually constitutive, and the differences between places can be disruptive of general economic processes, thereby impacting on the outcome. This is a central tenet of economic geography—the importance of difference, place, locality, unevenness, etc. (Massey 1995). In other words, increasingly global forces are working through at every geographical scale but constantly coming up against the obstinate variation of place, context, and resistance. In a globally interdependent system, economic activity is embedded in and disrupted by the geographies through which it takes place; practice and instance matter (Lee 2002).

Of particular importance for this research is how these formulations can be applied to urban analysis. At a general level, the movement of capital through the built environment in search of surplus value (through investment in industrial production, services, or real estate) is a primary general force underlying the restructuring of both the urban economy and the urban environment. This tendency toward equalization is offset by the highly differentiated outcomes across a variable physical and social landscape. For instance, the general processes of investment and disinvestment, boom and slump cycles, stop-go development patterns, growth, and decay can be recognized in every city, but the effects across a highly variable and dynamic surface of ground rent and land uses are unpredictable and sometimes surprising. The well-recorded cycles of inner-city underdevelopment and disinvestment (creating a rent gap) and, at a later point, reinvestment and recommodification lead to the local social effects of middle-class colonization and working-class displacement. However, the patterns vary and the end product is far from certain. For example, the nature and level of involvement of central and local state as an agent of such development cycles (e.g., by providing tax breaks or necessary collective consumption, which is beyond the logic of capital to provide) can vary temporally and spatially. Moreover, all of these projects are subject to contestation and resistance, and therefore remain, at least in theory, radically evitable. However, in many respects, the possibility of proposing and implementing alternative strategies seems ever more remote in a globalized era of interplace competition and neoliberal orthodoxy. Nevertheless, on the margins or beyond state and capital, resistances occur, and very local and contextual urban struggles complicate the story, depending on the balance of power and levels of militancy evident between different interests (city boosters, local development capital, neighborhood councils, grassroots coalitions, etc.). The narrative of urban social change is not simply scripted by the top-down, general forces and imperatives of capital in the built environment; rather it may also be colored and redirected by a complex of contextual factors, historic built forms, and the relative balance between resistance, consensus, indifference, or despair emerging at a local level.

This raises the important analytical question of the role of the state—and more specifically in recent years, the shifting tendencies and practices of urban governance—in regulating or influencing the broad patterns of uneven development and responding to the most overt contradictions and conflicts (Hall and Hubbard 1998; McLeod et al. 2003). Urban governance regimes variously emphasize economic priorities such as growth, competing for investment, city boosterism, etc., or social priorities such as public-housing programmes, social protection, services for vulnerable residents or the marginalized, and amenity provision (Harvey 1989b). Thus, a central question for the analysis of urban change and globalism relates to the balance of priorities, strategies, and policies adopted by city authorities to deal with the complexities and challenges of globalization at a local level. Perhaps, more importantly, we must ask, what are the consequences of all of these tendencies for different communities and locales (or for "these people in this place," to use Raymond Williams' formulation)?

In this regard, particular attention has been paid in the recent literature to the influence of neoliberal ideologies and practices in the arena of urban governance. Deriving from the conservative Anglo-American policies that gained momentum through the 1980s, which affected everything from welfare provision to the structural adjustment programmes imposed on the poorest, underdeveloped countries, the neoliberal orthodoxy is the doctrine of privatization, market approaches, deregulation, reducing social protection, and, effectively, promoting the interests of capital. At the city level, this has often translated into a withdrawal from an (essentially Keynesian) urban project based on considerable collective consumption provision (public services, social housing, etc.) and a reorientation toward marketized urban policies and entrepreneurial planning. In essence, this latter concept denotes a strategy of "selling the city" under conditions of increasingly mobile capital, whereby the neoliberal local state acts as agent rather than as regulator of the market (Smith 2002). Spatial policies such as urban renewal, fiscal incentives, microarea planning, and flagship projects are among the typical initiatives deployed, often alloyed with a conscious attempt to "reimagineer" run-down areas for high-grade functions and bourgeois consumption. In this manner, the local state becomes locked into a progrowth agenda, while privatizing many social services and retreating from direct public action as a means of influencing city futures and promoting more equitable outcomes. The new politics of urban governance and the role of planning within this institutional setting have been explored by a number of commentators (e.g., Brindley et al. 1996; Newman and Thornley 1997). Key concerns include the disempowerment of the local state and the reorientation of policy priorities within entrepreneurial urban regimes, characterised by public-private partnerships, appointed quangos, alliances with nongovernment actors, and "commercialized" public initiatives (Peck and Tickell 1994; Lovering 1995; Wilks-Heeg 1996; Edwards 1997).

The main dimensions of the theoretical discussion are summarized diagrammatically in figure 4.1. One analytical challenge is to engage with the operation of a number of global processes, principally, capital accumulation (the apparently ceaseless drive to make money out of money) and the related imperative, to seek out more profitable forms and patterns of investment (Harvey 1989a). This is one core force behind recent patterns of economic restructuring that have impacted at every scale. It is equally necessary, however, to explore the interpenetration of such processes with different individual biographies and different local environments with their own characteristic landscapes, histories, cultures, economic livelihoods, and social worlds. Taking a lead from Raymond Williams' cultural materialism (1973, 1977), the important point is the whole structure of feeling—a process of change and an unfolding collective experience that is immediately both general and particular—that defines "these people in this place" as part of a known and felt community and locale. In many respects, it is this complex social and cultural meaning that attaches to "places" that forms the generative basis for urban social movements, community mobilizations, and other forms of grassroots interventions. The policy environment raises a third problem for analysis, as we need to look at how the state intervenes at different spatial scales through various forms of public investment, regulation, place-promotion, incentivization, and social protection. Finally, in analyzing these mutually constitutive levels of the global-local nexus, it is important to remain sensitive always to the manifold inequalities, contradictions, and tensions in the global restructuring processes at work as well as in the responses (in the shape of formalized governance regimes and informalized grassroots resistances) that unfold at national, regional, urban, and local levels (see figure 4.1).

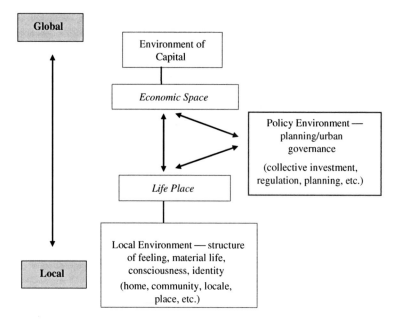

Figure 4.1   The global-local nexus.

CHANGING URBAN GOVERNANCE REGIMES: ENTREPRENEURIAL PLANNING IN DUBLIN

The rest of this chapter offers an empirical and experiential exploration of governance and conflict in Dublin's inner city, with a particular emphasis on the entrepreneurial realignment of planning and the contradictory results of this shift. The broader economic backdrop to this narrative can be sketched briefly. Arguably, Ireland's integration with an international capitalist system only approached maturity in recent decades, which witnessed a rapidly changing political economy, as global influences worked their way through various regions and urban areas with differential sociospatial effects. These changes were linked to (and in some respects were actively facilitated by) a particular kind of development model (essentially constructed from the late 1950s onward) founded on neoliberal export-led industrialization, which emphasized principles of free trade, free enterprise, foreign direct investment, and low levels of taxation on capital (O'Hearn 1992). The well-publicized economic boom of the late 1990s was driven by such policies, allied with a social partnership model of negotiating wage agreements (thus engendering some typical aspects of both American and European modes of regulation). This period also saw the reinforcement of Dublin as the main population and commercial center and as an emergent global site for back-office functions (particularly, financial services), electronics and computer software manufacturing, and personal and professional services. At the same time, much of its older manufacturing base eroded rapidly, with traditional, indigenous industries generally going into decline. In part, as a result, the boom years involved a process of deepening uneven development, characterized by rapid economic growth, considerable dependency on multinational (predominantly U.S.) capital, and social polarization (O'Hearn 2001; Kirby 2002; Punch 2004).

A number of analysts have traced the development of an entrepreneurial approach to planning in Dublin since the mid-1980s against this general backdrop of global economic restructuring, neoliberal macroeconomic policies, and local problems of urban decline (McGuirk 1994, 1995, 2000; McGuirk and MacLaran 2001; MacLaran and Williams 2003; Bartley and Treadwell Shine 2003). This research seeks to update these accounts with specific reference to the impact of entrepreneurial strategies on the regeneration of disadvantaged inner-city areas that have high levels of social housing present. In doing so, this research also aims to make a contribution to the broader international debate on entrepreneurial cities as exemplified by the recent work of Ward (2003).

Most of the above accounts are in general agreement with regard to the evolution of entrepreneurial planning in Dublin, its rationales, and its impacts. They develop a similar narrative showing the emergence of fairly crude market-led approaches to urban renewal in the mid-1980s and the early 1990s, based essentially on the introduction of tax incentives applied to a number of designated areas. The rationale for the introduction of this approach centered on a critique of existing local government policy and practice, which, it was argued, were reactive and had an antidevelopment ethos. Consequently, the new urban renewal policies sought to bypass established procedures through a mixture of fiscal incentives and the establishment of special-purpose planning and development bodies, which would operate outside the local authority structures. The net effect of such measures was to introduce significant risk reduction for private sector development interests, ensure far greater certainty in obtaining permission to develop, and fast-track bureaucratic procedures. The main consequence has been large-scale property development, the physical renewal of the inner city, and significant transformations in social geography. Since these schemes began in the mid-1980s, almost 17,000 new apartments have been built in the inner city, representing a massive physical but also social and economic transformation in inner Dublin (Kelly and MacLaran 2004).

After a decade of tax-led development from 1986 onward, this market-led approach was strongly criticized because of the absence of any local or community input into polices and the consequent negative social impacts, particularly for poorer city residents (Department of the Environment 1996). Indeed, this intense development has led to rapid land price increases, stimulating speculation in property, and to a local crisis of access to housing and the displacement of valuable low-grade community functions. Moreover, such an approach also substantially lessened the level and degree of local democratic or political accountability. The result, as McGuirk (1994, 1995, 2000) demonstrates, was the effective enfeeblement of the local authorities and the erosion of their powers and legitimacy. Indeed, evidence from McGuirk's research demonstrates that planners themselves became increasingly facilitative of development interests and began to assume a more entrepreneurial attitude to development proposals. While this approach certainly delivered some very substantial results in terms of extensive residential and commercial investment, official evaluations were critical of this marketized approach to planning as it was almost entirely property-led and either ignored or sidelined the need for socioeconomic renewal of local communities (Department of the Environment 1996).

As a reaction to this criticism, central government instituted, in 1998, collaborative or integrated approaches to urban regeneration, which, it was argued, would address community demands and thus generate local benefits and planning gain (McGuirk and MacLaran 2001). Five Integrated Area Plans (IAPs) were formulated for inner-city locales, which had a strong community emphasis with, in some cases, specific community-gain targets (MacLaran and Williams 2003). On the face of it, these plans were a significant reversal of earlier urban regeneration policy and suggested a new approach that would deliver elements of social renewal as distinct from purely physical-property renewal.

The more recent work of McGuirk and MacLaran (2001) and Bartley and Treadwell Shine (2003) is generally positive with regard to the potential of integrated planning and the possibility of community gain accruing. However, they also argue that local integrated planning can be manipulated as part of a neoliberal agenda and practice. In this regard, Bartley and Treadwell Shine (2003) argue that the Dublin City Council has in fact become an enthusiastic advocate of neoliberal entrepreneurial approaches, to such an extent that it is seen as being more enthusiastically probusiness than the Dublin Docklands Development Authority (one of the special-purpose agencies responsible or the redevelopment of the docklands area). McGuirk (2000) has claimed that the entrepreneurial approach to planning, which necessitated fluid relations among a variety of stakeholders, might allow the local authority room to generate positive social outcomes by taking a more central role in the new governance regime, whereas previously they had been excluded. However, while it seems that the local authority has become a stronger player in the new paradigm of urban governance, it is by no means clear that it has used this new situation to pursue social-inclusion aims. Rather, as the remainder of this chapter seeks to demonstrate, the local authority seems to have embraced a prodevelopment agenda, which looks likely to encourage the transformation of working-class and industrial parts of the city into overwhelmingly private enclaves, displacing an indigenous population with a long historic connection to the city in the process.

IMPACTS OF ENTREPRENEURIAL GOVERNANCE: THE CASE OF THE LIBERTIES-COOMBE

In distinction to previous phases of urban renewal, the current "integrated area planning" has specifically focused on the revival of some inner-city areas with significant levels of poverty and other social distress. The changes affecting most of these areas in inner Dublin since the late 1990s have followed a broadly similar pattern. In short, the promise of a community-oriented planning has been abandoned by the local state, with a strong progrowth and development agenda taking over with potentially calamitous impacts on local disadvantaged communities. What has gone wrong? The next section explores the implementation of the Liberties-Coombe IAP and identifies issues of concern for the local indigenous community relating to recent urban change, precipitated, at least in part, by the implementation of the IAP.

The Liberties-Coombe area takes in, broadly, the southwest quarter of Dublin's inner city and is renowned for its rich historical, architectural, and archaeological heritage as well as its complex and vibrant social fabric. There has long been a close organic interconnection between the indigenous working-class communities and the local industrial economic base. Traditional local industries included textiles (woollen and silk), iron works, brewing, distilling, printing, baking, shoe making, tanning, and furniture making and restoring. Until the 1970s, the Liberties area was a labor-intensive industrial locale with closely knit working-class neighbourhoods serving as a cheap and reliable resource for manufacturing (Aalen 1992; MacLaran 1993; SWICN 1999). However, the area was particularly adversely affected since then by economic restructuring (closures, decentralisation, technological change), resulting in the loss of labor-intensive indigenous manufacturing jobs. These trends resulted in the specter of mass unemployment and the serious fracturing of inner-city communities that were becoming increasingly marginalized, demoralized, and welfare dependent. Over the same period, urban policies favoured peripheral residential development rather than inner-city regeneration, and public and private disinvestment, along with road-widening schemes, created considerable urban blight. Such conditions created the typical environment for problem drug use, and a heroin crisis, which took hold in the early 1980s, has further devastated many neighbourhoods (Punch 2005).

Nevertheless, the area has seen considerable levels of vibrant grassroots organization and opposition to the contradictions and negative local impacts of economic change and urban policy priorities and to the changing "'place" of such inner-city locales within the broader structure and processes of capitalist globalization. The community sector of the southwest inner city has a tradition of drawing up local plans that are sensitive to the needs of inner-city residents and neighbourhoods. These bottom-up community-based plans include the "Back to the Streets" initiative developed by the South Inner City Community Development Association in the early 1990s and the "Area Action Plans" devised by the South West Inner City Network (SWICN, 1999), an umbrella network involving over 50 local community groups. The 1995 plan provided much of the basis for the 1998 Liberties-Coombe IAP. This IAP was initiated by Dublin Corporation (the local authority changed its name to Dublin City Council in 2002) and developed in close consultation with the SWICN, local representatives, local businesses, schools, and voluntary and statutory agencies. The IAP seeks to achieve sustainable urban regeneration through a three-pronged approach of economic, social, and physical renewal, and its stated vision is to "reinstate the dignity of the Liberties-Coombe as a living working locality fully participating in Dublin's entry into the next millennium" (Dublin Corporation 1998, p. 7). The objectives and renewal strategies contained in the IAP seek to attract significant investment to underpin this renewal (through the development of new industry locally), encourage the provision of a range of housing types and a variety of housing tenures, and improve educational and recreational facilities and the quality and appearance of the built environment (through a mixed land use policy, infill development, reinforcement of the coherence of streetscape, and the restoration of the civic character of a number of key urban spaces).

In line with the formal commitment to "integration and equity," the structures for implementation required the establishment of a cross-sectoral steering group "to guide the implementation" of the IAP (Dublin Corporation 1998). The steering group was subsequently changed to a monitoring committee in 1999. The monitoring committee originally comprised nine members—three from the local authority, three from community organizations (representing over 90 groups), one business representative, one trade-council representative, and one representative of architectural, historical, and conservational interests. A fourth community representative was subsequently added to the monitoring committee in 2001. A multidisciplinary project team and a project manager were responsible for the IAP's implementation and administration in consultation with the committee. To date, a key issue for the committee and for the community sector in particular has been the securing of community gain.

In order to qualify for tax incentives on designated sites, each development must contribute "community gain" to the IAP area. The Liberties-Coombe IAP stated that "a development levy of 15 per cent of the site value would be attached to key development sites [exceeding 350 sq. m. in gross floor area] designated for tax relief" (Dublin Corporation 1998, p. 109). To date, a total of 100 sites have been designated for tax incentives in the plan area. Types of community gain include the allocation of a percentage of residential development for social and/or affordable housing, a financial contribution based on a percentage of the current site value, and provision of facilities/opportunities within the physical development (e.g., play areas, youth club facilities, etc.) and/or the development itself, as in, for example, the preservation or restoration of a building of historical or architectural merit (Dublin Corporation 1999). Importantly, the local authority—Dublin City Council (DCC)—outlined in an annual report on the Liberties-Coombe IAP that the nature and amount of community gain to be extracted were *negotiable* with developers (DCC 2000).

The amount of revenue generated through the tax-incentive mechanism and the imposition of the community-gain levy had, by April 2004, yielded only !439,000 (less than the cost of two new one-bed apartments!). Furthermore, the acquisition of social-housing units for community gain has, to date, not been realized. Housing needs in the Liberties area have been highlighted repeatedly by community groups and organisations (see SWICN 1999), and the failure to secure social-housing units as community gain from the IAP has compounded the housing crisis in the area. The crisis has worsened as other policies of social mix, public-land sales, and the redevelopment of social-housing estates through public-private-partnership models have served further to reduce the current stock and potential future stock of social housing. There is also evidence to suggest that some developers are not availing themselves of the tax incentives provided under the IAP, in order to avoid involvement with a "community gain" clause. The failure to realize significant community gain and key social and economic objectives outlined in the IAP has been and continues to be a source of considerable frustration among community representatives on the monitoring committee and has served to undermine the implementation of the plan as agreed in 1998.

Another serious source of contention surrounds the recent granting of planning permissions for mixed-use developments on a number of sites. The design of the developments frequently runs contrary to the Urban Design Framework for the Liberties-Coombe IAP and, in some cases, to the recommendations of planning appeal inspectors. This seemingly contradictory outcome of microarea planning is explained by a senior planner in the DCC who, in describing the realignment of the operational activities of the local authority, suggests that "the potential of the entrepreneurial approach to enable planners to implement the social dimensions of planning schemes is compromised by a prodevelopment local authority corporate vision at the managerial level" (interview quoted in McGuirk and MacLaran 2001). This contradiction is manifested in the confusion surrounding the precedence of conflicting guidelines and plans, with the IAP guidelines, the Dublin City Development Plan (Dublin Corporation 1999), and central government's Residential Density Guidelines (Government of Ireland 1999) causing particular discord (for a more detailed discussion, see Brudell et al. 2004).

Criticism has also been directed at the implementation and monitoring mechanisms established by the local authority. Community and local elected representatives have pointed to a lack of clarity surrounding the agenda, with a blurring and confusion of roles and issues to be negotiated by the monitoring committee and the project team. No detailed guidelines or terms of reference have been devised as to the role and decision-making power of the various groups involved in the implementation of the plan. The SWICN (2002) suggested that the "precise provision and power vested in community representation should be formalised, if such representation is to extend beyond token." Other inadequacies with the implementation and monitoring mechanisms of the IAP, identified by the SWICN, include the weak links between the monitoring committee and the project group, the failure to "inform" and to "resource" the community representatives, and the insufficient frequency and duration of meetings of the monitoring committee. One community representative highlighted the broad frustrations in describing his experience of the monitoring committee as "the only group that I have ever been a part of that I feel excluded from" (personal interview).

The lack of progress in achieving the social and community aims has generated considerable conflict between the state and the community, leading to the resignation of two of the leading local representatives from the monitoring committee in November and December 2002. At the time of writing, the remaining two community representatives are refusing to sign off on the IAP's *Annual Report*, as dissatisfaction and frustration with the manner in which the regeneration is being implemented—and with the failures of the monitoring mechanisms to address these issues—continue to grow. Repeated appeals have been made to the city manager, the minister for the environment and local government, and to the European Commission to review and rectify the implementation structures and mechanisms. In his letter of resignation, a community representative illustrates the level of local frustration and discontent with the manner in which the plan is being implemented:

> Little did I, or my community, realise that the IAP would be implemented in a manner which would attribute wholesale precedence to market interests over the legitimate social and economic rights of the resident community. Little did we realise that . . . the maximum benefit of the urban renewal of a heretofore 'unfashionably' deprived area would accrue not to the deprived inhabitants of such areas but to the representatives of private capital who are moving in and reclaiming that land in their droves on the back of Government approved tax incentives. I am sorry to have to say that the last opportunity to do something helpful for the Liberties-Coombe area has been lost forever, in order to pander to the avarice of the private sector in the shape of developers.

This letter of resignation points not only to the general lack of progress on the IAP's social inclusion aims, but to the production in fact of opposite and exclusionary effects. This can be seen, for example, in the changes in the land market in the Liberties with dramatic increases in local property and land prices since the mid-1990s. For example, one-bedroom apartments experienced price increases of between 300 and 400 per cent from 1995 to 2003 (Kelly 2004; Kelly and MacLaran 2004). The IAP policy seems to be contributing to inflated property and land values with further pressure emanating from a proposed "Digital Hub"—a new cluster of digital media activity.

Although this research is at an early stage, it can be argued that the regeneration that has occurred in Liberties-Coombe so far, through the promotion of private capital as the sole motivator for regeneration, has proven insensitive to a procommunity agenda. While there has been a significant influx of private (and often gated) apartment complexes, the area has simultaneously experienced a reduction in social-housing units through the sale of public housing, the transfer/privatisation of social-housing estates and public land, and an increased number of vacant units in the remaining public stock (see Kelly and MacLaran 2004). Gentrification and social segregation have been facilitated and encouraged through past urban renewal schemes and are now being legitimised via quasi-participatory microarea planning mechanisms under the guise of "encouraging a variety of housing tenures." Where before, in terms of the structural requirements of capital, the most important local resource was a pool of low-skilled labour, now the prime resource of the Liberties-Coombe area is the land itself.

CONCLUSIONS

The analysis presented here represents only a small example of a general shift in urban governance priorities and strategies currently emerging in Dublin with potentially far-reaching consequences and many risks and unknowns. It would appear that much more is to come. In a broader sense, experiences in Dublin provide a telling insight into many dimensions of the uneven development of the contemporary city. The most important aspect of this is the movement of capital through the built environment, driven by the accumulation imperative (the global motive force at work), and this chapter has shown how urban policies have been reoriented away from social priorities and toward the "enablement" of this economic process. The effect has been to disadvantage and disempower working-class life places in the city, initially through the loss of the older industrial base as the city's role in the global division of labor changed, lately through the recommodification of nonmarket spaces for bourgeois consumption. In short, the local state is now heavily involved in preparing and selling the city for capital. As a result, the inner city and indigenous working-class communities are under severe pressure from powerful economic forces and the increasingly neoliberal priorities of urban policymakers, which are translating into a revanchist strategy of land and class clearance.

The research presented here provides some important insights from an "ordinary" smaller city undergoing rapid social and economic transformation, in part under the influence of an urban governance regime more attuned to economic than social priorities. Arguably, this tendency can be seen as a reflection of a broader developmental model pursued by the Irish state that has put considerable emphasis on issues of competitiveness, openness to foreign investment, and the search for new roles in the global division of labor (as older indigenous industrial sectors have fallen into decline). It is readily apparent how a policy emphasis on place promotion, tax incentives, and the transformation of decayed urban locales could come to dominate urban interventions in such a context. Moreover, as a capital and dominant city, the experiments carried out in Dublin have perhaps been pursued with particular gusto, almost as flagship projects, while the city remains particularly susceptible to intense cycles of private and public sector disinvestment, urban decay, social degeneration and (eventual) reinvestment, regeneration, and cataclysmic physical and social change.

In short, Dublin has essentially been a laboratory for a raft of marketized policy experiments since the mid-1980s, as well as an urban arena that has been substantially resculpted through the uneven flows of capital and the shifting priorities and practices of urban governance. It provides some critical lessons regarding the tensions consequent upon these processes of uneven development and urban intervention, which seem to have impacted cities almost universally (albeit in different ways and to various extents). Importantly, the shortcomings of the social agenda within the Liberties-Coombe IAP have already generated grassroots unrest and emerging opposition, and the progress of community movements and resistances of this kind will be instructive for urban analysis but (more importantly) potentially decisive for the possibility of exploring and implementing genuinely socially inclusive policies that might ensure a more egalitarian and sustainable city future.

CHAPTER 5

URBAN GOVERNANCE IN DEVELOPING COUNTRIES: EXPERIENCES AND CHALLENGES

RICHARD E. STREN

INTRODUCTION

To begin to comprehend the massive changes taking place in cities of the developing world, we need to start with some large demographic numbers. As the world moves inexorably toward the day when the majority of humankind will be living in urban areas (which will be some time during 2007, we are told by the United Nations), the fastest and most breathtaking population increases are taking place in the developing world: in Latin America, in Africa, and in Asia. Indeed, during 2000–2030, almost all the projected aggregate growth of the world's *total* population will be absorbed by cities of the less developed regions (United Nations 2004).

The aggregate figures on global urbanization set out in Chapter 1 hint at a more complex, regional story. Between the years 2000 and 2030, Africa's urban population is projected to grow at an average annual rate of about 15.1 million (a compound annual average rate of growth of 4.39 percent); Asia's at 42.2 million (an average annual growth rate of 2.22 percent); and that of Latin America and the Caribbean at an average annual rate of 7 million (a compound annual average growth rate of 1.42 percent) (United Nations 2004). And in these regions, it is generally in the poorest countries that urbanization is proceeding most rapidly. In Ethiopia, for example, a country with a per capita average income of $90 in 2003 (World Bank 2005), the rate of urban growth from 2000 to 2005 is projected at 5.75 percent per year. In Honduras, with a per capita average income of $970 (one of the lowest in Central America), the rate of urban growth from 2000 to 2005 is estimated at 3.25 percent per year. And in Asia, Cambodia, with a per capita average income of $310 in 2003, has a projected urban growth rate during the 2000–2005 period of 5.50 percent per year. Against typical European annual urban growth rates of 0.24 percent for France, 0.38 percent for the United Kingdom, and 0.32 percent for Spain, these growth rates are massive—between 10 and 20 times higher than in Europe.

And this rapid growth is taking place in countries with an incredibly low level of resources to meet this challenge.

But what, indeed, does this challenge involve? Or, to put the question more precisely, in what respects do cities in developing countries attempt to respond to their rapidly increasing population, given their extreme scarcity of resources? In a recent study I undertook with a number of colleagues, we considered this question in depth. In order to give some shape to the discussion, we determined that there were five major dimensions to this problem: a capacity dimension, a financial resources dimension, a diversity dimension, a security dimension, and an authority dimension (Montgomery et al. 2003). These five may be compressed to four, as the diversity and security dimensions have many points in common. As we discuss some of the major features of urban governance in developing countries, using these dimensions as signposts, we will look for patterns and regularities (as well as unique aspects) and consider the political implications of our findings. Among the most interesting findings are the special and, in many cases, unique connections between urban growth in many countries and the process of globalization. But, at the same time, many changes occur for purely local reasons. In this chapter, when we use the concept of "governance," we refer to the *relationship* between the government and the people, between the formal political structure and civil society (Stren 2003b). Given the very far-reaching political changes that are taking place in cities all over the developing world, the relational concept of "governance" can often serve our analysis better than the more positional and structural concept of "government'."

DIMENSION ONE: CAPACITY

During the 1980s, the rapid urban growth throughout the developing world began seriously to outstrip the capacity of most cities to provide adequate services to their citizens. The shortfall was most often filled not through government provision but rather through the informal sector. Already, by the 1960s, this incapacity to provide services had become increasingly visible through the increasing number and extent of slum and squatter settlements in the cities of developing countries. The 1960s and 1970s were a period of extensive contestation between municipal (and national) authorities on the one hand and low-income urban residents on the other hand. While the authorities sought to control the use of urban land for the purposes for which it was normally zoned (for example, residential, commercial, or industrial, with densities to match), people with low incomes attempted to build shelters on some of this land or to organize "invasions" in a more concerted attempt to convert the land for their own use. Clearly, the supply of cheap, serviced urban land fell far behind a rapidly growing low-income population's demand for such land—a population that, in addition, needed proximity to centrally located sources of income and employment in order to subsist economically. Government responses to this demand originally took the form of the setting up of centralized housing banks and construction agencies in many countries. For example, the National Housing Bank of Brazil (set up in 1964 and closed in 1986) produced around 4 million units; two major agencies in the Côte d'Ivoire produced close to 40,000 units during the 1960s and 1970s; in Egypt, public housing agencies built 456,000 units between 1960 and 1986; and, in Singapore, some 460,000 units were built from 1969 to 1985 (UNCHS 1996).

While these public-housing initiatives made up a substantial proportion of low-income housing projects in a number of countries by the 1980s, there were major problems: maintenance was poor, public subsidies were high, corrupt practices were hard to avoid entirely, and the pace of construction was, in any case, inadequate to respond to the level of in-migration (Cohen 1974; Mayo and Gross, J.S. 1989; Perlman 1976; Stren 1978). Partly as a result, international agencies encouraged low-income countries to turn to more collaborative approaches. Two policy responses stand out: *sites and services projects* in the 1970s and 1980s (Cohen 1983), in which minimally serviced plots were allocated in large subdivisions to low-income applicants, who would (with some assistance in the form of training and materials loans) be expected to build their own homes; and *squatter upgrading projects,* which regularized land tenure and improved services and infrastructure in "slum" areas in order to encourage the orderly improvement of neighborhoods without unduly displacing existing residents (Buckley and Kalarickal 2006). Variants of these approaches—promoted in many countries by assistance agencies and by the World Bank—are still operative now, but both involve complex, costly planning and administrative organization, as well as the designing of an incentive system that will encourage investment by the poor and discourage "leakage" to higher-income groups. From building housing units, public-policy approaches in developing countries have shifted to "enabling" strategies that encourage land and infrastructure development, as well as support for medium- and small-scale enterprises (UNCHS 1996).

Across the developing world by the end of the 1990s, however, a huge gap still existed between the effective supply of adequately serviced land and minimal standard housing, and the demand for accommodation as expressed through the disposable income that poor families are able to pay. Because land and minimal standard housing are, in general, not supplied as quickly as the need for them arises from low-income groups, the backlog is expressed in a very dramatic fashion in terms of the continuing existence of "slums," "squatter areas," and other forms of "informal housing" or "impermanent structures." The figures show that access to adequate housing is still a distant goal for large numbers of people living in Asia, Africa, and Latin America. For example, based on a UN-HABITAT definition of a slum as "a settlement in an urban area in which more than half of the inhabitants live in inadequate housing and lack basic services" (UN-HABITAT 2006, p. 19), slum populations have been rising steadily through the 1990s and the present decade to reach an estimated total of 998 million worldwide in 2005. Almost all these people live in so-called developing countries (UN-HABITAT 2006). The significance of this phenomenon has found its way into the list of important Millennium Development Goals and has, in addition, led authors to write important books with such imposing titles as *Shadow Cities. A Billion Squatters, A New Urban World* (Neuwirth 2005) and *Planet of Slums* (Davis 2006). Of approximately 100 developing countries tabulated by UN-HABITAT for their efforts and/or ability to reduce slums over the period 1990–2005, 8 were rated as "on track" in achieving a sustained decline in slum growth rates; 15 showed a "stabilizing" situation; 21 were "at risk" with a moderate increase of slums; and a total of 50 countries were "off track" with a high rate of growth of these slum populations. Of the 50 cases in the last category, fully 44 were among the lowest-income countries (UN-HABITAT 2006). In general, says Shlomo Angel, "while the formal housing sector [has] produced the bulk of housing for high-income groups, and while public housing [has been] of limited scope everywhere . . . most low-income housing in the developing market economies was and is produced by the informal housing sector . . . occupying land illegally (squatting) or built in land subdivisions that do not conform to zoning ordinances and planning regulations . . . without adequate infrastructure, without any state subsidies, and without any formal housing finance" (Angel 2000, p. 320).

This picture of housing supply badly lagging behind demand runs parallel to a variety of other statistical measures of urban service delivery. Based on a 1990s database of

Table 5.1   Percentage of urban households connected to utility services—in selected cities, grouped by region

Region	Water connections	Sewerage connections	Electricity connections	Telephone connections
Africa	37.6%	12.7%	42.4%	11.6%
Asia (Pacific)	63.2%	38.5%	86.1%	26.0%
Latin America and the Caribbean	76.8%	62.5%	91.6%	41.2%
Industrialized	99.4%	97.8%	99.4%	89.1%

Source: UNCHS (1999). *Global Urban Indicators Database.*

237 selected cities, we can observe in table 5.1 a major difference between the developed and developing world. In terms of water, sewerage, electricity, and telephone connections, the proportion of urban households receiving urban services is much lower in the developing world. By region, moreover, there is a clear gradation in terms of each of these services from a low in Africa, through Asia, through Latin America, to a high level in the industrialized north. The poorest countries (in this case those located in Africa) claim the lowest level of urban services, no matter which service is measured. A similar gradation of urban service levels—from the lowest in the poorest cities of Africa to the highest in the industrialized north—obtains for virtually all other major urban services: waste disposal, expenditure on roads per person, education, and health services (UNCHS 1999) (see table 5.1).

The figures are even more stark if we isolate the poor populations living in informal settlements. In Africa, in the 1990s, for example, only about 19 percent of households in informal settlements had direct connections to potable water (UN-HABITAT 2003).

Improving the level of basic service delivery is partly a question of sheer resources (as against a rapidly growing population), but it is also a question of governance and allocation. According to the 2001 census, the city of Bangalore, India, has a population of close to 6 million—4.3 million within the Bangalore municipal corporation and the rest in the larger urban agglomeration (Connors 2005). Charged with supplying clean and safe drinking water to this rapidly growing city anxious to attract overseas investment is the Bangalore Water Supply and Sewerage Board (BWSSB), established by the state of Karnataka in 1964. While the board operates within the municipality of Bangalore, none of the municipality's 100 local councillors is represented in its governing structure—the board is a parastatal, not a representative body in this sense. Since the BWSSB is required under law to be financially self-sufficient, it has been struggling to supply water to both rich and poor sections of the urban population while at the same time maintaining its network in good order and providing an adequate local supply in the face of a dwindling overall availability of water on the subcontinent. Although the Bangalore municipal corporation was paying the charges for unmetered public standpipes in poor areas of the city until recently, the corporation has decided to discontinue this policy (partially, it appears, because payments by the municipality to the board could not be aligned with the political interests of the councillors). One result is that the water agency has undertaken to phase out public standpipe services to both find and remove illegal connections (prevalent in poor areas) to encourage direct metering of water to all households, regardless of income. At the same time, it has developed a very sophisticated online management system for complaints, instituted regular meetings with low-income customers, and provided for the computerization of accounts and the elaboration of a "Citizen's Charter" to specify minimum standards of service and water delivery (Kanekanti 2006). Some of these important "pro-poor" governance initiatives have come about because of the presence of important local and international nongovernmental organizations in Bangalore, and because of the influence of an Australian aid initiative, but the board seems to be undertaking operational reforms (Connors 2005). Nevertheless, the BWSSB is still running a current-account deficit, and water outages are frequent all across the city—although they are less frequent in the upper- and middle-income areas than in the lower-income areas of the city. Policy tensions of a similar nature are prevalent in developing-country cities in many other regions. A parallel situation exists with regard to electricity supply and distribution agencies, except that the number of connections is even lower than that of water connections in the poorest countries.

DIMENSION TWO: FINANCE

Since the physical construction of water and electricity reticulation systems, to say nothing of transport, telephone, sewerage, or even high-speed cable networks, costs no less in developing than in industrialized countries, substantial financial resources must be found to finance major infrastructural investments. But because the bulk of their citizens are poor, and most municipal revenue is generated locally, developing-country cities have a very low revenue base. With per capita annual revenue figures at such levels as $13.20 in Nairobi, $2.60 in Lagos, $17.10 in Delhi, $27.70 in Dhaka, and $31 in Abidjan (figures from the 1990s), only the most elementary municipal activities and local services can be supported. While Latin American revenue figures are somewhat higher—again, depending on the wealth of the country in question—in rapidly urbanizing countries of the region such as Bolivia (where La Paz has a per capita revenue of $108) or Guatamala (where Guatamala City shows a per capita revenue of $26) (UNCHS 1999), services and infrastructure cannot even come close to keeping up with population growth. A UN-HABITAT survey indicates that in 1993 the average per capita revenue received by municipal governments in Africa was $15.20, in Asia (Pacific) $248.60, in Latin America and the Caribbean $252.20, and in the industrialized world $2,763.30. The ratio of the average per capita revenue between the lowest and the highest region was in the order of 1:182. This ratio is much higher than the ratio between the per capita income in sub-Saharan Africa and that of the "high-income" countries (1:51), as reported in 1998 figures in the World Bank's *World Development Report* (World Bank 2000).

While it is impossible to separate the capacity (or incapacity) of cities to deal with the service needs of their population from the financial resources they have at their disposal to manage the broad range of responsibilities for which they are responsible, it is also the case that the level of resources available is not a static or immutable quantity. Wealthy countries can direct much higher levels of taxes and fees for service to their municipalities and/or private service providers than can poor countries, since the elasticity of municipal revenue in relation to per capita income is clearly greater than zero. One of the reasons for this is that cities and their surrounding regions are often the most dynamic economic units in the country; the more effectively municipalities can build services and infrastructure to facilitate productive economic activity, the more will both the country and the individual urban citizens benefit. The logic behind this relationship was at least one of the factors underlying the major decentralization reforms in the 1980s and 1990s throughout the developing world. As a result of these reforms, local governments (and, in particular, cities) have been given substantially more power by central governments in many countries around the world (Manor 1999).

The nature of these decentralization policies varies tremendously—from incremental changes in protocols of intergovernmental relations on the one hand, to major constitutional amendments or even new constitutional dispensations on the other. Three large countries gave new constitutional powers to municipalities during this period. In Brazil, a new constitution in 1988 considerably increased the power of municipalities in relation to the states, assigning to them control of intracity transport, preschool and elementary education, land use, preventive health care, and historical and cultural preservation. On the participatory side, municipalities in Brazil were given the right to establish councils of stakeholders ("municipal boards" or "community councils"). These bodies, established in most of the largest cities in the country, include nonelected representatives of community groups and deal with such important matters as urban development, education, the environment, health, and sanitation.

In India, an important constitutional amendment in 1992 provided an illustrative list of functions that are henceforth considered appropriate for municipal government; among these functions are planning for economic and social development, urban poverty alleviation, and even urban forestry. The amendment also limited the degree to which state governments are able to suspend democratic local government (a practice that, until then, had frozen democratic local government in almost half of the largest cities in the country), provided for a revision of state-local fiscal relations, and required that no less than 33 percent of all elected local councillors be women.

The new South African Constitution of 1996 devotes a whole chapter (Chapter 7, containing 14 separate articles) to local government.[1] Among other things this chapter of the constitution states that the objects of local government (including municipal government) are:

> (a) to provide democratic and accountable government for local communities; (b) to ensure the provision of services to communities in a sustainable manner; (c) to promote social and economic development; (d) to promote a safe and healthy environment; and (e) to encourage the involvement of communities and community organisations in the matters of local government.
>
> (Section 152)

There are two clear messages in these reforms: first, that municipalities (and other local governments) are now expected to undertake *and to finance* a much wider and more inclusive range of services and other economic and social activities; and second, that the "community" and important local stakeholder groups must be engaged in the local governance process.

As a result of changes in intergovernmental relations, the financial health of municipalities is slowly improving—at least in some countries. A compilation of data from case studies carried out in the mid-1990s for Brazil, Bolivia, Colombia, Chile, and Peru shows that the scale of revenue transfers from other levels of government to the local level is now relatively high: 62.7 percent of the total of local revenue in Brazil, 54.7 percent in Bolivia, 47.8 percent in Colombia, 42.7 percent in Chile, and 58.1 percent in Peru (Aghón and Casas 1999). At the same time, property tax reforms in some countries have resulted in a much higher level of recovery. In La Paz, for example, after the *Ley de Participación Popular* (1994) devolved property tax collection from the central government to municipal jurisdictions, tax recovery increased considerably—from $4.6 million in 1993, before the new law took effect, to $9.3 million in 1996. In Bolivia, the new law also created "vigilance committees" at the central municipal level, composed of local citizens who were to monitor the use of resources by elected mayors and councils, who could propose investment projects and, in some cases, censure and dismiss the mayor (Grindle 2000). This clearly contributed to the heightened sense of local "ownership" in municipal government, and probably also to the higher rate of tax recovery. And in Bogota, Colombia, recoveries rose from approximately 9 million pesos in 1993 to 30 million pesos in 1996, once a system of self-evaluation of property tax was instituted (Aghón and Casas 1999). As a general rule, however, local tax collection has in most cases not kept up with the increased attribution of powers to cities as a result of decentralization.

That local tax collection and revenue generation may be as much a governance issue as a technical issue (requiring, for example, changes in tax codes, property attributions, and accounting systems) can be illustrated by the case of "participatory budgeting" (PB) in Brazil. The most well known example of a city practicing the participatory budget system is Porto Alegre, a city of about 1.3 million in the south of the country. The system—which essentially involves ordinary citizens in planning for the yearly capital budget (about 10–20 percent of the yearly budgetary total)—is based on the work of 16 forums based on local regions of the city. In addition, there are five thematic forums (created in 1994), involving education, health and social services, transportation, city organization, and economic development; and a municipal budget council with representatives from the regional and thematic forums. The system was originated in 1989 by the Union of Neighborhood Associations. By 1995, some 7,000 people were participating in the regional assemblies and 14,000 more in further meetings to negotiate compromises between the demands of one region and those of another. The system is complex and continues virtually throughout the year. The regional fora even micromanage the actual implementation of capital projects (Abers 1998). A research study of the city management process in Porto Alegre demonstrates that in only three years from 1992 to 1995, the city increased its total tax receipts by 34 percent (Pozzobon 1998); a former mayor of the city claims the popularity of the participatory budget system contributed to a tripling of the city's tax revenues over the period 1989–99 (Pont 2001).

While Porto Alegre is the best known of the Brazilian cities practicing PB, it is not the only, or even the first, city to have developed such a process. Yves Cabannes has argued that more than 130 other Brazilian cities adopted the participatory budgeting model during the period 1997–2000 and that subsequently, many European and other Latin American cities adopted different versions of the original model (Cabannes 2004). A recent estimate, which includes 800 Peruvian cities that are now working with PB, suggests the number of cities adopting some version of the model is as high as 1,000 (World Urban Forum 2006).

The needs of the poor are a long way from being solved by this process. As a knowledgeable Brazilian writer claims, referring to the PB process over the whole country:

[A]lthough some of the claims and results [of participatory budgeting] deserve more research, the experience does allow low-income segments of neglected areas . . . to decide on investment priorities in their communities. Furthermore, it also argues that encouraging participation in highly unequal societies like Brazil should be valued more for heightening citizenship rather than for the material gains it may bring to some areas of the cities.

(Souza 2001, p. 1)

DIMENSION THREE: HORIZONTAL AND VERTICAL DIVERSITY

As they grow and develop, many cities become increasingly diverse, both with respect to the cultural, ethnic, and even religious characteristics of their populations, and with respect to the nature of their economies and the differences in wealth and power that new economic structures are creating. It can be argued that one of the most important measures of a successful city—in both the north and the south—is the ability to deal effectively with diversity and to create structures of governance that integrate diverse communities and economic interests into a functioning system (Polèse and Stren 2000). In somewhat simplified terms, the two major axes of diversity are *horizontal* (comprising geographical and social differences) and *vertical* (comprising differences in wealth and political power).

Studies of the morphology of cities in developing countries almost always comment on the fragmentation of the population, from both a social and an infrastructural point of view. In his classic article on urban planning in developing countries, Marcello Balbo points out that although Western industrial cities are characterized by a certain coherence that is amenable to master planning (but see Graham and Marvin 2001), almost all cities in developing countries are more complex, both spatially and socially:

> [T]he city of the Third World is a city of fragments, where urbanisation takes place in leaps and bounds, creating a continuously discontinuous pattern. In the fragmented city, physical environment, services, income, cultural values and institutional systems can vary markedly from neighbourhood to neighbourhood, often from street to street. . . . Wealthy neighbourhoods provided with all kinds of services, such as exclusive schools, golf courses, tennis courts and private police patrolling the area around the clock intertwine with illegal settlements where water is available only at public fountains, no sanitation system exists, electricity is pirated by a privileged few, the roads become mud streams whenever it rains, and where house-sharing is the norm. Each fragment appears to live and function autonomously, sticking firmly to what it has been able to grab in the daily fight for survival.
>
> (Balbo 1993, pp. 24–5)

Toward the end of the 1990s, knowledgeable commentators were still observing social segregation in Latin American cities. Thus, Alan Gilbert (1996) observes that

> Latin American cities remain highly segregated . . . In Lima, everyone knows that San Isidro and Miraflores are rich while Comas and Villa El Salvador are poor; in Santiago, the extremes are found in affluent Providencia and Vitacura in the north-east and poor La Pintana and La Granja in the south. In Rio de Janeiro, the rich live in Leblon and Ipanema and the poor in the Baixada Fluminense.
>
> (p. 91)

While residential segregation is becoming more complex, he argues, there is no sign that it is declining: "Indeed, in some respects there is greater polarization" (Gilbert 1996, p. 93). The complex nature of this pattern can be illustrated through the case of São Paulo.

São Paulo

São Paulo, with some 10 million people, is one of the world's largest cities and is administered as a municipality. Greater São Paulo, which includes an additional 38 municipalities in a continuous urban area of 1,500 square kilometers, contains 17.9 million people (United Nations 2004, p. 7) and is the second-largest metropolitan area in Latin America after Mexico City. During the 1980s and 1990s, pockets of poverty and run-down housing development bedeviled the generally well-equipped central areas of the city, although more and more of the housing in the peripheral areas of the city, often on marginal land, was classified as "precarious," with low-quality materials, little or no infrastructure, and few social services. Aldaiza Sposati, a professor of social work and an elected municipal councillor, made the following observation:

If the city of Sao Paulo had eyes and could see itself in a large mirror, it would see the broken and shocking view of its inequalities. However, its two eyes would not be similar either. As in the popular song, maybe while one of them was staring, the other one would be floating. Because everything here seems unequal. The largest city in Latin America . . . is famous for the presence of the most advanced forms of technological development and the turnover of finance capital. It houses gardened neighborhoods, lavish mansions, imposing buildings, excellent teaching centers and first class hospitals. A numerous fleet of luxury and imported cars circulate through its avenues or stop in traffic jams. Nevertheless, Sao Paulo also lives with the most severe forms of deprivation and human suffering. A deprived and unemployed population seeks refuge in slums and shack houses, or is abandoned on the streets. They are daily victims of violence and do not have access to their rights and justice. They land on overcrowded buses and trains, and if they get ill, the health service is poor. Their children, when they manage to, attend deteriorated schools, and evasion takes place very soon.

(Sposati 1996, p. 5)

To some writers, this pattern is systemic. Raquel Rolnick, a senior planner, argues that the coincidence of precarious housing, low income, and low formal employment that characterizes many peripheral zones of the city actually constitutes a pattern of "territorial exclusion," whereby those groups consigned to live in these areas cannot fully realize the benefits of citizenship and economic growth that are available to people living in other areas of the city. She shows that the levels of violence and homicide in the city, and the level of basic services available are inextricably linked (Rolnick 1999). "Territorial exclusion," she explains, "makes daily life insecure and risky. It blocks access to jobs and educational and cultural opportunities, which are concentrated in small and protected enclaves within cities. Since most residences in excluded areas are illegal and mixed use is generally forbidden by municipal land regulations, people are denied the possibility of using assets, such as home ownership, to generate money and create jobs. . . . [In these excluded areas] living in a permanent condition of denial of basic human environmental needs makes inhabitants feel as if their lives are worthless" (Rolnick 1999, p. 17). In this analysis we have a very good example of the reinforcement of both horizontal and vertical disjunctures.

Another reflection of the fragmentation between rich and poor is the well-known fact that São Paulo is host to the largest fleet of private helicopters in the developing world. As a result of carjackings, kidnappings, and roadside robberies of those perceived to have money, "helicopters are increasingly used by privileged Paulistanos to commute, attend meetings, even run errands and go to church. Helicopter landing pads are now standard features of many of São Paulo's guarded residential compounds and high-rise roofs" (*New York Times* 2000). While the São Paulo municipal government is democratic in the sense that elections are held regularly based on strong political-party formations, governance, as a relationship between the rulers and the vast majority of the ruled, is a process that demands both great imagination and high levels of administrative and political agility.

DIMENSION FOUR: AUTHORITY AND THE RECOMPOSITION OF LOCAL GOVERNMENT

The basic parameters of urban governance in many developing countries have undergone a major transformation over the last decade and a half. The particular local governance structure currently in play in individual countries and cities is a result of the intersection between the decentralization process, the level of democratic reforms expressed through municipal restructuring, and local circumstance. Local circumstance, in turn, includes (but is not confined to) leadership, the national political situation, and the general involvement of civil society. Overall, Latin American urban governance seems most advanced in terms of staking out new modalities to manage and relate to urban growth; with Asia next (with China as a separate case); and Africa (at least outside a few selected "leaders" in urban governance reform such as South Africa and—at least until recently— Côte d'Ivoire) following.

Decentralization—in the sense of genuine devolution of power and financial resources (or the ability to raise finances) from the national to the local level—has had a rather limited trajectory in Africa. One of the reasons for this is certainly the centralized, statist bureaucratic regimes bequeathed by colonial powers that did not cede independence until the 1960s and even later (whereas formal decolonization took place 20 years earlier in South Asia and Indonesia, and a century earlier in Latin America). Another reason, however, is certainly political, since most postindependence regimes in Africa were ruled initially by powerful leaders and single parties who gave little ground to autonomous social formations or localities. By the 1980s, this picture began to change across the continent and, by the end of the 1990s, after the full democratization of South Africa in 1994 and the return to democracy of Nigeria in 1999, fully 29 African countries out of 53 evaluated by Freedom House were rated as democratic to some degree. The situation has remained more or less stable since then, with most democratic, or at least pluralistic, political systems remaining in the same category. However, the difficulties and challenges of competitive local politics can be illustrated by the evolution of the local governance system in Abidjan, Côte d'Ivoire.

ABIDJAN

A former French colony, Côte d'Ivoire has always been one of the francophone countries with the highest level of urban development and the most elaborate urban policy system (Cohen 1974). Its largest city, Abidjan, has a population estimated at 3.516 million (United Nations 2004, p. 127). This coastal metropolis represents some 40 percent of the total urban population of the country and about 75 percent of its formal employment (Attahi 2000, p. 10). Similar to other major cities in the West African francophone region, and in spite of its relative affluence in comparison to other sub-Saharan African cities, Abidjan still suffers from insufficient housing and infrastructure (at least 20 percent of its population lives in irregular or "spontaneous" housing in unserviced neighborhoods), struggles to remove ever-increasing amounts of household and industrial refuse, and cannot build enough roads to keep up with the growing number of motor vehicles. Often referred to as "the pearl of the lagoons," Abidjan's fabled high-quality infrastructure and large formal employment base have been deteriorating since the late 1980s, as population growth has fallen from a high in the 11 percent per annum range up to the late 1970s, to a figure closer to 3 percent now, a level lower than that of middle-sized towns in the region (Dubresson 1997, p. 266).

Like other ex-colonial states in Africa, Côte d'Ivoire emerged after independence (in 1960) as a relatively centralized country. Then, beginning in 1978, a decentralization process directed by the president (then Felix Houphouët-Boigny) saw, in succession, the restoration of "commune" status to the major cities in the country, including ten "communes" in Abidjan; the amalgamation of the ten Abidjan communes into a second-tier government known as the "City of Abidjan"; and the extension of communal status to 98 smaller towns (in 1985). Finally, three years after the death of Houphouët-Boigny in 1993, his successor extended communalization to the remaining rural areas of the country, taking the total number of local government units from 136 to 196 (Crook and Manor 1998, p. 141). In terms of the fastidious details of its planning, as well as the follow-up of support to local councils, the Ivoirian decentralization exercise stands as one of the most thoroughgoing and successful in Africa.

Two aspects of this exercise are worthy of mention here. First, beginning in 1990, the Ivoirian government loosened control over the political system, permitting parties other than the ruling party (the Parti Démocratique de Côte Ivoire) to contest both local and national elections. This resulted, in the 1990 communal elections, in independents and opposition parties (based on a list system) winning nine of the 135 communes; in the 1996 elections, the proportion grew to 27 of 196 communes (Crook and Manor 1998, p. 149). The 2001 local elections saw the party of President Laurent Gbagbo, the Ivorian Popular Front, winning only 34 of 197 communes, while the former government party (now the main opposition party) won 80 communes, and the Assembly of Republicans (RDR) 64 communes. The real possibility of opposition parties winning local elections and administering local councils has clearly enhanced the legitimacy of local government in many parts of the country. In fact, at the time of voting in 2001, observers said that "voter turnout has exceeded by far that of the parliamentary and presidential elections because of the participation of all the political parties, including Alassane Dramane Ouattara's RDR, which authorised its candidates to contest local polls" (Panafrican News Agency 2001).

Second, while it decentralized, the government also strengthened its advisory and central administrative systems, so that local councils could receive administrative and technical support when they needed it. The Department of Local Government (within the Ministry of the Interior) grew impressively, the strength of its professional staff reaching 108 in 1995 (Attahi 1996).

Until recently, when amalgamation took place, the governance of the Abidjan metropolitan area consisted formally of a two-tier structure: at the lower level were ten communes of differing size and wealth, each commune having elected councillors and an elected mayor; at the second level there was the "city of Abidjan," consisting of the mayors of the ten constituent communes, plus four more councillors from each commune. The mayor of the "city" was elected by the mayors of the ten communes at the first meeting of the collective legislative body, called the "grand council." After his election, he resigned from his communal position, handing the position over to his "assistant mayors" at the local level. The major functions of the upper-tier government were waste disposal and management; public lighting; sanitation; traffic regulation; maintenance of roads, parks, and cemeteries; and town planning. The communes administered markets, allocated plots for public purposes, dealt with the maintenance of primary schools and clinics (but not school or health policy, let alone the supervision and payment of professionals, which are national responsibilities), operated social centers, and shared functions with other levels of government with respect to pollution and hygiene. Major services, such as waste removal and electricity and water supply, were in the hands of private companies, albeit under some level of surveillance from either the local government or the national government. Problems with revenue existed at all levels, even in relatively affluent Abidjan, where the differences between communes were (and still are) palpable. In the early 1990s, for example, the three wealthiest of the ten communes of the city of Abidjan spent, per resident, an average of 49 times the amount spent by the three poorest communes on recurrent expenditures, and six times the amount in capital expenditures (Dubresson 1997).

Whatever successes the "city" of Abidjan may have enjoyed during the 20 or so years of its existence—and they were many—it was disbanded in August 2001 by the national government and replaced by the "district" of Abidjan, which consisted of the original ten communes (with their own governance systems) supplemented by three large subprefectures (which also include their own communal governments) on the outskirts of the city. The city has therefore expanded considerably in size from a much smaller central area and now includes some rural areas. Beginning in 2002, the new district of Abidjan was reconfigured administratively under the aegis of a governor, who, in turn, is appointed to a five-year term by the president of the republic. The governor is selected by the president from nominations by the party winning the majority of votes in the communal elections. The governor is the de facto mayor of the city, assisted by a district council of 51, whose members are two-thirds elected at large and one-third selected by the communes in the district as a whole. The current governor represents the president's party. He is Pierre Djédji Amondji, who had a very successful career as the mayor of the Abidjan commune of Adjamé during the 1990s. Since a virtual civil war has been in effect in Côte d'Ivoire following an attempted military coup in 2002, security issues have overwhelmed more normal service-delivery issues in Abidjan for several years. Urban planning in Abidjan is now fully a metropolitan—or district-level—function. (A similar district structure was imposed in Yamoussoukro, the official capital of the country.) In Abidjan, as throughout the country, communalization has been judged a relative success, but local resources are still very limited, the level of activity of civil society is highly localized and now becoming fractured by ethnic/religious issues (Leimdorfer 2003; Roubaud 2003), and larger political questions have dominated the agenda. On the positive side, however, one could argue that the maintenance of local democracy has been one of the major factors keeping the country functioning in spite of severe civil strife.

There are many other examples of local governance reform in developing countries. In terms of very large metropolitan areas, for example, Mexico City has seen drastic changes since the Mexican government permitted elections in the federal district in the late 1990s. First, the post of "head of government" was made elective; and then, elections took place in all 16 of the former *delegaciones* that became, in effect, local municipalities in their own right (Davis 2002). In South Africa, after the year 2000, the six largest metropolitan areas were amalgamated into "unicities," with provisions made for public participation in ward committees, which are made up of the councillors of the ward and up to ten members of the local community (Cameron 2005, p. 334). And in the Philippines, the Local Government Code of 1991 devolved some important responsibilities to local government units, including primary health care. While at first local governments did not have the capacity to absorb these new functions, they were assisted in many cases by community organizations and volunteer health workers in the transition to a better functioning system (Bautista 1998). To these examples we could add the reform of state and local financial institutions in India (Mathur 2003), the Law of Popular Participation in Bolivia in 1994 (MacLean 2004), and the local reforms in Chinese cities attendant on the use by local governments of market-based "off-budget" revenues (Gang 1999). The list is much longer than this, and it is growing.

CONCLUSIONS

In the developing world, cities are growing much more rapidly than in the developed countries. Basic challenges of urban growth involve the expansion and management of services, the collection and allocation of sufficient revenues to create infrastructure and to operate services in an adequate fashion, creation of a coherent planning framework for the city so that increasingly diverse populations can live together civilly and productively, and establishment of an institutional structure that both represents the constitutive parts of the growing city and at the same time generates adequate authority to govern effectively. These are not easy tasks even for developed countries; but they are much more challenging in developing-country cities when the majority of the population is very poor, and public resources are, as a result, extremely limited. In this chapter we have attempted to illustrate these challenges by classifying urban governance issues into four categories: capacity dimensions, financial dimensions, diversity dimensions, and authority dimensions.

Throughout the chapter the term "governance" has been used. Our understanding of this term, for the cities we have discussed, is in the sense of a relationship between governments and those who are governed, between—in the case of urban government—municipalities and their citizens. Since the 1970s there has been a steady improvement, not always directly visible, in the degree to which local governments have become more sensitive to the needs and even the rights of their people. This improvement has resulted in more and more cities having elected mayors and councils, generally more transparency and responsiveness in the operation of municipal services, and a greater sense of common identity and purpose between political leaders and their constituents. At the same time, global capital movements (which create economic and social divisions, ideas, and understandings of citizenship that transcend national boundaries) and the influence of both trading relations and external assistance agencies have created situations that harbor, for each city one can observe closely, both extreme complexity and great potential for local innovation. No two cities are alike, but by looking at their governance challenges closely through the four major lenses (or "dimensions") we have suggested, we can more effectively focus on the ways by which their elected (or selected) governments deal with the most crucial elements in their fluid and expanding environment. From a postcolonial world in which all initiative started with—and finished with—"the government," we are entering a period in which the responsibilities and actions of governments are being scrutinized and more closely influenced by ordinary people. This is no small accomplishment.

NOTE

1. The South African Constitution can be found at the Government of South Africa website: http://www.polity.org.za/govdocs/constitution/saconst.html.

INNOVATIONS IN URBAN GOVERNMENT

INTRODUCTION TO PART II

The six chapters in Part II of this collection examine the changing world of urban governance. Through case studies and comparisons, our authors explore the changes now taking place in local government and metropolitan governance. Some of the changes are intended efforts at reform; others are, perhaps, less visible shifts in power and authority. While in Part I of this collection our contributors were concerned with an exploration of the impact of macrotrends on cities, in Part II the spotlight is more sharply focused on the microlevel—on what is happening to local democracy and the institutions of urban government in particular localities and countries. In various ways all our authors consider the difficulties of maintaining governmental legitimacy in an era that is characterized by growing inequalities—in power, access, and resources.

In Chapter 6, Gross considers how local governing arrangements might be adapted to better engage the diverse urban populations now living in the complex, multicultural cities of North America and Western Europe. By choosing cities that are hyperdiverse—Toronto, for example, has a population that is 44 percent immigrant—she is able to illuminate challenges that, we believe, are now likely to confront multicultural cities across the world.

In Chapter 7, Swianiewicz examines the changing pattern of local government arrangements in Central and East European (CEE) countries. He explores various claims that are often made about the anticipated benefits of institutional reforms—for example, the claim that introducing directly elected mayors will strengthen local leadership and lift citizens' interest in local elections. He presents fresh evidence covering a range of CEE countries that should cause pause for thought.

In Chapter 8, Zhang shifts attention to the question of how Chinese cities might be able to generate adequate resources in a rapidly changing competitive environment. While the previous authors explored reforms in local democratic institutions, in the case of China Zhang suggests that it is helpful to focus on local resource needs and economic development reforms. He suggests that these changes, inevitably, then give rise to broader moves toward democratic reform. In Shanghai, a centrally planned push by national government has ignited urban economic growth. A by-product has been the emergence of a much wider array of private actors providing needed services and infrastructure. The central challenge for Shanghai and other Chinese cities concerns the relative absence of civil society. As Zhang reminds us, there are probably as many as 3 million migrant workers residing in Shanghai, but they appear to have little or no influence on decision making in the city.

One of the challenges identified by Zhang has parallels in many of the cities discussed in this volume. This is the emergence of "rent seeking" behaviors by central and local governments in which, in the name of economic development, the costs of paving the way for private sector investment are borne by local residents. In many cases we can see that as governments retract, to allow for a stronger private sector role, the potential for corruption grows. Betancur explores this theme in Chapter 9 by reviewing the changing political economy of Medellín, Colombia. He points to the dangers inherent in the movement from "government" toward "governance" in societies whose political structure relies heavily on the "informal" economy.

In Chapter 10, Kübler and Randolph remind us that local conflicts in complex multilevel governance arrangements may result in a situation that comes close to deadlock—a pattern familiar to scholars who have studied the fragmented patterns of government found in many U.S. metropolitan areas. In Sydney, fragmentation and conflict between local demands and metropolitan-wide needs create a challenge concerning the public interest: Who defines it? And how can we ensure that local, regional, and national concerns are balanced and incorporated? For Kübler and Randolph it is clear that higher levels of government need to take responsibility for ensuring that sound metropolitan governance arrangements are in place.

In Chapter 11, Judd and Smith draw attention to what they see as a most profound shift in contemporary urban governance in North America—the growth of special-purpose authorities (or public-private partnerships) that may be functionally adept but are democratically weak. They provide a forensic examination of these new urban development institutions and argue that, freed from the control of the municipal authority, they are becoming dangerously unaccountable. Judd and Smith argue that it is imperative to make these institutions more transparent so that they can become corrigible.

CHAPTER 6

DIVERSITY AND THE DEMOCRATIC CHALLENGE—GOVERNING WORLD CITIES

JILL SIMONE GROSS

INTRODUCTION

One of the hallmarks of globalization is increased mobility. While much research has explored the flows of capital, information, goods, and services to cities, less attention has been paid to the implication of popular mobility (e.g. influx of migrants and exodus of permanent residents) for governing the city democratically. Those who arrive in the city come with differing histories, cultures, skills, interests, priorities, and needs. Some come in search of jobs or education, others seek political, religious, or social asylum. All are seeking a better life, for themselves and their families. As urban populations grow, and diversity and densities increase, competition for access to power and resources often follows. Local governments sit at the center of these local contests. Their ability to respond can have profound impacts on the future of the city and its people.

Local governments play a central role in the democratic process. They are arenas for local policy formulation, serve as channels of communication for the representation of local interests, facilitate local elections, and promote varying degrees of political participation in governance. Given the state of urban demographic change, local governments face a potential crisis of legitimacy if they are unable to effectively engage populations in these governing processes. As Lijphart comments, "unequal participation spells unequal influence—a major dilemma for representative democracy in which the democratic responsiveness [of elected officials] depends on citizen participation" (1997, p. 1).

A local government that fails to manage tensions between urban dwellers, or that is unable to capitalize on the benefits of local diversity, is likely to experience disinvestment and decline. As Ray comments:

> It has long been recognized that urban areas, especially large cities, are places where cultural diversity flourishes . . . History demonstrates, however, that diversity is not a sufficient

condition to bring about the sustained inclusion of the different groups that populate a city. The collapse into inter-ethnic conflict of once relatively harmonious multicultural cities . . . highlights the fragility of cultural diversity.

(2003, p. 1)

Popular unrest in cities in recent years highlights the dangers when city governments become disconnected from urban populations.

This chapter explores how three local governments —those of Paris, Copenhagen, and Toronto—have grappled with the demands that "hyperdiversity" makes on governing, through an analysis of the "democratic capacities" of their local governing structures. It considers the impacts of different institutional structures for mitigating political exclusion and promoting greater political participation in local governing processes.

THE DIVERSITY-DEMOCRACY CHALLENGE

Paris, Copenhagen, and Toronto, like all global or globalizing cities, are heavily affected by immigration. As table 6.1 illustrates, all three cities have large foreign-born populations that are growing as a proportion of the urban population—they are what some researchers describe as the world's "immigrant cities" (Benton-Short et al. 2004). Copenhagen and Toronto have experienced growth both in population and in the proportion of immigrants residing there over the past decade. Though the population of Paris has declined, it has seen an increase in the proportion of urban immigrants.[1]

All three are home to the largest number of immigrants nationally; they are the prime receiving areas—or "immigrant gateways." They are all experiencing hyperdiversity of their immigrant populations—no single ethnic group dominates. As Benton-Short, Price, and Friedman point out, "The implications of large numbers of people from diverse countries settling in particular points on the globe have real consequences" (2004, p. 3), economically, politically, and socially.

A population that is disaffected is far more likely to turn away from formal mechanisms such as voting and to use informal forms of political participation such as direct action, protest, or even riot to express needs. These informal expressions can be costly.

Table 6.1   Copenhagen, Paris, Toronto: Total population and immigrant population change

	Population		%	Immigrants				%
	Total (year)	Total (year)	change	Total (year)	%	Total (year)	%	change
Toronto	4,647,960 (2001)	3,399,680 (1986)	31%	2,032,960 (2001)	44%	1,234,360 (1986)	36%	8%
Copenhagen	495,699 (2000)	466,723 (1989)	6%	58,535 (2000)	12%	33,570 (1989)	7%	5%
Paris	2,125,246 (1999)	2,176,652 (1982)	−2%	308,266 (1999)	18%	360,529 (1982)	17%	1%

Sources: Statistics Canada (2001), Citizenship and Immigration Canada (2005), Copenhagen City (2001) and INSEE (1982, 1999).

In Toronto, during the summer of 2000, a demonstration seeking greater resources and power for the municipality to grapple with poverty turned violent (Molotov cocktails, bricks, and bottles were lobbed at provincial government buildings), leaving dozens of protestors and police injured (CBC News 2000). The riots that began in Paris in 2005 sparked nationwide demonstrations that left almost 9,000 vehicles destroyed and resulted in the arrest of some 300 people (BBC News 2005). In Copenhagen, after the publication of offensive cartoons of the Prophet Mohammed, immigrants organized an international economic boycott of Danish products, which led to a 35 percent drop in national food exports to Muslim countries (Buch-Andersen 2006). For governments, these forms of informal participation can exert a high price on business and residents alike.

What many researchers agree upon is that immigrant minority communities tend to participate less in governance via formal institutional channels, such as voting, than natives (Maxwell 2005; Lijphart 1997; Parry et al. 1992). In turn, governments are less capable of representing the interests of these communities. Low voter participation, therefore, is an indicator of a potential crisis of legitimacy for local government (Giddens 1998; Putnam 1993, 1995, 1996). In the 2003 municipal elections in Toronto, for example, mean voter turnout in predominately Canadian wards (mean voter turnout in wards dominated by those of Canadian ethnicity) was 50 percent, while in immigrant-dominated electoral wards the average turnout was 32 percent (Siemiatycki 2006). Lower turnout at the polls by minority communities may also result in fewer ethnic candidates getting elected. Minority candidates in the 2003 elections won only 11 percent of Toronto's city council seats, though they represented 44 percent of the population (TCF 2004). With fewer representatives in positions of power, there is less likelihood that group interests will be reflected in local policy agendas.

Political participation can take a range of forms—formal participation through voting, the signing of a petition, community planning and policy consultation, as well as informal participation through involvement in voluntary sector organizations, protest, and riot. In this chapter, I present data on only one form of formal participation—voting. Whereas voting is one of many forms of formal political participation, it is the most common form. Its costs in time and energy to the individual and to government, relative to other forms of participation, are low.

There are, however, problems in using electoral turnout as a measure of participation. For example, turnout alone tells us only about the voters, and little about the broader population; new immigrants, for example, as noncitizens, are not usually captured by voting statistics. Of particular importance to this research is that in all three cities, large proportions of the foreign-born population have political rights at the local level, enabling them to vote and run for local office. Two of these cities (Paris and Toronto) are located in what Bird (2004) refers to as "relatively old immigration societies, such that the largest proportion of visible minorities are now second- and third-generation citizens," and have a sizeable number of "colonial" immigrants with citizenship status. Copenhagen accords foreign-born residents political rights in the municipality. While the sample of three cities is clearly too small to make broad generalizations from, my goal here is simply to look at the lessons that might be learned from the common experience of each of these city governments in their efforts to politically engage their populations, and to begin to develop a set of indicators to help municipalities better evaluate the capacities of their institutions to respond to the democratic governing challenge in conditions of increasing hyperdiversity.

THE DEMOCRATIC GOVERNING CHALLENGE

Comparative research on institutions reveals that differences in democratic structure can affect a municipality's ability to engage local populations and manage conflict in governing processes (Gunther and Mugham 1993; Franklin 2004; Guigni and Passy 2004). We know, for example, that the introduction of proportional representation boosts voter turnout (Lijphart 1997; Ladner and Milner 1999). We also know that simply creating more avenues for participation in local government does not necessarily mean people will utilize them (Gross, J.S. 1996); people need to feel that there will be some benefit from their efforts. Participation must be translated into influence. Creating governing institutions with adequate resources to carry out their functions, with power to set agendas, and ensuring that participation efforts occur early enough in a policy formulation process to affect its outcomes are all means of increasing popular participation in local governance (Gross, J.S. 2004 and 2005b). In table 6.2, I provide a summary of my central hypotheses and what indicators were used to explore the relationship between local democratic structures, capacities, and political participation.

Underlying this research is the belief that enhancing democratic capacity in these four areas is one path toward building more stable and politically inclusive cities.

Table 6.2   Indicators of democratic capacity

Democratic capacity measures	Hypotheses	Indicators
Representation	Local government systems, in which the geographic size and ratio of representatives to constituents is smaller, allows for closer links to the community and will therefore produce higher levels of popular participation	Geographic size of electoral districts Number of representatives Number of voters per representative
Responsiveness	Institutional mechanisms that can enhance the capacity of local government to respond in a timely and effective manner to the needs of the community will produce higher levels of voter turnout	Multilevel government Greater use of elected, as opposed to nonelected or appointed, governing bodies Control of resources Agenda-setting powers Veto powers
Salience	When channels for participation are structured such that residents perceive that their participation will influence the political composition of local government and its policy priorities and directions, they are more likely to participate	Local electoral systems based on proportional representation Two-way channels of communication Providing access during early stages of policy formation
Democratic norms	Local government systems that support direct forms of democracy will have higher levels of popular participation	Number and type of mechanisms in place for popular engagement

Table 6.3   Representation capacity

Toronto	Paris	Copenhagen
Low ⬅————————————————————➡ High		

REPRESENTATION

As table 6.3 shows, Copenhagen's local government system has a high level of representative capacity. Its largest district is smaller than the smallest districts in the other cities. Its city council members represent, on average, 9,000 electors, enhancing their capacity to represent local interests. Paris is not far behind on this measure. Despite the fact that Paris has four times the population of Copenhagen, its local government system offers small-scale representation—each council member represents 13,000 electors. In contrast, each of Toronto's elected council members represents almost 70,000 constituents. Thus, in Toronto, it is much more difficult for local representatives and their constituents to develop personal ties between them than it is in Paris and Copenhagen (see Appendix for further details on representation).

RESPONSIVENESS

As shown in table 6.4, from the perspective of multilevel government, Paris has the highest level of responsive capacity. There are three levels of government within the municipality—an upper tier to address strategic needs, a lower tier to address local needs, and a community-level body to respond to neighborhood concerns. Copenhagen has a single-tier authority but recently introduced a variety of community forums. Toronto abolished its lower-tier authorities in favor of a single, amalgamated metropolitan government.

On the scale of control of agendas and resources, or local autonomy, Copenhagen has a higher degree of responsive capacity within its local government system. Relative to the other cities, it has more control over resources, more independence in defining its policy paths, and greater independence from central government. Paris has gained more local control over the past two decades, despite being located within one of the most centralized governmental systems in Western Europe. Toronto falls at the low end on this scale: it is heavily controlled by the provincial government of Ontario, and the municipality here has very little direct control over resources, budgets, or agendas.

Table 6.4   Responsiveness scales

A. Degree of federation—multilevel government

Toronto	Copenhagen	Paris
Low ⬅————————————————————➡ High		

B. Degree of local control

Toronto	Paris	Copenhagen
Low ⬅————————————————————➡ High		

Table 6.5 Salience scale

Toronto	Paris	Copenhagen
Low ◄———————————————————————————————————————► High

SALIENCE

As table 6.5 illustrates, Copenhagen's local government system has high salience. Copenhagen uses proportional representation in elections, whereby parties that garner at least 2 percent of the vote are ensured 2 percent of the seats on its 55-member city council. In contrast, in Toronto, a simple majority in a ward brings all of the seats, excluding minority groups from direct power. In Paris, the arrangements are more complex—two rounds of elections are possible—during the first round, as many as nine political parties put forward lists of candidates. If one political party receives over 50 percent of the vote, it wins all the seats. However, more commonly, no party achieves this level, which leads to a second election runoff, in which the parties that reaped the fewest votes tend to throw their support to one of the lead runners. The negotiations between parties that are required to win a French election enhance its salience relative to other first-past-the-post systems because, even if one party does not win, its interests may be reflected in a coalition-style support base that generates the winning list.

Salience was also gauged in terms of local-agenda-setting capacities. Copenhagen operates under a doctrine of general competence—something akin to home rule in the United States. Thus, the city has greater control over its local policy agendas. Next in line is Paris, whose upper-tier municipal council has gained greater control and autonomy with regard to the agenda and local budget allocations since the mid-1980s, though the lower-tier districts have remained weak. As with responsiveness, Toronto has less local control, and provincial and national governments exert a heavy hand, particularly at moments when there is discord between governmental levels. Thus, overall, Copenhagen's local government system is characterized by the highest levels of salience, followed by Paris and lastly by Toronto.

DEMOCRATIC NORMS

In exploring the democratic norms, I considered those local government systems that supported popular access (in voting, policy formulation, planning, etc.) as having greater capacity than those that supported a more restrictive role for local residents. As table 6.6 shows, Copenhagen again scores highest, with recent democratic reforms offering residents forums for consultation in planning and policy. Of the three cities, only Copenhagen allows noncitizens to vote in local elections (after a three-year period of residency), suggesting a stronger attachment to local democracy. Paris is a somewhat unique case, because there has been an ongoing tension between the community and central government, dating back to the French Revolution—thus local democracy tends to be more narrowly defined and limited.

Table 6.6 Democratic norm scale

Toronto	Paris	Copenhagen
Low ◄———————————————————————————————————————► High

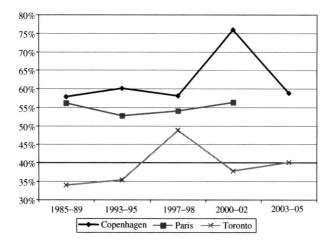

Figure 6.1   Voter turnout in Copenhagen, Paris, and Toronto municipal elections—1985–2005.
Sources: Copenhagen City (1999, 2001, 2004a, 2004b, 2005); TCF (2004), and Le Figaro (2006).

In both Paris and Copenhagen, recent efforts have been made to enhance local democracy. Both systems have introduced community-based forums at the most local level. While in Paris these reforms were mandated, localities in Copenhagen were given the option—thus, only a few of Copenhagen's city districts have put these reforms into place. In neither of these cases do these community-level institutions have more than advisory powers. This might offset their impacts by decreasing their salience. In Copenhagen, user boards have also been introduced to allow local service users to oversee day care and to assist the city council in planning and school governance. Both Copenhagen and Paris also introduced community forums for immigrants more recently. In Toronto, local communities have seen a decline in democratic access in recent years. Here, more emphasis has been placed on economic engagement in user boards.

Overall, we find that Copenhagen's local government system has higher democratic capacity than our other cases, closely followed by Paris. Toronto has the least democratic capacity. We would expect therefore to find the highest levels of political participation in Copenhagen, followed by Paris and Toronto. As figure 6.1 reveals, in the aggregate, this analysis is supported.

While democratic capacity appears to be meaningful for cities seeking to increase voter participation overall, we saw earlier that minorities tend to participate less. Given this fact, I felt it important to look a bit deeper into these hyperdiverse cities to explore whether reforms had equal impacts on minority populations.

CASE 1: COPENHAGEN—HIGH DEMOCRATIC CAPACITY

DEALING WITH THE DIVERSITY CHALLENGE

As figure 6.2 shows, for a comparatively small city, Copenhagen has attracted a very diverse group of immigrants. Many came as guest workers during the 1960s and later brought family members over for reunification.[2] As Goli and Rezaei comment, "As guest workers, their participation in Copenhagen civic life was minimal, they had no political rights[,] they were the unknowns—the strangers" (2005, p. 6). When economic downswings came,

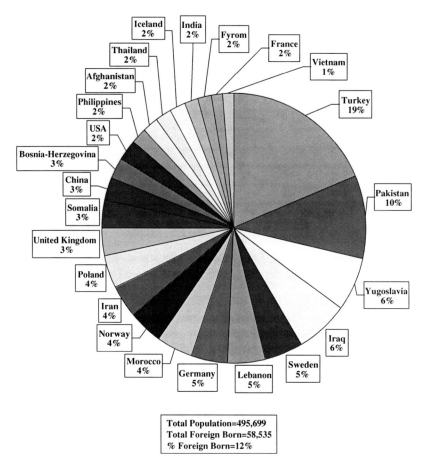

Figure 6.2 Distribution of foreign-born population in Copenhagen—2000.

Sources: Copenhagen City (2004) and GUM (2001a).

the municipality was faced with a problem—immigrant marginality, a potentially volatile situation. While national government introduced restrictions on the flow of immigrants, local government has been at the forefront of efforts to politically integrate and engage its immigrant minorities. The enhanced democratic capacity of the system enabled these governments to be quite innovative in this regard.

LOCAL ENGAGEMENT: ADMINISTRATIVE AND DEMOCRATIC CAPACITY

Danish local governments operate under the "doctrine of general competence," giving them powers akin to home rule in the United States. Thus, the Copenhagen City Council is responsible for most aspects of local welfare provision and has the right to undertake any activity it feels to be in the interests of the city.

Residential voting for immigrants and the right to run for office on the city council were instituted in the locality in 1981. What is interesting is that prior to this, immigrants were economically integrated as guest workers but politically isolated. During the 1980s, political integration was promoted, perhaps in part in an effort to counteract the effects of the growing economic isolation for many of Copenhagen's immigrants. Though immigrant local voting rights were granted, this initially had little effect on immigrant political participation, because many lacked the capacity to navigate the system owing to linguistic and educational barriers. During the early 1990s, in response, the municipality introduced of a series of support programs—language, culture, career, and educational services (Kobehavn Commune 2006).

In 1994, the 15 city districts were given the option to create community councils to aid the city council in planning, protecting the environment, and school governance; four were created. In 1999, the municipality introduced immigrant integration councils as a channel for immigrants to be involved in local immigrant policy and programs. Members were initially appointed, but in March 2006 membership was shifted to a system of locally based elections (Holck 2006). The shift was due to the fact these councils tended not to be inclusive. Researchers found that appointees tended to be drawn from long-standing ethnic groups (those who might be described as already integrated), and that new immigrant groups were either ignored or excluded from decision-making processes by local government.

There were larger problems of salience as well, in that many of these councils were used as one-way channels of communication from the city council to inform the immigrant community of policy being made in local government (Petersson and Nizam 2001).

POPULAR PARTICIPATION IN COPENHAGEN

The ability of local governments to develop locally responsive programming, and their efforts to engage residents (immigrant and native) in governing appear to be paying off in some areas. As we saw earlier (figure 6.1), in the aggregate, Copenhagen has the highest average turnout of our three cases—62 percent over the past 30 years (Copenhagen City 1999, 2004, 2004a, 2004b, 2005).[3] Not only does Copenhagen do well for aggregate voter turnout, but it is also showing signs of some success with immigrant political engagement.

In a detailed analysis of ethnic voting behavior in the 1997 elections, Togeby (figure 6.3) found that immigrants from Pakistan voted in numbers comparable with ethnic Danes. African populations however voted less. As Togeby (1999) comments, "The Danish local election system is not created to benefit immigrants, but it does serve to aid their political mobilization . . . and creates far better opportunities for collective mobilization" (1999, pp. 17–8). The patterns that Togeby saw in 1997 (figure 6.3) were slightly dampened in the 2001 and 2005 elections (figure 6.4): voter turnout in communities with large populations from Pakistan fell slightly below the citywide mean. Turkish turnout grew, and, while turnout in African communities increased, it remained below the citywide average.[4] The 2001 election produced quite different patterns because it corresponded with the national election, which always produces higher turnouts overall.

The small decline in participation by Pakistani residents, relative to the mean (as compared with 1997), may relate to broader political trends at the time. A more restrictive immigration and citizenship policy was implemented at the national level in the aftermath of 9/11, which may account for a minor electoral backlash. Variation in turnout suggests that the city is doing better at integrating in some areas and for some groups than in others. Slightly lower levels of turnout among African and Asian immigrants suggest that a more nuanced approach to integration is needed.[5] But, overall, data suggest that the efforts are paying off in the electoral arena. Less success has been found with Copenhagen's newly formed integration councils—the newest innovation in the city's efforts to engage immigrants.

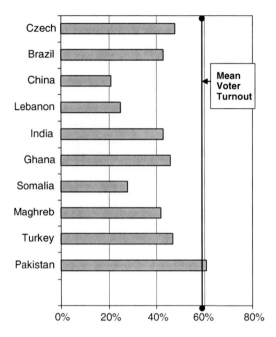

Figure 6.3　Voter turnout in Copenhagen municipal election by ethnicity—1997.
Source: Togeby (1999).

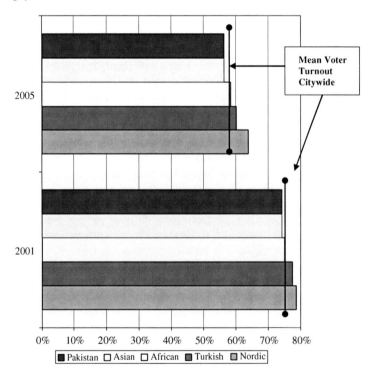

Figure 6.4　Voter turnout in Copenhagen municipal elections by ethnicity—2001 and 2005
Sources: Copenhagen City (2001 and 2005).

As the *Copenhagen Post* reported, "The first direct elections to the council were intended to give the city's nearly 53,800 immigrants and foreigners a voice in city affairs. Immigrants from ethnic minorities could choose a candidate from Africa, the Mideast, Asia, and Europe. Despite printing voter material in seven languages and running television spots and advertising in freesheets, turnout was a mere 13.8 percent" (*Copenhagen Post* 2006). Though pundits suggest that the lack of power accorded to these institutions has meant that they hold limited salience in the minds of voters, "Copenhagen City Councillor Ikram Sarwar said the turnout revealed that immigrants perceived the council as "an empty political initiative" (*Copenhagen Post* 2006).

CASE 2: PARIS: DENIAL OF DIVERSITY—OR CAPACITY BUT NO POLITICAL WILL

DENIAL OF DIVERSITY

In Paris, one finds a significantly different approach to dealing with diversity. As figure 6.5 illustrates, Paris appears less diverse than Copenhagen.[6] However, the proportion of immigrants residing in the city is greater.

As in our prior case, both local and national levels of government play a role in dealing with diversity. The national government regulates the flow of immigrants and promotes a policy of assimilation. "France has traditionally viewed the retention of ethnic

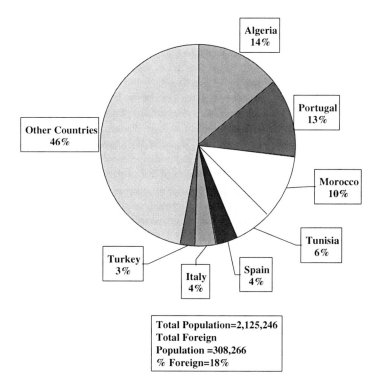

Figure 6.5   Distribution of foreign-born population in Paris—1999.
Sources: INSEE (1999) and GUM (1999).

identity as an obstacle to both integration and national solidarity" (Bird 2004, p. 16). Immigrants are expected to adapt. As Bird comments, "It would be an understatement to suggest that ethnic minorities in France tend to be politically marginalized. There is likely no democratic state in the world where ethnic minorities are excluded . . . to a greater extent than they are in France" (2004, p. 14).

Unlike Copenhagen, the local government of Paris has had to deal with diversity indirectly. According to Sabbagh, the result is that place, not race, becomes the focus of urban policies that seek to address "differences" in income, access to employment, educational qualifications, and housing. (Brouard S. et al. 2006)

LOCAL ENGAGEMENT AND INSTITUTIONAL REFORM

Historically, Paris has functioned within a highly centralized governing system. However, a series of reforms over the past 25 years has altered this. The first major reforms came in 1975, when an upper-tier, strong-mayor council system was introduced. Parisians were given the power to directly elect their city council. Mayors, however, remained State appointees, allowing the center to strongly influence the locality. Twenty lower-tier district councils were also created; however, they were given no real powers or resources. While the upper tier—the Paris Council—had enhanced responsive capacity, the lower tier remained weak (Kuhlmann 2004b).

During the 1980s, the upper tier was given greater decision-making capacity and administrative and budgetary power over local development and planning, enhancing the municipality's responsive capacity. There were also reforms that enhanced representation. Mayors became indirectly elected by the council. The lower tier remained weak, because the upper tier did not want to cede power to the arrondissements (Kuhlmann 2004b). The districts have no control over budget matters or resources. The power in the system is firmly rooted in the upper tier.

In 1995 six of the district councils were taken over by the left wing. Their mayors began to build their local power bases using a third, more local tier of government,[7] the community councils, to mobilize and engage local populations more directly in governing. In 2001 the upper-tier council was taken over by the Left. Then, in 2002, new laws were introduced to increase the power of the 20 districts councils in a wide variety of local policy and planning areas. In 2002 a new law was passed that mandated the creation of "neighborhood councils" across Paris to provide communities the opportunity to participate in major infrastructure projects and local service provision. Alongside of this, Paris has created "councils of citizenship" to provide foreigners a forum to discuss issues. Both are purely consultative.

IMPACTS

As we saw in figure 6.1, voter turnout in Paris is comparatively robust. More than half of the Paris electorate turn out for municipal elections. In the aggregate, we can note some interesting patterns. Variations can be seen at certain key reform moments. A small increase between 1977 and 1983 corresponds with the passage of laws that increased the responsive capacity of the local authority. However, the subsequent declines in turnout (till 1995) may reflect the failure of the upper tier to give the lower-tier authorities any meaningful power—lowering the levels of salience in the system. As Kuhlmann (2004b) points out,

> [T]he district . . . is suspiciously limited . . . the executive leaders at the upper level of the municipality, used a minimalist application of the [law] . . . amounting to what has been labeled by some observers as a real 'non-application' . . . a hybrid institutional setting has taken shape

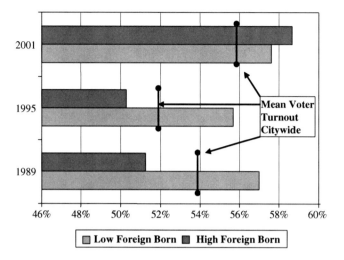

Figure 6.6   Voter turnout in Paris municipal elections by foreign-born population—1989, 1995, 2001
Sources: INSEE (1999) and Le Figaro (2006).

> which is characterized by a reinforcement of political participation and democracy on the one hand and a hitherto awkward lack of substantial functions and competencies on the other hand.
>
> (pp. 10–1)

Thus, the first election brought people out, but then the reality may have led to some disillusion and the declines. In 1995 we begin to see the beginnings of a turnaround; we may correlate to locally based efforts by left-wing candidates to bring real power to the district level (Kuhlmann 2004a, 2004b).

Turning our attention to minority participation,[8] figure 6.6 illustrates voting trends over the past decade in arrondissements with high and low proportions of foreign-born French citizens.[9] Until the most recent elections in 2001, communities with high proportions of foreign-born citizens voted at significantly lower levels than those dominated by French-born citizens. The 2001 elections however show a significant change; for the first time we see turnouts in the areas with high proportions of foreign-born citizens surpassing both the mean turnout for the city as a whole and that for the arrondissements dominated by French-born citizens.

This period corresponds to the introduction of reforms that enhanced local democratic capacity. In response, it would appear that foreign-born communities decided to vote in higher numbers. This may be an indication that in Paris, democratic reforms may be especially meaningful in politically engaging historically marginalized communities.

CASE 3: TORONTO'S SPLIT PERSONALITY—POLITICAL WILL BUT NO CAPACITY

DEALING WITH DIFFERENCE

Of our three case-study cities, Toronto has the largest number and proportion of immigrants, and, as figure 6.7 illustrates, it is incredibly diverse, with no single ethnic group dominating. In contrast to Paris's assimilationist approach, Toronto has promoted a policy of "multiculturalism," viewing immigration as an opportunity for the city rather than as a problem. I refer to the Toronto case as one of "split personality" because here we have a city that celebrates its diversity, yet lacks the capacity to politically engage that population.

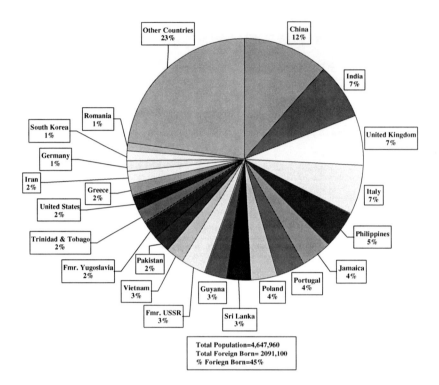

Figure 6.7   Percentages of foreign-born citizens in Toronto—2001.

Sources: Statistics Canada (2001) and GUM (2001a).

Thus, for example, in 1997, the province of Ontario transferred responsibility for housing, child care, public health, and social assistance to the municipality—services described as "vital to the immigrant settlement process" (Papillon 2002, p. 20). But, no funding was provided. The result is that the municipality has had to rely on outside providers in the nonprofit sector (adopting a governance approach). As Papillon (2002) reminds us, "Settlement services is largely a top-bottom process . . . While knowledge about needs (which vary considerably) lies mostly at the community level, programming is still for the most part developed vertically" (p. 20). The federal government regulates the flow of immigrants and distributes funds to the provinces to support local settlement and adaptation programs. The province, in turn, distributes those funds to community agencies to provide those services. Local government describes its role as advocacy for its residents to higher levels of government for fair treatment (Hoy 2004).

Thus, there is a real capacity deficit at the local government level. Though the city's motto, "Diversity is our Strength," is a celebration of diversity, there are few resources available. Thus, though the city has sought to promote a sense of belonging for newcomers, through outreach and public education campaigns, its efforts to promote political participation and engagement have been relatively unsuccessful by comparison to our other cases.

LOCAL ENGAGEMENT: ADMINISTRATIVE AND DEMOCRATIC CAPACITY

Toronto has no constitutionally guaranteed self-government (Wegener 2002). In recent years, the city has seen a reduction in its powers and a weakening of local democratic norms. Thus, of our three cases, the city should be viewed as having the lowest levels of democratic capacity overall, and recent reforms have only added to the problem.

From 1954 to 1997 Toronto was governed by a two-tier system—an upper-tier regional municipal government, also know as "Metro Toronto," and, below this, initially, 13 local municipalities, which were later amalgamated into five separate city governments. Since 1998, a single metropolitan-tier council has governed Toronto. In an effort to address community-level needs, planning, and development issues, there were six community councils established initially, which were later reduced to four covering areas with between 300,000 and 600,000 residents. These are, however, committees of the council and thus remain upper- rather than lower-tier authorities—tending toward top-down communication as opposed to bottom-up.

Currently, Toronto's residents can participate in governance via voting in elections; they can attend council and committee meetings, contacting their local councillor or via participation on local boards and commissions (though this is via appointment). Since amalgamation, the trend has been to involve residents in a dialogue concerning services—thus, task forces have been set up as a form of communication regarding service needs. The focus is on citizens as consumers of services, not on citizens as legislative advocates or policy developers.

The trend in municipal reform over the past decade has been centralization geared toward enhancing and streamlining government bureaucracy. There has been less emphasis here on municipal democracy than in our other case studies. This is not, however, to suggest that Toronto fails to acknowledge its ethnic diversity; quite the contrary, it celebrates it. However, it focuses upon "economic participation" and "responsive service" delivery. A reactive approach tends to be the path taken here, one that focuses on preventing discrimination, as opposed to promoting political integration (TCC 2003).

POPULAR PARTICIPATION IN LOCAL GOVERNMENT

Toronto, has low democratic capacity. Not surprisingly, we find relatively low voter turnout rates here.[10] As figure 6.1 shows, average turnouts rarely pass the 40 percent mark. The bump in turnout in 1997 correlated with the first elections postamalgamation, a highly contested race.

If we turn our attention to immigrant voting, we can quickly see that the system appears to do no better here (see figure 6.8). A simple contrast between high and low immigrant areas reveals that when it comes to voting patterns, clearly, "diversity" is not Toronto's "strength." Immigrant communities vote at signficiantly lower levels than Canadian-born Torontonians.

The exception for the immigrant vote came in 1997. Siemiatycki and Isin (1997) point out how much "emphasis the two front-runners placed on winning the immigrant and minority vote . . . Never before [had] Toronto's ethno-cultural diversity been so aggressively courted by candidates for civic government's highest office" (p. 97). This exception suggests that representation and responsiveness may be important for promoting minority political participation in Toronto.

What is especially worrying is that in the most recent elections the gap between immigrant and Canadian-born voting has grown, suggesting that the reforms to the Toronto municipal government may have led to higher levels of political marginality for these groups. Minorities also continue to be substantially underrepresented on the municipal council (Siemiatycki and Isin 1997).

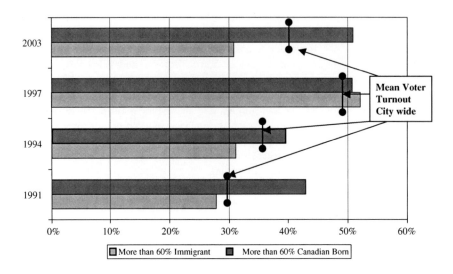

Figure 6.8 Voter turnout in Toronto municipal elections by high- and low-immigrant concentrations. *Sources*: TCF (2001a) and Statistics Canada (2001).

CONCLUSIONS

In Copenhagen, the existence of diversity was acknowledged and local government was empowered to create identity-based (ethnic, racial, religious, or gender) programs targeted at grappling with diversity and political exclusion. In Paris, programs were most commonly targeted at places based on deficits in services and economic opportunities. It is the responsibility of the immigrant to assimilate in Paris; not that of the municipality. At the same time, recent unrest in deprived communities that are heavily dominated by immigrants reveals the cracks in this system. The recent additions of enhanced democratic access at the most local level in Paris, and the creation of specific sites for the inclusion of immigrant voices may have positive affects on political participation for marginal communities in the future, provided a two-way flow of communication is preserved. Toronto leaders sought to celebrate their ethnic diversity—"Diversity is our Strength." But in a system in which the locality lacks the capacity to respond, these effects seem to have had little effect on local political participation. As Sisk observes:

> At the heart of all democracies is an essential trust that the individual places in others to fairly pursue the common affairs of all people. This basic trust . . . can only be built from the ground up, from the local level. A vigorous local democratic culture, a vibrant civil society, and an open, inclusive local government, are fundamental to the long-term viability of any democracy.
>
> (Sisk 2001, p. vii)

This small set of cases suggests that improving democratic institutional capacity can affect overall levels of political participation. However, some reforms may be more meaningful than others.

- Representation: We hypothesized that small-scale representation would enhance voter turnout. Our cases would support that finding. However, representation cannot be isolated from responsiveness.

- Responsiveness: We hypothesized that giving local government the capacity to innovate, to control resources and agendas would produce higher levels of participation, and again our cases would support this. Both cross-nationally, but also within the locality, the evidence would suggest that minority voters are savvy and are unlikely to participate in institutions that have no power to follow through or respond.
- Salience: This was particularly important across all systems. Higher turnouts were found in those systems in which voter preferences more directly influenced power distribution, and in forums with two channels of communication. When systems introduced reforms to enhance these features, increased participation followed.
- Democratic norms: When local governments increased the number of avenues for participation, and democratized them—emphasizing elected over appointed roles—higher levels of participation ensued. However, for this to be effective with immigrant communities, there must be strong educational components, as is the case in Copenhagen—not simply language, but civic education to enable new immigrants to better navigate the system.

A final lesson from this research was that "one size does not fit all" local populations. This is perhaps not surprising, given that each group comes with unique histories,

APPENDIX

Representation	Paris	Toronto	Copenhagen
Total population	2,125,000	2,988,102	499,000
Municipal districts/ boroughs	20 arrondissements	6 municipalities (preamalgamation) 1 megacity (post-1998) (44 electoral wards)	15 city districts
Mean population per municipal district	97,632	498,017 (preamalgamation)	36,122
Local government	Council of Paris 20 district councils Community councils (number varies by district)	Toronto Council (1998) 4 community councils (2003)/ 6 community councils (1998) 1 metropolitan government and 6 municipal governments (preamalgamation 1998)	Copenhagen City Council
Number of members	163 council 354 district	33 (pre-1997) 57 (1997–2000) 44 (since 2000)	55
Average number of electors per council member	13,037	72,285 (preamalgamation) 41,849 (1997–2000) 67,911 (since 2000)	9,072
Executive	Mayor and deputy mayors—indirectly elected from among council	Mayor directly elected	Borgmester (mayor) and deputies— indirectly elected from among council

cultures, and socioeconomic backgrounds. The moment of its arrival and duration of time in the city will affect political integration in a municipality. Given the growing diversity that globalization produces in the city, there is a surprising dearth of nuance in the ways that municipalities have dealt with difference. Or, more to the point, if different groups have different experiences and participate differently, might not cities need to begin to consider a more varied basket of policies for different neighborhoods? Targeted sets of policies are needed to respond to educational, linguistic, and economic barriers, as well as to racism and discrimination. While enhancing the democratic capacity of local government may be meaningful for cities seeking to engage traditionally marginalized populations, the cost of implementing a one-size-fits-all model may well be declining turnouts in other communities. Thus, a more nuanced application at the community level may be required with different strategies in different communities, depending on the composition of the population at a given time.

NOTES

1. In the case of Paris, for analytic purposes, we draw data at the level of the 20 arrondisements within the "commune" (note: within the broader metropolitan region—the "Ile de'France"—there have been small population increases. As regards Toronto, we are referring here to the amalgamated city, also known as the Greater Toronto Region, or GTA. In Copenhagen, data is at the level of the 15 city districts excluding Friedricksburg.

2. Danish law protects the right of immigrants to reunify with their families and, thus, immigrant numbers in Copenhagen rose from 8 percent in 1992 to 12 percent in 2001 (Copenhagen City 2001).

3. Voter turnout and ethnicity data were gathered at the level of the 15 city districts in Copenhagen from the Copenhagen City Statistical Office. As the data are not based on individual votes but rather those aggregated at the district level, we must look at the outcomes cautiously as indicators of trends and not as conclusive proof.

4. The data used by Togeby was much more locally sensitive, based on exits polls at a far more disaggregated level. I used census data to identify dominant demographic features of the districts and selected the districts with the largest concentrations of identified ethnicities.

5. Further research is needed in this area, as my data does not disaggregate in the detail that Togeby's does. Thus, while Togeby found that there was variation within African populations, my data are not sensitive enough to tease this out. In addition, African immigrants came as refugees, while Turkish and Pakistani immigrants came earlier, for the most part as guest workers, which may also affect participation and may warrant a slightly different approach by the city to civic education.

6. The data available are somewhat deceptive, as the French census does not ask questions regarding ethnicity, only nationality. Moreover, the French census treats second- and third-generation immigrants as "French." The point being that if we were to be able to identify populations by origin, it is likely that we would find a much larger number of immigrants in Paris. Even with these limitations, we can see that some 18 percent of the population is foreign, with the largest identifiable groups coming from North Africa (INSEE 1999).

7. Community councils were a part of the reforms of the 1980s, but were optional; thus, few districts at the time implemented them.

8. In an effort to tease out some of the difference in turnout by foreign-born citizens, I subdivided the data on turnout according to the proportion of foreign-born citizens overall (given the lack of information on ethnicity in the French census). Data here reflect the five arrondisements with the largest proportion of foreign-born citizens (twentieth, nineteenth, fifth, sixth and eighteenth) and those with the lowest proportion (eighth, second, tenth, thirteenth, and eleventh), according to the 1999 Census (INSEE).

9. I focus only upon this time period, owing to the fact that I was unable to access detailed census data on foreign-born populations and voting by arrondissement for the prior decade.

10. Voter turnout data for Toronto were highly problematic. No comprehensive data were publicly available on turnout at the ward level. Thus, these findings reflect data aggregated to the level of the former cities that made up the Toronto GTA—Etobicoke, Scarborough, North York, York, East York, and the city of Toronto. These outcomes, therefore, must only be looked at as indicators, and further local analysis is required to strengthen the claims made herein.

CHAPTER 7

CHANGING FORMS OF URBAN GOVERNMENT IN CENTRAL AND EASTERN EUROPE

PAWEŁ SWIANIEWICZ

INTRODUCTION—SETTING THE SCENE

The last decade of the twentiethcentury, which brought extremely important changes to the Central and Eastern European (CEE) political scene, was also a time of revival of local democracy in this region. After a long period of very centralist and undemocratic governance, devolution of power and strengthening local government seemed a natural direction to many politicians.

Nevertheless, no uniform model of decentralization or local government has been adopted in this part of Europe. Not surprisingly, many Eastern European debates concerning local government are rooted in a historical experience of centralization that took place during the communist period. It is not a unique phenomenon, characteristic of this region only. Hesse and Sharpe (1991) noticed that a tendency to automatically identify centralization with autocracy could be observed in Spain, Portugal, Austria, or Germany, but not in the Anglo-Saxon countries. This tendency is obviously related to earlier historical experiences of these countries. In CEE countries there is a very similar tendency of automatic identification of centralization with autocracy that arises from the communist centralist-state experience. Subsequently, strong local government is often believed to be valuable for its own sake. But this broad (and rather vague) verbal agreement on decentralization has not resulted in a common view of local governments' role and position. As Peteri and Zentai (2002) note: "Besides . . . broad principles, [there] rarely was any political consensus on a comprehensive model of state architecture, let alone elaborate blueprints for its establishment" (p. 15). This observation applies not only to the lack of consensus within individual reforming countries, but also to the absence of a common vision of local government that could be shared by different countries.

However, in this chapter, we try to go beyond discussion of the system changes in the countries of the region (which are briefly summarized in the next section).[1] Instead, we

concentrate on empirical examination of some claims that are often made in CEE countries about the impact of institutional settings on the functioning of local democracy.
Simultaneously, we refer to ongoing political debates and offer an empirical test of their
validity.

DECENTRALIZATION IN CENTRAL AND
EASTERN EUROPE—A TIME OF TRANSITION

There are three main dimensions (streams) of local government reforms in Central and
Eastern Europe after 1990. The first one, most commonly discussed in the literature on
this subject, is directly related to the political transformation from centralist, nondemocratic politics to pluralist democracy. This change involved both decentralization reforms
and the reintroduction of democratic local self-governments. The second stream of
reforms concerns the changes in institutional setting, which do not relate to massive systemic changes but rather to the more incremental corrections of the regulations related
to the local government institutional environment. Discussions relating to electoral systems, to the position of mayors or territorial organization, provide good examples of such
changes. The third stream concerns changes in the operation of local government, which
can be summarized as the self-reforming local governments that are looking to introduce
new, more effective ways of managing local services and/or to influencing important local
issues such as economic development. While the empirical part of this chapter focuses on
selected dimensions of the second stream, it is worth stating that countries of the region
differ significantly in all the three reform streams.

First of all, countries differ in the depth of the decentralization reforms. In some cases,
changes have been rather cosmetic, with local governments enjoying only very limited
discretion on important decisions relating to local issues. In some other cases, a significant range of functions has been assigned to local governments, which now enjoy considerable autonomy in deciding upon local matters. Most of the states established from
the former Soviet Union republics provide an example of the former, while Hungary,
Poland, and Estonia are in the latter group of the countries.

Also, details of the institutional setting of local government are very much diversified.
There are several countries with only one tier of elected subnational government (Bulgaria,
and most of the smaller countries of the region, such as Slovenia, Lithuania, Latvia, and
Estonia). At the other extreme there is Poland with three tiers of elected subnational governments. The Czech Republic, Slovakia, and Hungary all have two tiers and are located
between the two extremes. The common feature is that, even in countries with more than
one subnational tier, the middle level was usually created relatively recently (in 1998 in
Poland, and in 2000 in the Czech Republic and Slovakia) and is less powerful than the
municipal tier.

There are also significant differences between these countries in the territorial organization of the municipal tier and in electoral systems. Since these issues are directly related
to our propositions presented later on in this chapter, they are discussed in more detail
in empirical sections.

Table 7.1 summarizes basic information concerning a group of CEE countries that
became members of the European Union (EU) in 2004 or that are EU candidate states.
Usually, decentralization reforms in these countries have been faster and more radical
than in the remaining postcommunist countries.

The data provided in table 7.1 confirms that there is no common model of local government in Central and Eastern Europe. Significant differences occur owing to both

Table 7.1 Basic characteristics of CEE countries and their local government systems

Country	Total population (,000 in 2002)	Area (000, sq.km.)	Number of tiers of elected subnational governments	Average population size of municipal government	Method of mayor's election	Subnational government spending as % of GDP (2001)	Municipal government spending as % of GDP (2001)
Bulgaria	7,868	111	1	32,000	Direct	6.0	6.0
Croatia	4,440	57	2	8,800	Indirect	6.5	5.7
Czech Rep.	10,201	79	2 (1 till 2000)	1,700	Indirect	9.4	8.7
Estonia	1,359	45	1	5,700	Indirect	9.2	9.2
Hungary	10,159	93	2	3,300	Direct (in large cities since 1994)	12.8	11.1
Latvia	2,339	65	1	4,300	Indirect	10.2	10.2
Lithuania	3,469	65	1	66,000	Indirect	7.1	7.1
Poland	38,232	313	3 (1 till 1998)	16,000	Direct (since 2002)	11.5	8.8
Romania	21,795	238	2	7,600	Direct	6.5	5.5
Slovakia	5,379	49	2 (1 till 2000)	1,900	Direct	4.5	4.0
Slovenia	1,996	20	1	10,300	Direct	5.2	5.2

Sources: Population, area—Statistical Yearbook of the Republic of Poland 2003, Warszawa, Central Statistical Office; number of tiers, size of municipalities—Swianiewicz 2002; method of election—Swianiewicz 2005a; local government finance—Local Finance in the Ten Countries Joining the European Union in 2004 (2004).

variation in the policies of central government and different historical traditions (related, for example, to the shape of territorial organization) or various civic traditions of self-organization of local communities.

EXPLORING SOME CLAIMS ABOUT LOCAL GOVERNMENT IN CENTRAL AND EASTERN EUROPE

In this chapter, I now address two important debates on the institutional model of local governments in the analysed group of countries and—by referring to data from various research projects and surveys—try to determine how decisions concerning the institutional framework have influenced the functioning of local democracy. Empirical analyses focus on the municipal level, which is usually the most powerful tier of subnational governments in the region (Swianiewicz 2005a). The geographical coverage of individual empirical tests depends on the availability of data.

One of the widely discussed issues on which I focus in this chapter is *territorial organization*. In many countries the major political changes of 1990 were followed by radical territorial fragmentation.[2] The Czech Republic, Hungary, Slovakia, Croatia, Macedonia, Albania, and Ukraine are all examples of such a process. In some cases (Czech Republic, Hungary, Slovakia), the bottom-up pressure for fragmentation was a reaction to the forceful top-down amalgamation reforms of the 1970s. But other countries (Bulgaria, Montenegro, Poland, Romania) retained a more consolidated system (even though they experienced similar top-down amalgamation in the 1960s or 1970s) or even undertook amalgamation reforms in the late 1990s (Lithuania). Owing to these differences, the present territorial organization of the region is quite diversified. At the one extreme we have Lithuania where an average municipality has over 60,000 residents—more than most average European municipalities, except for those located in the United Kingdom. At the other extreme there is the Czech Republic and Slovakia, with an average municipality having less than 2,000 residents and nearly four in five having less than 1,000 citizens. The extreme cases of tiny municipalities include, for example, Prirky in Slovakia with two residents and Bidovce in the Czech Republic with just seven residents. This variation is illustrated by figure 7.1.

The other issue that I analyse in this chapter is the *role and position of the local leader (mayor)*, which has also been the subject of many debates in several countries of the region. At the present moment a tendency toward direct election of city mayors can be observed in several countries of Western Europe[3] (see Larsen 2002). The same trend may be noticed in Central and Eastern Europe. Direct elections of mayors were introduced at the beginning of the 1990s in Slovakia, Bulgaria, Romania, Slovenia, Albania, and Ukraine, in 1994 in Hungary,[4] and quite recently (in 2002) in Poland. Nevertheless, three Baltic States (Estonia, Latvia, and Lithuania) as well as the Czech Republic and Croatia still rely on either a system in which the mayor is elected by a council, or one in which there is a more collective form of leadership.[5]

Debates over these institutional factors are related to more general discussions on local governments' functioning. It is often assumed that we can influence (hopefully improve) local democracy mechanisms by changing the institutional setting. Some such normative assumptions are based on international experience (mainly of Western Europe), which supposedly may be useful for CEE countries as well. Changes in the electoral system or in territorial organization are often seen as remedies for such drawbacks as low citizens' interest in local public issues, devastating partisan cleavages in local politics, or the weak and unstable position of local executives.

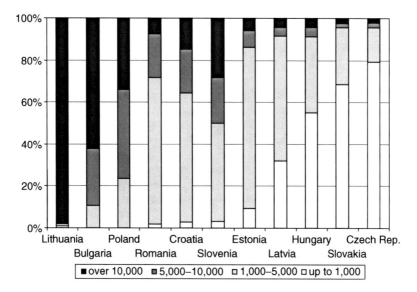

Figure 7.1   Distribution of municipal governments in Central and Eastern Europe according to their population size.

In this chapter, I am not going to discuss in detail the theoretical reasoning used for justifying various claims concerning institutional reforms. My task is much simpler—I will try to summarize those statements and claims about local government that are frequently referred to in public discourse; this summarization would help to verify to what extent they are confirmed by the actual behaviour of local actors.

The logic of empirical analysis in the chapter is that it uses a set of institutional factors as independent (explanatory) factors explaining various aspects of city governance.

The two independent variables are:

- Territorial organization—we distinguish territorially consolidated systems (with large local governments) from territorially fragmented systems;
- Formal position and nomination of local leaders—we limit our interest here to the distinction between leaders who are directly elected as opposed to those who are nominated by councils and/or operate in a more collective setting of the leadership model.

The three dependent variables are:

- Citizens' interests in local governments;
- The role of various actors in local decision making ("community power structure");
- The role of political parties in local politics.

FIVE PROPOSITIONS RELATING TO LOCAL GOVERNMENT IN CENTRAL AND EASTERN EUROPE

Our discussion is organized around five propositions, two of them referring to the level of territorial fragmentation and three to the method of mayor's election. On the one hand, territorial fragmentation is seen as a negative factor in most of CEE countries. It is argued that small local governments have higher unit costs of service delivery and are too weak to implement successful development policies. Although fragmentation is criticized on the economic effectiveness level, this type of critique will not be further discussed in this chapter.[6]

On the other hand, territorial fragmentation is defended by reference to the democratic and autonomy values of local governments. It is argued that in smaller units, the relations between councillors and citizens are much closer and that politicians are more accountable to local communities. In this chapter we aim to check whether these claims are confirmed by empirical data. Therefore, we formulate five propositions as follows:

1) Citizens in more (territorially) fragmented systems are more interested in local governments;

2) The role of parties in local politics is greater in countries with more consolidated territorial systems;

3) Direct elections of mayors lead to higher citizens' interest in elections and thus to higher accountability of elected politicians;

4) The role of parties in local politics is larger in countries with indirect mayoral elections and collective forms of leadership than in countries in which mayors are directly elected by citizens;

5) Direct election of mayors results in an increased role of mayors and decreased role of councillors in making crucial decisions.

We now consider each of these propositions in turn.

Proposition 1: Citizens in more (territorially) fragmented systems are more interested in local governments.

This claim is supported by numerous observations from Western Europe. According to this claim, " Social trust is based on strong personal ties in small communities. Decline of community and social trust resulting from increasing scale will be reflected in declining political trust" (Denters 2002, p. 796). Social trust should subsequently be reflected in generally positive attitudes toward the elected officials in small units. Advocates of fragmentation also use the classic Tiebout (1956) argument—that "citizens vote with their feet." Going by this analysis, smaller units offer more choice for citizens. It is also claimed that small local communities are more homogenous, which makes it easier to implement policies that go along with preferences of the majority of citizens. Finally, in small communities, there is more incentive for citizen participation, because a single individual's vote will "weigh more." This rational argument is additionally supported by a sociopsychological observation that people are more likely to develop a stronger sense of community and local identification in smaller, more homogenous settings. This in turn will strengthen interest in local affairs and stimulate political involvement. All of these arguments are recognized and often quoted in debates about local government in CEE countries.

We know also that political parties in Central and Eastern Europe are rather disliked by the public and that the dominant ideology of local government reform has been antipartisan.[7] A typical slogan used by many reformers, but also by local leaders, was that "a hole in the bridge is not a political issue." This is supposed to suggest that the issues local governments deal with are objective and do not leave much space for partisan-ideological debates. (Obviously, the slogan itself is highly controversial. One may argue that although a "hole" might not be political, the answer to the question, who should fix the hole and how? can be easily connected with ideological value choices). Baldersheim et al. (1996) provide information based on a 1991 Local Democracy and Innovation

(LDI)[8] project survey that "not being a member of political party" was perceived as one of the most desirable characteristics of an "ideal local councillor." The 1997 LDI survey found quite similar results.

This discussion can only be understood in the context of territorial organization. Political parties, as other organized groups, are usually more numerous and more active in larger communities (Dahl and Tufte 1973; Clark 1967). Also, observations from the Western part of the continent suggest that political parties are usually more significant in the more territorially consolidated countries of northern Europe than in the more geographically fragmented southern Europe (Fallend, Ignits, and Swianiewicz 2006). It may be argued that it is not just a coincidence that a rapid increase in the number of party members among councillors in Nordic countries (see data in Sundberg 1991) took place at the same time as territorial amalgamation reforms were implemented there. One may expect that the difference between big and small local governments will be even greater in Central and Eastern Europe where the party system is still far from being stable and fully developed. If parties are weak, then it is possible that they will hardly exist in several small communities. It is worth remembering that indices of party membership are in general lower in Eastern than in Western Europe (see Swianiewicz and Mielczarek 2005). This allows us to expect the following proposition.

Proposition 2: The role of parties in local politics is greater in countries with more consolidated territorial systems.
We can also expect that, within individual countries, the role of parties is greater in big cities (in which party organizations often play a decisive role in local politics) than in small communities (where parties are often almost nonexistent and most councillors as well as mayors are elected as independents).

Three other propositions refer to the mode of mayor's election. One of the most popular arguments in Eastern European discussions about the introduction of direct mayoral elections was that the change would invigorate local democracy through increasing citizens' interest in local elections. Directly elected leaders are supposed to be more accountable to their voters, and their legitimacy should be more clearly visible for an average citizen. This should result both in higher electoral turnout and in a higher level of interest in local government conduct in between elections. To reflect these discussions we formulate the following propositions.

Proposition 3: Direct elections of mayors lead to higher citizens' interest in elections and thus to higher accountability of elected politicians.
It should be noted that, although similar arguments were often used in Western European debates related to directly elected mayors, this proposition has been questioned by some analyses undertaken in countries that have experimented with direct elections (see, for example, Steyvers et al. 2003). Another explicit goal of the recent mayoral election reform in Poland (as well as in other countries of the region) was the desire to limit the influence of political parties on local governance. It should be noted that in the United Kingdom, the introduction of directly elected mayors resulted in the election of nonpartisan mayors in half of the 12 communities that adopted this institutional arrangement (Elcock and Fenwick 2003; Hambleton and Sweeting 2004). The mayor of London (Ken Livingstone) is, perhaps, the best known example of this phenomenon. Nevertheless, empirical data from other member countries of the Organisation for Economic Co-operation and Development (OECD) are not univocal. Mouritzen and Svara (2002, pp. 176, 184–90) notice, on the basis of their research in Western Europe and America, that in strong-mayor systems (parts of the United States, France, Italy, and

Portugal), the role of a local politician as a spokesperson for the party is usually perceived as much less important than in committee-leader or collective-leader systems (in, for example, Sweden, Denmark, the United Kingdom, and the Netherlands). Countries with council-manager systems (parts of the United States, Finland, and Norway) are much more diversified, but generally tend to regard the role of a local politician as the party's spokesman as rather less important.

This observation was made on the basis of chief executive officers' (CEOs') opinions on the characteristics of an "ideal politician," and Mouritzen and Svara (2002) note that "the attitudes of CEOs do not determine the behaviour of elected officials, but they presumably contribute to the definition of norms of appropriate behaviours that elected officials seek to meet" (p. 185). On the other hand, Mouritzen and Svara discovered, in the course of the same research, that in CEOs' assessment of the actual tasks performed by the mayors, partisan leadership was most often mentioned in committee-leader forms, followed by strong-mayor systems, and less frequently mentioned in countries with council-manager and collective forms of government (pp. 69–71).

Despite the seemingly conflicting conclusions that may be drawn from the study carried out by Mouritzen and Svara, we can formulate our fourth proposition as follows.

Proposition 4: The role of parties in local politics is larger in countries with indirect mayoral elections and collective forms of leadership than in countries in which mayors are directly elected by citizens.

Finally, the instability of executive leadership in systems characterised by council's control over the election of a mayor has been often regarded as a factor negatively influencing the effectiveness of local governance in Central and Eastern Europe. Although the style of politics in CEE countries is usually far from consensual, critics of collective forms of leadership have often pointed out the risks connected with unclear ("spread" between many actors) accountability for implementing decisions. Their arguments resemble those sometimes used in discussions about Scandinavian local government reforms (see, for example, Baldersheim 1993; Myrvold and Osttveiten 2000). Therefore, it has been claimed by some that the direct election of mayors would personalize and strengthen local accountability. Thus, we can arrive at our last proposition.

Proposition 5: Direct election of mayors results in an increased role of mayors and decreased role of councillors in making crucial decisions.

The five propositions discussed above are summarized in table 7.2.

Table 7.2   Summary of propositions—the impact of institutional factors on local politics in Central and Eastern Europe

	Territorial organization	**Position of the local leader (mayor)**
Citizens' interest in local governments	1) Territorial fragmentation leads to increased interest of citizens	3) Direct election of mayors leads to increased interest of citizens
The role of various actors in local decision making ("community power structure")		5) Direct election of mayors results in an increased role of mayors and decreased role of councillors in shaping crucial decisions
The role of political parties in local politics	2) Territorial fragmentation leads to lower role of political parties	4) Direct election of mayors leads to lower role of political parties in city governance

We now discuss each of the propositions in turn—first, the two relating to territorial organization and, then, the three relating to the position of the local leader.

THE IMPACT OF TERRITORIAL FRAGMENTATION

THE IMPACT ON RESIDENTS' INTEREST IN LOCAL GOVERNMENTS

Our first proposition assumes that territorial fragmentation is positively correlated with citizens' interest in local government issues. In our test we measure public interest in local government activities mainly with the simplistic indicator—turnout in local elections. We expect it to be larger in small local governments and, therefore, in more fragmented territorial systems. In figure 7.2, countries are ordered according to the degree of fragmentation in their local government systems—from those with the most consolidated to those with the most territorially fragmented local government systems. The figure does not show any systematic correspondence between the level of fragmentation and the turnout in local elections.

However, local level data are affected by several other (national) factors that determine that participation in politics is in general lower in some countries and higher in others. Therefore, to establish whether there is a relationship between the size of local government and electoral behaviour in Central and Eastern Europe, it may be more appropriate to look at the variation *within* individual countries. There is no doubt that—as public choice and localist theories suggest—small local governments help in building good and lively relationships between citizens and local authorities, as has already been noted in an article summarizing empirical evidence from four countries of the region (Swianiewicz 2001, pp. 34–5):

> [Citizens of small municipalities] feel better informed and they know local councillors more often. In all analysed countries the turnout in local elections is negatively correlated with the size (i.e. citizens of small towns and villages are more interested and more involved in local public affairs). Also, the larger the city, the higher the turn-over of mayors after elections, which may be interpreted by the lower voters' satisfaction with local governments' performance in big cities. . . .

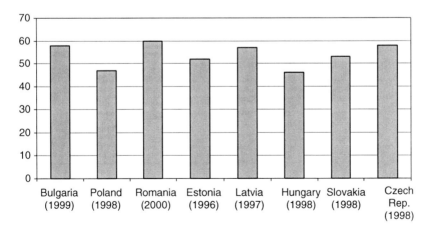

Figure 7.2   Turnout in local elections.

Sources: Horvath (2000), Kandeva (2001), Swianiewicz (2001).

But although in most cases the overall positive opinion is clearly related to the small size of the local constituency, the picture is not quite one-dimensional. The level of declared satisfaction with local governments' activity is usually negatively correlated with the size, but there are some exceptions to this rule.

In the Czech Republic opinions of citizens from villages below 500 inhabitants are less positive than those from 500–2000 population cohorts—although the difference is not statistically significant, but the trend at least stops around the size of 500. In Hungary, there was a clear (negative) correlation between size and satisfaction in 1990–91, but data for 2000 are not as clear. In the smallest group (below 1,000), the average opinion is negative, while the most positive opinions can be found in administrative units between two and five thousand citizens.

(Swianiewicz 2001, pp. 34–5)

The relationship between size and local democracy is, then, not entirely one-dimensional. Reformers seeking to introduce larger units of local government claim that politics is more pluralistic and less parochial. They also take the view that bigger governments are more trusted because of the more advanced development of civil society in larger communities (Dahl and Tufte 1973; Goldsmith and Rose 2000). This conviction is partly confirmed by data from Central and Eastern Europe. In Poland, the number of candidates in local elections sharply increases in bigger municipalities. Both in Poland and Hungary, there are more nongovernmental organizations (NGOs) and local newspapers in bigger local governments. But, in opposition to the reform theory expectations, neither the bigger pluralism nor the wider scope of functions in big governments leads to a larger degree of citizens' trust or interest in participation in local politics.

As figure 7.3 shows, turnout in local elections is negatively correlated with the size of municipality in three out of four countries for which relevant data is available (Hungary, Poland, and Slovakia, with Bulgaria as the exception[9]). Interestingly enough, in most of these countries, we can also observe a considerable increase in voters' turnout in the group of the largest local governments (simplifying matters a bit, we can call this phenomenon the "capital city effect"), but this does not change the general picture. The Bulgarian case does not go along with the rule of higher turnout in small municipalities, but accounting for that would require additional detailed investigation. One may speculate that the proportional electoral system in Bulgaria, which does not support the representation of small villages in municipal councils, may discourage voters from these

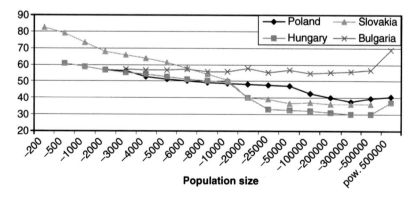

Figure 7.3   Turnout in local elections—1998.
Source: Swianiewicz (2002).

settlements from voting. And it has to be said, once again, that there are no really small local governments in Bulgaria, so the factor of closeness and openness in small communities cannot be really examined.

In summary, Proposition 1 has been confirmed by the variation within individual countries of the region. But, clearly, territorial organization is not the only factor that determines interest in local politics.

THE IMPACT ON THE ROLE OF POLITICAL PARTIES IN LOCAL GOVERNMENTS

It is worth repeating that parties are much less present in local governments of Central and Eastern Europe than in Western European countries (see Fallend, Ignits, and Swianiewicz 2006; Swianiewicz and Mielczarek 2005[10]). The first confirmation of this claim can be found in table 7.3. But we should also note that Western European countries enumerated in the table are usually located in northern Europe and are usually more territorially consolidated. According to Loughlin (2001), the situation is slightly different in more fragmented southern Europe. For instance, in France, political parties are virtually nonexistent in small localities. Only in towns with populations of over 30,000 do national parties exert real control over local coalitions.

In order to test Proposition 2, table 7.4 presents a summary of findings concerning the relationship between the size of local government units and the role of political parties—as measured by party membership, party role in local elections, and perceived influence of parties on local decision making. It is clear that the impact is very significant in most countries. We may conclude that fragmentation of the territorial system influences the character—partisan or nonpartisan—of local governments.

But the most comprehensive test of our propositions can be conducted through the analysis of statistical dependencies of the "index of party significance." The index is a weighted sum of following indicators:[11]

- Party membership rate of councillors
- Party membership rate of mayors
- Party support for councillors in the last election campaign
- Party support for mayors in the last election campaign
- Perceived influence of parties on local decision making
- Parties as the source of information for local councillors

Table 7.3 Party members as a percentage of total local government councillors in EU countries and Central and Eastern Europe

Western Europe		CEE countries	
United Kingdom (1997)	90.4	Bulgaria (2002)	86.4
Ireland (1991)	90.4	Estonia (2002)	49.4
Germany (1997)(*)	90.0	Slovakia (2002)	44.9
Sweden (1998)(**)	94.6	Poland (2003)	34.9
Denmark (1997)(**)	96.7	Hungary (2002)	34.7
Finland (1996)(**)	93.2		
Netherlands (1994)(**)	75.0		

Note: (*) Municipalities over 10,000 population, (**) excluding small, local parties.
Source: Western Europe—Loughlin (2001); CEE countries—Indicators of Local Democratic Governance Project (ILDGP) surveys.

Table 7.4   Pearson correlation coefficients between the size of local government and the role of political parties

Country	Party membership		Support or recommendation of the party in local elections		Perceived influence of political parties
	Mayors	Councillors	Mayors	Councillors	
Bulgaria					***
Estonia	**	***		***	***
Hungary	***	***	***	***	***
Latvia	**	NA	NA	NA	NA
Poland	***	***	***		***
Romania		NA	NA	NA	NA
Slovakia	**	***		**	***

Note: * correlation significant on 0.05 level; ** significant on 0.01 level; *** significant on 0.001 level; blank spaces mean insignificant correlations.
Source: Own calculations on the basis of ILDGP survey of councillors and mayors (2002–2003).

Table 7.5   Index of party significance in local politics

	Bulgaria	Poland	Hungary	Estonia	Slovakia
Mean value	73.6	47.6	33.9	50.8	49.5
Size standardized mean	70.9	43.3	44.5	53.0	48.9
Correlation of the index with population size	*	*	**	*	*

Note: 0 means no significance; 100 means a very large significance of parties in local politics; * means correlation significant at .001 level, **, significant at .0001 level.
Source: Own calculations on the basis of ILDGP survey of councillors and mayors (2002–2003).

The results of calculations are presented in table 7.5. The highest party significance can be noticed in Bulgaria, while in the remaining four countries it is by far lower. In all of the countries in question, it is significantly correlated with the size of local government—that is, the index grows with the size of municipality.

Although the correlation is significant at the .001 level in each of the countries, it is the lowest in Bulgaria and the highest in Hungary. In Bulgaria, Estonia, and Slovakia, the relationship is relatively flat (i.e., party significance grows with increasing size, but the change is relatively slow), while in Poland, and even more in Hungary, it is very steep.

As might be expected on the basis of Proposition 2, the party significance index is the highest in Bulgaria—that is the country with the most territorially consolidated system. But in Poland, the second country with large municipal governments, the index is very low. Therefore, our final conclusion is similar to that formulated in the course of discussing Proposition 1. The variation within individual countries confirms the significance of size in explaining the role of parties in local politics—the role of parties tends to be greater in bigger units. But differences between countries depend also on other factors, and territorial organization does not provide a sufficient explanation for that variation.

THE IMPACT OF DIRECT ELECTION OF MAYORS

THE IMPACT ON CITIZENS' INTEREST IN LOCAL POLITICS

Proposition 3 predicts that direct election of mayors leads to higher interest in local elections. But empirical data hardly support this claim. At the country level the relationship seems to be even the opposite—the mean electoral turnout in countries with strong mayors, who are directly elected, is lower than in those with collective leadership or mayors nominated by a council (see figure 7.4).

But, just as with Propositions 1 and 2, national data are distorted by several other factors (including the variation in territorial fragmentation), so they cannot give us an adequate answer to the question posed. In two of the countries of the region, the method of mayoral election changed only a short time ago. Thus, these reforms—in Hungary (introduction of direct elections in 1994) and in Poland (2002 reform)—give us an excellent opportunity to compare turnouts before and after the reform. The results are summarized in table 7.6.

It is clear that the switch to directly election of mayors did not have any dramatic impact on the voters' interest. We should add that the change between "before" and "after" did not differ significantly from the general trend in turnout in national elections during the period in question.

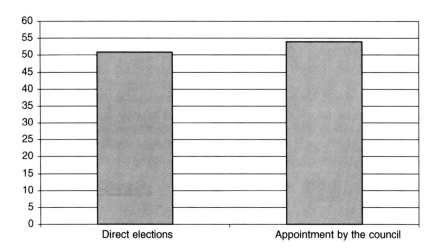

Figure 7.4   Turnout in local elections in countries with different systems of mayor's nomination.

Note: Direct elections—Bulgaria (1999), Hungary (1998), Poland (2002), Slovakia (1998). Indirect—Czech Republic (1998), Estonia (1996), Latvia (1997), Poland (1998).

Sources: Horvath (2000), Kandeva (2001), Swianiewicz (2001).

Table 7.6   Local turnout and method of mayors' election—the case of reforming CEE countries

	Turnout before the reform	Turnout just after the reform
Hungary	1990: 40%	1994: 43%
Poland	1998: 46%	2002: 44%

Source: Swianiewicz 2001, Swianiewicz and Mielczarek 2005.

In summary, data from Central and Eastern Europe provide no evidence to support Proposition 3 concerning the impact of direct election of mayors on citizen's interest in local politics. This is despite the fact that, according to numerous surveys, citizens support the direct mode of elections (Swianiewicz 2001).

THE IMPACT ON THE ROLE OF POLITICAL PARTIES

In relation to Proposition 4 we cannot rely on the party significance index (as we did testing Proposition 2) owing to the fact that necessary data are available for five countries only, out of which only one (Estonia) represents the indirect mode of nomination of mayors. Therefore, we cannot statistically distinguish the impact of "Estonian culture" from the impact of mayors' nomination method.

Our problem with determining whether the method of mayors' election has an impact on local government politicization may be partly solved by the analysis of CEOs' survey conducted in seven countries in the 2000–2001 period. The available data allow us to check the impact of methods of nomination on party membership of local mayors. In this survey we have three countries in which mayors are nominated by a council: Estonia, Latvia, and Poland (where the CEOs' survey was conducted before the 2002 reform that changed the method of Polish mayors' election). As a result, we can distinguish the impact of the mayors' election factor from the impact of the country variable.

What we find out from table 7.7 is that the method of mayors' nomination is insignificant when controlled by other independent variables in a regression model. The model confirms the significance of the size of local government, as well as the significance of most of the country dummy-variables.

But, at the same time, we know that in Poland the reform of the method of mayors' election coincided with a significant drop in partisan membership by local leaders. In 2001 (before the reform), as many as 57 percent of Polish mayors declared party membership, while in 2003 (after the reform) the proportion dropped to 40 percent. The change was especially significant in large cities in which well-recognized candidates did not need to rely on party coalitions within the council anymore in order to be elected. Furthermore, available case-study material indicates that directly elected mayors are less

Table 7.7   Factors influencing party membership of local mayors—results of multivariable regression model

R	0.589
R square	0.344
Significance of the model	0.0000
Independent variables:	
Size of local governments	+ +
Direct mayor elections	0
Bulgaria	+ +
Estonia	+ + +
Hungary	– – –
Slovakia	+ + +
Romania	+ + +
Latvia	– – –

Note: + means positive and – negative relationships. The number of pluses or minuses refers to significance of the variable. + + + means significance on .001 level, + + significance on .01 level, and + significance on .05 level. "0" means insignificant independent variable. Poland—reference group.
Source: Own calculations based on ILDGP surveys.

involved (than before the reform) in party negotiations related to everyday decision making (Swianiewicz, Mielczarek, and Klimska 2006).

In summary, it is difficult to formulate ultimate conclusions about the impact of the mode of mayors' election on the role of parties in local politics. The available analyses from Poland—the only country that has undertaken local electoral reform within the last few years—suggest that directly elected mayors are less dependent on party structures. But, at the same time, statistical analyses of data covering several countries of the region do not support this observation.

THE IMPACT ON COMMUNITY POWER STRUCTURE

Finally, we turn to consider Proposition 5, which claims that the introduction of direct elections of mayors with executive power will stabilize and strengthen the local executive. Has this really happened? In order to check this proposition, we used the reputational method of analysing politicians' (mayors, councillors) perception of community power structures. First, we look at two groups of countries: those with direct election and those with indirect nomination of mayors. We compare the average assessment of the influence of the council and of mayors on local decision making. The results of this comparison are presented in figure 7.5.

As we would expect, the local council is regarded as the most influential actor in the collective-leader systems, while the power shifts to the mayor in countries with the strong-mayor form of leadership. The same observation is even more striking when we compare the results from various surveys for the two countries that shifted from one form to the other during the last decade. In Hungary the direct election of mayors was introduced in 1994, while in Poland the change took place in 2002. Figure 7.6 reflects a very dramatic change in the structure of community power immediately after the change in the type of leadership.

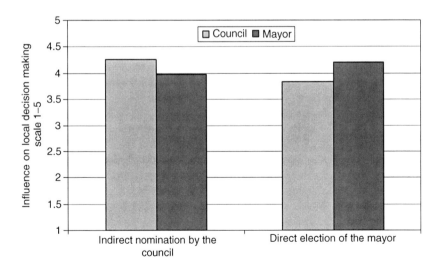

Figure 7.5   Councils' and mayors' influence on decision making in local governments in the CEE countries (1997–2003) as perceived by local councillors.

Source: A councillors' survey conducted within the framework of the LDI and ILDG research projects. The 'strong mayor model': Bulgaria, Slovakia, Hungary, Poland after 2002; the 'collective model': the Czech Republic, Estonia, Latvia, Poland before 2002.

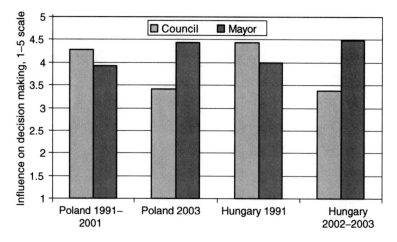

Figure 7.6 Changing influence of the council and the mayor on local decision making in the countries that introduced direct election of mayors after 1991.

Sources: Conuncillors' and mayors' surveys conducted within the framework of the LDI project (1991 and 1997); a councillors' survey of the IDLG research projects (Hungary 2002, Poland 2003); local political leaders' survey (2003).

The proposition assuming the impact of direct election of mayors on the community power structure is clearly supported by empirical data.

CONCLUSIONS

In this final section we return to the five propositions, formulated in the introduction, and consider whether we have been able to either confirm or falsify them.

Proposition 1: Citizens in more (territorially) fragmented systems are more interested in local governments.

This claim is fully supported by observations made within individual countries. Citizens in small local governments are more interested in local politics than those in large municipalities. This means that by extending territorial fragmentation we may be able to strengthen the citizens–local politicians relationship.

Proposition 2: The role of parties in local politics is greater in countries with more consolidated territorial systems.

This proposition is also supported. Although we have identified several other factors that have an impact on the role of parties—including country-specific variables, which can be associated with the broader issue of political culture in general—the relationship between the size and the role of parties has been recognized in the vast majority of the analyzed countries.

Proposition 3: Direct elections of mayors lead to higher citizens' interest in elections and thus to higher accountability of elected politicians.

No, there is no convincing evidence supporting this hypothesis. Neither in Poland nor in Hungary did the introduction of direct elections have a visible impact. Differences between countries with various types of leadership are not clear either.

Proposition 4: The role of parties in local politics is greater in countries with indirect mayoral elections and collective forms of leadership than in countries in which mayors are directly elected by citizens.

The available data are contradictory. In Poland the institutional change had this expected impact. On the other hand, comparing the impact of different types of leadership on the role of parties in different countries leads to somewhat confusing results.

Proposition 5: Direct election of mayors results in an increased role of mayors and decreased role of councillors in shaping crucial decisions.

Definitely true. This claim is confirmed by countries that have decided to change the system as well as by horizontal comparisons between countries with different types of leadership.

Our findings suggest that the two considered factors linked to the institutional setting of local government systems influence the practical operation of local democracy. But their impact is not as strong as it is often suggested by some participants of public debates. Decisions on institutional reforms are sometimes made on the basis of false, "ideological" assumptions and without examining practical experiences of other countries in the region.

In concluding this chapter, I now offer some comments on the shift from local government to local governance, identified by many of the contributors to this volume. Is this trend visible in the countries of Central and Eastern Europe? This question refers to the "third stream of reforms" referred to at the beginning of the chapter—that is, the efforts of self-reforming local governments looking for alternative methods of dealing with local issues. The complex answer to this question is not easy and goes beyond the frames of this chapter. However, we can offer some initial thoughts. Campbell and Coulson (2006) indicate the key difference between Eastern and Western Europe in the governance agenda: "CEE countries have had to introduce the Rule of Law [in the Weberian sense] and the New Public Management in parallel, whereas in the West the one preceded the other by many decades, so that in the East the tension between legalism and managerialism may threaten to fragment the local authority as an institution" (p. 544). But regardless of this very important difference, some authors have identified traces of the shift to local governance in Poland and Hungary (Swianiewicz 2005b, 2006; Soos 2006).

Based on my experience of working with many local authorities in the CEE countries, I believe that many local leaders in the region would feel very attracted to a broad definition of their role as guardians of the overall well-being of their communities, rather than limiting the scope of their activity to delivery of urban services. There are also several examples of innovations in management through partnership with NGOs or the private sector, as well as wide support for some the ideas associated with New Public Management. On the other hand, Djordjevic (2006), in her recent empirical analysis of strategic planning in Budapest and Warsaw, comes to the conclusion that attempts at governance often fail and that the traditional mode of local government is prevailing.

Perhaps, instead of slipping into simplistic generalizations about the shift or the lack of shift from government to governance in Central and Eastern Europe, we should talk rather about the increasing variation found among local governments in the region. We should also discuss the growing gap between a relatively small but visible group of innovators and the majority of local governments with a more traditional attitude toward the role of local government and the management of local services. We can also try to identify the main forces stimulating the shift as well as the most important factors that are barriers for the development of alternative (rather than traditional) modes of government.

Among the main factors pushing in the direction of local governance one may mention:

- The "vacuum" in the CEE experience with the management of local issues within a market economy framework. This was, in many instances, filled in the 1990s by foreign consultants funded by World Bank or the EU, or bilateral programmes such as those of the United States Agency for International Development or the British Know How Fund. Fashionable ideas from the United States or Western Europe were—in the absence of homegrown experiences—often taken for granted by newly elected Eastern European mayors;
- The process of European integration, which stimulates a growing number of contacts between the CEE countries and local governments in Western Europe. This process often results in cross-national trading of ideas and, in some cases, the transfer of approaches observed elsewhere. The stress on building partnerships, required by some EU-funded programmes, is also encouraging moves from local government to local governance.

On the other hand there are several factors that may be expected to slow down this process:

- In most of CEE countries, the development of civil society institutions is relatively weak. There is also a low level of social trust, which is a practical barrier in implementation of solutions based on voluntary, horizontal partnerships.
- The local private sector is also still weak, and is unable to fill the gap left by the large enterprises of the former era. Moreover, as identified in some empirical studies (for example, Swianiewicz, Mielczarek, Klimska 2006), partnerships with business actors are often met with the distrust of public opinion. There is a general fear of accusations of corruption, even if there are no solid, material reasons for such accusations.
- The traditional administrative culture in local city halls remains an obstacle. Even if, at the political leadership level, the postcommunist transformation has brought to power many innovative leaders, the culture of middle-level management and street-level bureaucrats is changing much more slowly. This is likely to continue to present a barrier to innovation in the coming period.

The list of factors identified above is far from complete and requires further empirical investigations. But it may explain why there is a frequent gap—identified, for example, in a study of the one of Polish regions (Swianiewicz 2006) —between the verbal declarations made by local leaders, who often refer to ideas of local governance, and the actual behaviour observed in many cities, where day-to-day practice remains close to the traditional local government mode.

APPENDIX

Most of the empirical tests referred to in this chapter are based on data obtained from surveys of local mayors, councillors, and CEOs in several CEE countries. Therefore, we mainly rely on the reputational method, basing our answers on subjective opinions expressed by the respondents—actors of local political life. However, in some cases, we also refer to more objective data, such as official statistics in local elections.

Empirical data have been obtained from a variety of sources related to different international research projects conducted in CEE countries. As a consequence, for each of the tests, we use data from several countries, but the set of countries may differ from one test to another. It should be stressed that our analysis is mainly limited to the part of Central and Eastern Europe that is more advanced in decentralization and economic reforms. Our data concern either the 2004 EU accession countries (Czech Republic, Estonia, Hungary, Latvia, Poland, Slovakia) or the "next wave" candidates for EU accession (Bulgaria and Romania). This means we leave aside—usually less advanced in political and economic postcommunist transformation—the countries of the south Balkans (Albania, Macedonia) or former Soviet Republics (Ukraine, Moldova, South Caucasus, or Central Asian states).

The specific empirical data have been obtained from the following studies:

1. *LDI project:* The project was sponsored by the Norwegian government and coordinated by Harald Baldersheim from the University of Bergen. The first stage of the project (1991) covered the Czech Republic, Hungary, Poland, and Slovakia and included extensive survey of local mayors, CEOs, councillors, and citizens. The second set of surveys (1997) was limited to mayors and included the Czech Republic, Poland, and Slovakia.

2. *ILDGP:* The project was coordinated by the Tocqueville Research Center and sponsored by the Local Government Initiative of the Open Society Institute, both in Budapest. Two sets of surveys were conducted in 2000–2003 as a part of the project, which also included two other extensive surveys:

- Of councillors and mayors (Local Representatives Survey—LRS) conducted in Bulgaria, Estonia, Hungary, Poland, and Slovakia;
- Of CEOs, from which, for the purpose of our paper, we derive information on the political composition of local councils as well as the political position of mayors. This survey was conducted in seven countries: Bulgaria, Estonia, Hungary, Latvia, Poland, Romania, and Slovakia.

3. *Local Political Leaders in Europe:* The project was coordinated by Annick Magnier from the University of Florence. Surveys were conducted in 2003 in local governments with more than 10,000 residents in 17 European countries. Three CEE countries were involved: Czech Republic, Hungary, and Poland.

Notes

1. For a more detailed discussion of various models of decentralization reforms in Central and Eastern Europe, see, for example, Peteri and Zentai 2002; Reid 2002; Swianiewicz 2005a, 2005b; chapters on Czech Republic, Baltic States, Hungary, and Poland in Kersting and Vetter 2003; and Coulson and Campbell 2006.
2. For a more extensive discussion of territorial organization in CEE countries after 1990, see Swianiewicz 2002.
3. To avoid confusion, I use terms "Western Europe" and "Central and Eastern Europe" in a sense that is popular in the literature and that refers to historical and political cleavages, although it is not consistent with any geographical definitions. In this somewhat strange terminology, Greece and Finland are part of Western Europe, while the Czech Republic

and Hungary are located in Central and Eastern parts of the continent. By CEE countries we mean the region that was a part of communist Europe until 1990.

4. Before 1994, Hungarian mayors of small towns (with populations below 10,000) were elected by citizens, while in larger cities they were appointed by councils.

5.   For a more detailed description of local leadership in CEE countries, see Swianiewicz 2005a.

6. For a more extensive discussion, see Swianiewicz 2002.

7. For an extensive discussion of the role of parties in local governments of CEE countries, see Swianiewicz and Mielczarek 2005.

8. The LDI international research project was financed in 1991–1997 by the Norwegian Council for Applied Social Sciences and coordinated by Prof. Harald Baldersheim. More information about the project can be found in the Annex on sources of empirical data.

9. In Slovakia, data on the size of local government from Figure 7.1 refer to the number of eligible voters (as opposed to the total number of citizens in local government unit)

10. This paper does not allow me to investigate in detail the causes of this difference. For more information, see Swianiewicz and Mielczarek 2005.

11. The index is calculated on the basis of mean values for each of the variables taken into account. To get a size-standardized index, means have been calculated individually for seven sizes of cohorts of local governments (below 1,000 residents, 1,000–2,000, 2,000–5,000, 5,000–10,000, 10,000–50,000, 50,000–100,000, over 100,000). In order to avoid strong domination of membership and support in elections in the index, first four variables weigh 0.5, while the last two weigh 1. The index is presented on a scale from 0 to 100, where 0 indicates lack of presence, while 100 means the domination of parties in local political life.

Innovation in Chinese Urban Governance: The Shanghai Experience

Tingwei Zhang

Economic Reform and Urbanization in China

Since the late 1990s, China has attracted world attention for its rapid economic growth. The country's average annual growth rate has been over 9 percent since 1995. Its gross domestic product (GDP) was $2,200 billion in 2005, and it is now the world's fourth largest economy, just behind the Unites States, Japan, and Germany, and over Britain ($2,000 billion) and France ($1,950 billion), according to the National Bureau of Statistics of China (NBSC 2006). China's GDP increased from about 5 percent of the world GDP in 1978 to 11 percent in 2004 (Hu 2004).

China's economic growth is coupled with its rapid urbanization. In 1951, just after the communist revolution, only one-tenth of the Chinese people lived in cities and towns. When China started its economic reform in 1978, 17.9 percent of its population was living in urban areas. In 2004, 40.1 percent of the population was officially recorded as urban residents, in addition to about 100 million rural-urban migrants who live in cities but are not recognized as "urban residents" under China's resident registration system (the *hukou* system in Chinese) (NBSC 2005, table 8.1).

The number of Chinese cities increased from 223 in 1980 to 660 in 2002, or by 196 percent in 22 years (NBSC 2005). This increase comes from two developments: the increase of urban population in some villages and townships, which makes them "cities" (i.e., areas with a population over 100,000); and the adjustment of administrative boundaries, which creates new cities through merging smaller townships. With a population of 1.35 billion and a rapid pace of urbanization, it is safe to declare that China provides an incomparable case of urbanization in world history.

In recent years Chinese leaders have adopted two strategies: (1) Maintain a high speed of economic growth to meet the pressures of the increasing population (especially in urban areas), and (2) Take advantage of cheap labor from the huge labor pool

Table 8.1 China's urbanization level (selected years)

Year	1951	1978	1995	2002	2004
Urbanization	11.8%	17.9%	29.0%	39.1%	40.1%

Source: China Statistical Yearbook (2005).

Table 8.2 Major cities of China (by population*, 2000)

Rank	Name	Population (in millions)	Location
1	Shanghai	12.72	East coast (middle)
2	Beijing	9.50	East coast (north)
3	Guangzhou	6.87	East coast (south)
4	Wuhan	6.56	Mid-China
5	Chongqing	5.68	West China
6	Shenzhen	5.57	East coast (south)
7	Tianjin	5.31	East coast (north)
8	Shenyang	4.34	East coast (south)
9	Dongguan	3.87	East coast (south)
10	Chengdu	3.82	West China

Note: * registered urban population, excluding nonurban population (peasants) and migrants living in the jurisdiction.
Source: China Census (2000).

to stimulate economic growth. In addition, China adopted a planned economy based on the socialist/communist ideology with a top-down decision-making structure from 1949 to the reform period of the 1980s. After 20 years of economic reform, however, China has shown fundamental changes in its economic life. Alternative business-ownership forms, such as joint venture, sole foreign ownership, and private ownership, have challenged the state-ownership regime. This change was recognized by the party-state in the 1982 constitution, in which legitimacy was given to various ownership forms. Following changes in ownership forms, the relationship between the central government and municipalities has been altered. It is clear that the lines of authority and the flow of resources between the central and local government have been changed as a result of the devolution of decision-making power. In the field of urban development, it is now municipalities rather than the central government that are shaping China's urban landscape (Naughton 1995; Yeh and Wu 1996; Zhu 1999; Zhang 2000, 2002).

Dramatic economic growth, rapid urbanization, and the decentralization reforms of the decision-making structure—these national trends paint the background to the changes in Chinese urban governance discussed in this chapter. Given China's huge population and its vast territory, the case of Shanghai should not be viewed as a "typical case" representing all Chinese cities. Rather, Shanghai's experience should be understood in the city's context—it is Shanghai's geographic location and its history and culture that define and give birth to the city's development strategy and policy, as correctly pointed by Friedmann (2005).

SHANGHAI—CHINA'S ECONOMIC CENTER

Located in the center of China's east coast and functioning as the nation's gateway to the outside world for one-and-a-half centuries, Shanghai has been the economic center of China since the 1850s when the city became an "open port" under a treaty between

China and the British Empire. In 2003, the city had an administrative territory of 6,341 square kilometers and a population of 17.11 million, of which 13.42 million were recognized as "registered permanent population" and 3.69 million were migrants living and working in Shanghai but without a permanent resident status (SMSB 2004). As shown in table 8.2, Shanghai is easily the largest Chinese city in terms of urban population.

The city consists of 18 urban districts and one rural county (Chongming County). Figure 8.1 provides a map of the city and the urban districts discussed in this study.

After the 1949 communist revolution, the city retained its economic position domestically but lost its economic connection internationally. From 1949 to 1978, Shanghai, with only 0.07 percent of China's land area and 1 percent of the total population, contributed

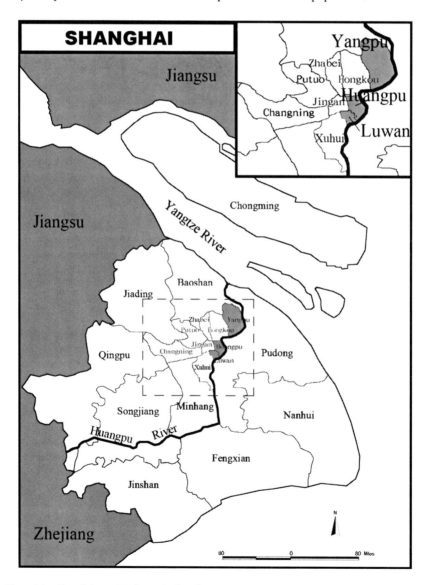

Figure 8.1   Shanghai municipality and urban districts.

Table 8.3   Shanghai's economic role in the YRDR and in the nation (2002) in U.S. dollars

	Total GDP (in billions)	GDP per capita	Industry output (in billions)	Revenue (in billions)	*FDI used & exports (in billions)	Total imports (in billions)
Shanghai	65.96	4,556	94.39	24.66	5.03	72.66
Ratio of Shanghai to YRDR	0.282	1.607	0.304	0.523	0.271	0.415
Ratio of Shanghai to nation	0.053	5.098	0.081	0.123	0.095	0.117

Note: One U.S. dollar equaled 8.21 renminbi (RMB, or yuan) in 2002.
* Foreign direct investment.
Source: Jin (2004).

17 percent of the country's national revenue and 10 percent of the total industrial output (Kong 2001). But Shanghai's outreaching function was reduced owing to China's "closed door" attitude to the outside world until 1978. However, Shanghai's economic importance has grown since the reform of 1978 and, in 2002, the city contributed 28.2 percent of the Yangtze River Delta Region's (YRDR) GDP, China's richest region, 30.4 percent of the YRDR's industrial output, 52.3 percent of the region's total revenue, and 41.5 percent of its foreign trade (table 8.3). Shanghai's per capita GDP was five times higher than the national average, and the city contributed 11.7 percent of the national foreign trade in 2002.

Another indicator of Shanghai's importance to China is its administrative status. Similar to a province, the city reports directly to China's national government. The mayor of the city traditionally holds a position in the central government as a vice-premier minister.

ECONOMIC RESTRUCTURING IN SHANGHAI

Shanghai was traditionally China's main manufacturing area, especially for labor-intensive industries such as textiles, garments, and family appliances. But the manufacturing-oriented economy has faced challenges since the 1980s. In the globalization era, other Chinese cities—cities in YRDR and in Pearl River Delta, in particular—have upgraded and strengthened their manufacturing bases with the introduction of foreign direct investment (FDI), which enables these cities to compete with Shanghai in manufacturing products. In light of the experience of cities in developed nations, the leaders of Shanghai are convinced that only a mixed economy—consisting of advanced services and high-technology manufacturing industries—can bring the city to the status of an "international economic, financing, trading, and shipping center" as defined by the municipal government in 2000.

Shanghai's total GDP increased from 27.3 billion yuan in 1978 to 625.1 billion in 2003, an increase of 2,215 percent in 25 years (SMSB 2004). This spectacular growth stemmed from economic restructuring. The city's economic transition gathered pace in the early 1990s. In May 1990, the central government approved Shanghai's proposal for developing the city's Pudong area (the east bank of the Huangpu River, a rural area which had few industries) into China's largest Special Economic Zone entitled to favored policies such as more decision-making power over taxation and land acquisition.

More importantly, the central government agreed to a better tax-sharing arrangement with Shanghai, increasing the city's tax allocation from the government from 13 percent to 30 percent (Kong 2001). The new sharing mechanism gave Shanghai urgently needed capital, and the Pudong New District provided the city with space for new development. The Pudong New District, as a "national project," received support not only from Shanghai but also from the entire nation. From 1990 to 2000, 32 percent of the FDI in Shanghai was accounted for by Pudong, and the district contributed about one-third of Shanghai's industrial output in the same period of time (Kong 2001). From 1991, when Shanghai launched its Pudong project, to the 2000s, most of its traditional labor-intensive textile and other light industries have been relocated to surrounding cities or suburban areas to make room for the financing, insurance, and real estate (FIRE) industry and knowledge-based manufacturing industries. The manufacturing sector is now represented by the "six key industries," including electronic information production, fine steel, automobile, petrochemical, complex equipment, and biomedicine manufacturing.

The new service sector includes FIRE, producer services, and the logistics/shipping industry. The service industry's share in the city's GDP increased from 18.6 percent in 1978 to 50.8 percent in 2004, or by 172 percent (SMSB 2005). The city has been becoming a leader in the financing sector not only in the YRDR but also in the whole nation. As a result, in 1999, for the first time in Shanghai's history, the tertiary industry's share of the city's GDP exceeded that of the manufacturing sector. The manufacturing industry share of the city's GDP, which was 75.7 percent in 1980, dropped to 47.4 percent in 2002 (table 8.4).

The composition of the service industry has also changed. In 1978, almost half (45.6 percent) of the tertiary industry comprised retail, wholesale, and catering. The real estate industry accounted for only 0.5 percent of the service sector, and the financing business's share was 13.8 percent. In 2003, the largest share in the tertiary sector was that of "others"—consulting, tourist, educational, and cultural businesses (22.8 percent)—followed by the financing industry (20.8 percent). The real estate industry's share increased to 15.3 percent, while the share of retail and wholesale industries dropped to 18.8 percent in 2003 (SMSB 2004). Tables 8.5 and 8.6 reveal the new role Shanghai

Table 8.4   Composition of Shanghai's GDP (in selected years)

Year	1980	1995	1999	2002
Primary industry	3.2%	4.3%	1.8%	1.6%
Secondary industry	75.7%	63.8%	48%	47.4%
Tertiary industry	21.1%	31.9%	50.2%	51.0%

Source: Shanghai Statistical Yearbook (2003).

Table 8.5   Distribution of the financial industry in Chinese cities (up to June 2004)

Location	Offices of foreign banks	Branches of foreign banks	Foreign insurance companies	Number of stock companies	Amount of class A stock issued
Shanghai	43%	37%	46%	11.3%	10.4%
Other Chinese cities*	57%	63%	54%	88.7%	89.6%

Note: *Excluding Hong Kong and Macao.
Source: The Industrial Map of the Yangtze River Delta (2005).

Table 8.6   Shanghai's share in China's bank assets (up to June 2004)

Location	Total asset of foreign banks	Total asset of national banks	Total asset of share-holder banks	Total asset of trust funds
Shanghai	53%	8%	17%	19%
Other Chinese cities*	47%	92%	83%	81%

Note: *Excluding Hong Kong and Macao.
Source: The Industrial Map of the Yangtze River Delta (2005).

is playing in China's financing industry. Since manufacturing is traditionally the mainstay of the economy, the city's strategy for economic restructuring has been to give more support to the service industry while retaining the manufacturing units that have a bright future. Today, Shanghai has become a mature economy, and the city is pursuing an even more ambitious goal of building "an international city" (Wang 2004).

Spatial Reorganization in Shanghai

Economic activities are delivered through land, and economic restructuring is reflected in Shanghai's spatial reorganization. With more emphasis given to the service industry, especially the financial business, the city needs an attractive, "world class" central business district (CBD) with office buildings armed with cutting-edge facilities. The increasing domestic "new rich" and foreigners brought by globalization to work in Shanghai seek better housing and entertainment amenities close to the CBD. Also, foreign investors seeking joint-venture opportunities prefer new factories served by good infrastructure and with sufficient space for potential expansion. These locations are available only in ex-urban areas. The new spatial demands push and drive the city's spatial reorganization, and six policies have been formulated and implemented since the 1990s in response:

1. Investing more in infrastructure improvement and beautification projects in the CBD for the service sector.
2. Promoting the service industry in the city's most attractive districts to replace existing manufacturing factories and the low-end housing stock.
3. Encouraging FDI enterprises in new industrial zones in Pudong and ex-urban areas through providing better infrastructure in these areas.
4. Transferring central industrial land to high-end housing and commercial buildings by relocating existing factories to ex-urban industrial campuses, especially in Pudong.
5. Reinforcing the CBD's position by increasing its population and activity through adjusting district boundaries—for example, the merger of Nanshi District and Huangpu District (the traditional CBD) to strengthen the CBD.
6. Revising the city's Master Plan through changing the development axis from north-south to west-east. Since Shanghai's main manufacturing factories are located in the north (the steel industry) and the south (the oil refining and chemical industry), and service centers are to the west (Hongqiao) and east (Pudong/ Lujiazui), the revision reveals the shift of the development strategy.

These policies are based on three strategies. First, the CBD is reinforced by relocating existing residents and factories from central districts to peripheral areas to support new

Table 8.7   Shanghai's building stock in selected years (million square meters)

Building type	1978	1980	1990	2000	Change 1990–2000	Change 1978–2000
Housing	41.2	44.0	89.0	208.7	134.5%	406.6%
Plant	25.4	26.5	48.2	57.4	19.1%	126.0%
Offices	2.3	3.4	6.0	24.2	303.3%	952.2%
Shops	2.3	2.4	4.0	11.9	197.5%	417.4%

Source: Shanghai Municipal Statistics Bureau (2003).

commercial developments in the central area. Second, creating inner-city residential zones for domestic elites and foreigners by reducing population density and building high-end housing in areas near the CBD. Third, creating industrial parks in ex-urban and peripheral areas to attract joint ventures and relocate profitable existing factories moved out from the central area. After 15 years, the positive results of spatial restructuring are evidenced in table 8.7.

Among all building types, office-building space has increased the most. From 1978 to 2000, office space increased by 952.2 percent, in which an increase of 303.3 percent took place from 1990 to 2000, the period Shanghai accelerated its pace to be an "international financing and trading center." The rapid increase of office buildings demonstrates clearly the city's economic restructuring toward the service industry. In the same periods of time, plants (factories) increased by only 126.0 percent from 1978 to 2000 and 19.1 percent from 1990 to 2000. This is the category that increased the least. Most new factories were actually built before Shanghai's race to "globalize" in 1992. With the increasing injection of FDI into Shanghai since 1990, new factories are generally built for and by joint ventures in the Pudong New District. Many "old" urban industrial districts, such as Yangpu, a traditional manufacturing industry base, experienced little change in manufacturing space (highlighted in figure 8.1) Shops increased by 417.4 percent from 1978 to 2000 and 197.5 percent from 1990 to 2000, the second largest increase among all building types. Meanwhile, housing increased by 406.6 percent between 1978 and 2000, and by 134.5 percent between 1990 and 2000. These changes in building stock reveal Shanghai's efforts in economic and spatial restructuring.

The distribution of spatial restructuring has been uneven. The city has deliberately given development priority to the CBD (consisting of north Huangpu District and Luwan District now, see figure 8.1), a strategy employed by many U.S. cities in the period of economic restructuring that took place from the 1970s to 1980s (Brenner and Theodore 2002; Rast 1999). Like the American case, the policy reflects the switch of the city's development goal toward a more service-oriented international economic center represented by the CBD, although manufacturing remains an important mainstay of Shanghai's economy.

CHANGES IN URBAN GOVERNANCE

The emergence of new economic activities and the creation of new urban spaces stimulate the need for innovative urban management arrangements. There have been new practices in city governance alongside the reform in economic life and the reorganization of urban space, the most important one being the decentralization of decision-making power in urban management. Having experienced poor government performance in managing resources under the centrally planned system, the central government initiated decentralization as a key component of the reform process. The motivation behind the devolution of decision-making power was primarily to improve efficiency in resource allocation (public investment funds and land in terms of urban development). The decentralization reform fosters the development of new mechanisms for the central-local relationship, such as the central government's partnership with localities on large-scale development projects. The reform creates a new relationship between the higher-level government and the lower ones. This dynamic relationship takes place at all levels of government: between the central and provincial/municipal governments, between municipal and district governments, and between district and subdistrict governments (street offices) in Chinese cities.

In the process of formulating the dynamic relationship, new players have been emerging on the stage of urban development and governance. At the municipal level, not only municipal bureaus, such as the planning bureau and the newly reinforced land bureau, have become influential, but also investor and developers of all kinds have become major stakeholders. In subdistricts, street offices are now playing an important role in shaping the community landscape. New players also include property owner association (POA), business owner association (BOA), and property management companies at the neighborhood level. In dealing with these new players, new mechanisms and strategies have been adopted by the municipal government in managing and governing the city, which opens the window for participation to a certain degree. The emergence of these players thus indicates the emergence of a new decision-making structure: a quasi-participatory decision-making structure in urban development in Chinese cities (Zhang 2002).

MUNICIPAL GOVERNMENT AND URBAN DISTRICTS

The Chinese administrative hierarchy has theoretically three levels of local government bodies in an urban area: the municipal government (*shizhengfu*), urban districts (*shiqu*) within the municipality, and street offices (*jiedao banshichu*) within an urban district. Street offices (SOs) represent district government as the basic administrative agency in urban areas. There is a fourth level of management body in urban areas: the residents' committees (*juming weiyuanhui*), but officially it is a resident organization, not a government institution, although in practice it functions as an extended administrative body at the lowest level.

The urban district has become an important stakeholder in city governance practice since the reform. A Chinese urban district could be as large as a big city in other countries. For example, with a population of 1.65 million and a jurisdiction area of 522.7 square kilometers in 2000, the Pudong New District, the largest urban district in Shanghai, is close to the size of the city of Chicago (2.8 million population and 584 square kilometers of jurisdiction area in 2000). The decentralization of decision-making power over land use and development funds takes place not only between the central government and local municipalities, but also between a municipal government and its local districts, and between a district and its street offices. Given the size and new decision-making powers of urban districts, devolving decision-making power to district governments has more impact on urban landscape than the devolution from central to municipal governments. Before the reform, urban districts had limited decision-making power over development funds and land use issues. Although most districts did have "district-owned enterprises" (*qu ban canyi*) before, most enterprises were simply workshops with aged machines operated by low-skilled workers. The main reason for setting up these workshops was employment rather than revenue. Districts had limited administrative power—even the district statistical year book did not show data for nondistrict enterprises (such as state-owned and city-owned enterprises) in the district—because they did not report to the district and their revenues were not shared with district government although they were located there. Municipal government funded most urban development projects at the district level. Also, the municipal government and its planning bureau made land use decisions. There were district planning offices, but these offices functioned as "supervisors" just to ensure the implementation of the city government's (or the central government's) land use decisions, rather than as "managers" to take care of district land management. In summary, before the reforms, neither development funds nor land use decisions, the two critical issues for urban development, were under the control of district government—despite the fact that a district might have a population of over one million.

After decentralization, considerable decision-making powers over local fiscal and land use issues were transferred to district governments. Not only can a district government now collect revenue from district-owned enterprises that have grown significantly in the last 15 years, but it can also share tax revenues with the municipal government, including tax on non-district-owned factories. In Shanghai, with the adoption of the "two levels of government, two levels of financing system" policy in 1987, district government has even been authorized to sign agreements with foreign investors in land leasing, real estate development, and other businesses (although guided by municipal regulations and limited to certain amounts). A director of an urban district (somewhat similar to an alderman in a U.S. city, although the director is elected only theoretically) has been called "semi-mayor" by China's ex-premier Zhu, the then Mayor of Shanghai (Kong 2001, p. 219).

The "two levels of financing system" include a responsibility-sharing arrangement between the municipal and district governments as well. Local financing is now essentially a district responsibility—each district government has to find its own resources to pay for most local expenses and projects. The burden of responsibility-sharing has forced district governments to seek new sources of revenue for the districts. Not surprisingly, land is viewed as the most valuable resource under local control, and making land use regulation less a barrier to investors is now seen as critical. Leasing land to investors of all kinds (foreign, overseas Chinese, and domestic real estate and business investors) has been a common practice in generating local revenue.

The practice of devolving decision-making power and sharing responsibility has mixed impacts on local life. One negative consequence is the growth of a "rent seeking" attitude in district governments, represented by the practice of "selling the place." This arises in all urban areas and imposes a cost on local residents, as relocation is needed to release land for leasing. There are positive impacts too. Compared with municipal governments, district governments know more about local needs and can make decisions reflecting local interests. To a certain extent, the decisions concerning a district have to be taken in line with the local residents' views, because the district officials have to report to the district people's congress, whose members are elected by residents. In practice, district leaders follow the municipal government's decisions in most cases because it is this government that nominates candidates as district officials for the approval of the district people's congress. However, district congress members are becoming more independent in making decisions on local issues, including local elections. Public participation at the district level is still limited and indirect, but decentralization has at least given local people improved access to their representatives, which pushes representatives to understand local needs better. In addition, initiating and practicing innovations and reform experiments first at the district level reduce the risks of reform both politically and economically.

At a lower level, with limited impacts, a reform mistake in a district costs less, while a successful experiment may easily be shared by, and spread over to, the whole city.

In summary, decentralization has made district governments much stronger in the process of urban development and governance. The district's active involvement in large construction projects is a major change in urban development in Chinese cities. However, decentralization with little public supervision may create opportunities for the abuse of power and corruption. There are potentially unwelcome by-products of decentralization.

THE GROWING INFLUENCE OF STREET OFFICES

In recent years, with the success of the "separating government administration from enterprise operation" (*zhenqi fengkai*) policy in production, a new policy of "separate government function from society function' (*zhenshe fengkai*) has been initiated. The purpose here is to reduce government's direct involvement in social services. The practice fosters the growth of SOs. As discussed above, SOs represent district government as the basic administrative agency in urban areas in China. With the municipal government's withdrawal, district governments and SOs are expected to play a more active role in community life. There is a "division of responsibility" between district governments and SOs: district governments focus on economic development issues, and SOs are expected to manage services for communities. In Shanghai, the SO's official functions have increased from three to eight, and areas in which SOs are involved have increased from three to fourteen. Today, the eight functions of SOs are leadership on local events, management of local businesses, services to community residents, coordination between various local groups, involvement in local economic development activities, communication between the government and the people, guidance on local social development, and monitoring of local safety and security. The SO's 14 new responsibilities include local justice, community security, traffic control, fire protection, sanitation, streetscaping, open space maintenance, environmental protection, family planning, employment and labor force administration, day care services, disaster protection, collective-owned businesses, community services, and farmers' markets (Zhang 2002).

These changes demonstrate a shift in the role of SOs from a low-level administrative body obeying higher government's decisions to an entity representing local interest with more independence. SOs are becoming more influential. In a study in Shi-ping Street Office, an average SO in Shanghai, it is found that the number of divisions of the SO increasing from eight to eleven. New divisions added are particularly related to economic development, financial, and labor administration—functions that have been devolved from a higher-level government after the reform. Another indicator suggesting that SOs have grown in local power is the increase in the SO staff strength. The Shi-ping SO had 74 staff members in 1999, an increase of 220 percent from 1963 when it had 20 members (no data were available for staffing in the 1970s and 1980s) (Zhang 2002). More staff members are deployed in divisions such as public works (sixteen members), economic affairs (eight members), social development (five members), and public relations (seven members). Since the public works division is in charge of infrastructure and housing construction in a street district, the growth of staffing and the expansion of the division's functions indicate that the SO has become more involved directly in infrastructure and housing issues, the areas in which community input and support are crucial. The Shi-ping SO has even issued local regulations to guide economic growth, including "Incentives to tax-revenue-increase projects," in which tax revenue from local businesses will be shared with the introducers of these businesses. In practice, the SO also functions as landlord in negotiating with investors who are interested in opening businesses in the community. The result is business is booming: in 1996 alone, 35 new businesses were established and 2,000 unemployed persons got jobs through the SO. Most new jobs are in service businesses established by the SO. With the increase of financial independence and responsibility for local issues, SOs are becoming stronger in decision making. Community interests, which also represent the interests of each SO staff member since they themselves live in the community, are given increased attention. In a sense, SOs can be said to be "selfish." Their decisions are more interest-driven—they now pay more attention to the local economic interests rather than the political interests of the municipal and district governments (Zhang 2002).

THE EMERGENCE OF NEW STAKEHOLDERS

Another new development in China's local life is the emergence of various interest groups, or "civic associations" (Pei 1998). In urban areas, these local groups include BOAs and POAs. They did not exist until the issuance of the 1982 constitution in which various ownership forms besides state ownership were allowed for the first time. Today, the number of employees in non-public-owned enterprises is more than that in state-owned ones in Shanghai in 2003 (SMSB 2005): 50.3 in nonpublic enterprises, 29.5 percent in collective-owned, and only 20.1 percent in state-owned enterprises . Business owners, especially those in sole-ownership and joint-venture categories, organize various BOAs to pursue their interest in relevant issues, especially urban development, infrastructure, and taxation issues. For instance, BOAs are actively involved in the development of retail and entertainment space in local commercial strips throughout Shanghai. Private and joint-venture business owners are the main investors in retail projects, and they approach local land bureaus and planning bureaus aggressively for land use permits, even through illegal means. BOAs represent owners' interests and receive government support. The government's positive attitude to BOAs is based on the consideration of channeling business owners' interest through these associations, so that the government can retain a certain influence over them and prevent illegal activities of individual owners through the use of BOAs as legal representative institutions.

POAs have emerged after the housing reform. With this reform, the home ownership rate has crossed 75 percent in Shanghai. Since the municipal housing department and its neighborhood branches have reduced their involvement in most of the housing service business after the housing reform, POAs have become a stakeholder in issues such as neighborhood safety, property management, open space maintenance, sanitation, and environmental protection. There has been more tension between the local government (represented by a resident committee, an elected resident governing body supported and influenced by the government), and other new players in day-to-day neighborhood management. For example, tensions arise because of challenges from nongovernment community organizations (such as POAs) to the traditional governing entity. Elected freely by all owners with little government intervention, POAs represent a more participatory decision structure to average owners.

In urban neighborhoods, BOAs and POAs have been involved in aspects of the development business that used to be the province of the public sector. With their financial means, they are increasingly challenging the public sector in local development decisions. Recognizing their importance, local governments (SOs, in particular) are recruiting members of these associations (BOAs, in particular) as "partners" of local government on local issues. Because members of BOAs and POAs are elected, their participation in local decision making should be viewed as positive, although this may not yet be a "real" participation in western terms. Nevertheless, it is possible to suggest that these moves represent the beginnings of a shift from urban "government" to urban "governance."

Conclusions

Since China's reform in the 1980s, Shanghai has experienced significant economic restructuring and spatial reorganization, guided and influenced by changes at the national level, such as the redirection of national development priority and the introduction of central-local tax-sharing arrangements. According to principles of political economy, any change in a society's economic foundation will eventually affect the realm of superstructure, including urban governance and urban spatial reorganization. The changes taking place in the economic structure, such as the emergence of various ownership forms and a much stronger private sector in economic life, are the main forces pushing the city government to create and adopt innovations in city management. In urban development, for example, the rising importance of district government and the emergence of community-level organizations are largely the reactions of the city government, as well as the local residents, to the more diversified economy and the space made available for innovation by decentralization. Currently, there is a debate among Chinese scholars and policy makers about the extent to which the government should represent the interests of the growing private sector. Proposals of adding an article on "protection of private property ownership" to the national constitution have been discussed since 2002. But no action has been taken partly owing to China's socialist ideology and, more importantly, owing to the government's (as well as people's) concerns about the increasing gap between the rich and the poor.

There are still challenges to be handled. China's rapid urbanization functions both as a positive force in terms of providing a huge amount of cheap labor to urban economy and as a negative one in terms of burdens imposed on urban public services and urban governance. For instance, for the three million rural-urban migrants in Shanghai, local districts and communities are the places where they work and live. But very little has been reported about their participation in development issues at the district and community level. The municipal government does not appear to be taking leadership in this realm. Devolving decision-making power from the municipal government to the urban districts may be viewed as a political strategy for reducing possible policy risks. There is still a tension between "the original city residents" and "new comers." New comers contribute to the success of the city, but they also need services and support. The importance of migrants' participation is not fully recognized by city leaders. But without support and legislative actions at the municipal level, district governments will tend to adopt a "wait and see" attitude in handling the migrant issue. It seems clear that successful urban governance involves constructive collaboration among a wide range of stakeholders. If this is the case, then moves to widen involvement in decision making will be needed in the coming period.

CHAPTER 9

Urban Challenges in Latin American Cities: Medellín and the Limits of Governance

John J. Betancur

INTRODUCTION

Governance now appears to be a critical feature of urban restructuring in modern society. It marks a shift from a belief that government can solve the problems facing society to one that implicates a wide range of stakeholders in the process of problem solving. A commitment to governance implies a process of bringing together the public sector, the private sector, and civil society around an agreed-on agenda. It stresses deliberation, partnership, shared responsibility, interdependence, and free dialogue. Governance has become such a powerful concept that entities such as the World Bank (1992), the United Nations (UNDP 1994), and the European Community (CEC 2001) have all adopted it as a major objective. Although it reflects real changes taking place throughout the world, governance may be still more a desired outcome than an accomplished reality. For example, it implies the government's ability to maintain social peace and guarantee acceptable levels of law and order. It also implies a basic societal consensus around the premises of (Western) democracy—human rights, the rule of law, and the marketplace. It assumes governability, development, opportunity, accountability, and trust. But what if these conditions are not in place? In this chapter I suggest that, in many of the developing regions of the world, these conditions are manifestly not in place. If this is indeed the case, we need to ask about the feasibility of a move from government to governance in such settings.

In this chapter, by examining the experience of Medellín, Colombia, I explore the following questions. Can cities with high levels of economic informality and social disorder maintain law and order without highly repressive regimes exercising power and authority? Is a governance approach feasible in such cities? Or, is governance an approach that is only suited to mature democracies supported by relatively developed economies and high levels of opportunity and stability for citizens? The study of Medellín sheds light on these questions as it illustrates in a concrete way some of the broader issues of urban governance in developing countries discussed by Stren in Chapter 5.

The city experienced economic downgrading and social chaos after the global crisis of the 1970s and 1980s, and, as a result, urban governance in such a context is problematic. In some ways it can be claimed that governance may be reduced to a process of transferring government's basic responsibilities to those lacking the capabilities to successfully address them. The dominance of para-economies (such as informal trading or crime for profit) and the presence of parastatal formations (such as armed militias, bands, gangs, drug cartels, mafias, and self-defense groups) speak to the inability of government to govern, the corruption of basic institutions, and, perhaps, the impossibility of governance.[1] This analysis starts with a brief examination of the trajectory of Medellín, followed by an account of the downgrading and informalization of its economy and workforce and the associated legitimacy crisis.[2]

THE TRAJECTORY OF THE CITY

Although Latin American countries have a relatively long history, they are at different stages in the construction of nationhood, state, and government. Rather than coinciding with preexisting social formations, national borders stem from artificial colonial partitions and adjustments thereafter. Colombia's current borders, for example, include historically disparate regions and geographies. In spite of a strong centralism, Colombia has been a country of regions with separate identities. *Gamonales,* or local elites, have often controlled local governments to their benefit. Although de jure the rule of law covers the entire country, de facto its exercise has been limited to the ability or willingness of localities to implement it. Similarly, Colombia has been a country of deeply entrenched and very powerful elite groups and families, and government legitimacy depends heavily on them. These elites have resisted the democratic demands of the masses and have imposed an inflexible, top-down public culture (Bergquist 1986; Uprimny-Yepes 2001). Such factors translate into the popular Colombian saying, "*las leyes son para los de ruana,*" which roughly translates as "the law is for the poor." In this context, it can be claimed that democracy has been highly symbolic. Even today, large portions of Colombia's national territory are contested by different entities—the government and groups such as guerrillas, paramilitaries, and drug barons fight for ascendancy. The state, then, has a weak presence in many urban and rural areas in Colombia. These brief remarks suggest that the local context needs to be factored into any assessment of the government's role and/or the potential for governance. For example, does government actually govern? How far does the rule of law go? What is the role of groups operating outside or in violation of the law? Whose interests are served by the police and the military?

Medellín, the second largest city and metropolitan area in Colombia, is the capital of Antioquia, first state in population in the country and one of the most entrenched and wealthy. The city's population grew from 168,000 in 1938 to 326,000 in 1951, to 1.7 million in 1993, and to 2,223,078 in 2005. The population of the rest of the metropolitan area increased from 77,000 in 1938 to 853,000 in 1993 and to 1.3 million in 2005. A successful rural economy based on coffee farming and gold mining generated enough primitive accumulation and trade to support the most impressive process of industrialization in the country. Through import substitution (helped by the 1914–1945 period of relative isolation from foreign trade and a high level of protectionism after that), Medellín grew into a prosperous city of trade and industry—in fact the most significant concentration of large-scale manufacturing in Colombia. A relative monopoly of the national market allowed for a system of mass assembly plants for consumer and other goods (textiles, apparel, tobacco, food, shoe and leather, cement, nonelectric machinery, home appliances, and cars) and a steel plant to be created. Along with them, smaller and midsize firms absorbed much population growth in the first half of the twentieth century.

Medellín became a major location of government as well as an important marketplace, a regional service center, a site of major educational centers, culture, and religion, and the main concentration of institutions and urban functions in northwest Colombia.[3] A strong compact between industrial, commercial, Catholic, and government elites provided the platform of legitimacy (Walton 1977). Together, they configured and directed the regulation of the local economy. By capitalizing on the "enclave culture" of hard work, family values, regional pride, and Catholicism, they managed to weave their vision and interests—particularly the centrality of manufacturing—into the core of the city's identity and economy. In the absence of any government social security or welfare system until the last decades of the twentieth century,[4] people relied on work-based pensions and mutual and extended family support. The upper and middle classes had work benefits—including government jobs and/or personal wealth.

A two-party system monopolized government to the point that, in the late 1950s, following a bitter civil war between the parties, they agreed to alternate power and share political positions, thus preempting the emergence of other political forces. Independent organization was discouraged or repressed. Other than unions, lower-class groups have consisted mostly of neighborhood-based nongovernmental organizations (NGOs) established to qualify for government assistance within a process combining unpaid labor with government-provided materials and a corrupt patronage system. In this context, left-wing organizations were always small and marginal. Mass mobilizations such as the 1960s' student movement and worker demonstrations have been closely watched or heavily repressed.

This social order has been reflected in the organization of the city, hegemonic ideology, the class system, and political, economic, cultural, and social life. The city is segregated by class, including a rich and exclusive enclave to the southeast (El Poblado), upper-middle-class areas near downtown (for example, Boston and Laureles) or bordering the upper class areas, working-class neighborhoods between these or near major industrial concentrations, and the massive collar of squatter settlements on the outskirts, usually in the steepest areas of the Aburrá Valley in which the city is located. Impressive churches, smokestacks, and high-rises dot the city, reflecting the strong presence and dominance of the church, manufacturing, and commerce.

Manufacturing was, for a long time, the major and best employer in the city, the pride of Medellín and its population. In the words of a labor leader, "The aspiration of a resident was to finish high school and get a lifetime job in one of the main factories; at the time, this was a real possibility." Labor organizing completed the picture within a paternalistic and highly co-opted process of demands and economic concessions— leaving politics and regulation to the elites.

Prosperity turned Medellín into an immigrant and development magnet assuring its primacy over the region and a central place in the country. Factors such as a bare-bones national system of roads, railroads, and airports maintained that sense of enclave and unity around the regional myths of entrepreneurship, industriousness, faith, family, independence, ethnicity, and adventure. Appointed by the president or the governor until the 1990s, for the most part, local and regional government was top-down/authoritarian.

Power resided with individual and party relations rather than with accountability to the citizens—although local government had to please local elites to remain in place. Despite the mass dislocations of the civil war in the late 1940s and through the 1950s, this political order managed to hold the city together until the 1970s. Then, as we explore in the next section, economic stagnation and massive shifts in society resulted in a major crisis in the life of the city—one that continues today.

THE IMPACT OF GLOBALIZATION—ECONOMIC RESTRUCTURING

The local economy started losing steam in the 1950s as import substitution, political and economic centralism, and locational advantages promoted industrialization in other cities, taking market from Medellín.[5] Still, the city continued to be the main concentration of large, assembly-line plants in the country. By 1970, however, the economy had stagnated, and major firms resorted to government bailouts, shrinkage or combined production, and commercialization of foreign products to remain afloat. Manufacturing entered a generalized structural crisis in the 1980s, dragging down all economic sectors. Initially viewed as a business cycle, it was soon linked to import substitution and overdependency on protected internal markets—along with rentierism (Garay and Angulo 1999; Garay et al. 1998; Chica 1983, 1994; Ocampo 1987; Paus 1983). Over time, commentators identified globalization as a key factor reshaping the local economy (Sarmiento 2000; Betancur et al. 2001).

To recap, by 1970, Medellín was producing a significant volume of low value-added mass-consumption goods in large assembly-line plants and smaller firms. High value-added multipliers accrued to foreign concerns providing technology and specialized services. Manufacturing demands on the local economy included materials, parts, repairs, and services. Reinvestment of earnings was low, and capital markets were down. A weak growth in demand was distributed between the products of local and nonlocal industries. Thus, industrial growth did not keep pace with the growth of the population. To aggravate things, mass migration after 1950 generated an ever-growing labor supply within an economy with declining absorption rates. Operating on the margins of global capital markets and corporations, businesses could not respond in the ways core firms and their outlets could. Instead, they turned to extreme labor-cost-cutting strategies, including (1) a virtual war on organized labor, (2) work reorganization, and (3) structural changes in labor-capital relations.

(1) The first sought to reduce labor power in the determination of compensation and working conditions. It consisted of a vicious and well-orchestrated offensive including contract violation, corruption of judges, government support of employers, threats, pitting of nonmembers against members, illegal breaking of strikes, weeding out job applicants with union experience or leanings, frontal attacks on independent unions and proworker associations, and replacement of seasoned with young workers.[6] Worse, the strategy included media attacks on union leaders, illegal firings, psychological warfare, killings, kidnappings, and the disappearance of leaders or threats to their families (interviewees and archives; also Puig-Farrás and Hartz-Son 1999; Betancur 1994; Toro-Vanegas et al. 1993).[7] In the end, a concerted effort among elites managed to replace union contracts with firm contracts, to reduce union membership and strikes drastically, to co-opt or paralyze the leadership, reduce wages and conditions, limit union prerogatives, and replace independent with employer-friendly unions or dismantle them altogether (ENS 1999). With a battered union movement, firms got the upper hand with the help of government and the courts.[8]

(2) Reorganization of work was a second major cost-saving strategy—mostly via productivity increases but also through further reductions in variable costs. Strategies here focused on: speeding up work (e.g., cutting dead time, introducing just-in-time management, and tying compensation to production); reorganizing production (e.g., around productivity circles and total quality control/management techniques); streamlining (limiting the firm to a basic core and subcontracting the rest or breaking it into horizontally integrated smaller firms); contracting out support activities (e.g., cleaning, maintenance, restaurants, and repairs); outsourcing and limited automation; reducing personnel to a core that worked in combination with temps as needed; and turning personnel management over to cooperatives. The result was a flexible network linking formal to informal operations and to home-based work; permanent to temporary workers; in-house core operations to outside peripheral and informal ones; and skilled core labor to outside consultants. Many firms introduced production systems isolating workers through chains of separate activities often performed in sweatshops or at home, eliminating ties among them and, hence, reducing opportunities for communication and unionization. Home-based work paid by the piece passed on space, utility, and machinery costs and defective parts to producers. A few facts on a selected set of these practices provide an idea of the savings involved.

- Temporary jobs grew at an annual rate of 25 percent in the 1980s alone (López 1996: pp. 32–3) and at higher rates thereafter (interviews). One-third of the workforce in firms with over ten workers had become temporary by 1990. The 1990 labor reform, allowing firms to resolve their fluctuations through temporary workers, gave the temporary employment sector a major boost.
- Subcontracting boomed from the 1980s as a tool to bypass unions and labor laws applying to large firms. The companies made enormous savings by accessing nonunionized, female and child labor working out of their homes.
- Hiring through worker cooperatives became a favorite way of bypassing labor legislation and worker organization/militancy. To join a cooperative and qualify for such jobs, the worker had to prepay social security and accident and health insurance. As an owner, he or she was not protected by labor laws and could not join unions or strike. Cooperative wages were lower than for those in firms contracting workers directly.

These changes are most dramatically reflected in the generalized informalization of the economy.[9] In Colombia, the informal economy became the main urban employer in the 1980s, rising to an estimated average of 54 percent of employment in the late 1990s compared with 33 percent in 1970 (Wickware 1999). In spite of having the lowest percentages among major Colombian cities, Medellín's figures went from 50.2 percent in 1984 to 55.7 percent in 2000 (DANE). Since the 1980s, 61.8 percent of new jobs in the Medellín metropolitan area have been created in this sector (López 1996, p. 176). The main components of the informal economy are retail (34.1 percent of jobs), services (26.8 percent), and manufacturing (18 percent) (López 1996, p. 181). Working conditions are much inferior to those in the formal sector. In 2000 over half (51.2 percent) of the workers in the informal economy made less than minimum wage compared with 14.5 percent in the formal sector (Gutiérrez 2002b, p. 20). Whereas 81.4 percent of workers in the latter have social security benefits, only 25.7 percent in the informal economy have these benefits (López 1996, p. 195). Contrary to a common perception that the sector is limited to the uneducated, in 2001, 44 percent had completed college and an additional 16 percent had some years of college (Gutiérrez 2002b: pp. 19–20).

(3) Lastly, changes in the system regulating capital-labor relations lowered costs further. By threatening to close down, firms sought exceptions from labor laws or operated in open violation of them. They lobbied for and obtained drastic labor reforms. Laws 50 and 60 of 1990 made major concessions in the process of firing, hiring, and contracting. Moreover, these laws freed employers from contributions to social security, and firms moved into an integral wage in which the worker bought his/her own social security in a privatized system; laws also allowed for the hiring of temps to deal with production peaks with the ability to extend their contracts indefinitely; and permitted employers to take back concessions above legally established laws (ENS 1999). Laws 31 of 1992 and 278 of 1996 tied adjustments in the minimum wage to the expected rate of inflation rather than to the actual rate. Finally, privatization had a critical impact both on the workers involved and on the negotiating power of public employees. Claiming inefficiencies such as inflated work forces, clientelism, artificial wages, and entrenched unions, privatization often assumed the form of subcontracting public functions to nonunion providers, including cooperatives.

ECONOMIC AND SOCIAL IMPLICATIONS

Although all economic sectors registered job growth in the 1973–1999 period, the growth of smaller firms and informalization has changed the economic structure of Medellín and the city region. Manufacturing went from mass operations, with thousands of workers under a single roof, to vertically integrated and independent smaller shops including home-based work and sweatshops. The global shift from a manufacturing- to a service-based economy is reflected in the 1999 distribution of employment. Manufacturing, construction, and agricultural shares declined. Some large manufacturing firms moved to the urban periphery. Subcontracting and informal production resulted in the transfer

Table 9.1   Employment and unemployment in Medellín and the metropolitan area for selected years, 1973–2000 (in percentages)

Year*	Working age (1)	Unemployed (2)	Economically inactive (3)	Occupational rate (4)	Dependency rate (5)
1973	70.0	14.2	58.4	35.6	4.0
1976**	72.5	14.0	53.3	40.2	3.4
1978**	76.2	12.7	50.6	43.1	3.0
1980**	76.2	14.7	46.5	45.6	2.9
1982**	76.3	12.5	49.5	44.1	3.0
1984	76.3	16.8	NA	NA	NA
1986	75.1	15.7	NA	NA	NA
1988	76.2	14.2	44.9	47.3	2.8
1990	76.2	11.5	45.1	48.6	2.7
1992	NA	15.2	NA	50.0	NA
1994	77.2	13.2	40.0	51.8	2.5
1996	77.4	11.6	42.5	50.9	2.5
1998	79.0	16.3	40.0	50.2	2.5
2000	78.5	22.2	39.0	47.5	2.7

Note: * March or April of each year; ** Medellín only (notice, however, that the rates of the city and the metropolitan area are very close); (1) Total unemployed/economically active population; (2) Total economically inactive/total population in working age; (3) Total employed/total population in working age; (4) Total population/total employed; (5) Population in working age/total population.
Source: DANE, Encuesta Hogares (household survey).

of many jobs to the informal sector. Meanwhile, the share of retail and services (the bulk of the informal sector) increased.

Indicators such as employment, income, crime, increases in the informal and criminal economies, and a generalized loss of faith in the new system reveal a societal paradigm in chronic crisis and an emerging formation that may be legitimized only through imposition and force. As table 9.1 illustrates, the last 30 years have witnessed very high rates of unemployment in Medellín and the wider metropolitan area. Not surprisingly, the highest levels are concentrated in lower-class neighborhoods. Rates ranged between 12.5 percent and 14.7 percent in the 1973–1982 period (beginning of the crisis); between 14.2 percent and 16.8 percent in 1982–1988 (employer-led adjustment); and between 11.5 percent and 2 percent in 1990–1996 (deregulation and brief recovery), and leapt to 16.3 percent in 1998, 22.2 percent in 2000 (bursting of a foreign-investment bubble), and 20 percent in 2001 (light recovery). They have swung between 15 percent and 20 percent thereafter. Interestingly, the educational level of the unemployed largely resembled that of the employed. In 2000, 30 percent of the jobless had completed secondary education, 24 percent had completed primary or less, and 13 percent had a bachelor's degree or some college education (Gutiérrez 2002a, p. 17). By 1999 women had become the main household-income source, a total reversal from the 1970s. There is a steady increase in the working-age group and the occupational rate and a smaller decrease in the dependency rate. These figures suggest a stagnant job market combined with labor-pool increases and higher participation rates—as more householders are forced into the workforce. Job transfers from the formal to the informal economy, from permanent to temporary categories, and deregulation are affecting incomes badly. Real wages have declined in the last three decades (Abello 1992, p. 54; ENS 1999; OEIS-MA 2002). The percentage of individuals in poverty grew from 37.8 percent in 1986 to 44.8 percent in 1992, to 50 percent in 1995, to 52 percent in 1998 (DANE), and to 55 percent in 2001 (*El Colombiano* 2001a, p. 5a).

Although limited formal-job absorption had always pushed residents into other job and income-earning options, after 1970 Medellín hosted an ever-growing criminal economy with its associated sequel of armed violence. A mass of refugees displaced by paramilitary, guerrilla, army, and police, or drug activity aggravated this situation (IPC 1999).[10] An estimated 250,000—children and women, mostly—entered the city in the 1990s. Armed conflict and disorder reached alarming levels in low-income areas, and parts of the city became a battlefield. With less than 7 percent of Colombia's population, the metropolitan area registered around 25 percent of public-order violations in the country. Medellín became one of the most violent cities in the world (*El Colombiano* 2001b, p. 10A) with a homicide rate of 169 per 100,000 people in 2001 (Arango and Jaime 2001, p. 61). Whereas before 1980 there were less than 1,000 homicides per year, they exceeded 3,000 thereafter (*El Colombiano* 2001b, 10A; Alcaldía de Medellín 1988, p. 461).

CURRENTS OF CHANGE AND THE CHALLENGE
FOR URBAN GOVERNANCE

With the undermining of the material basis of legitimacy—the possibility of a secure job; access to basic services such as education, health, and housing; and an adequate floor of stability and safety—the gap between the expectations and actual experience of the population has become intolerable. This growing gap raises major challenges for the role of government and governance. A generalized sense of insecurity (economic, social, and political) has set in. Squatter settlement after squatter settlement sprang up on the outskirts, especially in the period since the 1970s. These became vast territories of informality both economically and socially. Constructed through illegal land partitions, invasions, and self-help, these squatter settlements became a living testimony to the absence and indifference of the state and society. Lacking the most basic infrastructure and institutions, they became fertile grounds for predatory bands of drug dealers and delinquents who terrorized residents raping, killing, robbing, drug –dealing, and imposing protection fees, even curfews. In response, businesses owners and notables organized their own armed self-defense groups, taking justice into their own hands.

National insurgencies entered the fray with the alleged purpose of restoring order. Although militias and paramilitaries kept bands at bay in many areas, they imposed their own versions of order, charging protection fees and carrying out executions and exiles (Téllez 1995). Along with them, larger groups such as the Medellín Cartel—that staged an open war with government over extradition to the United States—terrorized the city. A criminal economy of killings and kidnappings for profit, extortions, smuggling, and assaults added to informality, confirming the existence of a generalized order of microstates and para-economies. Plagued by corruption and elitism, government intensified its repressive solutions.

Although the disintegration of the Medellín Cartel in the 1980s ended the most dramatic terrorist actions, the generalized conflict did not recede, and drug trafficking continues unabated. Armed robberies, petty thievery, rapes, and a drug epidemic are still the order of the day in significant parts of Medellín. Eventually, paramilitaries prevailed in many low-income areas. A recent agreement between these paramilitaries and government apparently led to the dismantling of these groups in some neighborhoods. However, local observatories and international agencies claim that all that has changed is their style of work. Under the guise of political or community groups, they are still strong in many of these areas and even in higher-income areas.

Ineffective in the 1970s and 1980s, government has engaged, since the 1990s, in more drastic actions. Operating around a neoliberal platform imposed by the capitalist core, the government has tried to restore governability through a combination of measures: militarism, authoritarianism, a total war on the Left, entrepreneurship (welfare for large corporations and microloans and microenterprises for the poor), a generalized ideological offensive, including a call to citizens to help fight criminality and disorder (e.g., a vast army of paid informants/vigilantes), enactment of pardons for paramilitaries, and symbolic interventions in low-income areas. A few independent nonprofits engaging in initiatives at democratization, human rights, and peaceful coexistence have become the target of both state and parastate organizations.

Public responses have tended to follow the approach of the old civic-military action of pacification coupled with a belief that the free market will take care of the economy. The first includes a military offensive (stick) accompanied by projects (carrot), particularly in the most conflictive areas. It seeks a demonstration effect to instill a positive image of the state and entice residents to work under the aegis of the law. Major projects are subcontracted, inviting participation of NGOs and residents (paramilitary groups and bands often use force to secure a share of the resources) to generate some jobs; residents carry out other services on an unpaid basis with public assistance in the form of materials and machinery. As much as these projects call for community-building within a context of local participation and transparency, government has been unable to shake off clientelism and corruption. Participation has been limited mostly to the recruitment of residents to work in the projects, to informational meetings or campaigns, and to cooperation of residents on issues such as the legalization of tenure and relocation (Betancur 2005).

In 1990, the presidency created a special office, Consejería, for the Metropolitan Area of Medellín. The office initiated public forums and negotiations with unlawful groups and called for peace along with the development of youth and sports centers, new NGOs, citizen nuclei, and highly visible public events. In turn, the city established a fairly decentralized pilot program, PRIMED, for overhaul of the worst areas (Betancur 2005). Both programs, however, ended with the administrations that created them. Although much infrastructure was developed, advances in education, health, job training, and jobs were always lagging, and poverty went untouched.

On the military side, tactics included extensive raids, new police stations, local self-defense groups, and an increase in the number of informants (legalized by the current president when he was governor of the state and later declared illegal) working in coordination with authorities, and negotiations with local bands (with a heavy involvement of the Catholic Church). Since 2002, newly elected President Uribe turned to an approach of repression, illustrated by a dramatic military takeover in 2003 of a commune contested between guerrillas and paramilitaries and an all-out war against the former.[11] According to observatories and watchdog groups, this action was coordinated with paramilitaries and focused particularly on militias. Accompanying it has been a "war" against independent NGOs, the Left, and other forces of civil society.

Although violent homicides have slowed down recently, their numbers are still high, and tensions loom large. As Harvey (1994) found in his own research, the push for competitiveness/entrepreneurship is actually replacing the early sense of collectivity in these neighborhoods with cutthroat competition within an already overcrowded informal economy. An economic agenda of self-employment via microloans and microenterprises has only helped enlarge the informal sector. In turn, government is expanding informality through privatization, labor deregulation, and corporate welfare, actually increasing poverty via unregulated wages. The outcome is clear: to throw the problem back on the poor, asking them to create their own jobs (the new poverty entrepreneur) and take care of themselves, on the one hand, and to deregulate the market so that employers get cheap and unprotected labor that they can overexploit, on the other. The alternative criminal economy of quick gains and predation becomes very attractive in this context.

The private sector made its move since the late 1970s when the chief executive officers of major industries in the city established a business group, Grupo Empresarial Antioqueño (GEA), or Sindicato Antioqueño—today's largest economic force in Colombia. Through the interlocking of boards, stocks, and decision making, the GEA has maintained control and ownership of strategic local firms and engaged in a coordinated set of measures to navigate the crisis, improve the competitive position of its firms, keep control of the local economy and system of regulation, and set direction vis-à-vis globalization (Betancur et al. 2001). The GEA undertook a well-orchestrated process of buying, selling, and merging of firms; streamlining; subcontracting; disinvesting in unprofitable firms; identifying and conforming a set of strategic industries; expanding financial operations; recruiting new talent; securing international advice; entering into strategic agreements with foreign capital; and penetrating the U.S., Central American, and Caribbean markets.

Today, the GEA is organized around three major subgroups—Inversiones Nacional de Chocolates (one of the ten largest food-production and distribution groups in Latin America with exports of more than US$60 million), Argos, a holding concern for firms in the construction and energy industries (controlling over half of the national cement market and exporting nearly half of its production), and Suramericana de Inversiones (a group with a large portion of the insurance, distribution, banking, investment, real estate, and pension market). The group established strategic alliances by specialized activity with overseas counterparts (e.g., Noel, a food plant, with Danone from France, and Exito, one of the largest box retailers in the region and country, with Casino, also from France). The GEA emphasizes alliances, globalization, investment, information, technology, and educational management. Although it includes goods producing concerns, it has prioritized financial and other services (Oriente Virtual 2005; Revista Dinero 2000; Jiménez 2005). All of this is part of its efforts to shape an ideological hegemony of free trade and to control the institutional and social fabric around its corporate agenda. The GEA's aim is to bring together major social forces behind a common agenda of growth, a condition for becoming competitive in the global economy (Borja and Castells 1997).

How has civil society responded to these major shifts? The answer is not very encouraging. Authoritarian, concerted, and paternalistic elites and their associates have been fairly effective in preempting the formation of a strong civil society. They have intensified their attacks on alternative social proposals (even those calling for compromise and the deepening of democracy). It is helpful to distinguish three kinds of civil-society organization: independent-progressive, clientelist-paternalistic, and elitist top-down (with overlaps among them). The first includes NGOs advancing self-determination among the poor and underrepresented (e.g., independent unions and advocacy or watchdog groups). Clientelist-paternalistic groups comprise the mass of community-based (both neighborhood and nonneighborhood) NGOs, promoted and controlled by government, churches, and elite philanthropy and dedicated to practical projects and paternalistic services. Lastly, elitist top-down groups include all noneconomic, nonpolitical NGOs created for cultural, philanthropic, and ideological work or neoliberal agendas such as the development of metropolitan and local plans of competitiveness or promotion of image and identity. Although most of them operate as nonprofits, in reality they promote elitist agendas.

What may be most promising vis-à-vis grassroots initiatives of social change is the emergence of citywide NGOs that are trying to redirect the conversation toward democratization, equal opportunity, transparency, solidarity, human rights, and conciliation. Lastly, some universities, international NGOs, and independent leaders have joined efforts to promote new perspectives. Their activities and voice have attracted the animosity of the presidency and an elite-controlled media that accuses them of playing into the hands of guerrillas and the Left. Although called on to abandon insurgency and engage in electoral politics, groups such as Union Patriótica, responding to such an approach, were exterminated by paramilitaries with the indifference of government.

IMPLICATIONS FOR URBAN GOVERNANCE

This analysis has identified two converging processes in Medellín after 1970: a process of economic crisis/restructuring and a process of social decomposition linked to a legitimacy crisis. The first was the result of the shift from a manufacturing-based economy—with fairly decent compensation and conditions, opportunities to secure a job in the formal economy, and the prospects of some mobility—to a service-based economy of devalorization and informalization with meager opportunities. The second includes social decomposition, a dramatic increase in criminality, escalating urban violence, and the associated formation of microstates. I am not here claiming a cause-effect relationship between these processes. But I am suggesting that the current crisis has much to do with the disintegration of the earlier "compact" between the economic and the social, and that, as global forces have ruptured established patterns, no adequate replacement "compact" has been found.

Without wishing to generalize too freely, a cursory review of Latin American cities reveals a similar picture of economic turmoil and loss of governability (Navia and Zimmerman 2004; Graizbord and Rowland 2003; CEPAL (Comisión Económica para América Latina) 2001; Tardanico and Menjívar 1987). Although contexts vary and each local version is different, many cities appear to be experiencing dramatic levels of informalization, a boom in criminal economies, and corresponding crises of social decomposition and governability. Perhaps the most revealing indicator is informalization: according to the CEPAL (2001), seven out of every ten new jobs created in Latin America are informal.

On the basis of this analysis, I suggest that the foundations for urban governance in Medellín, and possibly most of Latin American cities, are missing. Put more bluntly, the conditions for a move from government to governance are simply not in place. Contested for most of its history, the government sector—in the Medellín case, at least—does not abide by its own laws and, in fact, seems almost to compete with the outlawed in the violation of human rights. A private sector used to dictating its wishes to government and civil society or going by its own rules, at times in concert with paramilitary and other unlawful groups or individuals, has presided over a restructuring process involving violation of labor laws and agreements. Lastly, it would seem that a civil society, entwined with the power networks of elite groups, cannot be sufficiently independent to adequately represent its members. Absent a common grounding in the rule of law and well-established and legitimate public, private, and civil sectors, how can we expect transparent, accountable, and democratic governance or fair and legitimate partnerships among them? The Medellín case reveals a culture of domination and dependency—with the private sector imposing its agenda on an enfeebled civil society.

Similarly, this case shows the absence of accountability, transparency, debate, and deliberation, or the ability to resolve differences—all key characteristics of, or conditions for, governance. Although a foundation of the new Colombia announced by the 1992 constitution, governance has not, at this point, provided a vehicle for bringing all stakeholders into the governing process. Rather, the very concept of "governance" has been appropriated—as an excuse for private sector and government failures, as a mechanism of manipulation and convenient rhetoric, and as a great tool for passing on responsibility to those with the least power and resources to respond.

Regarding the relationship between governance and the economy and between informalization and governance, the experience of Medellín suggests that basic stability, the ability for a majority to achieve social citizenship through a secure and decent job, and the opportunity for job mobility and development constitute minimal conditions for legitimacy and hence governance. How much legitimacy or governance can a society have when working in the formal economy is a privilege rather than a universal possibility or when the rule of law is differentially applied? It is possible to conceive of a society in which the private and public sectors and civil society partner to confront crises and build governability. This, however, would require appropriate representation, common grounding, and full willingness on the part of each sector to compromise and live by the agreements.

The growth of the informal economy is particularly striking—and this is not a trend unique to this city. It is a troublesome development for those engaged in improving both government and governance. This is partly because a growing sector of the population is ending up in the informal economy and partly because there is a general feeling today that the informal economy is "a solution" or a necessary evil (Feldman and Ferretti 1998; Hassan Danesh 1991). The informal economy certainly has the elements of flexibility asked for by the prevalent accumulation regime. But it represents a deep social dilemma. Operating outside or in violation of the rule of law, it severs ties with the material and social basis of citizenship, legitimacy, and recognition. Illegal and unprotected, informal work becomes the most degraded and abused market form, in turn degrading all work as it drives down wages in those sectors linked to or in competition with it while giving a carte blanche to exploitation. The human being involved loses his/her rights, worth, and dignity.

The informal economy establishes an alternative order with its own social relations, value systems, and practices of violation (Alayón 1997; Mansilla 1992). In this way, the lives of a majority of the workers operate under, and are ruled by, an ever-repeated act of transgression. To the extent that values are based on and reinforce established orders, the operation, side by side, and actual integration, of the formal and informal economies represents a threat to sound government and governance. It dissolves the material basis of legality, turning the rule of law into a pragmatic ethics of convenience. To the extent that the majority may find jobs only in the informal economy, their relationship to the formal market becomes irregular or indirect. With a majority of workers and their families depending on the informal economy for a living, and with a growing dependency of the formal on the informal economy, de facto, the informal order and its relations may come to prevail over the formal and its supporting rule of law.

According to Mansilla (1992, p. 38), "the incessant repetition of the informal has turned it into something licit, habitual and quotidian." Once comfortable in the informal economy, the borders with criminality also get blurred. As a street vendor confided to this author, "I could not feed my family from the sale of the same products that many others sell around me. I felt more desperate by the day. Then, I used my business as a front for drugs. It works. I make more money now than other vendors or than people with regular jobs. I am not forcing anybody to buy. It is their choice!" The increasing "naturalness" of informality has evolved into, and is reflected in, a widespread culture of transgression (Betancur 2004) that amounts to an informal formality. Although the informal economy might represent a rational response to globalization and, in fact, somehow a response to employment problems, de facto it *legalizes* illegality. Hence, it may actually represent an effort to avoid the issue. As Itzigsohn (2000) argues for the cases of Costa Rica and the Dominican Republic, there may be more or less informality depending on the nature of government and its policies. Meanwhile, again, the repeated violation of the rule of law turns violation into the rule of law itself. Once informality becomes dominant, formality becomes less relevant, and the forces supporting it lose their legitimacy or relevance. How can we possibly build a society on such an order? How can we possibly build governance on equivocation? When work loses its role as a major foundation for recognition, stability, and citizenship, becoming instead a source of human devaluation, the social order is in jeopardy. Perhaps this issue—how to respond to the growth of the informal economy—is the major challenge for those who wish to strengthen democratic governance in the cities of Latin America and the developing world.

NOTES

1. This study is based on the author's research, including 30 long, formal interviews of labor leaders, informal workers and their organizations, public officials, industry representatives,

researchers, and NGOs; informal conversations with workers, union leaders, ordinary citizens, and ONG staff; participant observation; attendance of forums and encounters; conversations with researchers from Colombia and other parts of Latin America; archival research including newspapers, newsletters, and industry associations; and collection of data from public and private sources. This task was difficult, as Latin America does not have a long tradition of data production and analysis at the local, city level. This is further complicated by the sensitive nature of statistics, inspiring public agencies to control the data collected and released (Gutierrez 2002a, p. 13). Research for this study was supported by a Fulbright Grant in the first semester of 2001.

2. For two excellent reviews and compilations of this literature, see Feldman and Ferretti (1998) and Hassan Danesh (1991); also Rakowski (1994).

3. The city was the forerunner of industrialization, leading Colombia until the 1950s when it became second to Bogotá, the capital city. A national government centralizing resources and decision making in the capital eventually attracted businesses away from the rest of the country, making Bogotá the main business, trade, manufacturing, and cultural city in the country, indeed an international center.

4. In the 1980s, Colombia established a limited retirement system based on deductions; legislation included other benefits for workers holding formal jobs in the private sector. Most recently, privatization and an integral wage force workers to purchase retirement, health, and other plans directly from the private sector.

5. Aggregate industrial value as a percent of the nation declined from 22.6 percent in 1966 to 21.5 percent in 1985 (Gouëset 1998, p. 14) and to 18.1 percent in 1994 (CCM 2000).

6. Replacement of older with younger workers produced large payroll savings—workers with nine to ten years in manufacturing earned 75 percent more than new hires in the same occupations (López 1991).

7. Since the 1980s, Colombia holds the record for most assassinations of labor leaders. Most of these crimes remain unsolved and are blamed on the insurgency.

8. In many cases judges recognized the violation but agreed with firms' claims that they did not have the resources to comply (interviewees, archives, and cases learned by the author).

9. The informal economy is defined in Colombia as including all businesses with less than ten employees. Self-employed professionals are excluded. The reason for this definition is that firms of this size engage in some form of informality—from violation of established regulations to unethical employment practices.

10. According to Rueda B. R. (1998, p. 27), government lost the limited control and legitimacy it had: "Supposedly legitimate, the state here is an armed player, paradoxically increasing its illegitimacy through its [armed] interventions; it has lost its ability to be effective, which is the only guarantee of legitimacy."

11. According to independent observers such as Amnesty International, government supported paramilitaries in their fight against guerrillas and, in the case of the commune, it actually strengthened the former.

CHAPTER 10

METROPOLITAN GOVERNANCE IN AUSTRALIA—THE SYDNEY EXPERIENCE

DANIEL KÜBLER AND BILL RANDOLPH

INTRODUCTION

The organization of governance in metropolitan areas has been an issue ever since cities began sprawling over their jurisdictional borders in the late nineteenth and early twentieth centuries. Adapting the institutional map by the annexation of suburbs constituted a first approach to reducing governmental fragmentation in urban regions. Another approach, pursued mostly during the 1960s and 1970s, consisted in the creation of two-tier metropolitan governments to which competences and resources were transferred for the management of policy issues at the metropolitan scale. In the early 1980s these paths toward stronger metropolitan governance entered a major crisis. On an intellectual level, research in the wake of the public choice tradition had consistently pointed out the drawbacks of the big-government approach inherent in metropolitan government reforms. Politically, experiences with two-tier metropolitan authorities had proved disappointing, and many of them lost support or were abolished. However, since the mid-1990s, exposure to the global competition for capital investments has renewed the quest for strengthening regional governance in many metropolitan areas. In terms of strategy the "paths to new regionalism" (Savitch and Vogel 2000) are thought to be diverse. While structural territorial reform still is considered something of a distant ideal, new regionalist thinking advocates voluntary cooperation among governments, public agencies, nongovernmental, and private actors as a pragmatic and viable alternative for achieving regional objectives.

Against this general background, this chapter[1] discusses the recent emergence of an area-wide governance capacity in Sydney, Australia. After a brief presentation of the intergovernmental context relevant to governing cities in Australia, we will argue that urban and regional restructuring in the wake of globalization has produced new challenges for the governance of Sydney. We will then show the ways that have been explored to overcome the governance deficits that have led to unplanned urban growth and major infrastructure gaps. In particular, we will argue that area-wide governance capacity in Sydney is emerging mainly as a combination of State-led governmental initiatives as well as improved horizontal coordination at the subregional level.

GOVERNING AUSTRALIAN CITIES: THE INTERGOVERNMENTAL CONTEXT

Australia is a three-tier federalist polity. The Commonwealth forms the federal level. Six "States" and two "Territories"[2] are the federate entities that form the intermediate tier. The local level is formed by 667 "local councils."[3] All three levels play a significant, albeit different, role in governing Australian metropolitan areas.[4]

The Commonwealth (federal government) sets the context through its policies on immigration, trade, housing, and welfare. According to the rules of Australian fiscal federalism, the federal government also controls the flow of money raised as tax (especially income tax, corporation tax, capital gains tax, and the Goods and Services Tax) and then passed on to State and local governments in the forms of grants. The Commonwealth also regulates the extent to which States can borrow money, which has a major impact on the State's ability to fund expenditures on urban infrastructure, such as public transport. However, with a few exceptions, the federal government leaves direct policies on urban development planning and infrastructure provision to the lower levels. "State governments" are the "main players in the game" (Forster 2004, p. 142), as they are responsible for a number of policies crucial to urban development. They define area-wide planning strategies, they run the public housing bodies, they provide roads, public education, health, police, public transport, and recreational and cultural services, as well as other key utilities, such as water and sewerage. Local councils are the least powerful level of administration in Australia: they have no constitutional status and are basically creatures of the States, expected to provide services important to the local community on the basis of their own funds raised through property tax. Local governments are responsible for road maintenance, drainage, and sewage disposal, and administer local building regulations and health bylaws. In addition, they provide a range of community, recreational, and cultural services, for which they receive financial support from the higher levels of government. It has to be noted that, in comparison with other member countries of the Organisation of Economic Co-operation and Development (OECD), the range of services for which Australian local governments are responsible is rather narrow (McNeil 1997). These governments' genuine competences have been summarized as the "three R's": rates, roads, and rubbish. The real significance of local government in terms of urban planning lies in their local control of the development approval process, a role that has led to periodic scandals involving corrupt and dubious local development outcomes. Nevertheless, even this power is essentially controlled by the State, and there are several current cases where local councils have been forcibly removed, with State appointing an administrator to run council business, largely as a result of local development controversies. In addition, local councils are empowered to raise development levies from all new developments in order to pay for local infrastructure provision that is associated with the development. It is their necessary role in connection with development control that local government plays an important role in translating State planning policies into physical outcomes on the ground.

Stilwell and Troy (2000) have argued that this multilevel system of shared competencies and responsibilities has given rise to two major lines of conflict in the governing of Australian cities. The first line of conflict concerns the relationships between the federal and State governments. It feeds on vertical fiscal imbalance, that is, the discrepancy between the constitutional division of competencies and the actual distribution of resources engaged for action. Although the powers of the federal government are constitutionally restrained, it controls the bulk of tax revenues. Indeed, approximately three-quarters of the total tax revenues are raised by the federal government, whereas States raise about 20 percent and local governments 4 percent (Stilwell and Troy 2000). State governments are therefore dependent on fund transfers from the Commonwealth. The share of specific-purpose grants and payments has steadily increased since the early 1970s, thereby illustrating the expansion of federal control over expenditures administered by the States. This has led to conflicts between the States and the federal government, over who determines urban service investments and delivery. Such conflicts are particularly significant in periods of diverging political majorities on the federal and State levels. This is particularly the case at the time of writing, with a Liberal Commonwealth government and Labor governments in all the States and Territories.

The second and, with respect to urban governance, most significant intergovernmental tension is the one leading to conflicts between local councils and the States. It stems from the tension between local interests and the regional scope necessary for planning the development of the wider metropolitan area. It is clear that the implementation of area-wide planning strategies developed by the State government can only be successful if the regional goals and objectives translate into the local planning regulations made by local governments. But the compliance of local government to area-wide strategic objectives cannot simply be assumed. Australian local government has been described as an arena of "suburban backlash" (Forster 2004, p. 156), where elected council members easily back NIMBY protest against area-wide planning decisions. More sympathetic observers view such protests as an expression of a participatory political culture at the local level and welcome it as a corrective ensuring that urban policies cannot be colonized by developers' interests but produce some diffuse public interest (McGuirk 2003). In spite of limited statutory power, local governments represent major veto-players. Even though the States can be seen to "act as a metropolitan government" (Stilwell and Troy 2000, p. 910) on the basis of the formal division of powers, the behavior of local government, and especially its willingness or its ability to deliver planning decisions that comply with broader strategic plans, is decisive for governance in Australian metropolitan areas.

GLOBALIZATION AND URBAN-REGIONAL RESTRUCTURING IN SYDNEY

In many ways, the recent growth of Sydney represents an outcome of the process of integration of the city into the global economy that has effectively taken Sydney to the position of being Australia's only recognizably global city (Searle 1996; Connell 2000). National governments since the 1980s have pursued neoliberal economic and trade policies to better integrate Australia into the flows of international capitalism, especially through tariff reduction and financial deregulation. The consequential growth of business-to-business tertiary employment, especially in the financial and property services sectors, as well as the expansion of "knowledge" economy employment servicing a rapidly expanding Asia-Pacific region, has benfited Sydney much more than other Australian cities (NSW Department of Planning 2005; McGuirk 2005).

The result has been not only a rapidly expanding city that has achieved a position as the leading "gateway" city for immigrants to Australia, but also an increasingly economically polarized city (Randolph and Holloway 2005). Sydney's "Global Arc" of higher order internationally focused employment stretches from Chatswood and

North Sydney to the north of the Central Business District (CBD) through to the airport in the south (figure 10.1). Widened economic polarities have had a clear expression in a widening spatial differentiation, with parts of Western Sydney being effectively left behind in the globalized city economy (Fagan and Dowling 2005). Here, economic growth has been underpinned by decentralizing manufacturing, distributive industries, and lower-level service and public sector employment related to local population growth rather than to the global economy that dominates the east of the city.

This economic differentiation, plus the sustained low-density expansion of the western suburbs of Sydney after the 1950s, has resulted in the emergence of Western Sydney as a distinctive subregion in its own right. Over the last half century, the western suburbs have effectively accounted for much of the city's growth. In the 20 years up to 2001, 62 percent of Sydney's population increase took place in the 14 local government areas that make up Western Sydney. Future population growth is also expected to take place mainly in these areas (NSW Department of Planning 2005).

However, suburbanization in Western Sydney in the 1950s, '60s, and '70s was primarily fueled by the outward movement of moderate- to lower-income households seeking cheap, affordable homes. This was strongly linked to the postwar boom in home ownership, although large areas of housing were also developed by the public housing authority, the NSW State Housing Commission, both for sale and rental to low-income households. The resulting impact on Sydney's social geography, and the basis of its subsequent regionalization and political divisions, was profound. In the city's east, the increasing concentration of higher incomes in the northern suburbs, North Shore, and eastern and southern suburbs has only intensified in recent decades, as gentrification linked to global economy employment in these areas has effectively excluded those on lower incomes (Randolph 2004).

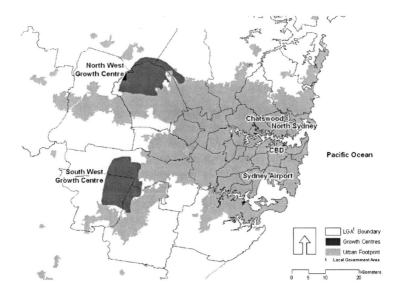

Figure 10.1 The Sydney metropolitan area.

The result has been the emergence of a strong regionalization trend, as Sydney has grown westward, reinforced by a bifurcation in the benefits of Sydney's global city status. The western suburbs, divided by class, politics, and attitude from the rest of Sydney, is now largely self-generating itself as the region grows further. A recent study of the attitudes of Western Sydney residents found that the vast majority identified strongly with the region and relatively few ventured to the eastern half of the city on a regular basis, except for the small minority who worked in the east or in the CBD (Randolph et al. 2001).

The local political impacts of rapid suburbanization of Western Sydney were profound. Growth proceeded with too little regard for the need for adequate infrastructure to support the population. As a result, by the 1970s, Western Sydney had developed major infrastructure deficits: roads, public transport, hospitals, schools, cultural facilities and local amenities, and sewerage, to name but a few. This infrastructure deficit was compounded by the region's relative lowly socioeconomic position. The political rivalry between west and east Sydney has been driven, in part, by the former's demands to "catch up" on this infrastructure deficit. The relatively low political clout of Western Sydney has meant this catch-up process has been slow. As a result, Western Sydney councils have long cooperated in order to conduct lobbying for greater resources, despite differing political allegiances.

THE FAILURE OF STRUCTURAL TERRITORIAL REFORM IN METROPOLITAN SYDNEY

As a consequence of exacerbated suburban growth and the lack of any political imperatives to reform local government structure, the geopolitical fragmentation of the Sydney metropolitan area is extremely high (table 10.1) but quite typical for Australia. Indeed, among other Australian cities, only Brisbane—thanks to annexation of suburbs in 1924—has an institutional structure that is comparable to the situation found in other OECD countries. All other major Australian metropolitan areas (i.e., Sydney, Melbourne, Adelaide, Perth) are roughly three to ten times more fragmented than their comparable counterparts in other countries (Hoffmann-Martinot and Sellers 2005).

This fragmented nature of the Sydney metropolitan area has led to calls for structural reforms in the past. Three avenues have been pursued, with different degrees of success. The first avenue was the idea of reducing fragmentation by creating new governmental authorities on an area-wide scale. This had already been conceived in the early twentieth

Table 10.1 Population, suburbanization rate and geopolitical fragmentation in Sydney: 1981–2001

Year of census	Overall population	Suburbanization rate	Number of local governments	Median population of local government areas	Local governments per 100,000	Index of geopolitical fragmentation*
1981	3,204,697	99.76 %	44	63,237	1.37	5.71
1991	3,518,773	99.69 %	45	63,524	1.28	4.13
2001	3,948,015	99.05%	45	70,009	1.14	1.2

Source: Australian Bureau of Statistics, Census Data for the Sydney Capital City Statistical Division.
Note: * This index was developed by Zeigler and Brunn (1980) and is computed by dividing the number of local governments per 100,000 inhabitants by the percentage of the overall metropolitan population of the core city.

century, mostly under the influence of experience in the United Kingdom and with the example of the London County Council in mind—the world's first metropolitan government, created in 1889 (Goldsmith 2005). However, an attempt to establish a metropolitan government for Greater Sydney foundered in 1915. As Spearritt (2000) argues, the main reason for the rejection of the relevant bill in the NSW State parliament was the opposition from the central city's financial and commercial interests, fearing loss of influence after a dilution of their electoral power basis.

Amalgamation of local governments into larger units has been a second route toward reducing governmental fragmentation in the Australian metropolitan areas (Forster 2004). In Sydney, however, this movement was heavily influenced by the differing attitudes of the various NSW State governments. Indeed, the history of local government amalgamations in the Sydney metropolitan area appears as a "one step forward, one step back" process, heavily driven by party political considerations. Whereas significant amalgamations were enacted by a Labor-dominated NSW government after World War II, some of them were undone again in the 1960s by a Liberal State government. In the following decades, amalgamations and reseparations more or less followed the change of political majorities at the State level, with the territory of the City of Sydney being the major issue at stake. Whereas Labor governments wanted it to be larger (and encompass suburbs with a strong Left electoral basis), the Liberal State governments advocated that the territory of the city of Sydney be confined to the CBD (where their electoral basis was strong). In the process, the borders of the city of Sydney expanded and contracted no less than five times since World War II, the latest move being an expansion that occurred in early 2004, when the City was amalgamated with the adjoining South Sydney Council by the current Labor government. Many observers have therefore claimed that, rather than driven by the objective to reduce institutional fragmentation, local government amalgamations in the Sydney metropolitan area essentially follow an agenda of gerrymandering in a "struggle for town hall" (Sproats and May 2004).

The third avenue toward structural reform—albeit of a less compelling type than area-wide authorities or amalgamations—has been the creation of Regional Organisations of Councils (ROC). These are joint bodies of local governments stabilizing voluntary cooperation in various policy fields. In some States (NSW and Queensland), regional groupings of local governments have been used for advisory purposes since World War II. In the 1970s, this approach was promoted on a national scale under the Whitlam federal government (see McPhail 1978), providing seed money for the setting up of ROCs, which were then used to direct federal funds to local governments. Although the following federal governments stopped this active support, voluntary regional cooperation had gained enough momentum for the ROCs to persist through joint funding by the constituent local authorities. In the Sydney metropolitan area, there are currently five ROCs. Although their relevance and their degree of activity vary considerably, some ROCs are well supported by their constituent local governments and effectively act as bodies for regional lobbying, research, and policy development. Nevertheless, they are limited by their nature as a nonautonomous political institution within Australian federalism and are, therefore, very weak.

To sum up, the existing institutional divisions of the Sydney metropolitan area have proven extremely resistant to change. In the face of the challenges ahead, the issue of governance in the metropolitan area has recently become a major topic of concern. But the capacity to govern this area, as we will see, flows from other avenues than structural institutional reform. On the one hand, efforts to define and implement area-wide frameworks of strategic planning have intensified since the late 1990s, and the latest developments suggest that the state of NSW has regained a willingness to exert political leadership on questions of metropolitan development. On the other hand, elements of subregional governance have emerged based on a variety of institutions, organizations, and networks. This is particularly noticeable in the Western Sydney region, where governance capacity has emerged as a response to the suburban expansion pushing ever westward in the 50 years after 1945.

STRENGTHENING GOVERNMENT CAPACITIES: THE LATEST METROPOLITAN STRATEGY

Given the highly geopolitical fragmentation of Australian metropolitan areas, strategic planning has traditionally played a major role for area-wide governance. Various strategic plans have been elaborated in all Australian metropolitan areas over the twentieth century, basically under the responsibility of the States. These "metropolitan planning strategies" are currently the only explicit guidance instrument for urban development at a metropolitan scale. They usually consist of an assessment of development trends and future challenges and outline the policies required to meet these challenges and channel future development in desirable paths (Gleeson et al. 2004).

Metropolitan planning in Sydney[5] goes back to early initiatives in the first three decades of the twentieth century, when planning emerged on the basis of environmental protest and lobbying, articulating planning ideals in a fragmented and issue-based way that eventually led to rudimentary ordinances enacted by local governments. More comprehensive efforts were taken in the period after World War II, characterized by the erection by the State government of an administrative planning machine, inspired by British town and country planning. The first area-wide plan for Sydney, the "County of Cumberland Plan," was elaborated in 1948, based on land-use and development control in order to manage the haphazard growth of suburban areas. However, in the face of rapid population growth that made predictions obsolete, the council came under increasing pressure to release more land for housing to the west of the city (Winston 1957). A new Strategic Planning Authority was created at the State level, which reviewed the Cumberland plan and came forward with the "Sydney Region Outline Plan" in 1968. The new plan, this time based on contemporary Scandinavian planning ideas, offered strategic guidance in a context of projected high rates of economic and demographic growth, identifying corridors of growth combined with suburban town centres, soon complemented with a matching metropolitan freeway network. In other words, it "planned for the suburban dream of a home in the sun and a car in the garage" (Spearrit and De Marco 1988, p. 29). However, during the 1980s, there were growing concerns over the environmental impacts of this low-density fringe development, the high costs of providing services (water, sewerage, and electricity), shortfalls in human services infrastructure, growing transport problems, and so on. In the search for an alternative to sprawling growth, a new strategic plan was developed by the State planning agency, the Department of Environment and Planning. The metropolitan strategy released in 1988 featured the goal of urban consolidation as one of its corner stones, that is, an increase of population density by the use of surplus land for housing, promotion of medium-density housing, smaller lot sizes, and an increased proportion of townhouses and flats in new release areas as well as within the existing urban footprint. This "historic shift in spatial orientation" (Freestone 2000, p. 129) of the 1988 plan was perpetuated in the subsequent plans, "Cities for the 21st Century" (1995) and "Shaping our Cities" (1999). Both built on the mix of critical planning issues familiar since the 1988 plan: sustained population growth, mismatches between jobs and homes, increased automobile use, and environmental stress. And both plans aim at tackling these issues through a policy mix organized around the promotion of compact urban form via consolidation and ecological sustainability via rigorous environmental assessment. This aim of working toward a more compact urban form through infill development (the process of developing vacant or underused land) is also emphasized in the latest Sydney Metropolitan Strategy, entitled "City of Cities" (NSW Department of Planning 2005). In some contrast to the tone of the other plans, the latest strategy contains a strong focus on the issue of maintaining the economic viability of Sydney as a global city. Indeed, it is primarily concerned with the economic structure of the metropolitan area, rather than its residential or other uses, with a transport framework designed in large part to circulate flows round the suburbs and into and through Sydney's "global" core.

The overall goals of metropolitan planning have roughly remained the same since the 1988 plan with its shift toward a concentrated rather than a dispersed pattern of growth. However, a change in the operational approach is clearly detectable in the plans elaborated since then. The blueprint approach geared toward goals over static outcomes evident in the earlier plans has gradually given way to a more de-spatialized and process-oriented approach. Metropolitan planning is no longer seen as the drafting of master plans to be implemented by State agencies, but more as an activity of managing a process that binds the agencies with a major stake in Sydney's development in a coordinated approach. Some writers see this as an expression of a supposedly neoliberal and antistatist climate. They fear that comprehensiveness of planning will be lost and planning will whither away in the process (Freestone 2000) or will be more and more geared toward the needs of the development industry demanding a watering down of the ecological and social emphases that are considered impractical (Khan and Piracha 2003). Others, however, see it in line with "scholarly and critical commentary [continuing] to oppose the rational technocratic idea that the public interest is a straightforward, unitary ideal, which experts can readily comprehend" and point toward "the need for more *negotiative* and *deliberative* policy making in planning, in which a plurality of (sometimes) opposing interests is assumed" (Gleeson et al. 2004, p. 353, original emphasis). The shift from outcome-oriented to process-oriented planning in Sydney's various metropolitan planning initiatives can be seen to echo the shift toward "new regionalism," emphasizing the idea that the area-wide governance ultimately results from the ability to produce coordination among stakeholders through collaborative processes and voluntary cooperation.

This collaborative approach toward area-wide governance notwithstanding, there is evidence that the State has reaffirmed and effectively strengthened its leadership in the process. The implementation of the 1995 and 1999 metropolitan strategies was hampered by the low profile that the State intended to play, restraining itself to the role of an enabler rather than actively regulating and/or engaging huge amounts of government money. In stark contrast to that picture, the release of the latest "City of Cities" metropolitan strategy has been accompanied by the creation of powerful instruments in the hand of the State, helping to ensure the implementation of the goals contained in the strategy. Among the more significant of these instruments, there is the imposition of levies on development profits in order to fund public infrastructure provision for new development areas, as well as a revision of the State's planning legislation, adopted in 2006, making it easier for the State government to amend or revoke local development control plans. Additionally, the State government has committed significant budget volumes to the deployment of public infrastructure (e.g., public transport) as part of the realization of the metropolitan strategy. It is yet too early to assess the practical use and useability of these instruments for realizing the goals of the current strategy—not least in the light of the turmoil they have caused with major stakeholders, such as the development industry (opposed to development levies) and the local councils (opposed to new State planning powers). Nevertheless, they are undoubtedly evidence to "suggest a marked return to the strong state institutional capacities and political drive of prior governance paradigm" (McGuirk 2005, p. 66).

GOVERNANCE FROM BELOW: THE EMERGING MOSAIC OF SUBREGIONAL GOVERNANCE IN WESTERN SYDNEY

The emergence of a distinct Western Sydney region as a political entity has been the second defining feature of the evolving governance of Sydney. This was stimulated by the formation of the Western Sydney Regional Organization of Councils (WSROC) in the mid-1970s, representing 11 councils to the west and northwest of the city, supported by funding from the councils. In many ways, it can be argued that the development of a strong regional voice has been the result of a deficit in governance at the regional level in Sydney. While Sydney's overall planning is a State responsibility, it clearly creates strong tensions at the local political level. State government has to play a role managing competing demands from across the State, notably between metropolitan and nonmetropolitan regions. It cannot be seen to be too preferential in its treatment of resource allocation between these competing regional demands (although this is far from the case in reality). WSROC has become the de facto voice of Western Sydney in the vacuum of any alternative vehicle to represent the region's evident problems (Gooding 2005).

These problems have their genesis in the unrestrained and largely unplanned suburban growth in the postwar period. The first strategic plan for Sydney released in 1952 did not anticipate the rate of the city's postwar population growth and therefore completely failed to restrain its suburban expansion (Spearritt 2000). However, as we noted above, this unplanned suburban expansion meant that many key infrastructure investments were not undertaken at the time. Additionally, new jobs were also difficult to attract to the region, especially more highly paid skilled trades in the manufacturing sector. By the 1970s, the onset of deindustrialization effectively took out many of those jobs that had moved west, and few were added in subsequent years. The net outcome was a major infrastructure deficit compounded by a deteriorating economic position. From this arose Western Sydney's increasing political and regional self-awareness, which has generated its own regional governance response.

In practice, what passes for regional governance at State level operates in the form of regional offices or districts of the various State departments. The result is a complex structure of power and resource allocation that militates against a unified and coordinated view of regional planning. Government tends to be conducted vertically through inward-looking departments and agencies, with little effective communication between them or an integrated approach to planning and implementation or much direct contact with the communities they serve. The proliferation of State-created quangos adds further to the chronic fragmentation of governance across the city with a lack of effective regional integration in planning. The latest addition in Western Sydney are the two Growth Centre Commissions set up in 2005 to oversee the rollout of the two major greenfield development areas on the southwestern and northwestern edge of the city designated under the 2005 Sydney Metropolitan Planning Strategy (under the 2005 "City of cities" metropolitan planning strategy).

However, in recent years, the incipient emergence of Western Sydney as a regional entity has led to a number of initiatives that have attempted to fill what is, to all intents and purposes, a regional governance deficit between the State and local levels. They also can be interpreted as expressions of the growing political clout of the region.

Demand for regional-level representation emerged in the 1990s from within the region in the form of a region-wide policy prioritizing initiative called TeamWest. Initiated by WSROC, TeamWest was launched in 1996 at a regional conference. TeamWest developed largely as a reaction to regional perceptions about the failure of earlier metropolitan strategies to deliver real results on the ground in Western Sydney. It was therefore very focused on implementation issues. It also explicitly recognized the need for a strong regional voice in an evolving global economy, one that operates between the levels of State government and local authorities on the ground. But in addition, TeamWest also recognized that "place management" approaches to specific localities where problems were deep seated, multifaceted, and long-standing would be critical to the success of policy implementation in the region. Place management approaches combine a focus on a locality—for example, town centres or neighborhoods suffering multiple deprivation—with an integrated and cross-agency approach to service delivery or planning. In other words, such initiatives tackle problems at the sub-local-authority spatial level. So, as well as recognising the need for regional level interventions, there was also a need for neighborhood-level interventions. A Greater Western Sydney Regional Priorities Group, made up of representatives from key regional organizations, including local councils (but not State or Federal government), was formed to coordinate and lead the identification of key regional policy priorities for the region.

However, the process was compromised by a reliance on financial support from both federal and State governments. This, together with the difficulty the process faced in getting its priorities adopted by the State government, despite the rhetoric of partnership and support for the process from the State, effectively neutered the effort. The initiative effectively petered out by 2003, by when the WSROC councils had become involved in their own response to the developing Metropolitan Strategy, culminating in the release of the "Western Sydney Regional Strategy" in 2004 (WSROC 2005). The strategy was an attempt to preempt the metropolitan strategy and set out the regions' own planning agenda. In the event, while the research and proposals contained in the Regional Strategy informed the State Department of Planning's deliberations about future development in the region, its recommendations were largely ignored in the actual rollout of the Metropolitan Strategy proposals. Nevertheless, the exercise of establishing TeamWest and the development of the Regional Strategy provided a major focus for the region's councils in developing a strong regional identity and profile and raised the bar in terms of how Western Sydney was perceived as a functioning urban region in its own right.

From this perspective, these regionally generated initiatives stimulated a very clear response from the State government. Shortly after TeamWest's launch, in December 1997, in what has been seen as a major breakthrough for the region and in response to strong lobbying by WSROC, the State government announced the creation of a new ministry, the minister assisting the premier on Western Sydney. The new minister established an Office for Western Sydney, based in the region, with a remit to provide strategic advice to the NSW government on Western Sydney issues and to facilitate partnerships between government agencies, regional businesses, and community organizations to encourage coordination of service delivery and regional initiatives in the Western Sydney region. In one stroke, the State government formally recognized the existence of Western Sydney as a regional entity and also that the particular problems associated with the region, noted above, required special treatment. At the same time, the NSW premiers department created its own Western Sydney Regional Coordinator in 1998, based in the region, to help "fast-track" strategic, large-scale, and complex investment projects in the Western Sydney region. Although these agencies still exist, their scope and functions have been substantially scaled back in recent years, to some extent reflecting the success in directing additional resources to the region and the more recent diversion of infrastructure issues into the development of the new Sydney Metropolitan Strategy.

The example of Western Sydney over the last 20 years illustrates the growing regionalization *within* Sydney of functional urban subareas with their own identity, as well as how government at State and local levels struggles to deal with spatially constituted issues that fall between the spatial scales at which their jurisdictional scope operates. The emergence of the regional governance "realms of action" might be taken to reflect the "globalization" of Sydney in the postindustrial era. But most significantly, while there are a number of other ROCs in the Sydney region, none have been able to project themselves to anything like the level of WSROC or attempted to successfully promote a regional agenda in the same way. As such, the case of Western Sydney has been very much a story of how the region's social and economic problems, compounded by its regional governance deficit, have found an expression in an emerging regional representational voice.

CONCLUSIONS

Sydney, as other Australian metropolitan areas, is increasingly exposed to the dynamics of a globalized capitalist economy, resulting in sustained urban growth. As it was largely unplanned and uncoordinated in earlier decades, this growth took place essentially as a low-density expansion of Sydney toward the west, lacking the adequate public infrastructure. In the process, the Sydney metropolitan area became increasingly polarized between the "global arc" of the city concentrated to the east, and the west being left behind. The changes in the regional structure of Sydney, in particular the growth of low-density suburban areas in the last 50 years, have been paralleled in other Australian cities, although the polarization effects of Sydney's global-city status since the 1980s have amplified the social differentiation here compared with these other cities (Forster 2006).

Today, Sydney faces increasing pressures to provide the urban amenities necessary for achieving or maintaining an internationally competitive urban economy. This means accommodating the ongoing and continuing growth in population, and particularly adapting and expanding the urban infrastructure capacity—especially in Western Sydney—needed to ensuring the functioning of the Sydney metropolitan area as a territorial system. Planning and public investments are clearly crucial to this process. In the past, strong intergovernmental conflicts and high fragmentation of the local government system, combined with strong opposition from the development industry against regulatory interventions, have resulted in a weakness of area-wide public governance. Recently, however, there is evidence that this governance deficit is being addressed, from above as much as from below. Indeed, current initiatives taken to strengthen area-wide governance capacity in Sydney not only entail the reaffirmation of the State's institutional capacities in the wake of the latest metropolitan strategy, but also the recognition of the role of regional bodies such as WSROC for the Western Sydney area.

At the time of writing, it is yet unclear whether this emerging metropolitan governance capacity will persist, especially in the face of increasing pressure from the development industry to loosen growth regulations and infrastructure requirements, as well as from the local councils opposed to the upscaling of planning powers at the State level. In this respect, it will be critical to find ways of increasing the legitimacy of governance measures taken for the sake of the metropolitan area as a whole. This suggests that the support of traditional government institutions at the State level, and, particularly, the involvement of elected politicians therein, remains a crucial resource for achieving public governance at the level of the Sydney metropolitan area.

NOTES

1. Research for this chapter was conducted during Daniel Kübler's visiting research fellowship at the City Futures Research Centre of the Faculty of the Built Environment at the University of New South Wales between December 2004 and April 2005.
2. The States (New South Wales, Victoria, Queensland, South Australia, Western Australia, and Tasmania) are the former British colonies that formed the Australian Commonwealth in 1901. There are also two major self-governing territories that are, de facto, treated as States. The Australian Capital Territory is a small area excised from the State of New South Wales in 1901 as the site for the national capital. The Northern Territory was excised from the State of South Australia in 1910.
3. Situation as of July 1, 2004 (ABS 2005, p. 19).
4. The expression "metropolitan area" echoes the concept of the Metropolitan Statistical Area (MSA), used by the U.S. Census Bureau to describe functionally integrated urban areas that have sprawled across institutional boundaries. The Australian Bureau of Statistics uses the concept of Capital City Statistical Division , representing "the city in a wider sense" (ABS 2005, p. 14), which is delineated on the basis of consultation with planners in order to contain the anticipated area of development of each State's or Territory's main urban region for a longer period.
5. For the following, see Spearrit and de Marco (1988), Spearrit (2000), Freestone (2000), McGuirk (2005).

CHAPTER 11

The New Ecology of Urban Governance: Special-Purpose Authorities and Urban Development

Dennis R. Judd and James M. Smith

Why Special Authorities?

Until very recently the literature on globalization mostly ignored the institutions of local governance and instead focused upon economic, social, and cultural transformations. But globalization has brought about a revolution in local political institutions that is as far-reaching as it is underappreciated. In recent decades, independent, quasi-public authorities have assumed most of the responsibility for major urban development projects and, in the process, become basic components in an increasingly complex local state (Erie 2002; Altshuler and Luberoff 2003; Flyvbjerg et al. 2003; Sellers 2002). In the United States, the United Kingdom (where they are referred to as quangos), and elsewhere, quasi-public authorities now administer undertakings ranging from huge megaprojects such as transportation networks and airports, to the infrastructure of tourism and downtown development, to neighborhood improvement and housing development. Nevertheless, most of the time, special-purpose authorities operate under the radar for most urban scholars and for broader publics. This is certain to change in the years ahead.

As Alan Altshuler and David Luberoff have noted, "Theorists of urban politics have paid scarce attention to mega-projects," because "mega-projects are usually constructed by regional and state agencies" and not by municipal governments (2003, p. 285). The tendency of scholars to focus on city governments has meant that urban scholarship has missed the most dynamic politics driving urban development for decades—the emergence of institutions that often dwarf the fiscal, administrative, and political capacity of general-purpose governments. Unless these institutions are taken into account, most of the development occurring within urban regions cannot be explained or even accounted for. Any discussion of urban development must go beyond municipalities, and any discussion of regionalism and regional development must go beyond general-purpose governments and their cooperative arrangements.

Within all large urban regions, a multitude of authorities have taken responsibility for transportation infrastructure (highways, roads, bridges, tunnels, mass transit, airports, seaports, harbors), water supply, wastewater management, solid waste disposal, and other services. In addition to these activities, special authorities by the dozen finance and manage tourism and entertainment facilities (such as convention centers, sports stadiums, museums, and urban entertainment districts). Even though these quasi-public authorities constitute much of the institutional fabric of urban governance, citizens are often unaware that they even exist. Paul Peterson believes that this is a good thing. In his view, special authorities are able to operate more efficiently than general-purpose governments because they are not bound by the rules that bind them to citizens:

> Operating like private firms, these independent authorities see little point in public discussion. Because it is in the city's interest to develop self financing projects that enhance the productivity of the community, there can be no place for the contentious group conflict that may characterize another policy arena.
>
> (Peterson 1981, P. 134)

General-purpose governments help support quasi-public authorities through subsidies and earmarked taxes; in addition these institutions are empowered to raise their own revenues by charging user fees, issuing tax-free bonds, establishing trust funds, and pursuing other financing mechanisms (Leigland 1995). Though they pursue public purposes and receive public funds, they generally conduct their business like private corporations. They do not have to hold public hearings and can claim proprietary control over information and financial information. And, most importantly, they need not worry about local electorates.

The rules under which special authorities operate help make them effective instruments of urban development because they can escape the political gridlock that often characterizes urban politics in the post-urban-renewal era (Altshuler and Luberoff 2003). The physical reconstruction of American cities in recent decades was made possible by a comprehensive restructuring of local public institutions and processes. Confronted by the fact that city government was too bureaucratic and fiscally limited to undertake expensive new projects, in the 1980s energetic mayors and other civic leaders pioneered the development of new institutions that could accomplish public purposes but would not be bound by the rules that frustrated general-purpose governments. These public-private authorities were able to operate much like private corporations, thereby avoiding public scrutiny of their operations (Perry 2003); they were often empowered to borrow money, issue bonds, and exercise critical powers such as eminent domain. These institutional arrangements are the key to understanding how fiscally strapped cities were able to build the facilities and undertake the ambitious projects necessary to support a local economy of tourism and entertainment.

Quasi-public authorities continue to multiply because they provide a mechanism for accomplishing development without the troubles associated with democratic participation and consultation. Public officials and the proponents of new facilities have become adept at bypassing the public (Eisinger 2000). Referenda on major capital projects were once the norm, but they had become increasingly rare by the 1990s. Where it was still necessary to ask voters to approve tax increases or bond issues for new facilities, a formidable coalition could be assembled to push for the new projects.

In this chapter, we begin our examination of quasi-public authorities by accepting the argument that they have been essential features of urban development in recent decades. Freed from the straitjacket of municipal authority, these new institutions have accomplished virtual miracles of urban revival. But the continuing proliferation of these institutions also raises fundamental issues about urban governance. To work as governance institutions, it is essential for them to make their activities fully transparent; by doing so they will become more corrigible, "capable of being corrected, reformed, or improved" (AHD 1982).

WHAT IS A SPECIAL AUTHORITY?

In the United States, special districts are the most common form of local government, as counted by the Census Bureau. Special districts have been growing in scope and power since the 1930s, during which they have become tools for distributing federal funds to local governments (Radford 2003). Though authorities have a considerable effect on governance, identifying one is not always easy task; most definitions within the literature remain ambiguous because the concept of special-purpose authorities covers a wide gamut—from authorities stretching across nations to finance megaprojects to tiny development districts (Axelrod 1992; Radford 2003). The U.S. Census Bureau's method for categorization is messy, and scholars have not always done much to clarify the definitions.

Kathryn Foster (1997) divides special authorities into two broad types—taxing districts and special-purpose public authorities. Taxing districts are entities "with the power to tax and levy special assessments" and comprise "elected governing boards," while public authorities are "government corporations without property-taxing powers" that "ordinarily operate under appointed rather than elected boards, with most appointments made by officials of the parent government . . . that created the district" (Foster 1997, p. 7). The distinction made by Foster is one often overlooked by scholars of public authorities, who tend to assume that all similar institutions are nonelected and nonresponsive to voters, when in fact large subsets of special districts have boards that are elected rather than appointed.

While Foster efficiently splits authorities into two groups, other scholars do not see the distinction so clearly. Jerry Mitchell (1999, p. 12) argues that "there is probably no such thing as a typical government corporation." In the United States, many doubts have been expressed about the Census Bureau's methods for identifying special district governments. Any census is unreliable because these governments come and go with some regularity; worse, they remain hidden even from the census because they are not required to register in most states. Some scholars assert that the count of special districts by the U.S. Census Bureau is almost useless because it leaves out many of the most influential agencies (Leigland 1990). In addition to single-purpose, small jurisdictional districts, Jameson Doig (1983, pp. 294–5) counted nearly 7,000 large public authorities and corporations that were left out of the Census Bureau's enumeration. The fact that scholars and government agencies are unclear as to what constitutes a special authority makes such authorities difficult to study, and this may be one significant reason why few scholars and agencies have attempted to do so.

URBAN DEVELOPMENT IN THE UNITED STATES:
A HISTORY OF CONSTRAINT

The projects undertaken by special-purpose authorities shape metropolitan growth and development at least as much as do elected local authorities. An inspection of city budgets can uncover only a portion—perhaps not even the most important portion—of the policy priorities of urban governments. City governments tend to provide basic services—what Paul Peterson (1981) has called allocational services utilized by all citizens, such as police, fire, and trash collection. These services tend to be noncontroversial and are often almost invisible because in most countries they are taken for granted as a part of daily life. But it is obvious that much bigger projects are being undertaken in the urban environment. If most of these projects cannot be found in city budgets, then where are they located? The answer to this question depends very much on the time period considered and the context in which the question is being asked.

Gerald Frug (1999) has issued a stern reminder that scholars have often overlooked the way in which state governments in the United States continue to limit their cities. In response, it should be noted that urban leaders have successfully devised a variety of strategies for overcoming constitutional and legal constraints. In the late nineteenth century, for example, the states reacted to the problem of municipal debt by trying to restrict the cities' ability to borrow and impose taxes. In 1868, an Iowa judge, John F. Dillon, led the charge to bring the cities to book when he enunciated the principle that cities "owe their origin to, and derive their powers and rights wholly from, the legislature" (1868). Still, cities found the resources to accomplish virtual miracles in expanding urban services and undertaking monumental capital works projects. The historian Jon Teaford has called these accomplishments an "unheralded triumph" (1984).

In the second half of the twentieth century, cities once again have accomplished an "unheralded triumph" in meeting daunting challenges. They came out of World War II facing a bundle of interconnected, intractable problems: the decay of downtown business districts, whole neighborhoods of obsolescent and dilapidated housing stock, and—something that would prove to be even more insidious in the years ahead—economic stagnation at the urban core. For the next half century, cities hemorrhaged population and business activity to the suburbs. In response, urban leaders have pioneered successive strategies of inner-city revival. From the 1950s to the late 1970s, urban leaders looked to the federal government to help bail them out of their problems. When federal funds began to dry up, a generation of "messiah mayors" (Teaford 1990) began preaching a gospel of self-help for their cities. Special authorities provided a way of escaping the limitations placed on municipal government; just as importantly, they offered a way around the equally severe limitations imposed by anti-tax sentiment among voters (Altshuler and Luberoff 2003). Many of the responsibilities of city government were off-loaded onto new institutions that could generate their own resources and that could be run like private corporations. It was the first step in the marriage between large infrastructure projects of the postindustrial city and the special-purpose authority.

Quasi-public authorities appeal to urban leaders for several reasons. First, they "represent a contemporary response to the need for alternative financing mechanisms. Because independent districts establish sources of revenue and spending capabilities separate from local governments and the general public, they are powerful tools for expanding the fiscal capabilities of communities that need more funds" (Porter et al. 1992, p. vi). Urban leaders came to understand that the capital available for urban development was not, and could not be, fixed by statute or otherwise. It could be created almost at will by creating new institutions capable of generating their own sources of revenue. This strategy is what has made the huge investment in urban infrastructure possible in the 1980s and thereafter. In only a few years billions of public dollars have been spent on urban entertainment and cultural districts, renovated waterfronts, aquariums, marketplaces, festival malls, and the other accoutrements of the tourism/entertainment complex. Municipal governments could not possibly have raised such resources. Cities have been involved in complicated deal making, offering to provide public infrastructure and amenities, to rezone or assemble parcels of land through the power of eminent domain, to reduce or withdraw taxes, or to subsidize private development. These activities have been essential but not sufficient. The new resources brought to the table by special authorities were crucial.

Second, these institutions provide a useful way for elected officials to play a kind of shell game in which they can take credit for new development but shift the actual process of development to an arena that seems nonpolitical. Because they rely on revenue rather than general-obligation bonds, and on revenue sources such as user fees rather than taxing authority, special authorities can undertake development projects without seeking voter approval. Special authorities often must lobby their parent governments for political or fiscal support, but because their activities are defined as nonpolitical and necessary for economic growth, they rarely encounter serious difficulties.

Third, quasi-public authorities can extend their reach beyond the borders of individual governments; geographic boundaries can be ambiguous and often undefined. This results in a "wider canvas" for government decisions and developmental visions (Doig 1983, p. 298). The broader an authority's power, the more ambitious development officials can be. What determines the breadth of an authority's canvas is typically its state enabling legislation, that is, the powers laid out for the authority by state officials. In some cases, the power of authorities may be very specific—aimed at enabling an institution to carry out one task within a very limited space. At other times, however, rules may be extremely vague, allowing the special authority to interpret its powers very broadly. The most famous case is the Triborough Bridge and Tunnel Authority, which was granted the power to build bridges as well as their "approaches." The master builder Robert Moses interpreted this to mean that the authority had the power to build roads throughout the boroughs of New York as well as all roads that indirectly led to his bridges (Caro 1975). Robert Caro's interpretation is that it was in Moses's nature, and in the nature of all public authorities, to interpret their powers broadly.

A great advantage of special authorities arises directly from their nondemocratic character. Because they operate essentially as private corporations, they are able to engage in the kind of complicated, fast-action deal making that private entrepreneurs rely upon. These were urban development practices that cities had not witnessed before, and many required new approaches to the process. The deals that public officials must strike with private developers to assemble land, provide public amenities, and guarantee sufficient profits are so complicated that it is often thought impractical to consult the public (Frieden and Sagalyn 1989). As large-scale public planning has given way to the deal making involved in the assembly of these types of development, the most important decisions tend to be made in behind-the-scenes day-to-day negotiations (Fainstein 2001).

The case of Boston's Quincy Market/Faneuil Hall development is instructive. The city of Boston provided $12 million—almost 30 percent of the total cost of the project—and gave the Rouse Corporation a ninety-nine-year lease on the property. In exchange, the city was guaranteed a minimum annual cash payment plus a portion of income from store rents (Frieden and Sagalyn 1989). This part of the deal was arrived at in intense negotiations and was not known by anyone outside an inner circle. Because of the significant risk to the city, public exposure would certainly have provoked opposition.

In most cases, deals such as Boston's were small compared with the activities of special authorities. Independent authorities gain access to taxes and other sources of revenue, sometimes in direct competition with cities and other governments. For example, the McCormick Place convention center, the world's largest, and the renovated Navy Pier entertainment complex in Chicago are administered by the Metropolitan Pier and Exposition Authority. This authority is governed by a board appointed by the Chicago mayor and the Illinois governor. The state of Illinois designates $98 million annually, derived from revenues from taxes (mainly a tax on cigarette sales) to pay off previous bonds for construction and remodeling (1998, 1999). Not only has the state paid for the convention center complex (which is undergoing another expansion), but the pier and exposition authority has also floated a $108 million tax-exempt bond issue to build and lease the building housing the Hyatt Regency McCormick Place Hotel (Fulton 2002).

It may be supposed that special authorities have a special appeal in the United States because of the structure of federalism that makes American cities more dependent on their own resources than elsewhere. H. V. Savitch and Paul Kantor (2002) have shown that intergovernmental support is a significant variable in determining development strategies and policies throughout Western Europe and North America. But there are striking similarities between cities that transcend differences in governmental structure and political culture: (1) all cities are dependent on their own capacities to generate revenue and (2) all cities are subservient to some higher level of government within their own national system (Gurr and King 1987). Constraints on local governments, then, are universal. In addition, since at least the 1980s, cities have become entrepreneurial everywhere as a result of changes in governmental policies aimed at reducing local dependence and forcing cities to assist in the restructuring their local economies (Judd and Parkinson 1989). Accordingly, special authorities have become ubiquitous features of urban governance in Europe and elsewhere as well (Graham and Marvin 2001).

THE CHALLENGE OF ACCOUNTABILITY

Assessing the accountability of special authorities is not as straightforward as it might seem. Because they are brought into being by general-purpose governments, it would appear that they remain accountable to elected officials. However, Foster (1997) argues that "districts have sovereignty over their administrative and financial affairs and enjoy substantial freedom from oversight by their parent government" (p. 10). In addition to the formal powers that give them substantial autonomy, special authorities also devise strategies to maintain their independence. And they often become major political forces in their own right. In their classic study of New York politics, Wallace S. Sayre and Herbert Kaufman (1960) found that, in the case of mid-twentieth-century New York, "the leaders of the authorities are major figures in the decisions and actions that distribute the prizes of politics" (p. 337). Attempts to make special authorities accountable must recognize that these authorities are political in nature, always on the lookout for ways to promote their own projects and enhance their fiscal and administrative capacity.

In the case of the professional football and baseball stadiums in Baltimore, an agency of the state government, the Maryland Stadium Authority, financed two stadiums through proceeds from a sports lottery offered through the Maryland State Lottery (Norris 2003). The campaign to build the sports stadiums was guided by this new agency, which commissioned studies to show that they would have a powerfully positive impact on Baltimore's economy. When another state agency followed with its own studies, it reduced the estimated impact, but independent studies sharply contested even these estimates as unrealistic, concluding that stadium development brought virtually no measurable economic benefit (Norris 2003).

The political nature of special authorities is illustrated in the case of the Denver Metropolitan Stadium District, which was created in 1990 by the Colorado legislature as a means of pushing forward plans for a new baseball stadium. The bill establishing the district did not contain financing mechanisms, because any that might have been proposed would have ignited controversy. Instead, the task of lining up political support for a new stadium was left to the seven-member Stadium District Board. Securing financing was more a political than a fiscal exercise. In close collaboration with the city of Denver, the board ran an astute campaign that kept voters in the metropolitan counties outside Denver in the dark about whether the stadium would be built close to or within their own jurisdictions. The uncertainties about location carried the day. In August 1990, voters in the six-county district passed a sales tax levy to build the stadium; large majorities in the city and an adjacent county overcame a losing margin elsewhere (Clarke and Saiz 2003: pp. 183–4). A few months later, just as many voters had suspected, the fix had been in all along, and the stadium was built in downtown Denver.

In addition to the special authorities established to finance and administer particular facilities, redevelopment corporations also have proliferated, often to administer the funds made available from tax incentive finance districts (TIFs). In the U.S. context TIFs are significant because they are a "departure from the traditional legal and political norm of uniform municipal action within a municipality" (Weber 2003, p. 622). TIF corporations capture a share of local taxing powers and keep it for themselves and are also able to market bonds to investors on the basis of the taxes that are expected to be collected on land that is slated for redevelopment in the future. The proceeds from bonds are generally used to make public improvements that will lure more private investment; to keep things going indefinitely, they are able to capture much of this benefit as well. In 2002, there were more than 130 TIFs in the city of Chicago and 217 in suburban Cook County (Weber 2003, p. 627). They are spreading rapidly across the United States, but not much is known about their effects upon urban fiscal structures.

TRANSPARENCY AND CORRIGIBILITY

The challenge of reform is to preserve some of the advantages of special authorities while making them transparent and corrigible. Mitchell (1992, p. 9) presents this paradox by observing, "The core issue is how to build an accountability framework that brings together political responsiveness and functional expertise . . . The difficult task is to find specific ways that authorities can satisfy the broad public interest as they develop narrowly focused projects." An absence of public accountability raises troubling questions. In the 1950s, urban renewal authorities regularly abused their powers. Transportation authorities rammed highways through urban neighborhoods. Today, convention centers, sports stadiums, and other undertakings connected to the infrastructure of urban tourism, generally, are built without attempts to seek public approval, even though general-purpose governments must often pledge their full faith and credit as backing for bonds.

The proliferation of special authorities also has significant ramifications for regional governance. Just as the intense competition among cities makes it difficult to achieve meaningful cooperation on the regional level, the entrepreneurial activities of special-purpose authorities fracture urban regions. The literature on public policy has shown that policy making at the national level tends to fragment into constellations of actors interested in particular issues and problems (Smith 1993). These constellations typically begin taking shape with an exchange of information between state actors and groups; as the policy community becomes firmly established, it attempts to police its ranks, keep out unwanted interlopers, and institutionalize its privileged status through the creation of administrative mechanisms of policy implementation.

Graham and Marvin (2001) have described the emergence of such networks in the building of urban infrastructure. In water and waste management, energy provision, telecommunications, and transport, specialized participants have sought to 'unbundle' infrastructure development from local power structures by establishing closed policy communities composed of local participants and actors embedded within globalized circuits of infrastructure development (Graham and Marvin 2001: pp. 172–3). In a similar vein, with respect to megaprojects for highways, airports, and rail transit, Altshuler and Luberoff have noted that "local interests gained leverage in national politics during the 1940s and 1950s by joining national industry-based coalitions with much broader agendas" (2003, p. 285).

The new generation of special-purpose authorities are not only local—they are both local and global. They interact with municipalities and with one another but also forge linkages with nonlocal interests, and these linkages are often crucial to their political autonomy and muscle. The politics surrounding convention centers illustrates this point. The staffs of convention centers are closely tied with and identify with the vast meetings industry, and they turn to this industry for information and support when pushing for expanded or new facilities. Consultants' studies are the necessary prelude to bond issuances and tax referenda (where these are necessary). Consulting reports establish an asymmetry of information that gives proponents a monopoly over information, so that opponents appear to be uninformed and biased. More generally, the reports also form the basis of a standard narrative of urban decline and growth that ties the construction or expansion of a convention facility to the future prospects and image of the city.

Because a broad array of consultants and industry specialists provide all relevant financial, public relations, marketing, and expertise to all cities, the same political process is replicated over and over again and from place to place (Sanders 1992). Engineering and architectural services are often offered by a handful of national firms. National public relations firms are also often hired to manage promotional campaigns, often from concept to tax approval campaign to construction. Likewise, national public accounting and public finance consulting firms with specialties in project finance and cost-benefit analysis provide the principal justifications for individual projects, and they justify public subsidies through feasibility and impact analyses (Sanders 1999). At the heart of these reports are data and information gathered from industry associations and publications. In turn, accounting and bond-rating firms rely on the same sources of data and on consulting reports from the same firms retained by cities. It is a remarkably closed community.

Sports stadiums provide a similar example. Special authorities established to promote stadiums have learned to be adept in building political support for new stadiums financed through public subsidies. Because teams sometimes move, or can threaten to do so, sports cartels and team owners find it easy to persuade cities to meet their demands. Studies consistently show that sports stadiums do not bring measurable benefits to local economies and that some may even have a negative effect by replacing some local spending with expenditures that exit the local economy quickly (Baade 1996; Rosentraub et al. 1994; Coates and Humphreys 1999). Nevertheless, in alliance with mayors, civic elites, and sports cartels, sports authorities have been generally successful in their bids to secure public funding.

In their ambitious study of megaproject politics in Europe and elsewhere, but with a special focus on the building of the English channel tunnel, the Great Belt link connecting Denmark and the European continent, and the Oresund link connecting Sweden and Denmark, Bent Flyvbjerg, Nils Bruzelius, and Werner Rothengatter (2003) found an interesting pattern: historically, advocates for these megaprojects have invariably overestimated use and revenues and underestimated costs. The reasons are not hard to find. Working in a closed world of supporters of their projects, participants and the consultants who advise them share an interest in moving forward and for generating the data to make this possible. As a result, "whether we like it or not, megaproject development is currently a field where little can be trusted, not even—some would say especially not—numbers produced by analysts" (Flyvbjerg et al. 2003, p. 5).

Flyvbjerg et al. propose that the only way out of this problem is to make the process of evaluating megaprojects far more transparent and participatory. Thus, they urge that all documents and relevant information must be made readily available to the public and other "stakeholder" groups. In this way governments may act less as the promoters of risky projects and more as intermediaries between the public and project managers, with the goal of ensuring that accountability is always given highest priority (Flyvbjerg et al. 2003). To support this process, Flyvbjerg et al. stress the importance of regular public hearings, frequent opinion surveys, and advisory committees for keeping project managers accountable.

As a way of formalizing these processes, Flyvbjerg et al. refer to a "regulatory regime" designed to limit the considerable fiscal risk associated with megaprojects. The principal value guiding this regime would be the assumption that the goal of a project should not only be its completion, but its completion in a specific fashion (here, their main concern is fiscal responsibility). The regulatory regime would require that investors assume the opportunities as well as the risks associated with large projects; governments would be barred from protecting private investors from losses (Flyvbjerg et al. 2003). Finally, all costs associated with a project, including other infrastructure required to make it accessible and useful, would have to be considered.

Though they are skeptical of voter referenda as a means of ensuring accountability (with well-financed referenda in California serving as a sobering lesson), Alan Altshuler and David Luberoff nevertheless believe that governments should make greater efforts to involve the voting public in some manner. They propose three necessary conditions: questions on referenda should be "restricted to up or down expressions of opinion on projects already approved by the locality's duly constituted representative institution(s)"; it should be a difficult task for development critics to put an issue on the referendum ballot; and "elected representatives should be free to reaffirm their original decision, even in the face of a referendum defeat" (Altshuler and Luberoff 2003, p. 293). It is obvious, however, that to some degree these recommendations contradict one another; additionally, Altshuler and Luberoff do not indicate how their proposal would be politically practical.

The way that special authorities were established in Los Angeles provides a model for achieving a level of accountability. Rather than turning to independent regional authorities for infrastructure development, as in New York, Los Angeles kept the departments of water and power, harbor, and airports within the city government. In doing so, the city kept them "under the nominal control of mayors and city councils," where they could "serve as coherent instruments of municipal policies involving central-city development, regional dominion, and global competitiveness" (Erie 2002, p. 139). The proprietary agencies claim nearly half of the city budget and, in 1996–1997, accounted for over three-fourths of city-issued debt (Erie 2002).

Jameson Doig (2001) has suggested that a sharp distinction be drawn between the narrowly focused work of "experts" and the broader responsibilities of politicians. He argues that

> "the decision on where to place an airport, and how large it should be depend mainly on the attitudes of elected officials and the region's voters . . . how to construct the airport, bring aircraft in and out safely, route ground traffic inside the airport, provide adequate security— should be decided mainly by experts not public vote".
>
> (Doig 2001, p. 21).

Any and all of these remedies would help to make special authorities more accountable. We agree with Flyvbjerg et al., however, that transparency is the singular issue. Development could still go forward even if special authorities were required to open their books for public inspection, hold public hearings on major proposals, release all consultants' reports, and issue comprehensive reports to the general-purpose governments that created them. "Transparency" is the mantra of economists who claim that it is the fundamental principle underlying free markets. It is also the fundamental principle underlying democratic governance. Quasi-public authorities must become transparent to become corrigible.

LEADERSHIP, PARTNERSHIP, AND THE DEMOCRATIC CHALLENGE

INTRODUCTION TO PART III

A theme that unites the four chapters in Part III of this book is a concern to enhance the quality of local democracy. When viewed in a historical perspective, democratic control of city government is a comparatively young phenomenon. Even in the so-called advanced nations of the world, it was only in the late nineteenth century that elected municipal authorities came into existence. The achievements of elected local governments in a large number of countries over this last century have been breathtaking, but the chapters in Part III suggest that these achievements are under attack. A subtle—in some cases, not so subtle—restructuring of urban power is taking place and citizens are the losers. But it is worse than that. This is because, even now, at the beginning of the twenty-first century, many countries have wholly inadequate structures in place to sustain local democracy. This is worrying as, if societies fail to cultivate a vibrant and influential local democracy, the foundations of national and supranational democracy will be fragile and could crumble.

In Chapter 12 Hambleton examines the way "new public management" has been introduced into local government in many countries. He argues that, while this move to introduce private sector management practices into public service bureaucracies has brought some benefits, the movement has limited potential because it does nothing to revitalize local democracy. He advocates a broader approach, which he describes as "new city management," in which public service managers strive to enhance the quality of government as well as work to modernize and improve the quality of services. He makes a plea for new approaches to urban leadership—approaches that combine significant improvements in participatory democracy with purpose-driven, outgoing leadership that shapes the behavior of other stakeholders in the city.

In Chapter 13 Bockmeyer examines the experience of immigrant communities in German cities and reveals what is best described as a democratic deficit. Her study of neighborhood management in three different German cities—Berlin, Dortmund, and

Hamburg—documents the efforts to bring about community involvement in the "Social City" approach to urban policy. While new settings for civic engagement have been created, she suggests that the model has been constrained by inadequate resources and conflicts between officials and local people. A concern here is that well-intentioned urban initiatives may fail to resonate with immigrant communities because cultural change within the city bureaucracies has been neglected.

In Chapter 14 Nalbandian takes forward the argument advanced by Hambleton in Chapter 12 and makes a powerful case for blending efforts to modernize public management with steps to foster the public good by enhancing civic engagement. He shows that, all too often, two important strands of local government reform have become isolated from each other. He argues that administrative modernization and the encouragement of civic engagement should be seen as two sides of the same coin.

In Chapter 15 Davies expresses strong reservations about the U.K. efforts to include communities in various local "partnerships." In his view, these efforts often end up attempting to submerge fundamental conflicts in values. Echoing themes articulated by Bockmeyer in relation to neighborhood management in the German context (Chapter 13), he suggests that public managers tend to see local partnerships as vehicles for improved coordination of public services, whereas many community representatives envisage the new partnerships as a vehicle for democratic inclusion. His conclusion is that, in a world characterized by vast inequalities in power, it may be more effective for communities to "exit" partnership settings and engage in community resistance in order to challenge the dominant neoliberal discourse.

CHAPTER 12

NEW LEADERSHIP FOR DEMOCRATIC URBAN SPACE

ROBIN HAMBLETON

INTRODUCTION

The rapid changes now taking place in society—particularly the changes in urban lifestyles and the creation of new social milieux—require us to rethink the nature of city leadership and city management. The forces of urbanization and globalization, discussed at length in this book, are causing cities to restructure both economically and socially, and this process of restructuring raises new challenges for those providing leadership to localities as well as those serving urban communities. Old stabilities have gone and models of urban leadership that may have served societies well in the past are unsuited to changing circumstances. This is not a new insight—in many countries national governments and city leaders are responding in a creative way to changing pressures from a variety of stakeholders, with the result that public service reforms, including efforts to redesign urban political institutions, now proliferate. For example, several countries, including England, Germany, and Italy, have witnessed the introduction of new local leadership models in recent years—such as directly elected mayors (Hambleton and Sweeting 2004; Egner et al. 2006; Procacci and Rossignolo 2006).

These innovations have been informed by a remarkable upsurge in cross-national policy learning in relation to the institutional design of local governance. In addition to the experiment with new leadership models, there is widespread innovation with various forms of "partnership" working, particularly in relation to urban regeneration, and considerable innovation with approaches to public involvement in decision making (Denters and Rose 2005a).

Notwithstanding this surge of innovation with approaches to urban governance, it can be claimed that much city management practice remains out of date. Traditional and fairly centralized modes of decision making characterize the practice of urban management in many city halls. Moreover, even where public service reform is under way, there appears to be, not in all but in many countries at least, a high reliance on private sector management models and concepts. These approaches—sometimes referred to as "new public management"—may inject fresh thinking and practice into slow-moving public service bureaucracies, but the benefits of these changes have often been overstated. Indeed, there is a risk that reforms advanced in the name of new public management could inflict lasting damage on city governance by eroding the democratic roots of local government.

In this chapter I discuss three major strands in the ongoing discourse about the governance of cities. These strands intertwine, but, for the purposes of analysis, it is helpful to separate them out. First, I consider shifts in thinking about the nature of "city management" and, in particular, focus on alternative ways of conceptualising the relationship between the state and the people it is designed to serve. As part of this I will suggest that it is a great mistake to collapse together the terms consumer, customer, and citizen—as often happens in new public management reforms. Second, I examine the concept of "city leadership." There is no well-developed theory of political leadership, still less city leadership, but helpful pointers from the literature and from the latest practice can be identified. Third, I explore the "modern urban leadership agenda" and will suggest that there are grounds for optimism if leaders and managers can focus more of their energy on democratic renewal alongside measures to improve service delivery to citizens. Before embarking on this review, it is important to clarify a few terms.

GOVERNMENT, GOVERNANCE, AND GOVERNING

Numerous writers have suggested that we are moving from an era of "government" to one of "governance" (Rhodes 1997; Andrew and Goldsmith 1998; Pierre and Peters 2000). But what do these terms mean? For the purpose of this discussion, "government" refers to the formal institutions of the state. Government makes decisions within specific administrative and legal frameworks and uses public resources in a financially accountable way. Most importantly, government decisions are backed up by the legitimate hierarchical power of the state. "Governance," on the other hand, involves government *plus* the looser processes of influencing and negotiating with a range of public and private sector agencies to achieve desired outcomes. A governance perspective encourages collaboration between the public, private, and nonprofit sectors to achieve mutual goals. While the hierarchical power of the state does not vanish, the emphasis in governance is on steering, influencing, and coordinating the actions of others. There is recognition here that government cannot go it alone.

Moving to the local level, "local government" refers to democratically elected authorities. "Local governance" is broader—it refers to the processes and structures of a variety of public, private, and voluntary sector bodies at the local level. It acknowledges the diffusion of responsibility for collective provision and recognizes the contribution of different levels and sectors (Andrew and Goldsmith 1998; Wilson 1998; John 2001; Denters et al. 2003; Boddy and Parkinson 2004; Denters and Rose 2005a).

The rhetoric about governance can be viewed as a way of shifting responsibility from the state onto the private and voluntary sectors and civil society in general—a point explored in this book by several authors, for example, Betancur, in Chapter 9. This displacement of responsibility can also obscure lines of accountability to the citizen, and the shift to governance certainly poses a major challenge to local democracy. For example, as Judd and Smith point out in Chapter 11, the growth of quasi-public authorities is undermining democratic accountability—hidden from the public gaze these special authorities can develop a life of their own. Going by this analysis, a move to governance is bad news for both government and democracy.

On the other hand the movement to local governance can, perhaps, be welcomed as an overdue shift from a perspective that, in Europe at least, sees local government simply as a vehicle for providing a range of important public services to a new emphasis on community leadership. This interpretation envisages the role of the local authority (or city hall) being extended beyond the tasks of service provision to embrace a concern for the overall well-being of an area (Clarke and Stewart 1998). This shift from government to governance is striking in the United Kingdom and other parts of Europe, but it is also visible in the cities of the developing world. For example, Stren (2003b) argues that the broadening of the contours of the discussion of urban challenges in developing countries from the technical confines of "urban management" and "local government" to "urban governance" is a healthy move because it focuses increased attention on issues relating to governmental legitimacy, citizen empowerment, and the vibrancy of civil society.

In any event, and regardless of whether it is a good or a bad thing, the shift from government to governance has profound implications for the exercise of local leadership. Out goes the old hierarchical model of the city "boss" determining policy for services controlled and delivered by the state, and in comes the facilitative leader reaching out to other stakeholders and local people in an effort to influence decisions made by others in order to improve the local quality of life (Svara 1994). Recognition of the shift from government to governance requires leading politicians and senior managers to adopt an outward-looking approach and, crucially, to engage with the economic and other interests that influence the current and future well-being of their locality.

As Stone argued in an early contribution to the literature on urban governance, as distinct from urban government, local politicians operate "under *dual pressures*—one set based in electoral accountability and the other based in the hierarchical distribution of economic, organisational and cultural resources" (Stone 1980, p. 984, emphasis in original). Elkin refined this approach, arguing that the division of roles between the state and the economy means that government must continually deal with the mandates of popular control and economic well-being. In the U.S. context the way the division of roles develops and is handled gives rise to specific "urban regimes" (Elkin 1987; Lauria 1997). These depend, basically, on the strength of political elites relative to economic elites. As discussed later in this chapter, modern approaches to local leadership need to understand these local power structures and use the unique positional power of local government to intervene in these processes. It follows that debates about local democracy could be more productive if they shifted their focus from a concern with the distinction between government and governance and gave more attention to the overall process of *governing*. It might then be seen that effective and accountable governing processes require locally elected governments to be robust in orchestrating the various stakeholders involved in governance.

UNDERSTANDING CITY MANAGEMENT

In parallel, and overlapping with, the movement from government to governance, there has been a significant shift in the way public services are organised and run. Simply stated, this shift can be described as a move from public administration to new public management (Hoggett 1991; Dunleavy and Hood 1994; Pollitt and Boukaert 2000). There is a good deal of rhetoric about these changes. Bold claims have been made about the virtues of private management practice and about the desirability of developing a more businesslike approach to the running of public services (Osborne and Gaebler 1993). But there is considerable confusion in the debate. In particular, the phrase "new public management" has several meanings (Wollman 2003). Because of the confusion, there is a risk that management-led reforms may come to lose sight of the underlying social purpose of public services. Researchers have also shown that new public management is taking different forms in different countries (Christensen and Laegreid 2001).

Figure 12.1 provides a way of unpacking the rhetoric surrounding new public management. It identifies the three currents of change that have characterized public service reform strategies in the last 20 years or so.[1] The first broad alternative, associated in the 1980s with the radical Right, seeks to challenge the very notion of collective and non-market provision for public need (Walsh 1995). Centering on the notion of privatization, it seeks to replace public provision with private. The second alternative, shown on the right of figure 12.1, aims to preserve the notion of public provision, but seeks a radical reform of the manner in which this provision is undertaken. Thus, it seeks to replace the old, bureaucratic paternalistic model with a much more democratic model, often involving radical decentralization to the neighborhood level (Burns et al. 1994). The market approach treats people as consumers of services, and the democratic approach treats people as citizens with a right to be heard.

In Hirschman's terms the political Right seeks to give individuals the power of *exit* and the political Left seeks to give citizens the power of *voice* (1970). In the market model, the consumer, dissatisfied with the product of one supplier of a service, can shift to another—the consumer has the power of exit. The democratic model recognizes that many public services cannot be individualized—they relate to groups of service users or citizens at large. Such collective interests can only be protected through enhanced participation and strengthened political accountability (Barber 1984; Wainwright 2003). The citizen, unlike the consumer, has the political power of voice. Hirschman is at pains to point out that, while exit and voice may be strongly contrasting empowerment mechanisms, they are not mutually exclusive.

The third broad strategy for public service reform shown in figure 12.1 attempts to distinguish a managerial, as opposed to a political, response to the problems confronting public service bureaucracies. This response borrows from the competing political models

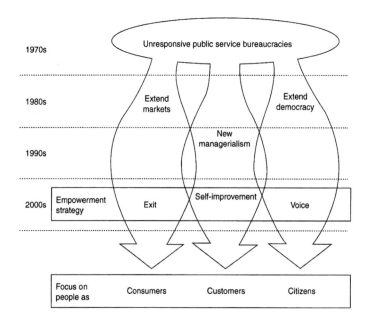

Figure 12.1 Public service reform strategies.

in a way that simulates radical methods but in a form that preserves existing power relations between the producers and users of services. In this model, citizens are redefined as customers. In place of the sometimes violent and unpredictable signals of exit and voice, the model introduces a variety of managerial techniques (market research, user satisfaction surveys, complaints procedures, customer care programmes, focus groups, call centers, interactive web sites, etc.) to provide more gentle and manageable "feedback." This model relies on self-improvement by managers—it is not a vehicle for user empowerment.

As shown in figure 12.2 we can now see that the new public management is associated with just two of the strands in figure 12.1—the market and managerialist reform strategies. This interpretation is consistent with the analysis put forward by Hood (1991), who suggests that new public management involves a marriage of two streams of ideas: the new institutional economics and business-type managerialism. This is a peculiarly narrow agenda for public management reform as it fails to recognise the vital importance of the third strand. Without a lively and empowered polity, there is no mechanism for holding decision makers to account.

By contrast, "new city management"—an approach that links management innovation into the process of democratic renewal (Hambleton 2002)—holds much more promise. The important point to note here is that while new public management can lead to service improvements, it is an approach that both skews and limits the potential of public service reform. As shown in figure 12.2 the "new city management" is a much broader concept that gives full attention to the politics of place. It is an approach that embraces democratic renewal and it requires managers as well as politicians to focus on people as citizens, not just customers or consumers.[2] This recognition that stimulating active citizen participation in local governance—complex and uncomfortable as it can be—is crucial to any successful strategy for public service reform has profound implications for managerial and political leadership in cities and neighbourhoods.

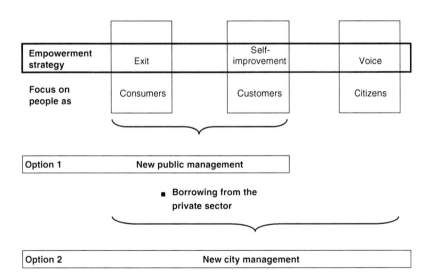

Figure 12.2   The new city management.

UNDERSTANDING CITY LEADERSHIP

Borrowing from Fainstein (1990), it can be suggested that there are two ways of entering a discussion of city leadership. The global approach scrutinizes the wider context within which cities operate and draws attention to the constraints on local leadership. Some, but not all, commentaries adopting this approach conclude that the scope for local leadership is trivial. Thus, according to one influential American study (Peterson 1981), cities are constrained by local and regional economic competition and must give priority to policies that promote economic growth. Cities that do not comply with these forces will be punished by loss of private investment, jobs, and tax revenue.

The second approach examines the forces creating the particularities of a specific place—its economic base, its social makeup, its constellation of political interests, and so on. In this formulation local political leaders and civic elites may turn out to have a considerable impact on the fortunes of the city, and this is the position adopted by Judd (2000). In practice both perspectives are helpful. The same city can be regarded as part of a totality and as a unique outcome of its particular history. Comparative academic studies that combine both a global and a local perspective are now on the increase, and this combination of perspectives is leading to a better understanding of the scope for and limits on local leadership (Di Gaetano and Klemanski 1999; Savitch and Kantor 2002; Haus et al. 2005).

While there is disagreement about what constitutes "good" leadership, we can identify four helpful pointers from the extensive literature on leadership—a literature that embraces psychology, sociology, and political science as well as organization theory. First, the personal characteristics of individual leaders matter. Qualities such as vision, strength, stamina, energy, inventiveness, and commitment are associated with successful leadership. As Jones (1989) observes, the biographical, or case study, approach to the study of leadership can, by examining the conduct and behaviour of known leaders, provide valuable insights on the exercise of leadership. Burns rightly argues in his classic book that "[t]he study of leadership in general will be advanced by looking at leaders in particular" (1978, p. 27).

In the field of urban politics there is, in fact, a considerable body of literature built around this approach. For example, the "fly on the wall" study of Ed Rendell when he was mayor of Philadelphia in the period from 1992 to 1997 provides an excellent, albeit journalistic, picture of personal emotion and energy in city leadership (Bissinger 1997). Other, more academic studies of U.S. city leaders include books on Robert Moses of New York City (Caro 1975), Mayor Richard J. Daley of Chicago (Cohen and Taylor 2000), and Mayor Harold Washington, also of Chicago (Rivlin 1992). A similar tradition exists in Europe with, for example, studies of Joseph Chamberlain, the mayor of Birmingham (Garvin 1932), and Herbert Morrison, leader of the London County Council (Donaghue and Jones 1973).

The second pointer is that context matters. An effective approach to leadership in one setting might not be appropriate in another. Going by this analysis, the accomplishments of individual leaders may be less important than forces—economic, political, institutional, and cultural—shaping the context within which they exercise leadership. Sometimes called situational leadership, at other times contingent leadership, this approach has become popular within the field of management studies as well as political science.

A recent U.K. study of leadership in urban governance, built around an examination of approaches to leadership in three localities, highlights the impact of contextual factors (Sweeting et al. 2004). By comparing experiences in different parts of the country, this study shows that the institutional design of the governance system of a city can be critical in shaping the leadership approach. The research shows, for example, that the constitution of the Greater London Authority provides a platform for high-profile, outgoing leadership by the directly elected mayor of London (Sweeting 2002). This institutional design provides both a strong legitimacy and a clear focus for leadership—the mayor enjoys a mandate from the citizens of the entire metropolis and is recognized by all concerned as the leader of the capital. This design contrasts with the governance arrangements in Bristol, where confusion reigns—hardly anybody knows who the political leader of any of the local authorities is. The poor institutional design of the governance of Bristol—a fragmented city region with confusing municipal boundaries and a proliferation of complex partnerships with overlapping responsibilities—constrains leaders. They are forced into an endless process of negotiation with diverse stakeholders. Nobody has the legitimacy to exercise strong leadership for the locality as a whole, with the result that even modest changes require leaders to participate in a delicate dance.

Our third point concerns the nature of the leadership task. Burns (1978) draws a helpful distinction between transactional and transformational approaches to leadership. Stated simply, the old paradigm has defined leadership as a "transaction" between a leader—often described as the "boss"—and a follower, or "subordinate." A typical exchange is pay for doing a job, but other exchanges can take place—such as the favours and feelings psychologists suggest are traded in social exchange theory.

Transformational leadership is different in nature from transactional leadership. It has been described as a process of "bonding" rather than "bartering" (Sergiovanni 2000). Burns argues that leadership is about transforming social organisations, not about motivating employees to exchange work efforts for pay. Sashkin and Sashkin (2003), in their excellent articulation of transformational leadership, build on the argument advanced by Burns and suggest that a shared approach to vision building is crucial. In addition transformational leaders couple self-confidence with an orientation toward the empowerment of others and recognize the importance of building a caring organizational culture.

The fourth point from the leadership literature concerns the interplay between leadership and management. Some writers attempt to draw a sharp distinction between "leadership" and "management." As Bennis and Nanus (1985, p. 21) put it, "Managers do things right, and leaders do the right thing." Kotter (1988) sees managers planning, organizing, and controlling, while leaders focus on the change-oriented process of visioning, networking, and building relationships. But Gardner counsels against contrasting management and leadership too much: "Every time I encounter utterly first-class managers they turn out to have quite a lot of the leader in them. Even the most visionary leader is faced on occasion with decisions that every manager faces: when to take a short-term loss to achieve a long-term gain, how to allocate scarce resources, whom to trust with a delicate assignment" (1990, p. 4).

This interplay between leadership and management is vital in local government. It is, as we shall see shortly, a mistake to claim that politicians "lead" and officers "manage." Both have roles in leadership and management, but the received models of political/administrative relations fail to recognise this. It has reached the point where these out-of-date models are impairing the development of effective local leadership in many countries.

LOCAL LEADERS—STAKEHOLDERS GREAT AND SMALL

Within government there are two main sets of players—elected politicians and appointed officers. It is normally the elected politicians who are seen as the main leadership figures in a locality. They enjoy a political mandate from local citizens and, even if voter turnout in local elections is not very high, their legitimacy to speak out on behalf of local people is difficult to challenge. In practice, elected politicians exercise a range of leadership roles in their locality. The nature of party politics can have a profound impact on the way leadership roles are exercised (Leach and Wilson 2000). In some situations the party group is enormously powerful, in other situations the political leader may have a wide area of discretion. In some countries individual leaders—for example, the directly elected mayor—may be pivotal. In others the city may be led by a group of senior politicians— sometimes described as a cabinet. And in some countries—for example, England and the United States—the institutional design of local leadership arrangements varies by locality (Hambleton 2000).

A long-standing myth in local government is that there is a sharp separation of roles between politicians and officers. The old adage that politicians decide on policy and officers implement it was challenged over 20 years ago by research on policy implementation. This showed that implementation is an interactive and negotiative process between those seeking to put policy into effect and those upon whom action depends (Barrett and Fudge 1981). More recently Svara (2001) has demonstrated how early contributors to the field of public administration acknowledged a policy role for administrators that has often been ignored partly because, over the years, the dichotomy became a "useful myth" (Miller 2000, p. 314–15). The dichotomy idea shields administrators from scrutiny and serves the interest of politicians who can pass responsibility for unpopular decisions to administrators (Peters 1995, p. 177–8). A more sophisticated conceptualization of the politician/officer interface recognizes that *both* groups contribute to both policy development and local leadership.

Mouritzen and Svara (2002) provide a valuable cross-national analysis of "leadership at the apex" of local government in 14 countries. The authors do not examine the role of leaders outside the institution of local government. Rather they provide a detailed and fascinating picture of the roles of mayors (and other leading politicians) and the way they interface with their chief executive officers (CEOs). This research shows that overlapping leadership roles between senior politicians and CEOs is the norm—a view confirmed by Nalbandian in Chapter 14.

Moving outside local government, attention needs to be given not just to the business interests highlighted by urban regime theory but also to a variety of other players who may, depending on the local context, be in a position to exercise decisive leadership. Sometimes these figures are to be found outside local government but inside other organs of the state. It may be, for example, that regional state bodies contain key actors who play a significant local leadership role. Certainly, as it becomes clearer that city regions form the effective spatial unit in an era of global economic competition, leadership for relatively large metropolitan regions is now receiving increased attention in many countries (Jouve and Lefevre 2002; Salet et al. 2002; Antalovsky et al. 2005). It is also the case that many important decisions affecting particular localities are made at higher levels of government, and this points to the value of understanding how cities fit within the multilevel system of governance (Carmichael 2005).

In some countries the nonprofit (or third sector) plays a vital role in local leadership. Religious groups, trade unions, and, at times, universities as well as charitable foundations can make a significant contribution in helping to set the local agenda as well as in relation to specific community projects. At the local level, community-based leaders can come to play a particularly important role, not least in situations where higher levels of government—perhaps national government, perhaps the European Community (EC)—have chosen to target regeneration or neighborhood renewal funds on particular localities. For example, the European Commission's URBAN program targets funding on specific neighborhoods and aspires to encourage the development of local leadership at the neighborhood level (European Commission 2003b). Research on community leaders in area regeneration partnerships in the United Kingdom suggests, however, that state agencies are still not that skilled at working with local people in ways that support their neighborhood leadership role (Purdue et al. 2000). Taylor (2003, 132–4) also shows how community-based leaders can be caught in a kind of no-man's-land between their communities and the decision makers, accused on the one hand of failing to deliver and on the other of being unrepresentative.

In summary, local leaders comprise a mixed bag. In some situations a powerful, directly elected mayor or council leader can give the impression of exercising decisive leadership of the locality, with other actors having relatively minor roles. This discussion has suggested, however, that it is more than likely that, in any given locality, there is, to some extent, a pattern of "dispersed leadership." In modern conditions of social complexity, power is fragmented, and this means that leadership involves a process of connecting the fragments. Elected politicians, appointed officers, business leaders, nonprofit organizations, religious groups, community representatives, and figures from higher education can all be found carrying out leadership roles in modern systems of urban governance.

THE MODERN URBAN LEADERSHIP AGENDA

Now that we have sketched the main dimensions of twenty-first-century city management and identified some pointers relating to city leadership, it is possible to explore some of the main challenges now facing local leaders. Earlier it was suggested that the context for leadership matters enormously—it follows, therefore, that there are dangers in generalizing too freely. In the discussion that follows, the aim is to hint at a "grammar" that the reader can revise in the light of his or her own experience (Cooper 1976). All urban leaders operate in a specific locality with its distinctive history and traditions.

Successful leadership may well involve leaders taking bold measures designed to challenge established patterns. Indeed, effective leadership takes the capacity to stomach personal hostility, as the many who gain from the continuation of the status quo will always be ready to attack an innovative leader. But experience suggests that in democratic contexts, as distinct from revolutionary opposition to an oppressive regime, successful leaders spend much of their time working "with the grain" of established cultures and traditions. Here we discuss three themes as pointers for possible practice: (1) Purpose-driven city leadership, (2) The relationship between leadership and community involvement, and (3) Leadership and the shaping of emotions and behaviour.

PURPOSE-DRIVEN CITY LEADERSHIP

Leadership is inextricably linked with purpose. As Stone (1995) observes, aimless interaction requires no leadership. In contrast, in cases where a compelling vision emerges from an inclusive process and is then articulated by a leader or leaders, the results can be inspiring. A clear statement of purpose (or mission) can provide a formative experience, shaping the identity of group members and articulating shared values and aspirations. In the mid-1990s Steve Bullock and I were commissioned to develop national guidance for the United Kingdom on local leadership (Hambleton and Bullock 1996; Hambleton 1998).[3] In carrying out this research we asked leading figures in U.K. local government what they thought constituted successful local authority leadership. The indicators of good leadership that emerged are summarised in figure 12.3.

This relatively early work on local leadership has been followed up in the U.K. context by more specific guidance from the Improvement and Development Agency for local government in England and by central government (IDA 2003; ODPM 2005b). In 2005 a Leadership Centre for Local Government was created to improve political and managerial leadership in English local government, and leadership development programs are now expanding.

There is no suggestion here that the indicators listed in figure 12.3 are comprehensive or appropriate in all settings. Rather they are offered as a possible set of aspirations for local leadership. The substantive objectives of leaders will, of course, vary depending on local trends and context. Leaders who can set out a convincing and hopeful vision for their area—and follow through with specific and practical actions in line with the vision—can be expected to enjoy stronger electoral support than those who seem more

---

- **Articulating a clear vision for the area**

    Setting out an agenda of what the future of the area should be and developing strategic policy direction. Listening to local people and leading initiatives.

- **Promoting the qualities of the area**

    Building civic pride, promoting the benefits of the locality, and attracting inward investment

- **Winning resources**

    Winning power and funding from higher levels of government and maximizing income from a variety of sources.

- **Developing partnerships**

    Successful leadership is characterized by the existence of a range of partnerships, both internal and external, working to a shared view of the needs of the local community.

- **Addressing complex social issues**

    The increasingly fragmented nature of local government and the growing number of service providers active in a given locality mean that complex issues that cross boundaries, or are seen to fall between areas of interest, need to be taken up by leaderships that have an overview and can bring together the right mix of agencies to tackle a particular problem.

- **Maintaining support and cohesion**

    Managing disparate interests and keeping people on board are essential if the leadership is to maintain authority.

Figure 12.3   Indicators of good political leadership.

Source: Adapted from Hambleton and Bullock (1996, pp. 8–9).

interested in obtaining and holding onto the power of office. All leaders and aspiring leaders will claim to have a vision for the area but only some will actually mean it. Relevant here is the notion of the "creative city." As Landry (2000, 2006), Florida (2005), and others argue, there is ample space for new kinds of thinking regarding the kinds of cities we want to create. Leadership that releases the creative talents of people in the city is now more important than ever before.

LEADERSHIP AND COMMUNITY INVOLVEMENT

How do local leaders relate to local citizens? Earlier it was suggested that the old, hierarchical models of leadership are out of date. A top-down approach in which the "boss" hands down instructions to a grateful—or not so grateful—band of subordinates or followers is anachronistic. We have seen how the politician/officer relationship in modern local governance is better seen as a kind of partnership with benefits flowing from mutual respect and role sharing. The same is also true in relation to citizen involvement in decision making. In all democracies well-informed and confident citizens are putting new demands on local government as well as other public agencies—to be more open, more responsive, and more accountable. As figure 12.1 makes clear, the bureaucratic paternalism of the past—in which politicians and officers made decisions over the heads of local people—has been challenged by new approaches to user and citizen empowerment. These changes have profound implications for the exercise of local leadership.

Three points stand out. The first concerns the need for leaders to develop the listening and organizational learning capacities of all those involved in leadership and management roles, whether senior or junior. In a complex and rapidly changing society, it is essential for leaders to be really well tuned in to the concerns of all groups in society. This is particularly important in multicultural urban settings where some groups in society can be marginalized as a result of poor communication and/or inadequate policies and institutionalized learning mechanisms. In the modern city it is essential for leaders and managers to have multicultural competence—a point brought out by Bockmeyer in Chapter 13. Stuart Hall put it this way: "Diversity is, increasingly, the fate of the modern world. The capacity to live with difference is . . . the coming question of the 21st Century" (Hall quoted in Zachary 2000, p. 222). As indicated in figure 12.1, leaders can enhance the way they interact with the population they serve by employing a *range* of empowerment mechanisms. The analysis suggests that, depending on the presenting problem, it can be effective, on occasions, to treat people as consumers and/or customers. On the whole, however, leaders need to give most attention to enhancing the voices of people as citizens with a range of rights and responsibilities.

Second, it is important to recognize the legitimacy of different viewpoints. Politicians, officers, and citizens draw on different sources of legitimacy—elected members enjoy a political mandate from citizens, officers bring managerial and professional skills as well as impartiality, and citizens have a democratic right to be heard and to hold government to account. Much of the management literature on leadership is built around practice in the private sector and this limits its usefulness in the context of democratic institutions where citizen rights are altogether different from the rights of the consumer or customer (Marshall 1950). Acceptance of this argument means that leaders need to do much more than listen—they need to empower neglected voices in the democratic process if decisions are not to be dominated by the powerful and the connected.

Third, while much has been written about leadership and about community involvement, there has been relatively little work that has examined the relationship between the two. This is surprising, given that these attributes are both central to the creation and operation of good urban governance. Recent comparative urban research in Europe and New Zealand has begun to fill this gap by examining the complementarity of urban leadership and community involvement in different settings.[4] This research suggests that, where the two are combined in a creative way, positive policy outcomes result—not least because the approach can build crucial support for urban policy interventions (Heinelt et al. 2006). Socially binding decisions that stem from a participatory process are not only likely to be more effective, but they can also enhance the legitimacy of urban leaders.

Leaders who promote participatory democracy may unleash critical voices. But, without active community involvement, how sustainable is local democracy? There is evidence to suggest that this point is well understood in countries with very different traditions—in, for example, Mexico (Flores 2005), Brazil (Wainwright 2003), and a number of other developing countries (McCarney 2003). In Chapter 14 Nalbandian explores the interplay between administrative modernization and citizen engagement in the United States context in more depth. His contribution is important as he shows how public managers are well placed to bridge the divide between managerial perspectives, which tend to downplay or ignore political dynamics, and a grassroots perspective, which strives to connect decision makers with communities of interest and place in an effort to advance democratic values.

LEADERSHIP AND THE SHAPING OF EMOTIONS AND BEHAVIOUR

Earlier a distinction was made between transactional and transformational approaches to leadership. It was suggested that a transactional approach implies a form of "trading" between leader and followers, whereas a transformational approach implies a process of "bonding" as all unite in common cause. My own definition of leadership is "Shaping emotions and behaviour to achieve common goals". In my experience—of working in government, of advising and consulting with governments and nonprofit organizations, and of practicing as a leader in a university setting—I have found the transformational approach to leadership to be more effective. This is not to say that transactional measures should be discarded—for example, granting a big pay rise to a star performer is good management as well as good leadership. But, in my view, truly significant and lasting changes occur when individuals and groups *feel* differently as well as act differently.

While the literature on "emotional intelligence" is relatively young, it does at least offer the insight that emotions matter. More than that it appears that leaders who manage their own emotions well and understand their own motivations may be better equipped to understand the emotions and feelings of others (Goleman 1995). This aspect of leadership is still not well developed, but there is the beginning of a literature that addresses these issues. Heifetz and Linsky (2002) offer a particularly helpful analysis when they argue that successful leaders inevitably generate opposition:

> The dangers of exercising leadership derive from the nature of the problems for which leadership is necessary. Adaptive change stimulates resistance because it challenges people's habits, beliefs and values. . . .
>
> (2002, p. 30)

For the most part, people criticize leadership initiatives when they do not like the message. Spirited debate about future direction is vital to organizational health—it resides at the heart of any democratically run organization. However, opponents of change will often avoid focusing on the substantive issues, preferring instead to attack the leader. For the leader this can be costly in emotional terms—opponents will often go after their competence or simply distort or misrepresent their views. Effective leaders do not cave in when faced with such attacks.

An example can illustrate the point. In 2000, shortly after his election as the first directly elected mayor of London, Ken Livingstone was advised that it was "madness" to introduce a congestion charge to discourage motorists from driving into central London. Focus groups were negative, and political and public opinion suggested that introducing a "new tax" would end Livingstone's political career at the next mayoral election. Livingstone ignored the advice and was vilified in the press and by his political opponents when he went about introducing the new tax. The congestion charge was introduced, the revenue generated was pumped into public transport, the environment of central London was dramatically improved, and Livingstone was returned to power at the next election with an enhanced electoral majority. Londoners loved the new tax because of the benefits that flowed from its imposition. Here, then, is a classic example of forward-looking municipal leadership going well beyond the limited thinking encountered in focus groups. Livingstone, to his lasting credit, took the personal flak, was not deflected, and has introduced an innovation that is so successful it has attracted worldwide attention. His leadership on this issue has improved the quality of life for millions of Londoners as well as visitors to London.

Conclusions

Ultimately, the "new city management" approach advocated in this chapter rests on the belief that any valid theory of local government must be a political theory. There are four main justifications for local government. First, local government supports political pluralism and is able to moderate a tendency or temptation toward autocracy that is itself destructive of good government. Second, it contributes to political education, acting as a school in which democratic habits are acquired and practiced. Citizens learn how to act politically and how to hold decision makers to account. Third, it can facilitate the growth of more self-organizing capacity in local communities. Fourth, it can improve the responsiveness of services to diverse needs and requirements. With the growth of complex multicultural communities in many cities, the importance of this fourth theme of enhancing responsiveness gains in importance.

The discussion of trends in city management suggested that the new public management is flawed because it ignores the political justification for local government. It is built around the notion that local government is nothing more than a convenient mechanism for the delivery of public services—a notion that, if it gains ascendancy, will clearly lead to the demise of local government. It was suggested that the broader conception—here described as "new city management"—is better suited to current challenges as it seeks to combine political and managerial innovation.

The analysis of city leadership has identified pointers for future practice and, in particular, it has been argued that many different stakeholders contribute to effective city leadership. Leadership in the modern city is inevitably dispersed, and important leadership roles exist not just at the "apex" of leadership in city hall but at every level of city governance—from street level to above the level of the city. Effective city leaders are purpose driven and good at relating to different communities of interest and place, and understand the emotional dynamics of urban politics. They know what good management looks like but, more important, they strive to revitalize the politics of democratic urban space.

NOTES

1. I would like to acknowledge the contributions of Danny Burns and Paul Hoggett in developing this framework in the early 1990s (Burns, Hambleton, and Hoggett 1994, p. 22).
2. I first set out the case for the "new city management" in Hambleton (2002). While I did not know it at the time, Denhardt and Denhardt (2003) had developed a very similar and more extensive critique of the "new public management." In their analysis they give particular attention to the damage that "new public management" is doing to the public service ethos and to public service values.
3. Steve Bullock was the leader of the London Borough of Lewisham in the early 1980s. He later became one of the very first directly elected mayors in U.K. history when he was elected mayor of Lewisham in 2002.
4. The idea that urban leadership and community involvement can be complementary lies at the heart of a major cross-national research project. Known as the Participation, Leadership and Urban Sustainability (PLUS) project, this EC-funded study in 18 cities in nine countries examined the impact of alternative "Combinations of Urban Leadership and Community Involvement" (CULCI). The cities were full partners in the project, and the findings have been published in two books: Haus et al. 2005; Heinelt et al. 2006.

CHAPTER 13

BUILDING THE GLOBAL CITY—THE IMMIGRANT EXPERIENCE OF URBAN REVITALIZATION

JANICE BOCKMEYER

IMMIGRANTS AND URBAN GOVERNANCE

The current peak in global migration is challenging norms for political engagement in the local state. To enhance the role of immigrant residents as participants in local civil society and foster integration, global cities are asking how they can engage their increasingly diverse populations. The Commission of the European Communities is giving new attention to enhancing "a shared sense of belonging and participation" in local democratic processes as a central part of the strategy to speed up integration of immigrants and promote "fundamental rights, non discrimination and equal opportunities for all" (2005, p. 3). The goal to enhance immigrant participation is now intersecting with new approaches to revitalize the most distressed urban communities, often in the same low-cost districts where immigrants have settled in pursuit of affordable housing. High demand in those districts for improved education resources, employment opportunities, and housing has added urgency to urban revitalization policies.

Reflecting global trends, new public management practices have emerged *in tandem* with civic engagement efforts that promote participation in district revitalization by the affected community residents and that make greater use of private sector partners as part of efforts to reduce public administrative costs and further devolve government (Clarke 2001; Franke and Löhr 2001; Mayer 2003). The resulting innovations in community revitalization pull disparate public and private neighborhood efforts into joint partnerships with common governance. Understood in Germany as *neighborhood management,* this approach to rebuilding distressed city neighborhoods emphasizes enhancing the organizational capacity of city administration and service-providing community nonprofit organizations in order to improve their ability to implement programs jointly. The approach also applies revitalization measures using an integrated, place-based method (Aehnelt et al. 2004; Franke 2003).

Place-based strategies address common needs for community-wide improvement and de-emphasize a sectoral approach that targets groups such as seniors, youth, or immigrants. To achieve their mandates, neighborhood management programs generally require governmental restructuring to integrate related agency resources and reapply them geographically. Particularly when neighborhood management is applied in high-concentration immigrant areas, redesigning how community services are delivered and who devises the content of programs presents a challenge to immigrant self-organization. After decades of settlement in European cities, immigrant communities are maturing. Many are well networked and intercity and transnational organizations support local efforts in providing neighborhood services and cultural institution building (Özcan 1992). This chapter addresses the neighborhood management approach as a new governance structure for urban community revitalization. It focuses on (1) the impact of neighborhood management on immigrant communities, exploring the potential of neighborhood management to expand immigrant participation, and (2) concerns that the access of immigrant networks that are already plugged into old decision-making structures may be diminished by some features of governance found in neighborhood management.

THE ORIGINS OF NEIGHBORHOOD MANAGEMENT

Neighborhood management priorities emerged from the now vast civil society research associating community-building efforts that began in the 1970s with social and economic improvement in urban areas. Putnam's (1993) research on regional decentralization schemes found that the presence of engaged local citizenry, able to take on joint governing, determined success. In particular, social capital is considered crucial by proponents in generating local civic engagement. Social capital is taken as "the *collective* capacity that has been built or exists within a 'community' and within a local context" (Evans et al. 2005, p. 14, emphasis in the original) to enable joint action. Whether scholars view the effect as coterminous with or as the product of civic engagement, the dynamics—generally including levels of trust, norms of reciprocity, the existence of partnerships and networks—are viewed as having a range of positive effects from reductions in crime to enhancing economic prosperity (Fraser and Kick 2005). As a result, public and nonprofit sectors have persistently promoted building stocks of social capital as essential to community development strategies (Lelieveldt 2004). These "community building" strategies emphasize building "community capacity"—"the interaction of human capital, organizational resources, and social capital . . . that can be leveraged to solve collective problems" (Chaskin et al. 2001, p. 7)—rather than the large-scale housing, commercial, and other construction projects associated with earlier phases of urban renewal. This has produced community programs with participatory or "capacity building" elements such as resident boards, councils, or teams for implementation.

In Germany, a neighborhood management approach was designed in 1999 to coincide with the administrative reforms initiated by the "Modern State-Modern Administration" program (Franke and Löhr 2001); and while it hews closely to global new public management goals, impetus for implementation generally arose from the need for cost-cutting measures following reunification (John 2001). The Social City program was intended as a social policy component to achieve citizen engagement in urban communities while winding down public service provision and "government"—"centralized government, assistance and welfare"—to be replaced by devolving responsibilities to state and city levels, and from "Government to Governance" (Franke and Löhr 2001). The shift is from government, as producer of public goods, to community governance, as a replacement strategy for intervention in distressed communities (Lepofsky and

Fraser 2003; Mayer 2003). Managerial and democratic trends, in other words, have merged to provide "the age of local governance" (Denters and Rose 2005a, p. 1).

With early international assessments now emerging, the findings on the ability of community-building strategies to generate community involvement and joint action are decidedly mixed, but the widespread adaptation of the social capital paradigm to urban policy continues its "sweep" through global policy networks (Mayer 2003). Diverse challenges are reported, including public administrators resisting the decentralized and integrated nature of the new community regeneration programs (Blanc 2002) and community residents opting out of participation (Hanhoerster 2000) or attempting to assert more control over decision making than administrators bargained for (Bockmeyer 2000). Blanc argues that difficulties are tied to implementing "ready to use" solutions universally. As he observes, "What is relevant in a specific context might be irrelevant elsewhere" (Blanc 2002, p. 224). What is absent in the growing body of community revitalization research is a focus on what impact the integrative, neighborhood management approach has on immigrant communities. The sections below assess the impact of the neighborhood management approach on immigrant, community-level participation in German urban regeneration programs, principally the 1999–2006 Social City program.[1]

NEIGHBORHOOD MANAGEMENT AND ENGAGEMENT

For community development practitioners and scholars, urban communities have widely come to be viewed as instruments for addressing the needs of disadvantaged sub-groups, including low-income families, seniors, and ethnic minorities, by generating investment in neighborhoods through links to public officials and private for-profit and nonprofit investors (Chaskin et al. 2001; Vidal and Keating 2004). The notion of community development as a "place-based approach" to generate assets for disadvantaged areas (Vidal and Keating 2004, p. 125) has become so extensive in the United States that building linkages to investors and securing funding have become dominant activities for community organizations engaged in neighborhood revitalization (Bockmeyer 2003; Silverman 2003a). One of the most extensive applications bringing both the social capital and new management reform components to community renewal practices is the European Union URBAN Community Initiative program. Germany's effort is the 1999 nation-state, "Districts with Special Development Needs—The Socially Integrative City" (Social City). Social City combined and reworked related extant revitalization efforts, including Hamburg's 1994 Project to Combat Poverty and North Rhine-Westphalia's 1993 "Districts with Special Development Needs" (Becker et al. 2002). Others were launched as new initiatives, but in districts where continuous and, at times, overlapping, urban renewal programs were applied since the late 1970s (Bockmeyer 2006; Schubert 2002). Whether the Social City program can make a unique and significant impact after decades of urban renewal strategies is contingent on the cooperation and active engagement of residents. The extent of voice residents achieve can ultimately determine whether revitalization programs elicit enthusiastic participation, disinterest, and disengagement, or, in the worst-case scenario, reinforce a sense of betrayal or distrust left from earlier renewal experiences.

IMMIGRANTS AND ENGAGEMENT

Even where urban regeneration plans elicit community input, immigrants and ethnic minority residents are those least often participating. Overcoming residents' concerns that inhabitant-led decision making is unimportant, unwelcome, or merely symbolic is difficult even in less diverse communities (Bockmeyer 2000). Establishing expectations that participation is necessary and genuine requires a long-term commitment that is stable and adequately funded (Fraser and Kick 2005; Silverman 2003b). Attempts in diverse communities to elicit resident participation through neighborhood councils and improvement associations have resulted in overrepresentation of middle-income homeowners and largely failed to engage immigrants and renters (Harwood and Myers 2002; Musso et al. 2004). Research on immigrant participation in the United States underscores the role of additional participatory skills (Bedolla 2000; Jones-Correa 1998; Verba et al. 1995). Periodic voting requires few political skills and is achieved relatively easily. For the problem-solving activities necessary to community revitalization planning, however, civic skills such as writing, public speaking, and organizational abilities are essential for prolonged engagement (Verba et al.1995, p. 359). As residents are asked to engage in neighborhood revitalization programs such as Social City, it often falls to public officials accustomed to controlling decision making not only to transfer parts of their domain, but to teach decision-making skills to lower-income residents with less experience in deliberative processes (Jacquier 2003). In what Jones-Correa (1998) characterizes as a catch-22 situation, however, immigrants not already mobilized are not valued by politicians and those who are mobilized do not need outreach by politicians (pp. 89–90).

Further development of immigrants' civic skills is now a goal supported by the European Commission as a mechanism for integration. Principally recognized is the need for support of immigrant self-organization and networking of existing immigrant nonprofits (CEC 2005). Indeed, after decades of urban settlement by Turkish immigrants, Germany's largest immigrant minority group, they have produced national networks as well as small self-help neighborhood groups, secular and mosque associations, and intercity parents' and professional associations, explicitly political committees targeting politics both in Turkey and in Germany as the "receiving" nation. Particularly before the German Republic took steps toward citizenship reforms in 1990 and 2000, voluntary organizations served the dual purposes of providing services to fellow immigrants and mobilizing immigrants under several large umbrella groups to advocate for citizenship reforms (Özcan 1992).[2] In Hamburg, the Hamburg Union of Migrants from Turkey serves as a citywide umbrella group since 1985. Berlin organizations are united into two large such umbrella groups, the Turkish Union in Berlin (*Türkischer Bund Berlin*) and the Turkish Community of Berlin (*Türkische Gemeinde zu Berlin*) (TGB). In addition, the Turkish Parents Associations are found throughout Germany, are members of the TGB, and keep close intercity ties between their member organizations (Özcan 1992; Soysal 1994). Within immigrant districts, additional neighborhood-based immigrant organizations also appear. In Berlin-Kreuzberg, for instance, over forty nonprofit immigrant organizations can be identified, many with ties to the larger umbrella groups. With extensive progress made in Turkish self-organizing, what remains to be addressed is the role immigrant groups have played in neighborhood management and what impact neighborhood management has had on immigrant participation in revitalization.

NEIGHBORHOOD MANAGEMENT AND
NEW COMMUNITY GOVERNANCE STRATEGIES

The recent concern over immigrant integration in Germany, as in other European Union (EU) nations, stems from increasing segregation in innercity urban areas (Faist and

Häussermann 1996) and increased levels of unemployment, poverty, and other indications of distress. Core city neighborhoods have been identified by German Institute for Urban Affairs (DIFU) researchers as "'gathering places' for disadvantaged population groups that are very heterogeneous and therefore often not in contact with one another." Diversity itself, in this view, becomes part of the problem, leading to polarization, fragmentation, and an image that "core society" develops, of a "loser district," nearly assuring a "downward spiral" (Frank and Löhr 2001).

The German antipoverty plan to the EU—National Action Plan for Inclusion (NAPincl)—found that on all measures of well-being, immigrants fall below the German population (Huster et al. 2003). Immigrants are overrepresented among unskilled laborers; over 50 percent of immigrants are unskilled compared with 10 percent of Germans. The German NAPincl reported that three-fourths of foreign unemployed residents did not complete vocational training, 19 percent of immigrant students dropped out of school (compared with 8 percent of Germans), and only 10 percent of immigrant students, contrasted with 26 percent of Germans, who completed school and took qualifying exams passed them (European Union 2003: pp. 10, 36). Unemployment and poverty rates are also alarming, with both over 21 percent by 2003 (Huster et al. 2003, pp. 15, 37).

To combat economic distress in immigrant communities, the German NAPincl claims the Social City program as its most important strategy, setting as its key goal "obtaining equality for socially disadvantaged citizens." Necessary to achieving Social City goals is "involv[ing] local players in processes and decisions." "The activities of the players on the spot are a key prerequisite for the longer term success of the programme" (European Union 2003, p. 23). As the social capital model has taken hold of service delivery, immigrant-serving nonprofits have been encouraged in some European countries for their presumed ability to create social capital, to deliver community services, and, as Huntoon (2001) observed in Spanish cities, to act as a "communication channel" between immigrants and government (p. 158).

To participate in EU-funded programs, however, immigrant associations enter a competition with strong charity organizations such as the social democratic welfare organization Arbeiterwohlfahrt (AWO), which has been traditionally tapped by the German state to serve Turkish immigrants (Soysal 1994). AWO, Caritas, Diakonisches Werk, and other major social work nonprofits are working on both the national and the EU level through networks such as the European Anti-Poverty Network to build local horizontal partnerships and vertical EU-local ties, promote major nonprofit interests, and build multilevel governance. Germany's federal system has now made "subtle re-orientations within the policy networks" (John 2001, p. 83) to disperse EU program administration to public and private, formal and informal "partners." Welfare nonprofit organizations exerted influence to shape the social inclusion elements of Germany's National Action Plan, the formal statement to the EU on national social welfare policies and goals. German charity organizations were a presence in EU negotiations over urban renewal policies and have been viewed as successful in expanding the role of the charities in URBAN programs. And while this can result in giving a greater role to community-level nonprofit organizations, it can also aggravate the competition between them for public contracts. As Huster et al. (2003) write of the role of social inclusion policy partners, "[O]n a number of concrete topics, there is also a competition between the partners, either in improving living conditions or in economizing, or in reforming the use of the legal and financial resources" (p. 44). In other words, social policy interests— whether immigrant-based organizations seeking support for their community projects, traditional charity groups, or community-based nonprofits that in many cases have become a hybrid of German and immigrant activists—compete to serve overlapping constituencies and geographical districts. In the competition, better-resourced groups are well positioned to assert their interests in a larger arena that small community organizations are ill equipped to master. As a result, immigrant-based organizations giving voice to a minority population may see weakened access to public officials and funding and a smaller role in policy decisions vital to their communities.

Scholars now liken these trends toward *governance*—through the use of informal networks of individuals and interests in decision making, rather than traditional formal, governmental structures—to the United States' long experience with urban regimes, nonprofitization, and the growing use of informal governing structures at the local or neighborhood level (Hambleton 2002; John 2001).[3] In the United States, these processes have produced larger, professionalized community development corporations and comprehensive community initiatives rather than broadband participation by neighborhood residents (Bockmeyer 2003). An examination of the impact of these processes on community residents' engagement in community decision making in both the United States and Europe indicates similar concerns with increased complexity, fragmentation of political institutions, and diffuse policy networks (John 2001). In addition, some scholars warn that "community building" revitalization efforts reflect market-place interests to "(re)claim" high poverty districts as good social policy and to enhance residential and entertainment marketability (Fraser and Kick 2005). Conflict potentially emerges, as not only diverse resident concerns clash, but also those of national and local officials, social workers, housing, and other development interests (Uitermark 2003). As Peter John concluded, current transformations converting government to governance threaten the possibility that "governance can weaken democracy." Representative government is designed to provide accountability and opportunities to organize new populations through political institutions, such as parties, to "achieve political action" (John 2001, p. 155). Many non-EU immigrants such as the Turks, however, are not citizens and do not enjoy voting rights or the ability to participate in political parties. A 2001 survey of Berlin residents of Turkish ancestry, for example, indicated that only 20 percent had German citizenship (Senatsverwaltung für Arberit, Soziales und Frauen 2002, p.3). Given the lack of formal political rights, their access to informal arrangements should have the potential to democratize decision making for them by opening access. Survey research on Turkish immigrants in Germany found that decades of political exclusion have fostered a deep sense of political alienation (Diehl and Blohm 2001) that will not be easily modified by community-building efforts. Whether the neighborhood management approach has made progress in that direction will next be assessed.

HOW DOES NEIGHBORHOOD MANAGEMENT IMPACT IMMIGRANT PARTICIPATION?

The Social City program holds to three ambitions: to encourage resource "pooling" in targeted urban districts with special needs, to generate integrative administration through "flexible management," and to utilize district-level resident networks and organizations to enhance citizen engagement. The built-in contradiction appears in the top-down management required by the two former goals, which discourages inhabitant participation required in the latter; the commitment to resident inclusion is threatened with becoming an outside target, and one that, in some cases, is missed even when projects achieve other goals (Blanc 2002). The clearest emphasis is on "pooling resources" drawn from various public departments and private sector resources, including community nonprofit organizations and housing companies. This aspect of Social Cities raises one of the most widely held critiques of the community development approach: that it converts community advocacy groups into "more formally structured organizations focused on policy implementation" (Silverman 2003a, p. 2731). How extensively residents are able to participate in advance of program implementation is a key test of the resident engagement goals.

The integrative approach has the most potentially potent effect on immigrant participation. Community-wide representatives are seated on neighborhood management panels to deliberate on issues that can be viewed as addressing community-wide concerns. They endeavor to find common themes in which all community "stakeholders" share a general purpose interest. As a result, attention focuses on the least common denominator: services viewed as benefiting all and deliverable at the lowest cost, such as playground improvement and street—or sometimes, public school bathroom—beautification. In Berlin-Kottbusser Tor,[4] for example, the ongoing priorities of existing immigrant nonprofit organizations—to mobilize immigrant parents as advocates for an increased presence of Turkish-ancestry teachers in public schools and for bilingual education—in the neighborhood management project become enlisting parents to create after-school homework help centers for all children. *Mobilizing capacity*—the ability of one population sector to organize its members to advocate for and jointly address common goals— becomes secondary in the neighborhood management approach to administrative or *organizational capacity,* which includes achieving reduced public expenditures through low-cost resident self-help projects.

Social Cities also aim to weaken bureaucratic territoriality. Bringing together departments responsible for education and youth, immigrant affairs, planning, urban development, and housing requires centralized management to gather diverse players and interests and achieve coordinated implementation. As DIFU researchers acknowledge: "[T]he implementation phase generally require[s] more top-down proposals to get the ball rolling" (Becker et al. 2002, p. 16). Centralizing administrative elements, however, creates obstacles that are common to social capital model programs. In Detroit, Silverman found that community development groups, under similar circumstances, became "sub-contractors in a subordinate position to government, private and larger non-profit sector organizations." This hampered their ability to play an advocacy role in policy formation (2003a, p. 2736). Social Cities encountered similar challenges, particularly in the earliest phases as top-down decision making was used for early-stage implementation (Becker et al. 2002, p.16). Program expectations were that residents would participate by voicing ideas and "'cooperating," but without scrambling new managerial goals. As DIFU found in its Social City assessment, residents' demands "often clash with municipal government's concrete project design concepts, timetables and performance indicators" (Becker et al. 2002, p. 26).[5]

IT'S ABOUT DOMINANCE BY POLITICIANS

Globally, and across a variety of revitalization programs, the programs' inability to engage neighborhood residents appears to be their most fundamental weakness. Field research points to a variety of explanatory variables, with the dominance of party officials occurring as a common theme. Van den Berg et al. (2003) attributed Strasbourg's low engagement level in part to partisan factors: links to the community were undermined by elections and the decline of public support for officials associated with the program. In French Social City programs, Blanc (2002) found that officials were hesitant to relinquish control over local programs. In Dortmund-Nordstadt, some residents indicated frustration with party officials' involvement: "[A]t the neighborhood level they try to control the process. They are reluctant to give away decision making." One observed that "'[a]s long as parties play a role, there is no real benefit from the process to immigrants. There is no chance to decide anything. There are many reasons not to get involved."

IT'S ABOUT OLD PRODUCTS WITH NEW LABELS

Although the administrative structure for Social Cities differs from earlier urban renewal programs, sponsored community projects are either closely similar in approach or, more commonly, use projects created by nonprofit organizations prior to URBAN II. A chief criticism of many current national neighborhood revitalization programs has been that cities are simply making use of "an accumulation of existing projects" (Kloosterman and Broeders 2002, p. 136). Dortmund provides one illustration of a city applying many revitalization approaches since its decline as a coal and steel producer (Högl 1994; Staubach 1995). Dortmund-Nordstadt was particularly hard hit by high unemployment and outward migration by German-ancestry residents. In its three districts of Hafen, Nordmarket, and Borsigplatz, the immigrant concentration is, respectively, 33 percent, 44 percent, and 45 percent, with majority Turkish ancestry residents (Stadt Dortmund Statistik und Wahlen 1999, Tables 25, 26). Dortmund-Nordstadt, where urban renewal had a lengthy history, was chosen as one of North Rhine-Westphalia's "Areas with Special Development Needs" in 1993. It was not a radical break with old approaches, but a more subtle knitting together of ongoing efforts. Under the original effort the state administrative offices for economic development had the primary responsibility for choosing projects within revitalization areas drawn by municipalities. City development officials then prioritized the slate of projects, at times taking cues from political relationships. The designation of Nordstadt as an URBAN II site in 2000 added a new layer of funding and, in 2002, added three neighborhood management teams (Stadt Planungsamt Dortmund 2003). In this sense, it may be more accurate to characterize URBAN II as a contributor to the ongoing state-city Dortmund effort in Nordstadt rather than as a unique effort. Some of the neighborhood management staff worked previously in funded community organizations and projects; a significant number of projects had been proposed earlier, but rejected by the City of Dortmund Department of Urban Development. Thus far, the managers appear to have made some gains over the more centralized administration of "Communities with Special Renewal Needs." Of the three neighborhood management offices, at least two have immigrant community residents and long-time community nonprofit activists in positions as managers. Two previously rejected projects—long proposed by nonprofits as promoting the interests of resident immigrants—have become URBAN II projects: a house of culture, or meeting place and office space, long sought by immigrant nonprofits, and a conflict resolution project sponsored by Nordstadt's leading participatory community planning nonprofit.

IT'S THE PROCESS

As an effort to restructure community development administration, the Social City program battles severe internal discontinuities. As a top-down structure, residents' input comes into play only in the final stages of program construction. In this late stage, residents are invited to cooperate with professional district-level administrative staff to devise an "Integrative Action Plan" as a tool "to establish a common self-image and group awareness in the neighborhood and discuss urban measures, projects and procedures" (Becker et al. 2002, p. 16). The critical role of opening the process is left entirely to "neighborhood managers," who are to network local actors, connect them to district and city administrators, and promote "self-reliant and permanently effective personnel and material structures for the development of a neighborhood" (Franke and Löhr 2001). The choice of neighborhood managers as connective for residents, organizations, city officials, and other development actors is key to opening the Social City process. Processes, however, are site specific and sensitive to local political conditions. In the Berlin sites, for instance, managers were selected through a competitive search conducted by private consultants. District resident status was not a hiring criterion. For nonresidents, the initial task of managers is to identify residents' organizations, networks, and potential participants and create strategies to generate their involvement, primarily through juries, given the task of voting on projects to be funded by the district neighborhood management offices. Even on juries, immigrant nonprofit organizations (NPOs) are structurally underrepresented through the selection process for choosing jury members. In order to avoid dominance of neighborhood management decisions by assertive neighborhood organizations, jury membership for existing groups was held to 49 percent; of that, seats are designated for specific sectors such as seniors and youth, again limiting immigrant representation. Jury members were selected by phone invitation from neighborhood managers using a randomly generated list of district residents created by Social City consultants, again limiting the selection of experienced immigrant activists. In Berlin-Wrangelkiez, these administrative strategies did not appear to create severe limits on immigrant participation in neighborhood management activities overall. Both of the team managers were of immigrant ancestry. Also, immigrant representation on the district jury was characterized as strong. In Berlin-Kottbusser Tor, however, team members are of German ancestry and had greater difficulties identifying local immigrant organizations, generating their participation, and addressing key immigrant concerns (Bockmeyer 2006).

It Lacks Incentives

Since the areas of decision making in which residents may be involved are limited primarily to selecting projects and participating in them, projects are both of short term and of limited funding, and since improvements in poverty levels and educational attainment for immigrants appear beyond the scope of neighborhood management projects, immigrant organizations have few compelling incentives to work Social City activities into their existing agenda. Interviews with Berlin immigrant nonprofits found some that declined to submit project applications to neighborhood management juries. To invest staff time needed for proposal preparation and submission, program areas and funding levels must be meaningful. DIFU concluded in 2002 that Social Cities were "failing to reach certain people (e.g. migrant families, the long-term unemployed, the elderly) in many districts. Many activities remain middle-class affairs" (Becker et al. 2002, p. 28). A 2004 interim assessment drew similar conclusions: "[A]s regards the involvement of the migrants, little progress becomes visible in many areas, despite considerable efforts undertaken" (Aehnelt et al. 2004, p. 10). Indeed, as analysts have noted, expanding the significance of the Social City program into areas of more fundamental concern and drawing on federal financing would require lifting constitutional barriers that limit federal involvement in urban investment. Currently, headway in improvements on economic and education measures has not occurred under Social City projects and, in some areas, these measures are "often even worsening" (Aehnelt et al. 2004, p. 11).

COMMUNITY PLANNING: A DIFFERENT APPROACH

Hamburg-Wilhelmsburg takes a unique position among the cases presented here. As a large and diverse community on an island in the Elbe River, it seems to have slight connections with the bustling commercial and cultural center of Hamburg. Historically, Wilhelmsburg was Germany's shipping port and point of emigration. As such, it has represented a point of departure; ironically, it is now one of Hamburg's three areas with the highest concentrations of immigrants. By 2003 the immigrant proportion of Wilhelmsburg was almost 35 percent, the majority of which was Turkish. (Statistisches Landesamt 2003). There are also indications of economic distress similar to Social City sites: nearly 38 percent of the neighborhood's housing is publicly supported, in contrast to Hamburg's 17 percent; unemployment was high at 10.7 percent in 2003, compared with Hamburg's 7.3 percent; and the proportion of public assistance recipients is almost double that of the larger city (Statistisches Landesamt 2003).

To address the district's social isolation and economic distress and to create resident engagement, in 1997 a group of city planners, working with the Hamburg Department of Urban Development, created *Mitwirken in Wilhelmsburg* (MIT-Wil), a community planning group. The organizational office, *MIT-Büro*, takes the work and functions of neighborhood management (Machule et al. 2003), but is not a designated URBAN II or Social City area. MIT-Wil divided the island into three regions and formed a project group for each. Relevant community organizations and individuals were then invited to create community plans and projects at regular meetings. Anchored by a core group of volunteer professional planners, MIT-Büro worked to conceptualize plans and pull community members into monthly meetings. Planners then worked with the Department of Urban Development for funding and plan execution. Documentation of meetings indicates that they are well attended and have maintained stable membership. In interviews, planners explained that they used every possible tactic to keep community residents engaged, including visiting immigrant nonprofit offices, "knocking on doors," or "doing whatever it takes." Although immigrant residents recounted similar feelings of general social exclusion heard in interviews in Berlin and Dortmund, when questioned about the planning efforts in Wilhelmsburg, responses were more positive. A number of small immigrant nonprofit organizations are present in Wilhelmsburg, and many of Germany's largest and most influential immigrant nonprofits are also active in Hamburg and Wilhelmsburg specifically, but ethnic, political, gender, and religious differences create strong barriers to working together on the neighborhood level. To overcome these obstacles, MIT-Wil creates narrow community planning areas and brings immigrant residents together to identify needs and work toward solutions. This approach addresses immigrant concerns that when Germans become involved they make the decisions and fail to hear local immigrants' views: "The problem is that no one asks immigrants. The needs are assumed." According to MIT-Wil's planners, the alternative approach is conceived as bringing parts of the community together "like a salad: The discussions are to fill in the gaps . . . Not partnerships, though, they don't have to leave their worlds, but find some common ideas. MIT-Büro tries to stay in the background." Given the difficulty of participatory planning for diverse communities, perhaps what is most impressive is that MIT-Wil has survived and continues to hold bi-monthly planning meetings.

CONCLUSIONS

Social City uses an integrative approach to focus resources from a number of policy areas on distressed communities in a manner that attempts community building by engaging local residents and enhancing community capacity. The question remains whether this approach can be effective in communities where immigrants are concentrated. In comparing the effects of the urban revitalization strategies discussed above, there are early indications that levels of immigrant participation in most Social City sites are unlikely to increase significantly (Aehnelt et al. 2004). The Social City/Neighborhood Management program is young and final assessments are not yet possible. From early data collected, however, it is clear that Social City faces four key challenges with relevance to immigrant community residents. First, funded projects are often either previously unfunded nonprofit programs or ongoing projects. The nature of Social City decision making encourages organizations to "follow the funding" and apply for Social City designation if it increases opportunities for funding. This would suggest a new incrementalism emerging in Social City sites that works against generating innovations.

Similarly, city and political party officials play the role in some sites of steering URBAN funding toward political supporters and favored economic development projects (see also Krummacher et al. 2003; van den Berg et al. 2003). Particularly in Dortmund, local officials appeared most successful at maintaining close control over regeneration processes (Aehnelt et al. 2004), but this is consistent with wider European experiences, as city administrators and politicians hesitate to relinquish local decision making (Blanc 2002).

The short-term and limited nature of neighborhood management projects may also confound efforts to achieve the program's ambitious engagement goals. In what Krummacher et al. (2003) call "go and stop" support, Social City initiatives must continuously seek funding or end before they see results. Globally, scholars have identified the fragility of neighborhood processes for building networks and trust and generating political identity (Clarke 2001). Stable public and private resources and long-term public commitment to programs are essential to maintaining resident participation (Fraser and Kick 2005; Silverman 2003b). Hamburg-Wilhelmsburg's MIT-Wil effort appeared better able to meet these criteria.

Most crucially, administrative reform elements inherent in neighborhood management dilute the engagement of immigrant residents in community revitalization decision making. While immigrant residents are present in some Social City endeavors, the minority demographics of most Social City sites examined here indicate a severe underrepresentation. More to the point, the highlighted social capital model goals of the Social City program to enhance networking on the community level and build bridges to city administration and the private sector appear unlikely to be achieved for immigrant community residents, given the political dynamics of development politics and the nonprofit sector. Particularly where neighborhood management increases competition between NPOs, and when larger well-established charities are present to "represent" the interests of immigrants, the necessities of organizational maintenance will likely not align with the long-term goals of enhancing immigrant engagement. The greatest concern that we might have about Social City is that its place-based approach will diffuse particularized immigrant demands and rewire those immigrant networks that have been constructed. More importantly, the inability of neighborhood management to generate substantial immigrant engagement is a firm reminder that governance mechanisms cannot replace a legal framework for participatory rights in an arena where the full spectrum of policy issues meaningful to urban immigrant residents is open to deliberation.

NOTES

1. The research presented in this chapter was supported in part by grants from the City University of New York PSC-CUNY Research Award Program and by a John Jay College—CUNY Fellowship leave. An earlier version of this paper was presented at "City Futures: An International Conference on Globalism and Urban Change," University of Illinois at Chicago, July 2004. The author thanks Jill Simone Gross and Robin Hambleton for helpful comments and insights and the City Futures participants for excellent feedback. The author takes all responsibility for the final product and any flaws therein.

2. The Naturalization Reform of January 1, 2000 granted German citizenship to children born in Germany of non-German parents if at least one had been a legal resident of Germany for eight years or more with a residence entitlement for at least three years. At age 23, to keep German citizenship, one must choose to give up one's non-German citizenship or to relinquish German citizenship. The law also sped up the residency requirement needed when applying for naturalization to eight years from fifteen; see Europäisches Forum für Migrationsstudiun (EFMS 2001).

3. Stone's (1989) urban regime theory generally has been applied to citywide, not community-level governance; this is in contrast to neighborhood councils or panels that give some form of input to residents in European community revitalization programs. As John (2001) notes, governance may operate through relationships between individuals "in a diverse set of organizations located at various territorial levels" (p. 9).

4. The project examines three urban neighborhoods with high immigrant concentrations: Berlin-Kreuzberg, Dortmund-Nordstadt, and Hamburg-Wilhelmsburg. The three districts are also targeted as urban revitalization or Social City sites and were selected in order to assess levels of immigrant inclusion in community revitalization. Qualitative analysis of planning documents, materials from nonprofit organizations, and archival data were combined with 39 semistructured personal interviews with 45 interviewees conducted between August 1999 and January 2004, including 15 interviews in immigrant and German nonprofit organizations and interviews with city and state urban development and planning officials, neighborhood management leadership, and immigrant, political party, union, and housing officials responsible for immigrant affairs as well as other relevant actors. Relevant events and meetings were also observed.

5. DIFU, a research institute founded in 1973 by the German Association of Towns and Cities, works under contract to the Berlin state government as the Social City evaluation team of the Berlin Kottbusser Tor site.

CHAPTER 14

Professionals and the Conflicting Forces of Administrative Modernization and Civic Engagement

John Nalbandian

As governments worldwide give more responsibility to local authorities, it makes sense to examine emerging roles of the local government professional. These roles are developing in a contemporary context that features the conflicting forces of administrative modernization and civic engagement (Nalbandian and Nalbandian 2002, 2003; Naschold and Daley 1999a, 1999b, 1999c; for a global perspective see Barber 1995; Friedman 1999; Kettl 2000a; Sacks 2002; Yergin and Stanislaw 1999). Modernization creates an administrative culture driven by efficiency and the pervasive influence of technique. This trend is increasingly divorced from a second force that involves citizen engagement, participation, and the passion of local politics. In Chapter 12, Hambleton describes these forces succinctly in figure 12.2, as he outlines what he refers to as the new city management.

Local government professionals experience tension between these forces along five dimensions described in this chapter. Successfully bridging the gaps along these dimensions connects the culture of professional management with the culture of citizen engagement and participation in the effort to build community. The effectiveness of local government professionals depends upon their acceptance of responsibilities and roles associated with this bridge building.

Complicating their task is an increasing reliance in governance worldwide on partnerships between the public, private, and /nonprofit sectors, multiplying the number of actors and contexts in which bridges must be built. The unique value of local government professionals in these multisector partnerships centers on recognizing that the strongest bridges are built on solid foundations of public values—values that local government professionals have embraced and should not shy away from advocating.

MODERNIZING THE ORGANIZATION

At the level of the local jurisdiction, modernizing the organization is a trend that focuses on managerial practices and the scope of government. Organizational modernization, the so-called new public management or managerialism, emphasizes service delivery and performance with the instrumental goal of enhancing administrative capacity. The overall intent is efficient resource utilization and more effective and innovative policy support in the search for credibility, accountability, and improved trust in governing institutions. The characteristics of local government modernization include

- Connecting administrative processes to strategic goals
- Integrating personnel and financial systems
- Organizing around problems, not departments
- Decentralized decision making for timely, customized response
- Market and competition orientation, including privatization
- GIS/GPS-related activities and Internet-based innovations
- Results-based performance measurement and bench marking
- Goal-based performance appraisal
- Performance budgeting
- Flexibility in organizing work and in personnel policies

Every progressive local jurisdiction will have incorporated some, if not all, of these elements into its administrative practices along the lines indicated in the new public management literature (Heinrich and Lynn 2001; Lynn 1998; Salamon 2002b). The ubiquitous nature of the trend is based in part on technological innovation (especially in communication), specialization of knowledge, technical skill (and the rise of the technical specialist or technician), an emphasis on the professions and professionalism, and on the image of private enterprise as a model for management.

The "best practices" metaphor symbolizes this trend. These are not "good" or "better" practices. They are the best. They are said to result from objective scrutiny and rigorous measurement. Best practices are amenable to importation from one jurisdiction to another, with just marginal change to accommodate context. The jurisdiction-by-jurisdiction diffusion of best practice "innovations" contributes to an increasingly homogenized administrative world. Furthermore, the hegemony of modern best practices, and the hard data upon which they are presumably based, drives out conventional wisdom and discounts the importance of local knowledge and tradition.

CITIZEN ENGAGEMENT

The forces of civic engagement are widely evident both locally and globally (Halvorsen 2003; Haus and Klausen 2004; Lukensmeyer and Brigham 2002; Smith and Huntsman 1997). The emphasis and value of engagement and participation are seen in Putnam's (2000) work on social capital and in the communitarian movement (Etzioni 1995), as well as in the work programs of several philanthropic organizations such as the Charles F. Kettering Foundation. One of the key responsibilities of local leaders, elected and appointed, is building and maintaining a sense of community that engages citizens in social, economic, political, and civic activities. The characteristics of the forces of civic engagement and citizen participation are

- Recognition of neighborhoods as the base unit of the community
- Engagement of citizens in administrative processes
- Acknowledgment of expressions of direct democracy
- More jurisdictional accountability and transparency with citizens
- More two-way communication with citizens about policy, service delivery, and citizen obligations to the collective good
- Partnerships with other nongovernmental sectors—private sector, nonprofit sector, faith-based organizations—as a way of creating a social fabric

The driving force behind this trend is the desire for identity, connection, preservation of tradition, and at least some measure of control over one's life (Bellah et al. 1985; Etzioni 1993; Fowler 1991; Sacks 2002; Selznick 1992). People want to be part of creating and maintaining a community they identify with, and they are willing to contribute to protecting a sense of community whether it is in Fairfax County, Virginia, or Fremont, California. The social anchors that community provides—the opportunities to build trusting relationships in a world where relationships have become fragile and temporary and to influence one's fate through personal involvement—drive this trend. While civic engagement of this kind does not occur all the time, the spirit of public service and respect for the ideal of citizenship demand that elected and appointed officials act as if it does.

The force of modernization homogenizes our lives whether in Chicago or Melbourne—no one can mistake a suburban mall, everyone recognizes the term "Big Mac," a roundabout puzzles few of us. Modernization erases identity. The forces of civic engagement represent a countervailing trend—the wish to create or preserve something unique within one's control, something that signals identity. Community connotes anchors and resting points. Community is narrative—a soap opera with episodes of virtue, vice, and intimacy—a novel without an ending. But, most importantly, community is expressed and experienced uniquely when built authentically.

Is the civic engagement trend as powerful and important as the modernizing trend? Yes, but civic engagement is expressed in greater variety.[1] And, it is naïve to think the trend is unique to the United States. The "Participation, Leadership, and Urban Sustainability" research project involves nine universities in nine countries excluding America. It documents eighteen successful cases that combine political leadership and citizen engagement.[2]

The forces of administrative modernization and civic engagement conflict fundamentally, and the resultant tension brings these questions to us: Is there a way to purposefully connect the competing trends so as to achieve both modernity and community? How do we mobilize the force of modernization to create communities with individual character? (Harvey 1990).

The answers to these questions are found in the world of local government professionals whose responsibilities, roles, and values place them squarely in the center of the conflict. Table 14.1 shows how local government professionals experience the conflict. It identifies five dimensions along which local government professionals find the collision between modernizing and community building. Located in the first column are professional staff, departments, governing institutions, technical/specialized orientations, and a policy perspective. Together, they do much to capture the culture of professional

Table 14.1   Gaps between modernizing and civic engagement perspectives

Modernizing the organization	Gaps	Civic engagement
Professional staff	←———→	Elected officials
Departments	←———→	Chief administrative officer (CAO)
Institutions	←———→	Community-based politics
Specialist	←———→	Citizen focus and community problems
Policy	←———→	Place

management. In the other column are elected officials, the chief administrative officer (CAO), community passion, citizens, and an attachment to place. These attributes are meant to connote a culture of civic engagement and participation. There are profound differences between the two orientations or cultures. The space between the columns presents gaps to be bridged to answer our fundamental questions. In short, the argument is that effective bridges connect the two trends. More generally and importantly, they join administrative/bureaucratic with grassroots democratic perspectives and, in doing so, add to a jurisdiction's capacity to join administrative capacity with political accept-ance— key components in any community's ability collectively to chart and implement a desired future. Public leaders—governmental, private, nonprofit, or simply citizens— who understand the need to build these bridges, who have skills, and who respect the democratic foundations of local government will add value to their communities.

THE GAP BETWEEN ELECTED OFFICIALS AND PROFESSIONAL STAFF (BUREAUCRATS)

The first gap identifies the difference in perspective between elected and appointed officials. Svara has examined these differences empirically in terms of time spent on mission, goals, administration, and management (1999). Elsewhere, I have described them in terms of contrasting constellations of logic (Nalbandian 1994). Here, I look at these differences in another way, with figure 14.1 depicting the first gap in terms of the accumulated learning of professionally trained staff compared with local elected officials (Nalbandian 2000a). The argument is that, over time, professional staff have learned to do their work more effi-ciently and more effectively than have elected officials. In other words, today's profession-ally trained staff have more knowledge, better tools, and more skills to do their work compared with their predecessors. To some degree, this can also be said about local elected officials, but not to the same extent. Thus, the gap grows over time.

There are several ways that professional staff accumulate competence at a faster rate than their elected counterparts. The nature of the professions is at the center of the learning. Professional education, while dramatically different in content from one profession to another, systematically conveys learning from one generation to the next while each generation builds new knowledge through research and practice within accepted paradigms.

There is no comparable systematic way for one generation of elected officials to learn from another. Term limits accentuate this learning problem. Many local elected officials practice their craft from scratch without the benefit of the accumulated learning of past generations. To some extent, the problem is ameliorated with training that the National League of Cities, the National Civic League, state leagues, and individual jurisdictions

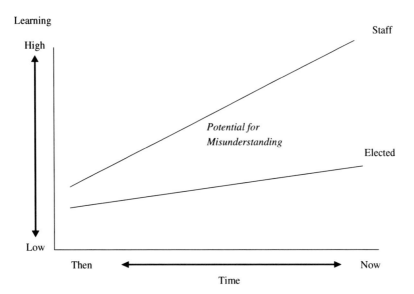

Figure 14.1   Gap between professional and political learning.

Source: Nalbandian (2000a).

conduct. In addition, one should acknowledge that the learning needs—both substance and depth—of elected and appointed officials are different (Freeman 1992; McDonough 2000; Nalbandian 1994). But while this training and the kind of learning needed may warrant less divergence than I have drawn in figure 14.1, the gap cannot be expected to close without conscious attempts to close it. This might not cause concern if the tasks elected officials face were inconsequential. But today's elected bodies worldwide face greater challenges associated with diversity, economic complexity, and citizen expectations than did their predecessors (Zakaria 2003).

The crucial consequence of this widening first gap is greater potential for misunderstanding and mistrust between the perspective of elected officials and the jurisdiction's professional staff and more difficulty getting things done. This leads directly to the second gap in table 14.1, between the CAO and department heads.

THE GAP BETWEEN DEPARTMENT HEADS AND THE CHIEF ADMINISTRATIVE OFFICER

The CAO in local government has always had the responsibility of bridging the perspectives of the elected officials to whom he or she reports and those of the jurisdiction's professional staff—especially technically trained staff, who believe that there are right answers to the problems they confront. As gap one grows, the challenge of gap two increases. To bridge the gap between elected officials and professional staff, the city/county manager spends more time with elected officials than did his/her predecessor. The challenge here is that the CAO risks being seen by professional staff as the "sixth" council member (often, there only are five council members in American cities), thus losing credibility with the staff. The extreme alternative is the CAO's blind defense of staff with the attendant risk of losing the council's trust. One of the ways that city and county managers bridge this gap is to promote/hire staff into positions as department heads who understand and respect the governing body's perspective and role. To take an engineering example, I suspect that hiring nonengineers as public works directors will continue as CAOs attempt to find allies in their challenge of bridging the second gap so they can work on the first. In fact, based on anecdotal evidence, I am not at all surprised to find department heads who are expected to think like deputy city/county managers.

THE GAP BETWEEN GOVERNING INSTITUTIONS AND COMMUNITY-BASED POLITICS

The third gap contrasts the deliberative processes of governing institutions and what they are prepared to do with the passionate expressions of community wants. Newspapers are filled with stories reflecting passions that are carried into relationships among governing body members and their engagement with citizens alongside charges that government institutions are slow and unresponsive.

THE GAP BETWEEN TECHNICAL SPECIALISTS AND CITIZENS

This gap revolves around communication between technically sophisticated professional staff and citizens with issues that cross the professions and departments (Smith and Huntsman 1997).

Professions are ways of mastering knowledge, utilizing it ethically, and transmitting it systematically from one generation to the next. But, as the knowledge base becomes more sophisticated, professionals run the risk of distancing themselves from the people they serve (Charles F. Kettering Foundation 2005; Schon 1983). Modern local government administration is filled with "go betweens." Even though governing body members may expect them to fill the role of technical expert, increasingly, I argue, it is the role of the CAO and department heads to serve as "go betweens" (Nalbandian 1990).

THE GAP BETWEEN POLICY AND PLACE

The last gap juxtaposes policy and place. Affordable housing is a key economic driver for the Silicon Valley in California. Which political jurisdiction will authorize high-density, low-cost housing to solve the problem? This tension is captured in the Not in My Back Yard (NIMBY) phenomenon. Policy that is sound when framed regionally fails when the issue spawning the regional solution is dealt with locally—at least in America where local governments exercise significant authority. Public managers, oriented toward problem solving, create formal and informal interlocal agreements in response to regional policy and managerial problems. Frederickson notes that this kind of networking is much more likely to occur at the administrative than at the political level (1999; Thurmaier and Wood 2002).

BRIDGING THE GAPS

Bridges come in many forms and are found in every city, county, and region. They may be as simple and temporal as a meeting between staff and a neighborhood association regarding a land use issue scheduled for a planning commission. But, they may be complex, as well, including partnerships to build major civic projects or deliver public services (Agranoff and McGuire 2003).

For example, at Iowa State University, professors Ho and Coates are engaged in a statewide project designed to promote citizen-initiated performance assessment of municipal services including public safety. The goal is to develop citizen-driven measures that matter to residents, as residents understand them. Those familiar with the closed culture of public safety agencies will understand the remarkable challenge this project has taken on and the potentially fruitful bridges that can result (Iowa State University 2003).

In Lewisham, England, a working class borough of London, a stratified demographic sample is drawn to create a citizens' panel of 1,000. These citizens agree to participate in citizen surveys for three years, to be included in a pool from which citizen public policy juries are drawn, and to participate in a number of public forums annually.[3]

In metropolitan Kansas City, the Mid America Regional Council (MARC) acts in a brokering role, providing an interjurisdictional bridge for networks involving regional planning, transportation, and homeland security. In addition, MARC sponsors two important forums monthly, where CAOs and their assistants gather and discuss regional issues (Thurmaier and Wood 2002).

Intersectoral bridges are facilitated as local jurisdictions utilize their authority to create tax increment financing (TIF) districts. These districts permit private investors to leverage their wealth, to cushion their financial risk, and to tackle projects that at least in part advance public purposes. My intent here is not to evaluate the effectiveness or appropriateness of TIF, but rather to illustrate how local jurisdictions utilize their authority in partnership with others to join what is politically acceptable with what can be accomplished.

Every local jurisdiction and region has examples of these activities. The more effectively a community connects the forces by building bridges and creating intersections, the more successfully it closes the gaps and puts itself in a position to positively answer the crucial question we started with: how to utilize the tools of modernization to build and preserve unique communities. In other words, bridging the gaps is the key to successfully joining modernization and citizen engagement, especially where power in government institutions seems increasingly irrelevant (Salamon 2002a; Kettl 2000b; 2002b) (also see Judd and Smith in Chapter 11 in this volume).

BRIDGE-BUILDING RESPONSIBILITIES, ROLES, AND VALUES

We now turn to the responsibilities, roles, and values that guide local government professionals as they seek to bridge the gaps, creating capacity for local jurisdictions to reconcile administrative modernization with citizen engagement that leads to community building.

Table 14.2 identifies the work that contemporary local government professionals perform in terms of responsibilities, roles, and values. I first utilized these three categories to examine professionalism in local government with research grounded in interviews with a representative group of local government professionals (Nalbandian 1991). That research documented the role of the city manager as policy maker, negotiator, and broker of community interests and grounded the CAO's actions in responsibility to the value diversity of the community as well as the wishes of a governing body. The value diversity was expressed in terms of representation, social equity, and individual rights, as well as efficiency.

A decade later I revisited the interviewees (Nalbandian 1999). Adding a few new members to the group, I asked what had changed. Enhanced responsibility for community building within the organization as well as outside of it was newly evident. Managers moved from policy makers, negotiators, and brokers to facilitators, indicating a less

Table 14.2 Contemporary professionalism in local government

Responsibilities	Roles	Values
• Citizen engagement	• Facilitate partnerships	• Representation
• Modernizing the organization	• Build bridges	• Efficiency
• Closing gaps in divergent perspectives	• Create community intersections	• Social equity
		• Individual rights

authoritative, controlling position. In the newer role the manager had become less the "boss" and more an authoritative "convener."

I illustrated this responsibility and role in a case study involving site selection for an automobile speedway. The case reinforces the grounding contribution of the values (Nalbandian 2000b). The case placed the CAO squarely in the middle of an issue where some expected him to be a crucial political advocate while others expected him to be a critical analyst. His credibility in bridging these expectations, I concluded, was due to his having internalized the public service values identified in table 14.2.

BRIDGES AS THE FOUNDATION OF CIVIC DISCOVERY

Taken in whole, the bridges constitute a new kind of infrastructure. Rather than physical infrastructure, these bridges represent capacity to help jurisdictions make difficult political decisions—ones that can tear communities apart. The bridges with the most carrying capacity are constructed through deliberative thought and action that engage traditional democratic values—representation, efficiency, social equity, and individual rights—with conflict in values at the root of difficult local issues (Kirlin and Kirlin 2002). In the absence of credible legislative forums, the bridges become critical elements in advancing democratic values, but only if the values are engaged authentically.

Authenticity is crucial as the critique of postmodernism by Box et al. (2001), Harvey (1990), and Stivers (1994) reminds us. One important reason why modernizing and civic engagement are so difficult to reconcile is that building something unique and valued is rare. It is efficient to replicate what exists or what existed (Harvey 1990). But one cannot replicate the adjudication of democratic values. Each community that works must survive its own struggles, which increasingly, I argue, are taking place on the bridges and less frequently solely in executive and legislative bodies.

Not all bridges are equal when set against the challenge of fostering authentic decisions based on deliberative engagement. Complicating the challenge are the multiple arenas and actors that now are part of determining the successful engagement of politics and administration. In his review of large-scale development and infrastructure projects in urban areas, Judd and Smith point out in Chapter 11 that today "most ambitious undertakings are not located in municipalities at all, but in a panoply of special authorities." Further, "The politics of urban redevelopment is rapidly moving from the arena of electoral and municipal projects into an expanding number of institutions that operate with little public accountability. These institutions, in turn, seek to enhance their political authority by seeking support from a constellation of supportive actors." With implied understanding of this phenomenon, Behn points out that traditional public administration that relates politics and administration in hierarchical fashion may suffer empirically. But as a template to examine issues of accountability and to convey the axiom of political supremacy over administrative discretion, nothing is better (Behn 1998b). Whitaker et al. (2004) might argue that their concept of mutual accountability modifies Behn's assertion. Nevertheless, in a networked world where privatization is advocated and intersectoral partnerships are touted for their political attraction as well as their ability to produce results, accountability to a full range of public values may take a back seat (Gilmour and Jensen 1998; O'Toole 1997; Salamon 2002a, p. 603; Terry 1998).

If the significance of jurisdictional hierarchy is diminished, and if traditional forms of accountability are disabled, then professionals play a particularly important role in constructing bridges that introduce and authentically engage public values (Romzek and Dubnick 1987). Rohr (1978) and Rosenbloom (1983) have been reminding us for years that professionals could and should carry regime values into their work. Cooper (1998) and Green et al. (1993) convey a similar message. They see it as an ethical obligation. Their message is especially timely as we create and reinforce a hollow state (Milward and Provan 2002). Kettl (2002a) writes, "An important but often overlooked fact is that this (indirect government) is not just a production function—delivering goods and services in exchange for a fee. It is also a value-transfer function" (p. 507). Similarly, Feldman and Khademian (2002) argue, "Managers are involved not only in producing results that consist of numerical policy goals, but also in facilitating the creation, development and change of various governing structures that enable and constrain actions" (p. 542). Finally, Behn (1998a, p. 221) asks pointedly, "Why would we assume that the manager of a business firm, the manager of a nonprofit social-service agency, the manager of a religious organization, or the manager of a political party would have something useful to contribute to the political process but a public manager would not?"

It is not enough to argue that public managers can and should convey public values. How they do this will determine their effectiveness. Without traditional authoritative forums, the competencies necessary for the effective public manager center on educating, facilitating, listening, helping, and enabling—and doing so in ways that embody regime values. In this sense, the public manager becomes a midwife to civic discovery.

CONCLUSIONS

Encouraging modernization is necessary to bring the most efficient and effective methods to administrative aspects of governing to produce measurable results (Osborn and Hutchison 2004). Equally important is fostering effective citizen investments that create the public good through engagement. But, as stated at the outset, most important is building bridges between the two forces. Closing the gaps between techniques and approaches associated with modernization and the passion and perspectives of citizen engagement to create and preserve communities with character requires connections and networks—in short, a panoply of arrangements represented by the bridge metaphor.

I believe that when local government professionals fulfill the roles and responsibilities charted here and embrace public values, they contribute significantly to their communities. Their value lies in two areas. First, they provide bridges that connect political culture and acceptability with administrative culture and feasibility. Second, and equally importantly, they facilitate the creation of paths to civic discovery.

NOTES

This chapter is a condensed and edited version of a published article: J. Nalbandian, (2005) "Professionals and the Conflicting Forces of Administrative Modernization and Civic Engagement," in *The American Review of Public Administration,* Vol. 35, no. 4, pp. 311–26. It is reprinted here with the permission of Sage Publications. It was originally presented at the City Futures Conference, Chicago, July 8–10, 2004. The College of Urban Planning and Public Affairs, University of Illinois at Chicago, sponsored the conference. I want to thank Robin Hambleton for the invitation to participate in the conference. I am indebted to George Frederickson for his many reviews of this chapter.

1. For example: Collaborative Communities, http://www.collaborativecommunities.org; Community Building Resource Network, http://www.commbuild.org; Community Tool Box, http://ctb.ku.edu; and the National Community Building Network, http://www.ncbn.org.
2. Participation, Leadership and Urban Sustainability, http://www.plus-eura.org/index.html (Haus et al. 2005; Heinelt et al. 2006).
3. See http://www.ronneby.se/dialogue/ENG/cpanel.htm.

CHAPTER 15

AGAINST "PARTNERSHIP": TOWARD A LOCAL CHALLENGE TO GLOBAL NEOLIBERALISM

JONATHAN S. DAVIES

INTRODUCTION

The purported shift from "government" to "governance" is a dominant theme in the urban politics literature. For Rhodes, "governance" refers to "self-organising, inter-organisational networks" (1996, p. 660). Networks are characterized, he says, by interdependence between organizations, continuing interactions between network members, and game-like interactions rooted in reciprocity and trust and subject to rules negotiated by network participants. This conception of governance has gained a "semblance of orthodoxy" in the past decade (Marinetto 2003, p. 593) with a considerable body of scholarship sharing its core assumptions. According to Pierre and Stoker:

> Today, the role of the *government* in the process of *governance* is much more contingent. Local, regional, and national political elites alike seek to forge coalitions with private businesses, voluntary associations and other societal actors to mobilize resources across the public-private border in order to enhance their chances of guiding society towards politically defined goals.
>
> (2002, p. 29)

Local governance, then, refers to the ways in which a variety of public, private, community, and voluntary sector organizations collaborate at different levels to produce valued governing outcomes (see Hambleton, Chapter 12). Thus understood, local governance could be seen as an umbrella concept, encompassing approaches such as urban regime theory (Stone 1989) and neoinstitutionalism (Lowndes 2001).

This interpretation of local governance underpins the case for partnership building. In 2002, the report of the second World Summit on Sustainable Development in Johannesburg declared (UN 2002, p. 4):

We recognize sustainable development requires a long-term perspective and broad-based participation in policy formulation, decision-making and implementation at all levels. As social partners we will continue to work for stable partnerships with all major groups respecting the independent, important roles of each of these.

The word "partnership" occurs 137 times in the report, "local" 119 times. The rhetoric suggests that partnership is the dominant organizing principle in global-local politics, the key to social inclusion. Urban partnerships are found everywhere. From London to Manila, Atlanta to Mexico City, collaborative governance is the favored governmental strategy for goals as diverse as development, public service coordination, and democratic participation (Geddes 2005).

But does partnership work? This chapter builds on Judd and Smith's critique of special authorities in Chapter 11 and presents a critique of the global fashion for partnership. Collaborative structures may be judged against two main criteria—the achievement of joined up governance and democratic inclusion. These ends become the means to achieving policy goals, such as development, social regeneration, or better educational attainment in a complex polity. In the New Labour outlook in the United Kingdom, community engagement is instrumental to coordination. For example, community activists sitting on partnership boards are able to send messages to public agencies and other providers of public services about whether they are delivering their commitments: Is the refuse collection service working as effectively in neighborhood "A" as in neighborhood "B" (Davies 2005a)? Without democratic inclusion, coordination and public service responsiveness are very difficult. Hence, democratic inclusion is the main criterion against which partnership is evaluated in this chapter, and it is found wanting.

REGIME POLITICS AND DEMOCRATIC INCLUSION

There are two basic partnership models: the semiformal or formal governing network promoted by New Labour in the United Kingdom and the bottom-up informal governing regime, of which Stone's (1989) urban regime in Atlanta is emblematic. The latter type is fundamentally undemocratic in virtue of its informality. Stone's study of Atlanta explained how the city-business coalition excluded interests concerned with poverty and lower-class opportunities. He went on (Stone 1993) to argue that lower-class opportunity regimes are the hardest of all to build. But recently, he has discovered opportunity regimes such as the school-based human capital regime in the U.S.-Mexico border city of El Paso. Stone (2004) explains how this coalition generated better educational opportunities for poor African American and Hispanic children. He has since moved further, arguing that the original regime concept did not sufficiently take account of the role of citizens in local politics (Stone, forthcoming). He uses the El Paso example to support his valid contention that local politics matters. But he provides no indication that the El Paso coalition is democratically accountable, or that it gives voice to the aspirations of the urban poor. Thus, even where informal local regimes pursue what they see as lower-class interests, they are still fundamentally undemocratic, out of the public realm, if not clandestine.

But what of the "visible" partnership institutions, occupying the boundary between the public and private domains? The remainder of the chapter explores recent partnership initiatives in the United Kingdom. It is argued that these partnerships represent a top-down, technocratic mode of public service coordination, supporting neoliberalism. While Britain is a good example of the partnership technocracy, it is far from unique (Jessop 2002; Geddes 2005). The partnership model found in the United Kingdom may not be pervasive, but it has global reach. Where it exists, it conflicts with democratic values.

THE PARTNERSHIP NARRATIVE: A NEOLIBERAL CONSENSUS

Jessop's (2002) discussion of the World Commission's *World Report on the Urban Future 21* explains the global context in which the partnership paradigm is situated. Key principles of global governance are the centrality of cities to economic growth, prosperity and innovation, cutting welfare state provision and partnership. Partnership is intended to draw together state, market, and civil society in pursuit of entrepreneurial goals. As Betancur argues in Chapter 9, the rhetoric of governance and partnership also shifts responsibility from states onto communities. According to the *World Report*, partnerships should work with the grain of market forces. They require a retreat of the state, which takes a back seat, steering, not rowing (Jessop 2002: pp. 465–6). Hence, "urban poverty results not so much from capitalism as from ineffective local administration—which a judicious combination of mobilization from below and capacity-building from above can correct" (Jessop 2002, p. 468).

This global narrative is reflected at the national scale. For New Labour, partnership is the institutional mechanism through which a social consensus is mobilized in pursuit of neoliberal socioeconomic goals. Said Tony Blair:

> The creation of an economy where we are inventing and producing goods and services of quality needs the engagement of the whole country. It must be a matter of national purpose and national pride.
>
> (cited in Fairclough 2000, p. 87)

And, "competing on quality can't be done by government alone. The whole nation must put its shoulder to the wheel" (Blair, cited in Fairclough 2000, p. 28). Competitiveness requires partnership, and neoliberalism is the "seemingly natural, almost self-evident economic, political and social imaginary" of the global capitalist renaissance (Jessop 2002, 455). The neoliberal common sense is inscribed in the rules of the partnership game.

These values underpin the government's approach to community engagement and democratic renewal. David Blunkett, former U.K. Home Secretary (2003, p. 11), explained that "only by engaging and developing citizens . . . will there be hope of achieving ambitions for a robust, knowledge-driven economy, for vibrant, self-sustaining communities and for a universal culture of lifelong learning." The government has introduced a wide range of methods to promote community engagement. Participation in partnership is at once constitutive of political freedom and social inclusion and functional for equity in service delivery, as statutory partners respond to the local needs and demands expressed by community activists (Davies 2005a). Partnership is an important element in the local institutional apparatus needed for community to thrive within the parameters of a global market economy.

To what extent are these assumptions borne out in local partnerships? In the following sections, I argue that community participation is being subverted to managerial and technocratic ends. I then venture an explanation for the congruence of neoliberalism with managerialism before finally suggesting that exit from partnership may be a more effective strategy for democratic empowerment than participation (see Davies 2006).

THE PARTNERSHIP TECHNOCRACY

In this section, I draw on evidence from a study of the local politics of social inclusion in Dundee and Hull. Dundee and Hull are coastal cities, the former in Scotland, the latter in England. Both cities have suffered major economic and social crises with the decline of the jute industry in Dundee and the fishing industry in Hull. Both continue to feature prominently in government deprivation indices. The study, undertaken during 2004 and 2005 (see Davies 2006), sought to surface the political controversies that remain disguised beneath the superficial consensus projected by partnerships. The intention was to draw respondents into a space for dialogue about the politics underpinning the "social exclusion" debate and the efficacy of partnership for "social inclusion."

The research suggested that the rhetoric of democratic inclusion was trumped by the practice of managerialism. Skelcher et al. (2005, p. 586) argue that in partnerships and governing networks, "technical expertise is privileged and decisions proceed through a rational process little impacted by the political world." The managerialist approach eschews democratic deliberation for the pursuit of goods deemed self-evident and beyond deliberation. It is undemocratic, antipolitical, paternalistic, and instrumental. Managerialism, thus understood, was a major barrier to democratic inclusion in the partnerships studied. Interestingly, public managers and community activists in Dundee and Hull had contrasting commonsense views about the function of collaboration, framed respectively as "coordinating" and "democracy" purposes. These contrasting perspectives were a root cause of disagreement, but inhabiting the subconscious common sense, they were closed to deliberation.

In both England and Scotland, local authorities are required (in Scotland by statute) to establish city strategic partnerships. In Scotland, these are called Community Planning Partnerships (CPPs), in England Local Strategic Partnerships (LSPs). Both CPPs and LSPs are charged with producing strategic plans reflecting a "holistic" approach to the socioeconomic needs of the city. The goal of the strategic partnership is to mobilize governing resources to secure the delivery of this plan. Local communities are supposed to be involved as the "main partner in the process" (Scotland) (Scottish Executive 2002, p. 14) or as "one of the most important aspects of LSPs' work" (England) (Johnson and Osborne 2003, p. 148). However, the development of strategic partnership working in both cases appeared to have reenforced managerialism. The following passages draw freely from material discussed in greater detail in Davies (2007).

In Dundee, there was a controversy over the absorption by the CPP (known as the Dundee Partnership) of a small government regeneration fund, the Social Inclusion Partnership (SIP), which had previously been controlled by local community activists. The goal of community planning is to improve the strategic coordination of public services and to increase community influence over strategic decisions. As a "stakeholder" group, community activist members of the Dundee Partnership are, in theory, able to influence local public spending but, conceded a senior city council manager, at the cost of community "sovereignty over decisions of a smaller nature." This senior manager also conceded that public agencies under fiscal pressures will want to "realign SIP funding" against priorities governed by the Scottish Executive. In other words, community planning gives communities a smaller say in bigger decisions. The risk was that the community voice would be lost in an environment where governmental and local agency imperatives to deliver dominate, (Fairweather 2005).

This is certainly what many community activists in Dundee thought was happening. Scottish communities had been given no say at the outset about whether they wanted a

CPP. But partnership activists in Dundee were now concerned about how this imposed framework would function. One activist, already concerned about a "them and us" relationship between activists and public managers, feared that community planning would lead to "an even higher them and us." A second said, "I'm frightened of community planning. I really am, 'cause I get a feeling that Council officials will say, 'I'm no' gonna let go what's mine." For a third activist, "I don't think there's going to be any community involvement. As a matter of fact, they shouldn't have put 'community' in there at all, like, they should have just made it 'The Partnership.'"

This rhetoric of marginalization reflected a genuine democratic deficit. If misgivings were expressed in a forum where all parties had an equal voice in decisions, the sceptics might hold sway through force of reason; not possible in this context. One senior council manager conceded that community concerns were valid. But, like other colleagues, he considered community planning to be instrumental for better strategic coordination and therefore more responsive public services. In this context, the opportunity structures for community influence over partnership decisions were severely constrained, managerial priorities coming into conflict with those of activists demanding a democratic voice. The move to community planning can therefore be interpreted as part of a managerialist trend in the local politics of Dundee, placing functional efficiency over democratic inclusion.

In Hull, this trend was even more pronounced. In England, as in Scotland, strategic partnerships are charged with involving communities and creating joined up governance. LSPs were created in the late 1990s as part of the U.K. government's strategy for joined up governance. Localities are tasked with creating inclusive partnerships and mobilizing a coordinated cross-sector effort to deliver against priorities set out in local strategic plans.

Collaboration in Hull was defined by the difficult relationship between public managers and the government-funded Hull Community Network (HCN) on the LSP, Hull CityVision. The government's Neighbourhood Renewal Fund (NRF), allocated to deprived areas in England, had been a source of conflict. A partnership manager in Hull commented that the Hull City Council had "a particularly unpleasant relationship with our community network," which used the partnership as an opportunity to "bash the council." However, the community activist perspective was that the city council was trying to control the funds for its own ends. Said one, "The city council has decided what's going to happen to that money. They've kept the bulk in the city centre to support the local services."

Thus, the community activists saw the NRF as a vehicle for community projects, in contrast with the official purpose, to stimulate public service innovation in deprived neighborhoods and thereby (narrow the gap) with prosperous areas (ODPM 2005a). The city council perspective was explained by a senior councillor:

> The community and voluntary sector have seen it as their own bank account, which it isn't. There's been endless wars about how much of NRF is spent in local government. There's this constant row about what schemes have got it and who's going to get it next year and who didn't get it this year.

According to a partnership manager, the partnership structure was a contributory factor in these difficulties. S/he explained that it was designed on a slate model, where each constituency—business, local authority, public agencies, and community activists—had a fixed number of seats on the board. S/he commented that this was "just a disaster" because it gave a block vote to dissidents:

> And I mean LSPs aren't about voting. They are about consensus politics, but unfortunately, with our Community Empowerment Network there is a real desire to, you know, dictate the agenda and to behave in ways that aren't conducive to partnership working.

The managerialist response to these difficulties undermined the prospects for a deliberated solution. When the study in Dundee and Hull concluded in June 2005, the partnership was engaged in a restructuring exercise designed to improve strategic focus and produce network structures more functional for effective decision making, coordination, and performance management. One proposal for achieving this was to reduce the size of the board and curtail community representation on it. Said a leading city councillor on CityVision:

> I mean, putting it bluntly, there's too many of them. We have three members of the private sector around the table and something like eight members of the community and voluntary sector, so they can dominate things.

This proposed course of action was at odds with what the HCN wanted—a more substantial voice and greater influence on CityVision. A partnership manager anticipated trouble over the restructuring, warning that a forceful approach would be taken:

> I think what we will have to say is, 'Look, you know, this is some work. It's based on best practice. NRU [Neighbourhood Renewal Unit] wants this to happen and it's going to happen'. And I think, you know, then just be prepared for all sorts of you know, awful sort of repercussions. But I think that that's the only way we're going to, you know, succeed'.

Asked whether the partnership reflected on the meaning of terms such as "social inclusion," s/he commented that government had given CityVision "a set of indicators to monitor our progress against . . . and we've just got to get on and do it." To this end, s/he found the authority of a government-appointed advisor helpful, someone able to say: " . . . [L]ook. You're not doing this. It's not appropriate and this is why. I'm here . . . to make sure that this LSP is turned around."

This "reform" strategy is a form of agenda gate-keeping (Bachrach and Baratz 1962), where organizational principles are removed from the democratic realm. In Hull, the managerialist culture was being rolled forward by public managers under pressure from central government to deliver, but also with a better feel for the game of coordination than for democratic deliberation. Their approach was based on a tacit appeal to the public good over the heads of recalcitrant activists: if strong managerial control leads to better public services, quality of life will improve and the people of Hull are thereby served. This approach might also be defended on the grounds, almost certainly true, that members of the activist group lacked representative legitimacy. The point, however, is that as a government-funded "stakeholder" group, the HCN was excluded from decisions about the purpose and future structure of CityVision to which it would have been party, given equal access to agenda setting and decision making. Moreover, if it is accepted that democracy is functional to coordinative efficiency, this exclusionary strategy is likely to be self-defeating.

But perhaps the most important point emerging from the study of Hull was that the public managers and the community activists interpreted partnership in radically different ways, each appealing to a distinct commonsense view of the world: coordination and delivery on the one hand, democratic inclusion on the other. Effective deliberation was precluded by mutual incomprehension. Terms such as "engagement" and "empowerment" were contested, but the protagonists lacked a common discursive repertoire sufficient to recognize why they differed, let alone achieve agreement. With more governing resources at their disposal, Hull's public managers were, with the best of intentions, sidelining the group of activists who participated in this study. For them, as for their colleagues in Dundee, it was self-evident that the top priority had to be the creation of strategic governing capacity in pursuit of government targets.

Hull may be an unusual example in that it was the only English city council labelled "poor" under the U.K. government's Comprehensive Performance Assessment (CPA) inspection regime for local government. A poor CPA score results in local authorities being subject to special measures up to and including a wholesale takeover by government-appointed officials. As such, Hull may be an extreme example of the democratic deficit in partnerships. Nevertheless, this democratic deficit is widely reported in the U.K. literature (Jones 2003; Davies 2004; Diamond 2004; Skelcher et al. 2005). Where the governance of towns and cities is contested, the solution seems to be not democratic debate but control by public managers acting as agents of the centre.

But is Britain's "partnership technocracy" typical of patterns globally? Jessop's (2002) analysis of the *World Report* suggests that it may be (see also Jayasuriya 2003). The instrumental and nondemocratic character of U.S. regime politics has already been discussed. Flores (2005), examining community participation initiatives in Mexico, argues that they are ineffective and that community leaders organizing outside participative structures have more influence than those inside. Forde (2005), examining local government reform in Ireland, argues that top-down and managerialist tendencies undermine the democratic and participative ethos proclaimed by the Irish government. Townsend et al. (2002), in a powerful critique of the "donor culture" in the developing world, argue that nongovernmental development organizations have acted as a powerful transmission belt for the culture of managerialism. For Thake (cited in Townsend et al. 2002, p. 831):

> Community capacity building has become the mantra of those who don't want to give up power. The language used by professionals (in the UK) sounds horribly similar to that used around the time of the break-up of the British Empire.

This perspective resonates with De Beer's review of development studies in Southern Africa. He fears that the rhetoric of empowerment disguises the practice of managerialism— "a technical process of social engineering based on Western models for the transformation of traditional societies" (De Beer 2003, p. 487). These perspectives cast major doubt on the efficacy of partnership for democratic empowerment and suggest that governmental rhetoric of "participation" and "empowerment" cannot be taken at face value.

However, it would be wrong to infer that the diffusion of neoliberal partnership and empowerment strategies is completely pervasive. Geddes' wide-ranging review of "regimes of local governance in a neoliberalising world" highlights regional variance. Beyond Europe and North America, he finds that the transformation to local governance in Japan has been "very slow and limited," while Morocco, under pressure from the European Union and the World Bank, is developing neoliberal partnership modes of governance. Geddes concludes that there are "shifting patterns of accommodation and resistance to neoliberalism, producing overlapping clusterings around variations on a theme" (2005, p. 372–3). Nevertheless, where it develops, local partnership tends to go hand in hand with neoliberal goals, as Jessop (2002, p. 469) puts it, rallying "the good and the great, the movers and shakers, the rich and poor, shanty dwellers and property capital, men and women, to the banner of 'good governance.'" Leading Blairite and former government minister Alan Milburn (2006) seemed to give the game away when he argued that the government must " . . . redistribute *power* so that *responsibility* for meeting the challenge of economic, demographic, environmental, social and cultural change is shared between citizens, states and communities" (emphasis added). If "empowerment" means the capacity to engage in critical debate and decision making about politics and policy, then partnership is found wanting. But what explains these trends?

THE CONJUNCTION OF MARKETS AND HIERARCHIES

The basic goal of neoliberalism is an open market society governed by entrepreneurial, minimal states. Jessop (2002, p. 454), however, notes that it has resulted in a "paradoxical" increase in state intervention. Apologists, he says, argue that this is legitimate and temporary. After a short transitional period, the state can retreat to its proper light-touch supervisory role. Jessop concludes that this argument is spurious, and I concur, arguing (Davies 2005b) that a strong state is the condition for a "free" economy (Gamble 1994). Polanyi (1957) argued that a free market was a "utopian chimera." He identified an irreconcilable contradiction in market capitalism (cited in Marquand 2004, p. 42):

> Thus even those who wished most ardently to free the state from all unnecessary duties, and whose whole philosophy demanded the restriction of state activities, could not but entrust the self-same state with the new powers, organs, and instruments required for the establishment of laissez-faire.

But what explains this unholy dependence of market on state? Mrs. Thatcher's governments were relatively successful in suppressing direct political resistance to market reform; but quiescence is not sufficient, activism is required. Analyzing conflict in British partnerships (Davies 2005b), I argue that neoliberalism requires enthusiastic compliance—active, entrepreneurial citizenship commensurate with Blair's one-nation aspirations. The problem is that citizens active in the partnerships discussed above drew on different values. While they were not engaged in open resistance, they did interpret the function of partnership rather differently from public managers: as vehicles for democratic inclusion rather than as vehicles for the coordination and delivery of public services. Disagreements of this nature can undermine collaborative structures, rendering them dysfunctional. The case of New Deal for Communities (NDC), further illustrates this argument. The following passages draw freely from Davies (2005b, pp. 320–324).

The NDC is a flagship neighborhood regeneration programme established in 1999. Some £50 million was allocated to each of 39 English neighborhoods over a ten-year period. Funding was conditional on the establishment of a local multiagency partnership to deliver the program, in which local residents were to play a leading role (DETR 1999). The NDC was therefore emblematic of the U.K. government's commitment to put communities at the centre of the local regeneration process. In some ways, it has been very effective. Local residents are elected onto partnership boards, often constituting a numerical majority. Partnerships have experimented with democratic reforms, some lowering the voting age from 18 to 16, others attracting a voter turnout double that in local authority elections (Shaw and Davidson 2002). However, despite this, the NDC partnerships seem to have been subjected to ever-greater managerial constraints, undermining the original aspiration for community leadership. Resident voting majorities have not translated into effective political control. One reason for this is that in many cases community activists did not conform to the New Labour model of regeneration "good practice."

From 2001 to 2005, I was part of a consortium undertaking the government-funded national evaluation of the NDC program. I was responsible for evaluating the program in the city of Wolverhampton. In the early years of the Wolverhampton program, influenced by governmental rhetoric about community leadership, resident activists behaved as if they could spend NDC funds as they pleased. They put forward certain project proposals, which were rejected by the local and regional regeneration managers responsible for delivering and auditing the program. The managers felt that these proposals were economically unsustainable and that they had little relevance to the "strategic" regeneration needs of the area. Residents felt cheated when such proposals were vetoed by public managers citing "value for money" regulations designed to ensure that NDC money was spent responsibly.

NDC managers were charged with managing a closely audited programme and at the same time with mobilizing residents in deeply deprived areas. This mix had conflict, not consensus, built into it from the outset. The residents wanted goods such as subsidized community facilities, while the managers, backed by government officials, wanted "leverage," supporting developments only if they were deemed sustainable in the market place. While this conflict had no evident ideological character, it derived from different political and economic values—a politics of entitlement on one side, a politics of entrepreneurialism on the other. These competing values remained largely unspoken, but nevertheless lay at the heart of the problem. The moral of the tale is that the representatives of deprived communities—market losers—cannot be relied on simply to defer to the philosophies of governing elites (Davies 2005b, p. 322).

Conflicts over program strategy undermined the functional capacity of some NDC partnerships. As a consequence, program delivery was very slow, and central government, frantic to ensure that NDC partnerships delivered, quickly reneged on its commitment to community leadership. In his valedictory on four years as chair of the local NDC Board in Liverpool, the then Bishop, a renowned partnership activist, urged Tony Blair to keep faith with his promise to empower communities. He feared that the government was backtracking and bypassing residents in favour of managerial solutions (Jenkins 2004). Perrons and Skyer's study of the Shoreditch (London) NDC partnership found that centrally imposed performance management regimes rendered "the task of adequately representing the community difficult—'virtually impossible'" (2003, p. 278). Describing the programme as a potentially "volatile political cauldron" (Lawless 2004, p. 399), the director of the government-commissioned national evaluation of the NDC program argued that "the original assumption that partnerships should be given a strong degree of local flexibility and freedoms has been steadily eroded" (Lawless 2004, p. 383).

It is arguable, then, that noncompliant community activists provoked government to intervene and roll back local autonomy in ways it would not have in an ideal world of active and entrepreneurial citizens. In this interpretation, the partnership technocracy is a necessary flanking measure to neoliberalism. It is a mechanism, deployed perhaps reluctantly, to manage uncooperative "stakeholders." This, then, may help explain the conundrum of why, contrary to philosophical tradition, liberalism cannot do without authoritarianism. Loser compliance cannot be secured solely by ideological manipulation; it requires coercion. And, if liberalization cannot proceed without centralization, this points toward an irreconcilable contradiction in the neoliberal project. This contradiction plays out in partnerships where the rhetoric of community empowerment is accompanied by the practice of technocratic managerialism. It is hard to see how neoliberal partnerships can be made functional for democratic empowerment, if this entails the freedom to advocate an alternative political agenda. In the final section, therefore, I consider an alternative to the partnership model.

PARTNERSHIP EXIT AS A STRATEGY FOR DEMOCRATIC INCLUSION

There has been an interesting debate recently among a group of scholars whom I call "network egalitarians" about how partnerships might be democratized. This debate takes the current hegemony of managerialism as its problematic (Skelcher et al. 2005, p. 586). The potential of network egalitarianism depends on the feasibility of deliberative democracy. Sorensen and Torfing (2005), for example, argue that all affected actors should be included in the construction of an open-ended policy discourse. However, oppositionists may still be excluded by nondecisions or manipulation of their wants and needs. Therefore, the political agenda must be "so broadly and vaguely defined" that it is accessible to all relevant actors. Second, protagonists must show respect for other opinions and be committed to transparent, responsible decision making. They may engage in robust, confrontational debate, but should be committed to reaching a "rough consensus," for which all share responsibility (Sorensen and Torfing 2005, p. 213). These procedures depend on integrity, reflexivity, and mutual respect among democratically minded protagonists prepared to engage in relatively unconstrained debate.

Network egalitarians also suggest institutional reforms—nondeliberative mechanisms to level the deliberative playing field. For example, Klijn and Koppenjan (1999) recommend the appointment of neutral arbiters to guarantee open debate and arbitrate disputes between network actors. Skelcher (2005) advocates a more radical solution, where disadvantaged groups are given a veto over partnership decisions. He believes that this "consociational" approach could underpin a democratic "polity forming" model of governance, where subordinate groups have an equal voice in networks.

Such proposals are radical in that, if implemented, they would be incompatible with the partnership technocracy. However, they may be impractical for two reasons. First, a reform movement, unlike a revolutionary movement, requires a reformist government. The continuing geographical advance of neoliberalism suggests that in many parts of the world we will wait in vain for governments prepared to devolve sufficient power for such measures to be implemented. Within the dominant global governing paradigm, network egalitarianism appears utopian.

But, second, even if they were implemented, it is possible that these measures would merely reproduce the power inequalities they were designed to counter. Pierre Bourdieu pointed to the subtle ways by which class domination is secured and maintained: through speech, body language, culture, and taste, as well as the more transparent forms of domination apparent in Dundee and Hull (see Bourdieu 1984). As noted, network reforms rely on the possibility of deliberative equality. But, as Crossley (2004, p. 108) argues, communication or deliberation is always "systematically distorted" by the commonsense assumptions, habits, and dispositions embedded in the structured personality.

Interpreted in Bourdieusian terms, network reforms such as the neutral arbiter or the consociational veto would fail to insulate partnerships from culturally embedded structures of power. How might the neutral arbiter recognize and enter into a struggle with the structural capacities that s/he embodies? If s/he could, how would s/he recognize and overcome the subtle exercise of power by others in what might appear to be an open debate? Even if governments conceded a veto over partnership decisions to community representatives, cultural power would govern the interpretation and exercise of that veto. The meaning and appropriateness of "veto" would be produced by convention and common sense, the symbolic capital accrued by dominant groups in past struggles (see Davies 2007 for a detailed account). Consequently, in a world characterized by vast social inequalities, the prospect of equitable deliberation appears very limited, particularly when the rules of the game are set by governmental actors who appear to be part of the problem. In Dundee and Hull, the problem was not that public managers did not want to engage in partnership with communities, but that they were unable to grasp perspectives that conflicted with their commonsense understanding of good governance.

If not partnership, then what? One answer lies in the traditions of resistance reflected in the social movement and community-organizing literatures. Kohn (2000, p. 425) argues that critical distance permits the creation of protected space where social movements can "explore and test genuinely alternative ways of framing collective problems." If governing institutions reproduce power inequalities, then disempowered groups have to build new institutions, incubating alternative approaches and gaining strength. But creating a separate space is not sufficient. Says Kohn (2000, p. 426) " . . . realizing abstractions such as reciprocity, equality and opportunity is usually a process of historical struggle rather than theoretical consensus." This struggle takes place not through deliberation, but at "concrete sites of resistance, the . . . barricades, forums, and fortresses where the people mount challenges to currently hegemonic visions of collective life." Separation can be an act of resistance, but it must be complemented by coercive action to overcome dominant interests.

Medearis (2005, p. 55) develops this theme in a critique of deliberative democracy. He argues that where hierarchical power is pervasive, "marginal groups must often act coercively in order to achieve democratic aims." Commitment to collaborative values requires activists to concede the positional legitimacy of local elites and give up the right to act coercively against them in favour of persuasion. The freedom to act coercively therefore requires that they reject the politics of collaboration. With this freedom secured, argues Medearis, coercive action is capable of restructuring the dominant discourse and altering "the social relations in which discourse is situated." Coercion threatens dominant interests, disrupts alliances, and creates crises (Medearis 2005, p. 55). Medearis argues that coercive strategies have often been used very effectively by social movements seeking to "regenerate democracy," notably the U.S. civil rights movement (2005, p. 75). The community-based anti-poll-tax movement is a fairly recent example of a coercive strategy in the United Kingdom. The victorious movement in 2006 against the deregulation of youth employment law in France is another. If this analysis is right, community activists may achieve greater governing influence by organizing against elites than by collaborating with them (Davies 2007).

This does not mean that community activists ought never to cooperate with state actors. Saegert's overview of the U.S. community-organizing and development literatures examines the effectiveness of collaborative and confrontational strategies. Each approach can, depending on circumstance, "partially succeed and partially fail" (Saegert 2006, p. 292; see also Stoecker 2003). But where neoliberalism dominates local politics, it is unlikely that partnership will be empowering in the sense of offering communities a democratic voice or allowing those with critical perspectives to challenge the dominant understanding of "good governance." Participation then depends on a judgment call about whether partnership enhances the political power of poor and oppressed communities or not. In New Labour Britain, the prognosis is negative.

CONCLUSIONS

Judd and Smith's contribution (see Chapter 11) demonstrates that statutory development partnerships, such as special authorities, are designed specifically to avoid democratic scrutiny. This chapter argues that partnerships that are nominally open to local communities are also becoming increasingly undemocratic and authoritarian. The rise of neoliberal partnerships as "an elite form of local governance" (Geddes 2005, p. 363) seems inimical to the ideal-typical model of collaborative democracy, where local state actors engage communities and other "stakeholders" in open, relatively unconstrained deliberation.

Unfortunately, the fashion for partnership in local governance shows no sign of passing. Partnership is considered by many left-of-centre scholars to be, if not a panacea, then an important part of the solution to growing pubic alienation from official politics and public bureaucracies. The challenge they face is to demonstrate that reform is feasible and, if so, that reformed partnerships will not reproduce the power inequalities they seek to counter. In the mean time, "exit" is a practical alternative. Where democracy is undermined by the neoliberal partnership technocracy, community activists should consider abandoning participation for organized resistance.

ACKNOWLEDGEMENT

This chapter draws on research entitled *Interpreting the Local Politics of Social Inclusion* funded by the U.K. Economic and Social Research Council (award RES-000-22-0542).

DISCLAIMER

I was a member of the national consortium undertaking the 2002–2005 evaluation of New Deal for Communities funded by the Office of the Deputy Prime Minister (ODPM). The views expressed here are not those of the ODPM, now renamed Department of Communities and Local Government.

PART IV

GOVERNING CITIES IN A GLOBAL ERA

CHAPTER 16

FROM GOVERNANCE TO GOVERNING

ROBIN HAMBLETON AND JILL SIMONE GROSS

INTRODUCTION

In our opening chapter we argued that two major changes are transforming the agenda of those concerned with the governance of cities: globalization and urbanization. These are both words that are used frequently in modern discourse about societal change—they trip off the tongue with ease. A consequence is that the true significance of their meaning may sometimes escape us. We suggested in Chapter 1 that both these trends are not just dramatic—they are unprecedented in human history. It follows that those concerned with the governance of cities need to recognize that minor adjustments to past practice are unlikely to be successful in meeting the new challenges that now confront them. We take the view that the pace and dynamism of modern change require leaders to make bold, imaginative leaps if they are not to be overtaken by events.

The challenges are many. In this book we have sought to address three major questions:

- What are the implications of globalization for urban government and governance?
- How are cities and metropolitan areas responding to these unprecedented economic, social, environmental, and political changes?
- What are the implications for those who must lead and manage increasingly complex multicultural cities and city regions?

The preceding three parts of the book have spotlighted each of these questions in turn. Through vivid case studies as well as comparative analyses and overview commentaries, our contributors have addressed these questions in an imaginative way. Many of our authors have, of course, offered insights that throw light on more than one of these three questions. This is as it should be—it is not necessary, or even desirable, to compartmentalize discussion of these inter-related topics. Thus, global trends stimulate responses and, in turn, the process of examining how cities are responding to these trends in different geographical contexts generates new ways of thinking, not just about alternative responses but also about the nature of the trends themselves. In this final chapter we offer some broad reflections on the evidence presented in this volume as well as our thoughts on possible ways forward in relation to both urban practice and comparative urban research and lesson drawing.

THE WORLD IS NOT FLAT

As we mentioned in Chapter 1, major steps forward in global horizontal connectivity, aided by computers, e-mail, and the Internet, have led to the suggestion that the "world is flat" (Friedman 2005). The evidence presented in this book rejects this view. Friedman and others, who have studied the rapid expansion of global communication systems, are right to highlight the way space is no longer the obstacle to interpersonal exchange that it once was. Startling advances are taking place in communication technologies and we can expect these technologies to become even more influential in the future. But, the role of this new technology in creating a level, global playing field for would-be economic and social entrepreneurs is in danger of being overstated. These new and improved communication systems are being laid down onto an *uneven* landscape of differential advantage. The contributors to this book show that the world continues to be characterized by sharp divides in power, access to knowledge and wealth—and that huge divides are to be found even within cities and city regions that, in aggregate terms, appear to be prosperous. More than that, our authors also illustrate the importance of local institutions, actors, culture, and context in understanding the dynamics of urban change. Localities situated at strategic nodes in the world communications system—such as New York and London—compete in an entirely different way from places that lack these advantages—such as Abidjan and Medellín.

A key lesson to emerge from this volume is that, given the significant differences that continue to exist (within cities, between cities, between nations), it becomes even more critical for policy makers and community leaders to take great care when considering (1) what models and theories to turn to and apply; (2) what policies and programs to select and seek to promote; and (3) what approaches to leadership and management to adopt for their cities. In offering this comment we are not suggesting that countries, cities, and communities cannot learn from each other—indeed, later in the chapter, we will offer some suggestions on how to improve cross-national learning. Rather, we want to sound a warning note at the beginning of this chapter about the dangers of generalizing too freely about global trends and approaches.

Context and place are critical elements in understanding globalization and urbanization. Staunch "localists" may even take the view that there is nothing to be gained from studying experience abroad. They will argue that societal differences are simply too great for comparative urban studies to offer useful insights, let alone wise and helpful proposals, for busy national policy makers and city leaders. We are not so pessimistic. We take the view that, despite the existence of powerful global forces driving sameness and homogenization, it is clear that communities are responding in a variety of ways— ways sometimes similar to each other, sometimes not. Different cities and communities are carving out diverse patterns of response to global pressures. Individual cities and communities can learn by examining these differences to see whether they prompt fresh ideas for local consideration. Communities of place and communities of interest, such as transnational ethnic communities, are interpreting global changes in their own way. Moreover, our authors identify similar tensions and conflicts in very different contexts— for example, frictions between established communities of place and newly arrived migrants and immigrants appear to be widespread. In our view there is every reason to share understanding and cross-national insights as this may assist cities in improving the way they respond to these relentless international pressures.

GOVERNMENT, GOVERNANCE, AND GOVERNING—CLARIFYING MEANINGS

In Chapter 1 we suggested that, in the ongoing discourse about how to govern and manage cities, there is a fashionable view that "government" should give way to "governance." While this is a trend that has been examined in numerous chapters in this volume, we should hesitate before generalizing too freely—it may be that the terms have slightly different meanings in different contexts. This is, however, a crucial debate that goes to the heart of the leadership task now facing just about all cities—what role should "government," as distinct from "governance," play in the future strategy for "governing" cities and city regions?

Let us examine these terms more closely. In Chapter 1 we defined local "government," in its ideal form, as the democratically accountable formal institutions of the state operating in the locality—providing services, acting as channels for the representation of local interests, and generating a secure environment for residents, businesses, and visitors alike. Thus, local government in many countries is empowered to, for example, regulate the use of private land, permit or disallow urban development, decide on how to spend public money, raise or lower local taxes, and so on. In established democratic systems, citizens grant local governments legitimacy to exercise these powers through a democratic political process—usually voting at the ballot box.

The degree of power that local governments have does, of course, vary. For example, many cities in the United States have local "home rule charters" that provide for a high level of local autonomy, while cities in China remain largely controlled by higher levels of government. Most cities lie somewhere between these two extremes. In any given country the arrangements for "government" may be "democratically accountable," but this is not necessarily the case.

"Governance" is broader than "government" and, as defined by Hambleton in Chapter 12, it "involves government *plus* the looser processes of influencing and negotiating with a range of public and private sector agencies to achieve desired outcomes." In governance models, attention focuses less on the role of the state and more on the need for collaboration between different stakeholders in the public, private, and nonprofit sectors. In the U.K. context Stewart describes governance as "a process of multi-stakeholder involvement, of multiple interest resolution, of compromise rather than confrontation, of negotiation rather than administrative fiat" (Stewart 2003, p. 76).

If we stick with this distinction for a moment, we can see that local "government," in its ideal form, is a democratically accountable institution of the state enjoying specific administrative and legal powers that enable it to make collective decisions on behalf of the local population. "Governance," which brings together a wider range of actors (from civil society and the private sector), involves different interests working in partnership to address shared concerns.

Twenty years ago, the urban studies literature in both the developed and the developing world focused on "government." Initially, government was looked at almost exclusively through the lens of institutions and structures and then, later, researchers branched out to explore actors and behaviors. Local government was perceived narrowly as an arm of the state operating in the locality. There is a substantial pre-1980 literature describing and analyzing local government and not a small amount examining proposals for reforming the institutions of local "government" and approaches to urban "management." In those days many countries placed great faith in the role of the state to solve societal problems.

While varying cross-nationally in scale and scope, we can see the emergence—in the 1980s and the 1990s—of a case for moving from "government" to "governance." The oil shocks of the 1970s, the recessions in the 1980s and the 1990s, and global economic restructuring, left many governments scrambling for resources. Couched differently in different countries, common themes in the debates that brought about the shift from government to governance were a recognition that the state cannot go it alone; that working in partnership with other stakeholders can improve problem-solving capacity; that no one organization has a monopoly of wisdom in relation to solving urban challenges; and that new and more inclusive approaches to community representation and leadership needed to be developed. Driven by public purpose all these motivations signaled a desire to strengthen the government's capacity to work with a range of stakeholders to solve societal problems.

"Governance" came to be seen as an increasingly attractive option and, as Stren contends in Chapter 5, it is a relational concept. He sees it as describing the "relationship between the government and the people, between the formal political structure and civil society." Governance, then, acknowledges the diffusion of responsibility for collective provision and recognizes the contribution of different levels and sectors to the well-being of the community. But, as we describe below, there appear to be limitations to the "governance" approach. The dialogue we have had with our authors on this important theme has taught us that local context, history, and experience matter enormously in this debate.

Critics of the "governance" approach point out that some protagonists sought a shift from "government" to "governance" for ideological reasons. Politicians on the radical right—and this was particularly noticeable in the United Kingdom and the United States during the Thatcher (1979–1990) and Reagan (1981–1989) years—were attracted to the notion of "governance" because they saw it as a way of "rolling back the state" and enhancing the role of the private sector in public affairs. Nicholas Ridley, when he was U.K. Secretary of State for the Environment in Prime Minister Thatcher's Conservative government, argued that the government should be cut back dramatically: "This government goes in for private ownership, because assets in *private* hands are cared for and used efficiently, while assets in public hands have too often been allowed to decay and stagnate and become a burden on the community" (Ridley 1988, p. 23, author's emphasis). Ridley advocated selling off city halls, arguing that the local "government" could function by hiring a tent once a year to hold a meeting at which it could let the contracts for running public services to private companies. While relatively few politicians are quite so antigovernment, it needs to be acknowledged that neoliberal politicians still see "governance" as a way of off-loading state responsibilities onto civil society and as a way of saving public money.

GOVERNMENT, GOVERNANCE, AND GOVERNING—ARGUMENTS AND ISSUES

In this volume we see the presentation of varying views on the "governance" theme. Thus, Stren, in Chapter 5, argues that, so far as the developing world is concerned, it is highly desirable to move toward a "governance" approach. In some countries, the local government may be corrupt and a governance approach to decision making, by bringing in a range of stakeholders, could lead to a strengthening of accountability. In many localities, it may well be the only way for city governments to "govern" amid the challenges of urbanization and globalization. In Chapter 9 Betancur offers a cautionary tale about the viability of such a strategy in Columbia, mainly because civil society is relatively weak. He notes that effective "governance" requires a careful balance of actors, or risks potential local failure, manifested in breakdowns in services and infrastructure or popular unrest. In his view the shift from "government" to "governance" implies an ability on the part of the government to maintain social peace and law and order. He notes that this may not always be the case and asks how the concept of governance can work in countries where these conditions do not arise.

The literature on urban governance in developing countries is rich in insights on this theme. A position that, perhaps, unites many policy makers, activists, and scholars is that it is essential for countries that have relatively young traditions of local democracy to secure legitimacy for those expected to lead. While there is no standard recipe for success, legitimacy is likely to flow, in many settings, from an approach that combines multiple actors drawn from the local state and civil society, from public, private, and nonprofit sectors. It may be that "government" and "governance" models can be combined. Governance, in the absence of government, risks throwing localities into crises of legitimacy, while government, in the absence of governance, risks throwing localities into crises of capacity.

Two of our chapters present a robust critique of "governance" models as introduced in the United States and the United Kingdom. Judd and Smith in Chapter 11 argue that unaccountable special-purpose authorities are now in control of the important decisions shaping U.S. cities. Going by this analysis, "governance" has gone too far—important private stakeholders have been brought into the process to the point where they have actually taken it over. U.S. city leaders can be expected to contest this interpretation, but it is difficult to dispute the demonstrable growth in power of quasi-public institutions in U.S. urban governance or to contest the view that they patently lack transparency. In Chapter 15 Davies offers a similarly trenchant critique of developments in U.K. local governance. He argues that the patterns of partnership working that have emerged in recent years in U.K. localities are, essentially, top-down affairs designed to orchestrate a neoliberal agenda. Again, we find evidence of "governance" concepts being used to privilege certain stakeholders at the expense of others. Given the distorted power structures encountered in U.K. local partnerships, Davies advises community activists to "exit" partnership structures and engage in organized resistance.

In summary, this discussion suggests, in a positive vein, that "government" *can* serve public purpose. Elected representatives and hard-working public officials are to be found across the world who deserve our admiration for the way they pursue the public interest in a selfless way. But "government" can also be corrupt, and strong mechanisms for holding leaders to account are clearly needed in all cities. "Governance" can lead to imaginative new approaches to collaborative problem solving at the urban scale. But it can also be a vehicle for advancing a neoliberal agenda or local patronage. In both instances the system does not serve the interests of all citizens. We take the view that there is now a danger of the discourse about the future of cities descending into a sterile exchange between those who favor strong government and those who favor a weak role for the state, placing their hopes in governance models. A better course of action is to focus on the desired outcomes. What kind of city do urban dwellers want? How can such a city be created? What institutional arrangements can further democratically identified aspirations? How can those aspirations be implemented? An approach of this kind would, in our view, lead to new thinking about the overall process of governing cities and city regions. Both "government" and "governance" can be expected to play a role in an effective and accountable approach to governing. The successful city of the future, as the contributors to this collection argue, is one that values social cohesion as well as economic prosperity and sustainable development. City leaders must be concerned with more than efficiency—to govern effectively they also need to be concerned with legitimacy, responsiveness, fairness, and capacity. We can anticipate, therefore, that successful cities of the future will have created more transparent and inclusive forms of decision making than tends to be the case in most cities today.

In our view a focus on "governing" is desirable as it can blend together an interest in using the *legitimate* hierarchical power of the state (i.e., government) with an *inclusive* approach to partnership building (i.e., governance). If we can move the discourse beyond a contest between "government" and "governance" approaches, it may be that we can arrive at a sharper focus on the desired outcomes of societal action.

DYNAMIC DIVERSITY IN THE MODERN CITY

An important theme identified by many of the authors in this collection is that globalization and urbanization are generating new patterns of what we would like to term "dynamic diversity." While the reasons why people choose to reside in the city vary, it is clear that more and more are following this path globally. In Chapter 1 we presented evidence to show that the world will soon be predominately urban. At the same time, we recognize a dynamism that is inherent to this process. As Brenner argues, "[T]he urban scale is not a pre-given or fixed platform for social relations, but a socially constituted, politically contested and historically variable dimension" (2000, p. 367). Cities and city regions are in flux—some are expanding at a breathtaking pace, some are actually shrinking. Within cities some areas are receiving truly massive injections of capital investment—often in association with various kinds of megaproject—while other neighborhoods are turning into vacant wastelands. While some groups within cities have become extremely wealthy as a result of urban restructuring, others have lost out completely.

In Chapter 4 Punch, Redmond, and Kelly review some of the theoretical approaches that can help us understand the patterns of uneven development, or dynamic diversity, now encountered in modern cities. They challenge the narrative about urban social change that sees the imperatives of capital accumulation as the only significant driver of economic restructuring. In contrast they posit a "global-local" nexus in which the top-down forces of capital —the apparently ceaseless drive to make money out of money— encounter local cultures and social worlds that may not share this imperative. People living in particular places have their own history, experiences, and views of the world. They attach cultural meaning to local landscapes, traditions, and community activities. This sense of home, history, and engagement with locale gives rise to what these authors term "life place." The chapter provides a case study of urban conflict in Dublin's inner city. In an important sense, however, the chapter illuminates a wider pattern found in many of our other chapters—the interplay between global forces driving homogenization and "life place" forces insisting on diversity. The importance of recognizing this interplay finds support in other studies of urban change—see, for example, Savitch and Kantor (2002) and Ranney (2003). It is a framework that challenges the neoliberal view that globalization in the interests of capital is an inexorable force that cannot be stopped.

Population movements are contributing to new patterns of dynamic diversity. In some cities of the world, the population is dominated by youth, in other cases the urban population is aging. Immigrant flows are constantly changing in response to the changing geopolitics of host and sending nations, creating new ethnic and religious mixes at different points in time. Economic restructuring elevates some workers while subordinating others (Sassen 2006). And while diversity—ethnic, social, economic, and political—can, under optimum conditions, enable cities to offer remarkable opportunities for both established residents and those newly arrived, it can, if poorly governed, become the basis for exclusion, division, and social breakdown. This is especially the case when ethnic, social, economic, religious, or political differences become the basis for unequal access to jobs, housing, and urban services. The authors in this book suggest, in different ways, that the diversity of needs now found in the modern city requires differentiated policies and programs or, as Gross argues in Chapter 6, that "one size does not fit all" in the contemporary city.

Both Gross in Chapter 6 and Bockmeyer in Chapter 13 document troubling spatial divisions and patterns of social and political exclusion in a number of cities based on race, religion, and class. In Chapter 8 Zhang's examination of urban change in Shanghai also identifies tensions between different groups—in this case between "the original city residents" and the "new comers." Chinese policy makers, as with city leaders elsewhere, need to guard against allowing their bold efforts to attract inward investment into major Chinese cities to obscure the importance of addressing the needs of the floating migrant population. In many cities, and this is particularly true of cities in the developing world, social divisions are growing, and this, at the very least, should raise serious questions for urban leaders. Urban economic growth that creates tension and conflict does not provide a sustainable platform for lasting urban prosperity.

Various chapters in this volume suggest that those lacking in social or economic status often find themselves spatially segregated in the modern city—in ghettos or shantytowns—or situated in the most environmentally vulnerable parts of the city, such as flood plains or brown fields. Gated communities for wealthy residents—essentially fortified enclaves surrounded by walls and high levels of security—now proliferate in cities in Latin America, North America, and Western Europe and are also on the increase in China. These spatial trends point toward the disaster scenario for cities that we sketched out in Chapter 1—this scenario suggested that the modern city is in danger of becoming a balkanized world, with consumers living isolated lives in separate fortified enclaves. A central cause of this pattern is, we would argue, the political inability of some cities to respond to and manage diversity.

The challenge is a demanding one. Both national and city leaders are faced with unprecedented transitions as a result of population movements. There are regional differences here between cities in the north and the south, the east and the west—and this can lead to significantly different policy responses. As various authors have explained, in the developing world, the fundamental challenge relates to rapid migration to the cities from the countryside. But the causes of migration vary. In parts of Africa, the city is often safer than the countryside, where conflicts over territory and ethnicity have resulted in violent civil wars. In China, India, and Latin America, the city often offers economic opportunities that are absent from the rural countryside. While the underlying reasons for migratory movements to the city may be different, the central task of incorporating the voices of these groups into urban governing processes is transcendent. One pointer from our chapters on developing countries is that more should be done to improve understanding of the causes of migration in different contexts. Better understanding may enable policy makers to take steps to diminish the pace of movement to the cities to the benefit of both urban and rural areas.

In Western European cities, we find very different patterns of dynamic diversity. Rapid population growth, of the kind now being experienced in Asia, Africa, and Latin America, occurred during the period of urban industrialization over a century ago. The major migratory challenge is, on the whole, no longer how to accommodate population growth. Indeed, many European cities are experiencing out-migration of certain groups, with the result that city leaders are increasingly concerned with slow or zero growth and with meeting the needs of an aging population. In relation to the dynamic diversity agenda, the key challenge for city leaders is how to respond to the distinctive needs of newcomers and to head off a rise in social and economic inequality. As Bockmeyer suggests, in her analysis of neighborhood management in German cities in Chapter 13, measures to improve the capacity of newcomers through training and skill development programs, as well as an emphasis on legal frameworks for political inclusion, are becoming increasingly important. She notes that new immigrants may, in fact, posses the requisite job skills but lack the capacity to access employment opportunities—due to either lack of information or transportation or, at times, deliberate exclusion.

Shifts in world politics following the terrorist attacks on New York City and Washington, D.C. on September 11, 2001 have added a new and unwelcome dimension to analysis of diversity in the modern city. The thoughtless rhetoric about a "war on terror" has generated a climate of fear and tension in many cities. Misguided U.S. foreign policy, particularly the incompetent and damaging invasion of Iraq, has done untold damage to community relations in multicultural communities across the world. Fear and misunderstanding are—in many settings—on the rise and are contributing to a growth in anger and hate. As Levin and Rabrenovic (2004) argue, expressions of hate are trumpeted each evening on the television news and, over time, this has a disturbing effect. Spurred on by failures of political leadership as well as poor coverage on the part of the mass media, "organized hate," in the form of white supremacist and extremist ethno-religious groups, is clearly on the rise. In their examination of this phenomena, Levin and Rabrenovic (2004) offer many insights on "Why we hate," as well as provide inspiring examples from sites of conflict around the world, including Northern Ireland, that show astonishing cooperation between ethnic and religious groups that have transcended hate.

MULTILEVEL GOVERNANCE AND THE CITY

Globalization, as we have seen, unleashes competition not only between groups within the city, but also between cities in the global system. Thus, London now competes with Tokyo to lure or maintain corporate finance, and Pittsburgh competes with Shanghai for steel industry contracts. This leads governments at all geographic scales to pay more attention to urban economic development and, more specifically, to take steps to support projects and infrastructure designed to attract private sector inward investment. As cities come to be recognized as serious players in the international economy, their role is changing and, in some countries at least, higher levels of government are paying much more attention to the performance of their urban economies. As Jouve and Lefevre (2002) point out, central government policy makers have come to realize that cities and city regions are key drivers of national economies and that, therefore, the local institutions running cities can come to play a crucial role for national economic policy. In the European context Le Gales (2002) confirms that economic growth has tended to become an urban phenomenon, partly because of the growth in the importance of the "knowledge economy." In Europe, then, cities and city regions are now seen as engines of national economic prosperity (Antalovsky et al. 2005). Not surprisingly, this has led to the introduction of new forms of city leadership designed to enhance the visibility and effectiveness of city governments as leaders of economic development. In Chapter 12, for example, Hambleton notes that directly elected mayors have recently been introduced in England, Germany, and Italy, partly for this reason.

In Chapter 2 Tsukamoto and Vogel examine the roles of different levels of government in the operation of some twenty "globalized cities" and conclude that significant territorial rescaling is occurring around the world. Some of this rescaling is in line with the conventional wisdom, implicit in the literature on globalization, which suggests that national policy makers should build the "institutional capacity" of their cities so that they can compete in the global marketplace. Thus, there is evidence of political decentralization taking place in some countries. For example, in London, a new metropolitan authority—the Greater London Authority—with a directly elected mayor, was created in 2000 partly to strengthen the institutional capacity of London to act as a global city. However, in some instances, power is being moved upward, and Tsukamoto and Vogel suggest that central governments are becoming more actively involved in the strategic development of their global cities than is commonly recognized—Paris provides a classic example.

In Chapter 3 Röber and Schröter examine the historical evolution of big city government in Berlin, London, and Paris and identify a moderate convergence in the institutional design of the government arrangements for these three capitals. They sketch the emergence of two-tier systems of government in these big cities—with the upper tier focusing on strategic planning functions and internationally visible cultural events and economic projects, and with the lower tier handling local decision making and the delivery of a range of welfare services. Other chapters also point to the importance of policy makers taking active steps to manage what is increasingly recognized as a multilevel process of governance. For example, Kübler and Randolph, in their study of the Sydney experience with metropolitan governance in Chapter 10, show how the city has become both the leading "gateway" city for immigrants to Australia as well as the only recognizably global city in the country. The current fragmented governmental arrangements in the Sydney metropolitan area are identified as providing an unsatisfactory basis for a global city. They note that moves are afoot to improve area-wide public governance—although, as with many cities in the United States, this is a fraught process as parochial vested interests often strive to cling to the status quo.

According to Zhang in Chapter 8, it is now municipalities rather than the central government that are shaping China's urban landscape. This is a very significant shift as it suggests that, in the case of Shanghai, a centrally planned push to ignite urban economic growth has, as a by-product, encouraged the emergence of "quasi-participatory decision-making structures" and the generation of an array of private actors providing needed services and infrastructure. From a democratic governance point of view, the missing piece, in this example, relates to the role of civil society—as Zhang reminds us there are several million migrant workers residing in the city, but they have no legitimacy in the decision-making system that is shaping the future of Shanghai.

There is not space here to examine the role of supranational institutions in the multilevel governance of cities and city regions, but we must note that the role of the European Union has grown in importance in European urban governance (Carmichael 2006). Indeed, it has stimulated considerable innovation, particularly in cross-border collaboration (Church and Reid 2002). One lesson to emerge from this discussion concerns the role of higher levels of government in supporting the emergence of effective arrangements for governing cities and city regions. There are no "off the shelf solutions" here, but it seems clear that higher-level governments have a responsibility to ensure that effective governance arrangements and resources are in place. In too many countries national governments are failing to rise to this challenge. As discussed in the next section, local leadership and an enlivened local democracy are crucial for urban success, but these local energies need to be orchestrated and supported by higher levels of government (state and federal in federal systems, national in unitary systems). This means ensuring that the powers, funding, and the configuration of local democratic institutions are suited to modern challenges rather than to a bygone era.

LEADERSHIP AND LOCAL DEMOCRACY

It is too easy for city leaders to blame higher levels of government for all their woes—and the best do not do this. As Hambleton argues in Chapter 12, bold, outward-looking city leadership is essential if cities are to compete successfully in a global era. He notes that individual characteristics matter. Strong, effective leaders—Ken Livingstone, the mayor of London, provides a striking example—make a significant contribution by virtue of the sophisticated leadership skills they bring to the task. But Hambleton also notes that context matters enormously—the local institutional design and configuration of metropolitan governance can help or hinder the emergence of visionary city leadership. Thus, in the London case, it is clear that the institutional design introduced by the U.K. Labour Government in 2000—a Greater London Authority (exercising strategic planning and economic development powers) headed by a directly elected mayor—provides a splendid platform for the exercise of high-profile leadership by whoever is elected mayor of the capital. The design provides for legitimacy, visibility, accountability, and authority—a powerful combination. In terms of the international projection of the city, it is at least debatable whether London would have been able to win the competition to host the Olympics in 2012 had the city governance arrangements been as feeble and opaque as they were in period before the Labour Government came to power in 1997.

In Chapter 7 Swianiewicz offers a detailed examination of the changing pattern of local government arrangements in Central and Eastern European (CEE) countries and concludes, inter alia, that the introduction of directly elected mayors (in Bulgaria, Poland, Romania, Slovakia, and Slovenia) has strengthened the role of executive leadership. This may enhance the competitive position of cities in these countries. Perhaps disappointing for advocates of the directly elected mayor model, his evidence from the CEE countries does not suggest at this point that directly elected mayors have been able to heighten citizen interest in local elections. This is an important finding for, without the legitimacy that comes from strong political support, city leaders—whether directly elected or not—will not be able to command the necessary authority to shape the behavior of the many stakeholders in the modern city. Gross found similar outcomes in London voting patterns following the introduction of an elected mayor (2004).

A key challenge facing all cities is how to combine modern management practices with strong and effective citizen involvement. In Chapter 12 Hambleton examines the way "new public management" has been introduced into local government in many countries. While this move to introduce private sector management practices into public service bureaucracies has brought some benefits, the thrust of his argument is the suggestion that the movement has limited potential. He advocates a broader approach, which he describes as "new city management," in which public service managers strive to enhance the quality of government as well as work to modernize and improve the quality of services. Nalbandian takes this idea further in Chapter 14 where he makes a powerful case for blending efforts to modernize public management with steps to foster the public good by enhancing civic engagement. He notes that, all too often, two important strands of local government reform have become isolated from each other. Administrative modernization promises reliability, consistency, and low variation in quality. However, at the same time, it can drive out spontaneity, tradition, identity, and preservation of community. Citizen engagement resists uniformity of treatment. Communities strive to create something unique and within one's control—something that signals identity. The challenge is to build bridges between these two forces for reform. Nalbandian believes that public managers can work closely with politicians to convey public service values and promote civic discovery.

Several of our authors have drawn attention to the limitations of centralized forms of decision making in local governance. Neighborhood management (or neighborhood decentralization) has gained in popularity in many countries as it can enhance responsiveness to the needs of particular localities as well as create opportunities for community involvement. In Chapter 13 Bockmeyer examines the emergence and performance of neighborhood management in Germany. In this study she focuses on the experience of immigrant communities in neighborhood decision making and concludes that, while new settings for engagement have been created, the effectiveness of the model has been constrained by inadequate resources and conflicts between local officials and local people. As revealed by other studies of neighborhood decentralization—in, for example, the United Kingdom (Burns et al. 1994), Mexico (Flores 2005), and Sweden (Tedros and Johansson 2006)—devolved management presents major challenges to vested interests and, if citizen involvement is to thrive, there has to be significant cultural change within the public service bureaucracies.

Participatory budgeting offers another way of engaging local citizens in decisions that affect their locality. As Stren observes in Chapter 5, this model first gained real momentum in Brazil, with Porto Alegre providing a fine example (Wainwright 2003). However, the approach is now spreading across international frontiers, and Stren suggests that as many as 1,000 cities may now have adopted this approach.

As city authorities strive to develop more inclusive approaches to decision making, they will need to pay even more attention to the "dynamic diversity" we discussed earlier in this chapter. In Chapter 6 Gross examines this theme in some depth. Using the cases of Paris, Copenhagen, and Toronto, she concludes that simply creating channels for popular involvement in decision making, or even offering new city dwellers the opportunity to vote regardless of citizenship status, is not enough. If local governments lack the resources or political will to directly respond to popular input, then local residents are far more likely to turn to less formal methods of influence, such as direct action, protest, or riot. She finds that different communities within cities are participating in very different ways. The divergent histories and experiences that urban populations have had with democratic government and governance will shape how they approach political participation in the locality. Gross suggests that because cities are becoming more ethnically diverse, city leaders may need to develop more differentiated approaches and paths to promoting political engagement in different ethnic and, possibly, religious communities—one size does not fit all.

CROSS-NATIONAL POLICY TRANSFER

Earlier in this chapter we suggested that there is a great deal of scope for cross-national learning and exchange in relation to urban government and governance. Rose (2005) offers some helpful advice on how to go about what he calls "instrumental learning" from other countries. He suggests that policy makers do not seek fresh ideas for their own sake but to promote political satisfaction. This lays down a significant challenge for academics. Comparative research on public policy, including comparative research on urban governance, is an expanding field. But when this work is limited to advancing understanding—the traditional focus of scholarship—it falls short of instrumental learning. Cross-national lesson drawing requires investigators to go beyond description and analysis and offer evidence-based advice to policy makers.

There are four main reasons why those concerned with the future of cities—whether as academics or practitioners—should devote more time to instrumental learning from abroad. First, as Rose observes, learning can focus on actual accomplishments in another setting. This, he argues, can provide a better basis for policy innovation than merely making up ideas and speculating about what might happen if they were adopted. Second, in a rapidly globalizing world, citizens expect professionals to be up to date with the latest developments—wherever they take place. As emphasized in Chapter 1, information, people, and money now flow almost effortlessly across national frontiers in the worlds of science, business, the arts, and culture. Why should public policy be walled into national enclaves? Third, city leaders, planners, and managers operate in an increasingly multicultural world. Examining experience in other countries can enhance the "cultural competence" of both politicians and professionals by exposing individuals to different ways of doing things. A fourth reason for studying experience overseas is that—as revealed by many of the chapters in this book—common problems do *not* produce an identical response. It is the *differences* in the responses that governments make to common problems that can offer powerful and compelling insights for both theory and practice.

True, there are pitfalls to avoid in cross-national learning, but if the process of transfer is handled carefully, we believe that lesson drawing from overseas can provide substantial gains for both academic understanding of urban governing and for the practice of governing cities.

CITY FUTURES

In Chapter 1 we sketched out two alternative scenarios for the future of cities. The alarming scenario envisaged globalization threatening local jobs, widening social divisions, and damaging social relations. In this scenario the politics of fear and hate gain ascendancy and the city spirals downward into a balkanized world with self-interested consumers living empty lives in fortified enclaves protected from the poor by expensive security systems. The optimistic scenario suggests that global awareness grows in leaps and bounds. Transnational migrants continue to refresh the culture, economic vitality, and politics of vibrant urban areas. Tolerance between different ethno-religious groups improves as diverse communities come to understand each other and work out ways of living together. Local democracy is revitalized and the public realm is expanded and cities reestablish themselves as centers of culture and civilized living. It is not difficult to identify the scenario that maximizes the quality of life for all urban dwellers. We hope this book helps city leaders, managers, academics, and activists steer cities toward the optimistic scenario. We have stressed that local culture and context are the lifeblood of the city and that cities should differ. But in one sense they should be the same. They should stand for the notion of democracy—for the creation of an inclusive public realm in which all voices are influential, not just the voices of the rich and powerful.

BIBLIOGRAPHY

Aalen, F. H. A. 1992. "Health and Housing in Dublin c. 1850 to 1921." In *Dublin City and County: From Prehistory to Present,* edited by F. H. A. Aalen and K. Whelaned. Dublin: Geography Publications.

Abello, A. 1992. "Reestructuración Industrial o Desindustrialización?" *Deslinde,* (January/February): 54.

Abers, R. 1998. "Learning Democratic Practice: Distributing Government Resources through Popular Participation in Porto Alegre, Brazil." In *Cities for Citizens. Planning and the Rise of Civil Society in a Global Age,* edited by M. Douglass and J. Friedmann. Chichester, UK: John Wiley.

Abrahamson, M. 2004. *Global Cities.* New York: Oxford University Press.

ABS (Australian Bureau of Statistics). 2005. *Australian Standard Geographical Classification.* Canberra: Australian Bureau of Statistics.

Abu-Lughod, J. L. 1999. *New York, Chicago, Los Angeles: America's Global Cities.* Minneapolis: University of Minnesota Press.

Aehnelt, R., H. Häussermann, W. Jaedicke, M. Kahl, and K. Toepel. 2004. *Interim Appraisal for the Federal-Länder-Programme "Districts with Special Development Needs—the Social City."* Short version. September. Berlin: IfS Institut für Stadtforschung und Strukturpolitik GmbH.

Aghón, G., and C. Casas. 1999. "Strengthening Municipal Financing: Difficulties and New Challenges for Latin America." In *Fiscal Decentralisation in Emerging Economies. Governance Issues,* edited by K. Fukusaku and L. R. de Mello. Paris: OECD.

Agnew, J. A., S. Michael, and G. Bettoni. 2002. "City Versus Metropolis: The Northern League in the Milan Metropolitan Area." *International Journal of Urban and Regional Research* 26: 266–83.

Agranoff, R., and M. McGuire. 2003. *Collaborative Public Management: New Strategies for Local Governments.* Washington, D.C.: Georgetown University Press.

AHD (American Heritage Dictionary). 1982. Second edition. Boston: Houghton Mifflin.

Aja, E. 2001. "Spain: Nation, Nationalities, and Regions." In *Subnational Democracy in the European Union: Challenges and Opportunities,* edited by J. Loughlin. Oxford: Oxford University Press.

Alayón Monserrat, R. 1997. "No Todos Subirán al Tren: Globalización, Pobreza y Eclosión." *Revista Venezolana de Análisis de Coyuntura* 3, no. 2: 221–43.

Albrechts, L. 2001. "Devolution, Regional Governance and Planning Systems." *International Planning Studies* 6: 167–82.

Alcaldía de Medellín. 1983, 1988. *Anuario Estadístico Metropolitano.* Medellín: Departamento Administrativo de Planeación Metropolitana, Alcaldía de Medellín.

Alden, J., S. Crow, and Y. Beigulenko. 1998. "Moscow: Planning for a World Capital City Toward 2000." *Cities* 15: 361–74.

Altshuler, A., and D. Luberoff. 2003. *Mega-Projects: The Changing Politics of Urban Public Investments.* Washington, D.C.: Brookings Institution Press.

Amin, A., ed. 1994. *Post-Fordism: A Reader.* Oxford: Blackwell.

Amin, A., and N. Thrift. 1994. "Living in the Global." In *Globalization, Institutions, and Regional Development in Europe,* edited by A. Amin and N. Thrift. Oxford: Oxford Unversity Press.

Andrew, C., and M. Goldsmith. 1998. "From Local Government to Local Governance—and Beyond?" *International Political Science Review* 19, no. 2: 101–17.

Angel, S. 2000. *Housing Policy Matters. A Global Analysis.* New York: Oxford University Press.

Antalovsky, E., J. S. Dangschadt, and M. Parkinson, eds. 2005. *European Metropolitan Governance. Cities in Europe—Europe in Cities.* Vienna: Node Research Program of the Austrian Federal Ministry for Education, Science, and Culture.

Arango D., and H. Jaime. 2001. "Medellín: a Reducir Índices de Homicidios." *El Colombiano,* February 18: 6A.

Atkinson, R. D. 2004. *The Past and Future of America's Economy.* Northampton, MA: Edward Elgar.

Attahi, K. 1996. "Côte d'Ivoire." In *The Changing Nature of Local Government in Developing Countries,* edited by P. McCarney. Toronto and Ottawa: Centre for Urban and Community Studies and the Federation of Canadian Municipalities.

———. 2000. "Gouvernance Metropolitaine en Afrique Occidentale." Paper to the National Academy of Sciences meeting, Wood's Hole, Massachusetts, September.

Axelrod, D. 1992. *Shadow Government: The Hidden World of Public Authorities—And How They Control Over $1 Trillion of Your Money.* New York: John Wiley.

Baade, R. A. 1996. "Professional Sports as Catalysts for Metropolitan Economic Development." *Journal of Urban Affairs* 18, no. 1: 1–17.

Bachrach, P., and M. S. Baratz. 1962. "Two Faces of Power." *American Political Science Review* 56, no. 4: 947–52.

Badcock, B. 2000. "Australia: Post-Fordist Transition." In *Globalizing Cities: A New Spatial Order?* edited by P. Marcuse and R. V. Kempen. Oxford: Blackwell.

Baeten, G. 2001. "The Europeanization of Brussels and the Urbanization of "Europe." *European Urban and Regional Studies* 8: 117–30.

Balbo, M. 1993. "Urban Planning and the Fragmented City of Developing Countries." *Third World Planning Review* 15, no. 1: 23–35.

Baldersheim, H. 1993. "Local Government in the Nordic Countries." Paper presented at the conference "Kommunalpolitik in Europa," Stuttgart, September 13–17.

Baldersheim, H., M. Illner, A. Offerdal, L. Rose, and P. Swianiewicz. 1996. *Local Democracy and the Process of Transformation in East-Central Europe.* Boulder, CO: Westview.

Barber, B. R. 1984. *Strong Democracy. Participatory Politics for a New Age.* Berkeley: University of California Press.

———. 1995. *Jihad vs. McWorld.* New York: Times Books.

Barlow, M. 1993. "Large City Reforms." In *Local Government in the New Europe,* edited by R. J. Bennett. London and New York: Bellhaven.

Barrett, S., and C. Fudge. 1981. *Policy and Action.* London: Methuen.

Bartley, B., and K. Treadwell Shine. 2003. "Competitive City: Governance and the Changing Dynamics of Urban Regeneration in Dublin." In *The Globalized City: Economic Restructuring and Social Polarization in European Cities,* edited by F. Moulaert, A. Rodriguez, and E. Swyngedouw. Oxford: Oxford University Press.

Barzel, Y. 1989. *The Economic Analysis of Property Rights.* Cambridge: Cambridge University Press.

Bauman, B. 1998. *Globalization: The Human Consequences.* Cambridge: Polity Press.

Bautista, V. A. 1998. "Reconstructing the Functions of Government: The Case of Primary Health Care in the Philippines." In *Local Government in the Philippines: A Book of Readings.* Vol. 2. *Current Issues in Governance,* edited by P. Domingo Tapales, J .C. Cuaresma, and W. L. Cabo. Quezon City: Center for Local and Regional Governance and National College of Public Administration and Governance, University of the Philippines.

BBC News. 2005. "France Extends Laws to Curb Riots."

Beauregard, R. A. 1995. "Theorizing the Global-Local Connection." In *World Cities in a World-System,* edited by P. L. Knox and P. J. Taylor. Cambridge: Cambridge University Press.

Beaverstock, J. V., R. G. Smith, and P. J. Taylor. 1999. "A Roster of World Cities." *Cities* 16: 445–58.

Beck, U. 2000. *What is Globalization?* Cambridge: Polity Press.

Becker, H., T. Franke, R. Löhr, and V. Rösner. 2002. *Socially Integrative City Programme—An Encouraging Three-Year Appraisal.* Berlin: Deutsches Institut für Urbanistik.

Becker, H., T. Franke, R. Löhr, and U. K. Schuleri-Hartje. 2003. *The Socially Integrated City Programme: From Traditional Urban Renewal to Integrative Urban District Development.* Berlin: Deutsches Institut für Urbanistik.

Bedolla, L. 2000. "They and We: Identity, Gender, and Politics among Latino Youth in Los Angeles." *Social Science Quarterly* 81, no. 1: 106–22.

Behn, R. D. 1998a. "What Right Do Public Managers Have to Lead?" *Public Administration Review* 58, no. 3: 209–25.

———. 1998b. "The New Public Management and the Search for Democratic Accountability." *International Public Management Journal* 1, no. 2: 131–64.

Bellah, R. N., R. Madsen, W. M. Sullivan, A. Swidler, and S. M. Tipton. 1985. *Habits of the Heart: Individualism and Commitment in American Life.* Berkeley: University of California Press.

Bennis, W. G., and B. Nanus. 1985. *Leaders: Strategies for Taking Charge.* New York: Harper Collins.

Benton-Short, L., M. Price, and S. Friedman. 2004. *Global Perspective on the Connections between Immigrants and World Cities.* Occasional paper. Washington: George Washington Center for the Study of Globalization.

Bergquist, C. 1986. *Coffee and Conflict in Colombia: Origin and Outcome of the War of the Thousand Days 1886–1910.* Durham, NC: Duke University Press.

Berselli, E. 2001. "The Crisis and Transformation of Italian Politics." *Daedalus* 130: 1–24.

Betancur, J. J. 2004. "Medellín y la Cultura del Rebusque." In *Las Ciudades Latinoamericanas en el nuevo [des]orden mundial,* edited by M. Zimmerman and P. Navia, pp. 273–92. Mexico: Siglo XX Editores.

———. 2005. "Approaches to the Regularization of Informal Settlements: The Case of Medellín, Colombia." Proceedings of the Second World Bank Urban Research Symposium, sponsored by the World Bank and the Instituto de Pequisa Economica, Brasilia, Brazil, April.

Betancur, M. S. 1994. *La Reconversión Industrial en Colombia y sus Efectos sobre los trabajadores.* Medellín: Instituto Popular de Capacitación.

Betancur, M. S., A. Stienen, and O. A. Durán. 2001. *Globalización, Cadenas Productivas y Redes de Acción Colectiva.* Bogota: Tercer Mundo.

Bird, K. 2004. "Unequal Gains: Patterns of Ethnic Minority Representation in the Political Systems of France, Denmark and Canada." Paper to the International Political Science Association RC14 "Ethnicity and Politics" meeting, Ottawa, Canada, October.

Bissinger, B. 1997. *Prayer for the City.* New York: Vintage Books.

Blanc, M. 2002. "Strategies for the Social Regeneration of Disadvantaged Neighbourhoods in France (1977–2002)." In *Soziale Stadt—Zwischenbilanzen: Ein Programm auf dem Weg zur Sozialen Stadt?* edited by U. Walther, pp. 211–27. Opladen, Germany: Leske and Budrich.

Blunkett, D. 2003. *Active Citizens, Strong Communities—Progressing Civil Renewal.* London: U.K. Government, The Home Office.

Bockmeyer, J. 2000. "A Culture of Distrust: The Impact of Local Political Culture on Participation in the Detroit EZ." *Urban Studies* 37, no. 13: 2417–40.

———. 2003. "Devolution and the Transformation of Community Housing Activism." *Social Science Journal* 40, no. 2: 175–88.

———. 2006. "Social Cities and Social Inclusion: Assessing the Role of Turkish Residents in Building the New Berlin." *German Politics and Society* 24, Winter 2006.

Boddy, M., and M. Parkinson, eds. 2004. *City Matters. Competitiveness, Cohesion and Urban Governance.* Bristol: Policy Press.

Body-Gendrot, S. 2000. *The Social Control of Cities?* Oxford: Blackwell.

Boone, C., and A. Modarres. 2006. *City and Environment.* Philadelphia: Temple University Press.

Borja, J., and M. Castells, in collaboration with M. Belil and C. Benner. 1997. *Local and Global: The Management of Cities in the Information Age.* London: Earthscan.

Bourdieu, P. 1984. *Distinction: A Social Critique of the Judgement of Taste.* London: Routledge.

Box, R. C., G. S. Marshall, B. J. Reed, and C. Reed. 2001. "New Public Management and Substantive Democracy." *Public Administration Review* 61, no. 5: 608–19.

Brenner, N. 1999. "Globalisation as Reterritorialisation: The Re-Scaling of Urban Governance in the European Union." *Urban Studies* 36: 431–51.

———. 2000. "The Urban Question as a Scale Question: Reflections on Henri Lefebvre, Urban Theory and the Politics of Scale." *International Journal of Urban and Regional Research* 24, no. 2: 361–78.

Brenner, N., and N. Theodore. 2002. *Spaces of Neoliberalism: Urban Restructuring in North America and West Europe.* Malden, MA: Blackwell.

Brindley, T., Y. Rydin, and G. Stoker. 1996. *Remaking Planning: The Politics of Urban Change.* London: Routledge.

Brouard, S., J. Gehring, E. Lepinard, O. Ruchet, D. Sabbagh, and V. Tiberj. 2006. "Was Paris Burning? Power and Politics in France." Roundtable discussion at the American Political Science Association, Annual Meeting, Philadelphia, August.

Brudell, P., C. Hammon, and J. Henry. 2004. "Urban Planning and Regeneration: A Community Perspective." *Journal of Irish Urban Studies* 3, no. 1: 65–87.

Bruna, G. C. 2000. "The Sao Paulo Region." In *Global City Regions: Their Emerging Forms,* edited by R. Simmonds and G. Hack. London: Spon.

Buch-Andersen, T. 2006. "Denmark Row: The Power of Cartoons." http://news.bbc.co.uk/go/pr/fr/-/1/hi/world/europe/5392786.stm.

Buckley, R. M., and J. Kalarickal, eds. 2006. *Thirty Years of World Bank Shelter Lending. What Have We Learned?* Washington: World Bank.

Burns, D., R. Hambleton, and P. Hoggett. 1994. *The Politics of Decentralization. Revitalising Local Democracy.* Basingstoke, UK: Palgrave.

Burns, J. M. 1978. *Leadership.* New York: Harper and Row.

Cabannes, Y. 2004. "Participatory Budgeting: A Significant Contribution to Participatory Democracy." *Environment and Urbanization* 16, no. 1 : 27–46.

Cameron, R. 2005. "Metropolitan Restructuring (and More Restructuring) in South Africa." *Public Administration and Development* 25, no. 4 : 329–39.

Campbell, A., and A. Coulson. 2006. "Into the Mainstream: Local Democracy in Central and Eastern Europe." *Local Government Studies* 32, no. 5 : 543–61.

Carmichael, L. 2005. "Cities in the Multi-Level Governance of the European Union." In *Urban Governance and Democracy. Leadership and Community Involvement,* edited by M. Haus, H. Heinelt, and M. Stewart. London: Routledge.

———. 2006. "Local Leadership in Multi-Level Governance in Europe." In *Legitimacy and Urban Governance. A Cross-National Comparative Ctudy,* edited by H. Heinelt, D. Sweeting, and P. Getimis. Abingdon, UK: Routledge.

Caro, R. 1975. *The Power Broker: Robert Moses and the Fall of New York.* New York: Vintage.

Castells, M. 1989. *The Informational City: Information, Technology, Economic Restructuring, and the Urban-Regional Process.* Oxford: Blackwell.

———. 1996. *The Rise of the Network Society.* Oxford: Blackwell.

CBC News. 2000. "Protests at Queens Park."

CCM (Cámara del Comercio de Medellín). 2000. *La Ventaja Competitiva Empresarial Antioquña hacia el Siglo XXI.* Medellín: Editorial Colina.

CEC (Commission of the European Communities). 2001. *European Governance, A White Paper.*

———. 2005. *"A Common Agenda for Integration Framework for the Integration of Third-Country Nationals in the European Union,"* September 1, COM (2005) 389 final.

CEPAL (Comisión Económica para América Latina). 2001. *Panorama Social de América Latina 2000–2001.* Santiago de Chile: CEPAL.

Charles F. Kettering Foundation. 2005. "Citizens and the Work of Self-Government. Theme Three: Professionals and Public Life," *Connections.* Dayton, OH: Kettering Foundation.

Chaskin, R. J., P. Brown, S. Venkatesh, and A. Vidal. 2001. *Building Community Capacity.* New York: Aldine de Gruyter.

Chica, R. 1983. "El Desarrollo Industrial Colombiano 1958–1980." *Desarrollo y Sociedad* 12 (September): 19–123.

———. 1994. *Crisis y Reconversión en la Industria Colombiana.* Bogotá: Pontificia Universidad Javeriana.

Christensen, T., and P. Laegreid, eds. 2001. *New Public Management.* Aldershot, UK: Ashgate.

Church, A., and P. Reid. 2002. "Local Democracy, Cross-Border Collaboration and the Internationalization of Local Government." In *Globalism and Local Democracy. Challenge and Change in Europe and North America,* edited by R. Hambleton, H. V. Savitch, and M. Stewart. Basingstoke, UK: Palgrave Macmillan.

Church, C. H. 2000. "Switzerland: A Paradigm in Evolution." *Parliamentary Affairs* 53: 96–113.

Citizenship and Immigration Canada. 2005. "Recent Immigrants in Metropolitan Areas: Toronto—A Comparative Profile Based on the 2001 Census."

Clark, T. N. 1967. "Power and Community Structure: Who Governs, Where and When." *Sociological Quarterly* 8, no. 3: 291–316.

Clarke, M., and J. Stewart. 1998. *Community Governance, Community Leadership and the New Local Government.* York, UK: Joseph Rowntree Foundation.

Clarke, S. 2001. "The Prospects for Local Democratic Governance: The Governance Role of Nonprofit organization." *Policy Studies Review* 18, no. 4: 129–45.

Clarke, S. E., and G. L. Gaile. 1998. *The Work of Cities: Globalization and Community.* Minneapolis: University of Minnesota Press.

Clarke, S. E., and M. Saiz. 2003. "From Waterhole to World City: Place-Luck and Public Agendas in Denver." In *The Infrastructure of Play,* edited by D. R. Judd. Armonk, New York: M. E. Sharpe.

Coase, R. 1937. "The Nature of the Firm." *Economica* 4, no. 16: 386–405.

Coates, D., and B. Humphreys. 1999. "The Growth Effects of Sports Franchises, Stadia, and Arenas." *Journal of Policy Analysis and Management* 18, no. 4: 601–24.

Cohen, A., and E. Taylor. 2000. *American Pharaoh.* Boston: Little Brown.

Cohen, M. 1974. *Urban Policy and Political Conflict in Africa. A Study of the Ivory Coast.* Chicago: University of Chicago Press.

———. 1983. *Learning by Doing. World Bank Lending for Urban Development, 1972–82.* Washington: World Bank.

Colton, T. J. 1995. *Moscow: Governing the Socialist Metropolis.* Cambridge, MA: Belknap Press of Harvard University Press.

Connell, J., ed. 2000. *Sydney. Emergence of a World City.* Melbourne: Oxford University Press.

Connors, G. 2005. "When Utilities Muddle through: Pro-Poor Governance in Bangalore's Public Water Sector. *Environment and Urbanization* 17, no. 1 : 201–17.

Cooper, D. 1976. *The Grammar of Living. An Examination of Political Acts.* Harmondsworth, UK: Pelican.

Cooper, T. 1998. *The Responsible Administrator: An Approach to Ethics for the Administrative Role.* San Francisco: Jossey Bass.

Copenhagen City. 1999, 2004a, 2005. "Copenhagen in Figures." Copenhagen City: Statistical Office.

———. 2001, 2004. "Statistical Ten-Year Review." Copenhagen City: Statistical Office.

———. 2004b. "Valg-Elections." Copenhagen City: Statistical Office.

Copenhagen Post. 2006. "Integration Council Vote Flops." Copenhagen, May 17–19.

Coulson, A., and A. Campbell, eds. 2006. "Local Government in Central and Eastern Europe." Special issue. *Local Government Studies* 32, no. 5: 537–696.

Crevel, P., and N. Wagner. 2003. "Dezentralisierung in Frankreich—ein großes Vorhaben der Regierung Raffarin." Edited by Konrad-Adenauer-Stiftung. *Auslandsinformationen* 30, no. 5: 58–78.

Crook, R. C., and J. Manor. 1998. *Democracy and Decentralisation in South Asia and West Africa. Participation, Accountability and Performance.* Cambridge: Cambridge University Press.

Crossley, N. 2004. "On Systematically Distorted Communication: Bourdieu and the Socio-Analysis of Publics." In *After Habermas: New Perspectives on the Public* Sphere, edited by N. Crossley and J. M. Roberts, pp. 88–112. Oxford: Blackwell.

Cullinane, S. 2003 "Hong Kong." *Cities,* 20: 279–88.

Dahl, R., and E. R. Tufte. 1973. *Size and Democracy.* Stanford: Stanford University Press.

DANE (Departamento Administrativo Nacional de Estadisticas). Encuesta Hogares 1973–2000 and Censo Nacional de Hogares y Vivienda 1973 and 1993.

Davies, J. S. 2004. "Conjuncture or Disjuncture? An Institutionalist Analysis of Local Regeneration Partnerships in the U.K." *International Journal of Urban and Regional Research* 28, no. 3: 570–85.

———. 2005a. "The Social Inclusion Debate: Strategies, Controversies and Dilemmas." *Policy Studies* 26, no. 1: 3–27.

————. 2005b. "Local Governance and the Dialectics of Hierarchy, Market and Network." *Policy Studies* 26, no. 3: 311–35.

————. 2007. "The Limits of Partnership: An Exit-Action Strategy for Local Democratic Inclusion." *Political Studies* 55(4) (forthcoming).

Davis, D., R. Kraus, B. Naughton, and E. Perry. 1995. *Urban Spaces in Contemporary China: The Potential for Autonomy and Community in Post-Mao China.* New York: Cambridge University Press.

Davis, D. E. 2002. "Mexico City: The Local-National Dynamics of Democratization." In *Capital City Politics in Latin America,* edited by D. J. Myers and H. A. Dietz. Boulder, CO: Lynn Rienner.

Davis, M. 2006. *Planet of Slums.* London: Verso.

DCC (Dublin City Council). 2000. *Liberties/Coombe Integrated Area Plan Annual Report 1999–2000.* Dublin: Dublin City Council.

De Beer, F. 2003. "Whither the Study of Development in South Africa?" *Development Southern Africa* 20, no. 4: 477–89.

Debofle, P., et al. 1979. *L'Administration de Paris (1789–1977).* Geneva and Paris: Librairie Droz.

DeLeon, R. E. 1992. *Left Coast City: Progressive Politics in San Francisco, 1975–1991.* Lawrence: University Press of Kansas.

Denhardt, J. V., and R. B. Denhardt. 2003. *The New Public Service. Serving, Not Steering.* Armonk, NY: M. E. Sharpe.

Denters, B. 2002. "Size and Political Trust: Evidence from Denmark, The Netherlands, Norway and United Kingdom." *Government and Policy C: Environment and Planning* 20, no. 6: 793–812.

Denters B. and L. E. Rose, eds. 2005a. *Comparing Local Governance. Trends and Developments.* Basingstoke, UK: Palgrave Macmillan.

Denters, B., and L. E. Rose. 2005b. "Local Governance in the Third Millennium: A Brave New World?" In *Comparing Local Governance: Trends and Developments,* edited by B. Denters and L. E. Rose. New York: Palgrave Macmillan.

Denters, B., O. Van Heffen, J. Huisman, and P. J. Klok, eds. 2003. *The Rise of Interactive Governance and Quasi-Markets.* Dordrecht, The Netherlands: Kluwer Academic Publishers.

Department of the Environment. 1996. *Study of Urban Renewal Schemes.* Dublin: Stationery Office.

DETR (Department of the Environment, Transport and the Regions. 1999. *NDC Phase 1 Proposals: Guidance for Ppplicants.* HMSO (Her Majesty"s Stationery Office).

Diamond, J. 2004. "Local Regeneration Initiatives and Capacity Building: Whose 'Capacity' and 'Building' for What?" *Community Development Journal* 39, no. 2: 177–89.

Diehl, C., and M. Blohm. 2001. "Apathy, Adaptation or Ethnic Mobilization? On the Attitudes of a Politically Excluded Group." *Journal of Ethnic and Migration Studies* 27, no. 3: 401–20.

Di Gaetano, A., and J. S. Klemanski. 1999. *Power and City Governance. Comparative Perspectives on Urban Development.* Minneapolis: University of Minnesota Press.

Dillon, J. F. 1868. Decision in *City of Clinton v. Cedar Rapid and Missouri River Railroad Co., 24 Iowa,* pp. 455–75.

Dillinger, W. 1994. *Decentralization and Its Implications for Urban Services Delivery.* Washington, D.C.: World Bank.

DiMaggio, P. J., and W. W. Powell. 1983. "The Iron Cage Revisited: Institutional Isomorphism and Collective Rationality in Organizational Fields." *American Sociological Review* 48, no. 2: 147–60.

Djordjevic, M. 2006. "The Effect of Strategic Planning on Urban Governance Arrangements: The Politics of Developmental Planning in Budapest and Warsaw." PhD dissertation, Central European University, Budapest.

Doig, J. W. 1983. "If I See a Murderous Fellow Sharpening a Knife Cleverly . . . : The Wilsonian Dichotomy and the Public Authority Tradition." *Public Administration Review* 43, no. 4: 292–304.

————. 2001. *Empire on the Hudson: Entrepreneurial Vision and Political Power at the Port of New York Authority.* New York: Columbia University Press.

Donaghue, B., and G. W. Jones. 1973. *Herbert Morrison—Portrait of a Politician.* London: Weidenfeld and Nicholson.

Dublin Corporation. 1998. *Liberties/Coombe Integrated Area Plan.* Dublin: Dublin Corporation.

————. 1999. *Dublin City Development Plan.* Dublin: Dublin Corporation.

Dubresson, A. 1997. "Abidjan: From the Public Making of a Modern City to Urban Management of a Metropolis." In *The Urban Challenge in Africa: Growth and Management of its Large Cities,* edited by C. Rakodi. Tokyo: United Nations University Press.

Dunleavy, P. 1991. *Democracy, Bureaucracy and Public Choice: Economic Explanations in Political Science.* New York: Prentice Hall.

Dunleavy, P., and C. Hood. 1994. "From Old Public Administration to New Public Management." *Public Money and Management* 14: 9–16.

Eagleton, T. 2003. *After Theory.* London: Allen Lane.

Eckstein, H. 1975. "Case Study and Theory in Political Science." In *Handbook of Political Science: Strategies of Inquiry,* edited by F. I. Greensein and N. W. Polsby, Vol. 7, pp. 79–137. Reading, MA: Addison-Wesley.

Edwards, J. 1997. "Urban Policy: The Victory of Form Over Substance." *Urban Studies* 34, no. 5/6: 825–44.

EFMS (Europäisches Forum für Migrationsstudien). 2001. *Migration Review.* Bamberg, Germany: University of Bamberg.

Egner, B., M. Haus, and C. Konig. 2006. "Strong Mayors and Policy Innovations: Lessons from Two German Cities." In *Legitimacy and Urban Governance. A Cross-National Comparative Study,* edited by H. Heinelt, D. Sweeting, and P. Getimis. Abingdon, UK: Routledge.

Eisenger, P. 2000. "The Politics of Bread and Circuses: Building the City for the Visitor Class." *Urban Affairs Review* 35, no. 3: 316–33.

Elcock, H., and J. Fenwick. 2003. "Lesson Drawing Can Fail: Leadership in Local Government." Paper to the ECPR conference, Marburg, September 18–21.

El Colombiano. 2001a. "Editorial. El Agobiante Desempleo," March 13, p. 5A.

———. 2001b. "La más violenta de América Latina," May 6, p. 10A.

Elkin, S. L. 1987. *The City in the American Republic.* Chicago: University of Chicago Press.

Engeli, C. 1986. *Landesplanung in Berlin-Brandenburg: Eine Untersuchung zur Geschichte des Landesplanungsverbandes Brandenburg-Mitte 1929–1936.* Stuttgart: Kohlhammer-Verlag.

ENS (Escuela Nacional Sindical). 1999. *Cultura y Trabajo* 49 (August).

Erie, S. P. 2002. "Los Angeles as a Developmental City-State." In *From Chicago to L.A.: Making Sense of Urban Theory,* edited by M. J. Dear. Thousand Oaks, CA: Sage.

Etzioni, A. 1993. *The Spirit of Community: Rights, Responsibilities, and the Communitarian Agenda.* New York: Crown.

———, ed. 1995. *New Communitarian Thinking.* Charlottesville: University Press of Virginia.

European Commission. 2003a. *Partnership with the Cities.* Luxembourg: Office for Official Publications of the European Communities

———. 2003b. *Urban Actions in Objective 1 and Objective 2 Programmes.* Brussels: Commission of the European Communities.

European Commission. 2005. *Strategies to Enhance Social Integration: National Action Plan against Poverty and Social Exclusion, 2003–2005.* http://europa.eu/employment_social/social_inclusion/docs/nap_03_05_3n_fassung.pdf.

Evans, B., M. Joas, S. Sundback, and K. Theobald. 2004. *Governing Sustainable Cities.* London: Earthscan.

Ezquiaga, J. M., E. Cimadevilla, and G. Peribanez. 2000. "The Madrid Region." In *Global City Regions: Their Emerging FormsI,* edited by R. Simmonds and G. Hack. London: Spon.

Fagan, R. H., and R. Dowling. 2005. "Neoliberalism and Suburban Employment: Western Sydney in the 1990s." *Geographical Research* 43: 71–81.

Fainstein, S. 1990. "The Changing World Economy and Urban Restructuring." In *Leadership and Urban Regeneration,* edited by D. Judd and M. Parkinson. London: Sage.

Fainstein, S., N. Fainstein, R. Hill, D. Judd, and M. Smith. 1983. *Restructuring the City.* New York: Longman.

Fainstein, S. S. 2001. *The City Builders: Property Development in New York and London, 1980–2000.* 2nd ed. Lawrence: University of Kansas Press.

Fairclough, N. 2000. *New Labour, New Language?* London: Routledge.

Fairweather, S. 2005. "Services for People's Needs: Power in People's Hands." *Concept* 15, no. 3: 3–6.

Faist, T., and H. Häusserman. 1996. "Immigration, Social Citizenship and Housing in Germany." *International Journal of Urban and Regional Research* 20, no.1: 83–98.

Fallend, F., G. Ignits, and P. Swianiewicz. 2006. "Divided Loyalties? Mayors between Party Representation and Local Community Interests." In *The European Mayor: The Role and Position of Political Leaders in European Cities in Transformation*, edited by H. Bäck, H. Heinelt, and A. Magnier. Opladen, Germany: Verlag fur Sozialwissenschaften.

Feldman, M. S., and A. M. Khademian. 2002. "To Manage is to Govern." *Public Administration Review* 62, no. 5: 541–55.

Feldman, S., and E. Ferretti, eds. 1998. *Informal Work and Social Change: A Bibliographical Survey.* Ithaca and London: ILR Press / Cornell University Press.

Flores, A. 2005. *Local Democracy in Modern Mexico: A Study in Participatory Methods.* Bury St. Edmunds, UK: Arena Books.

Florida, R. 2002. *The Rise of the Creative Class.* New York: Basic Books.

———. 2005. *Cities and the Creative Class.* New York: Routledge.

Flyvbjerg, B., N. Bruzelius, and W. Rothengatter. 2003. *Megaprojects and Risk: An Anatomy of Ambition.* Cambridge: Cambridge University Press.

Foot, J. 2001. *Milan since the Miracle: City, Culture and Identity.* Oxford: Berg.

Forde, C. 2005. "Participatory Democracy or Pseudo-Participation? Local Government Reform in Ireland." *Local Government Studies* 31, no. 2: 137–48.

Forster, C. 2004. *Australian Cities. Continuity and Change.* Melbourne: Oxford University Press.

———. 2006. "The Challenge of Change: Australian Cities and Urban Planning in the New Millennium." *Geographical Research* 44, no. 2: 173–82.

Fosler, R. S. 1996. "Forward." In *Globalization and Decentralization: Institutional Contexts, Policy Issues, and Intergovernmental Relations in Japan and the United States,* edited by J. S. Jun and D. S. Wright. Washington, D.C.: Georgetown University Press.

Foster, K. 1997. *The Political Economy of Special-Purpose Government.* Washington, D.C.: Georgetown University Press.

Fowler, R. B. 1991. *The Dance with Community: The Contemporary Debate in American Political Thought.* Lawrence: University Press of Kansas.

Franke, T. 2003. "Neighborhood Management—A Critical Tool for Integrative District Development. Soziale Stadt. Berlin: Deutsches Institut für Urbanistik.

Franke, T., and R. P. Löhr. 2001. "Neighborhood Management—A Key Instrument in Integrative Urban District Development". Paper delivered at EURA-Conference, Copenhagen, May 17–19.

Franklin, M. 2004. Voter Turnout and the Dynamics of Electoral Competition in Established Liberal Democracies since 1945. Cambridge: Cambridge University Press.

Fraser, J., and E. Kick. 2005. "Understanding Community Building in Urban America." *Journal of Poverty* 9, no. 1: 23–43.

Frederickson, H. G. 1999. "The Repositioning of American Public Administration." John Gaus Lecture presented at the American Political Science Association meeting, Atlanta, September.

Freeman, J. F. 1992. *Government is Good: Citizenship, Participation, and Power.* Columbia: University of Missouri Press.

Freestone, R. 2000. "Planning Sydney: Historical Trajectories and Contemporary Debates." In *Sydney. The Emergence of a World City,* edited by J. Connell. Melbourne: Oxford University Press.

Freund, B. 2003. "The Frankfurt Rhine-Main Region." In *Metropolitan Governance and Spatial Planning,* edited by W. Salet, A. Thornley, and A. Kreukels. London: Spon.

Frieden, B. J., and L. B. Sagalyn. 1989. *Downtown, Inc.: How America Rebuilds Cities.* Cambridge, MA: MIT Press.

Friedman, T. L. 1999. *The Lexus and the Olive Tree.* New York: Farrar, Straus, and Giroux.

———. 2005. *The World Is Flat. A Brief History of the Twenty-First Century.* New York: Farrar, Straus, and Giroux.

Friedmann, J. 1986. "The World City Hypothesis." *Development and Change* 17: 69–83.

———. 2001. "World Cities Revisited: A Comment." *Urban Studies* 38: 2535–6.

———. 2005. *China's Urban Transition.* Minneapolis: University of Minnesota Press.

Friedmann, J., and G. Wolff. 1982. "World City Formation: An Agenda for Research and Action." *International Journal of Urban and Regional Research* 6: 309–44.

Frug, G. 1999. *City Making: Building Communities without Building Walls.* Princeton, NJ: Princeton University Press.

Fujita, K. 2003. "Neo-Industrial Tokyo: Urban Development and Globalisation in Japan's State-Centred Developmental Capitalism." *Urban Studies* 40: 249–81.

Fulton, W. 2002. "Paying the Hotel Bill." *Governing* 16 (August): 60.

Gamble, A. 1994. *The Free Economy and the Strong State.* 2nd ed. Basingstoke, UK: Macmillan.

Gang, F. 1999. "Transition to Fiscal Federalism: Market-Oriented Reform and Redefinition of Central-Local Relations in China." In *Fiscal Decentralisation in Emerging Economies. Governance Issues,* edited by K. Fukusaku and L. R. de Mello. Paris: OECD.

Garay, L. J., and A. Angulo. 1999. *Construcción de una Nueva Sociedad.* Bogota: Tercer Mundo Editores-Revista Cambio Santa Fe de Bogotá.

Garay, L. J., L. F. Quintero, J. A. Villamil, J. Tovar, A. Fatal, S. Gómez, E. Restrepo, and B. Yemail. 1998 *Colombia: Estructura industrial e Internacionalización 1967–1996.* Bogota: Departamento Nacional de Planeación.

Gardner, J. W. 1990. *On Leadership.* New York: Free Press.

Garrett, G., and J. Rodden 2001. "Globalization and Fiscal Decentralization." In *Governance in a Global Economy: Political Authority in Transition,* edited by M. Kahler and D. Lake. Princeton, NJ: Princeton University Press.

Garvin, J. L. 1932. *The Life of Joseph Chamberlain.* London: Macmillan.

Geddes, M. 2005. "Neo-liberalism and Local Governance. Cross-National Perspectives and Speculations." *Policy Studies* 26, no. 3: 359–77.

Gel'man, V. (2003). "In Search of Local Autonomy: The Politics of Big Cities in Russia's Transition." *International Journal of Urban and Regional Research* 27: 48–61.

Giddens, A. 1998. *The Third Way. The Renewal of Social Democracy.* Cambridge, U.K.: Polity Press.

Gilbert, A., ed. 1996. *The Mega-City in Latin America.* Tokyo: United Nations University Press.

Gilmore, R. S., and L. S. Jensen. 1998. "Reinventing Government Accountability: Public Functions, Privatization, and the Meaning of 'State Action,'" *Public Administration Review* 58, no. 3: 247–58.

Glass, G., B. McGraw, and M. Smith. 1981. *Ethnography and Quantitative Design in Educational Research.* Orlando: Academic Press.

Gleeson, B., T. Darbas, and S. Lawson. 2004. "Governance, Sustainability and Recent Australian Metropolitan Strategies: A Socio-Theoretic Analysis." *Urban Policy and Research* 22, no. 4: 345–66.

Glum, F. 1920. *Die Organisation der Riesenstadt. Die Verfassungen von Paris, London, New York, Wien und Berlin.* Berlin: Verlag von Julius Springer.

Gobernación de Antioquia. 1986, 1998. Anuario Estadístico de Antioquia. Medellín: Departamento Administrativo de Planeación, Gobernación de Antioquia.

Godfrey, B. J. 1997. "Urban Development and Redevelopment in San Francisco." *Geographical Review* 87: 309–33.

Goetz, E., and S. Clarke, eds. 1993. *The New Localism.* London: Sage.

Goldsmith, M. 2005. "The Experience of Metropolitan Government in England." In *Metropolitan Governance: Capacity, Democracy and the Dynamics of Place,* edited by H. Heinelt and D. Kübler. London: Routledge.

Goldsmith, M., and L. Rose. 2000. "Constituency, Size and Electoral Politics: A Comparison of Patterns at Local Elections in Norway and the UK." Paper to the IPSA World Congress, Quebec, Canada, August 1–5, 2000.

Goleman, D. 1995. *Emotional Intelligence.* New York: Bantam Books.

Goli, M., and S. Rezaei. 2005. "Active Participation of Immigrants in Denmark." Report by the European research project POLTIS.

Gooding, A. 2005. "In the Saddle or the Burr Underneath—The Role of Regional Organisations of Councils in Metropolitan Planning." Paper presented at the Second State of The Australian Cities Conference, Griffith University, Brisbane.

Gouëset, V. 1998. *Bogotá: Nacimiento de una Metrópoli. La Originalidad del Proceso de Concentración Urbana en Colombia en el Siglo XX.* Bogotá: Tercer Mundo.

Government of Ireland. 1999. *Residential Density: Guidelines for Planning Authorities.* Dublin: Stationery Office.

Graham, L. S., and P. Jacobi. 2002. "Sao Paulo: Tensions between Clientelism and Participatory Democracy." In *Capital City Politics in Latin America,* edited by D. J. Myers and H. A. Dietz. Boulder, CO: Lynne Rienner.

Graham, S., and S. Marvin. 2001. *Splintering Urbanism. Networked Infrastructures, Technological Mobilities and the Urban Condition.* London: Routledge.

Graizbord, B. and A. Rowland. 2003. "México City as a Peripheral Placer: The Two Sides of the Coin." *The Annals of Regional Science* 37: 501–18.

Gratz, R. B., and N. Mintz. 1998. *Cities Back from the Edge: New Life for Downtown.* New York: Wiley.

Green, R. T., L. F. Keller, and G. L. Wamsley. 1993. "Reconstituting a Profession for American Public Administration." *Public Administration Review* 53, no. 6: 516–24.

Grindle, M. S. 2000. *Audacious Reforms. Institutional Invention and Democracy in Latin America.* Baltimore: Johns Hopkins University Press.

Gritsai, O. 1997. "Moscow under Globalization and Transition: Paths of Economic Resturcturing." *Urban Geography* 18:155–65.

Grogan, P. S., and T. Proscio. 2000. *Comeback Cities. A Blueprint for Urban Neighborhood Renewal.* Boulder, CO: Westview.

Gross, J. S. 1996 "British Local Government: The Demise of Local Democracy." *New Political Science,* no. 33/34 (Fall/Winter 1995–1996).

———. 2004. "Local Government and Local Stakeholders: Building Bridges in the Global City— Lessons from London." Paper to the City Futures Conference, Chicago, Illinois.

———. 2005a. "Cybercities." In *Revitalizing the City: Strategies to Contain Sprawl and Revive the Core,* edited by F. Wagner, T. Joder, A. Mumphrey, K. Akundi, and A. Artibise. London: M. E. Sharpe.

———. 2005b. "Local Governance and the Global City: Institutions, Ethnic Communities and Access." Paper to the Urban Affairs Association Conference, Salt Lake City, Utah.

Grunsven, L. V. 2000. "Singapore: The Changing Residential Landscape in a Winner City." In *Globalizing Cities: A New Spatial Order?* edited by P. Marcuse and R. V. Kempen. Oxford: Blackwell.

Gualini, E. 2003. "The Region of Milan." In *Metropolitan Governance and Spatial Planning,* edited by W. Salet, A. Thornley, and A. Kreukels. London: Spon.

Guigni, M., and F. Passy. 2004. "Migrant Mobilization between Political Institutions and Citizenship Regimes: A Comparison of France and Switzerland." *European Journal of Political Research* 43, no. 1: 51–82.

GUM (Globalization, Urbanization, Migration). 1999. http://gstudy.com/gum/France/Paris1999.htm.

———. 2001a. http://gstudy.com/gum/Denmark/Copenhagen2001.htm.

———. 2001b. http://gstudy.com/gum/Canada/Toronto2001.htm.

Gunther, R., and A. Mughan. 1993. "Political Institutions and Cleavage Management." In *Do Institutions Matter?* edited by R. K. Weaver and B. Rockman. Washington, D.C.: Brookings Institute.

Gurr, T. R., and D. S. King. 1987. *The State and the City.* Chicago: University of Chicago Press.

Gutiérrez, J. F. 2002a. "Informales: cada vez mas numerosos, profesionales, y con bajos ingresos." *Observar: Desempleo e Informalidad en Medellín,* December 8, pp. 18–21.

———. 2002b. "Desempleo en Medellín, Cifras Cambiantes de la misma Urgencia." *Observar: Desempleo e Informalidad en Medellín,* December 8, pp. 12–17.

Hall, P. 1986. *Governing the Economy: The Politics of State Intervention in Britain and France.* New York: Oxford University Press.

———. 2004. "World Cities, Mega-Cities and Global Mega-City-Regions." GaWC Annual Lecture.

Hall, T., and P. Hubbard. 1998. "The Entrepreneurial City and the 'New Urban Politics.'" In *The Entrepreneurial City: Geographies of Politics, Regime and Representation,* edited by T. Hall and P. Hubbard. Chichester, UK: Wiley.

Halvorsen, K. E. 2003. "Assessing the Effects of Public Participation." *Public Administration Review* 63, no. 5: 535–43.

Hambleton, R. 1998. "Strengthening Political Leadership in U.K. Local Government." *Public Money and Management,* January–March, 41–8.

———. 2000. "Modernising Political Management in Local Government." *Urban Studies* 37, no. 5–6: 931–50.

———. 2002. "The New City Management." In *Globalism and Local Democracy. Challenge and Change in Europe and North America,* edited by R. Hambleton, H. V. Savitch, and M. Stewart. Basingstoke, UK: Palgrave Macmillan.

———. 2006. "US Public Policy for Cities—Insights from Abroad." Report to the Joyce Foundation, Chicago. Available at www.uic.edu/cuppa/cityfutures.

Hambleton, R., and S. Bullock. 1996. *Revitalising Local Democracy—the Leadership Options.* London: Association of District Councils/Local Government Management Board (now Local Government Association/Improvement and Development Agency).

Hambleton, R., H. V. Savitch, and M. Stewart. 2002. "Globalism and Local Democracy." In *Globalism and Local Democracy: Challenge and Change in Europe and North America,* edited by R. Hambleton, H. V. Savitch, and M. Stewart. Basingstoke, UK: Palgrave Macmillan.

Hambleton, R., and D. Sweeting. 2004. "US-Style Leadership for English Local Government?" *Public Administration Review* 64, no. 4: 474–88.

Hamilton, D. K. 2002. "Regionalism in Metropolitan Chicago: A Work in Progress." *National Civic Review* 91: 63–80.

Hanhoerster, H. 2000. "Renewal and Integration in Ethnically Diverse Neighborhoods in Germany. Case Study: Duisburg-Marxloh." Paper to the Urban Affairs Association Annual Conference, Los Angeles, May.

Harrigan, J. J., and R. K. Vogel. 2003. *Political Change in the Metropolis:* 7th ed. New York: Longman.

Hartman, C. W. 2002. *City for Sale: The Transformation of San Francisco.* Berkeley: University of California Press.

Harvey, D. 1989a. *The Condition of Postmodernity: An Enquiry into the Origins of Cultural Change.* Oxford: Blackwell.

———. 1989b. "From Managerialism to Entrepreneurialism: The Transformation in Urban Governance in Late Capitalism." *Geografiska Annaler* 71B, no. 1: 3–17.

———. 1994. "Flexible Accumulation through Urbanization: Reflections on Post-Modernism in the American City." In *Post Fordism, A Reader,* edited by A. Amin, pp. 361–86. Oxford and Cambridge: Blackwell.

———. 1996. *Justice, Nature and the Geography of Difference.* Oxford: Blackwell.

———. 2000. *Spaces of Hope.* Edinburgh: Edinburgh University Press.

Harwood, S., and D. Myers. 2002. "The Dynamics of Immigration and Local Governance in Santa Ana: Neighborhood Activism, Overcrowding, and Land-Use Policy." *Policy Studies Journal* 30, no. 1: 70–91.

Hassan Danesh, A. 1991. *The Informal Economy, A Research Guide.* New York and London: Garland.

Hauck Walsh, A. 1968. *Urban Government for the Paris Region.* New York, Washington, and London: Frederick A. Praeger.

Haus, M., H. Heinelt, and M. Stewart, eds. 2005. *Urban Governance and Democracy. Leadership and Community Involvement.* Abingdon, UK: Routledge.

Haus, M., and J. Klausen. 2004. "Urban Leadership and Community Involvement: Ingredients for Good Governance?" Findings from the PLUS Project. Paper presented at the City Futures Conference, Chicago, July.

Heifetz, R. A., and M. Linsky. 2002. *Leadership on the Line. Staying Alive Through the Dangers of Leading.* Boston: Harvard Business School Press.

Heinelt, H., D. Sweeting, and P. Getimis, eds. 2006. *Legitimacy and Urban Governance. A Cross-National Comparative Study.* Abingdon, UK: Routledge.

Heinrich, C. J., and L. E. Lynn, Jr., eds. 2001. *Governance and Performance: New Perspectives.* Washington, D.C.: Georgetown University Press.

Her Majesty's Stationery Office (HMSO). 1998. A Mayor and Assembly for London. Cmnd 3897. London: HMSO.

Hesse, J. J., and L. J. Sharpe. 1991. "Local Government in International Perspective: Some Comparative Observations." In *Local Government and Urban Affairs in International Perspective,* edited by J. J. Hesse. Baden-Baden, Germany: Nomos Verlagsgesellschaft.

Hill, R. C., and K. Fujita. 2003. "The Nested City: Introduction." *Urban Studies* 40: 207–17.

Hill, R. C., and J. W. Kim 2000. "Global Cities and Developmental States: New York, Tokyo and Seoul." *Urban Studies* 37: 2167–95.

———. 2001. "Reply to Friedmann and Sassen." *Urban Studies* 38: 2541–2.

Hirschman, A. O. 1970. *Exit, Voice and Loyalty.* Cambridge, MA: Harvard University Press.

Hitz, H., C. Schmid, and R. Wolff. 1994. "Urbanization in Zurich: Headquarter Economy and City-Belt." *Environment and Planning D* 12: 167–85.

Hofer, A. 2004. "Postindustrial Zurich—15 years in Search of a New Paradigm of Public Planning." In *The Contested Metropolis: Six Cities at the Beginning of the 21st Century,* edited by R. Paloscia. Basel, Switzerland: Birkhauser.

Hoffmann-Martinot, V., and J. Sellers, eds. 2005. *Metropolitanization and Political Change.* Opladen, Germany: Verlag Für Sozialwissenschaften.

Hoggett, P. 1991. "A New Management in the Public Sector?" *Policy and Politics* 19, no. 4: 243–56.

Högl, G. 1994. "Das 20 Jahrhundert: Urbanität und Demokratie." In *Geschichte der Stadt Dortmund,* edited by D. Stadtarchiv. Dortmund, Germany: Harenberg Verlag.

Holck, L. 2006. "The Integration Council, City of Copenhagen, Denmark." Presentation to the Hearing on Immigration and Integration Cooperation between Regional and Local Governments and Civil Society Organizations, Barcelona.

Hood. C. 1991. "A Public Management for all Seasons." *Public Administration* 69: 3–19.

Horn, M. 1995. *The Political Economy of Public Administration.* Cambridge: Cambridge University Press.

Horvath, T., ed. 2000. *Decentralisation: Experiments and Reforms.* Budapest: LGI-OSI.

Hoy, S. 2004. "Immigration Framework in Toronto." Presentation to the Chinese Professional Association of Canada, Toronto, October 17.

Hu, An-gong. 2004. Zhingguo xing fazhang guang [China: New Development Strategy]. Beijing: Zhejiang People's Press.

Huntoon, L. 2001. "Government Use of Nonprofit Organizations to Build Social Capital." *Journal of Socio-Economics* 30: 157–60.

Huster, E., B. Benz, and J. Boeckh. 2003. "First Report on the Implementation of the German NAPincl. 2001—2003." Unpublished European Union document. Hutton, W. (2002) *The World We're In.* London: Little Brown.

Hutton, W., and A. Giddens, eds. 2000. *On the Edge. Living with Global Capitalism.* London: Jonathan Cape.

IDA (Improvement and Development Agency). 2003. *An Emerging Strategy for Leadership Development in Local Government.* London: Improvement and Development Agency (on behalf of the Leadership Development Commission).

Immergut, E. M. 1992. *Health Politics: Ideas and Institutions in Western Europe.* Cambridge: Cambridge University Press.

INSEE. (Institut National de la Statistique et des Etudes Economique). 1982. *Recensement de la population 1982.* [Census for the population.] Paris: INSEE.

———. 1999. *Recensement de la population 1999.* [Census for the population.] Paris: INSEE.

Iowa State University. 2003. *Annual Report.* Public Policy and Administration Program.

IPC (Instituto Popular de Capacitación). 1999. *Antioquia, fin de Milenio: Terminará la Crisis del Derecho Humanitario?* Medellín: IPC.

Itzigsohn, J. 2000. *Developing Poverty: The State, Labor Market Deregulation, and the Informal Economy in Costa Rica and the Dominican Republic.* University Park: Pennsylvania State University.

Jacquier, C. 2003. "Inhabitant Participation and 'Politique de la Ville' in France." In *Soziale Stadt Info* 14, October. Newsletter. Berlin: Deutsches Institut für Urbanistik.

Jayasuriya, K. 2003. *'Workfare for the Global Poor': Anti-Politics and the New Governance.* Working Paper No. 98, Asia Research Centre, Murdoch University, Perth, Australia.

Jenkins, R. 2004. "Bishop Tells Labour to Keep Faith with Poor." *The Times,* London, April 5.

Jessop, B. 1993. "Towards a Schumpeterian Workfare State? Preliminary Remarks on Post-Fordist Political Economy." *Studies in Political Economy* 40: 7–39.

———. 1999. "The Changing Governance of Welfare. Recent Trends in its Primary Functions, Scale and Modes of Coordination." *Social Policy and Administration* 33: 348–59.

———. 2002. "Liberalism, Neoliberalism, and Urban Governance: A State-Theoretical Perspective." *Antipode* 34, no. 3: 452–72.

Jessop, B., and N. Sum. 2000. "An Entreneurial City in Action: Hong Kong's Emerging." *Urban Studies* 37: 2287–313.

Jiménez Morales, G. 2005. "El Sindicato Antioqueño Tiene Ahora Tres Líderes" *El Colombiano,* June 6. http://www.elcolombiano.terra.com.

Jin, T. 2004. *Zhongguo quyu jinji fazhang baogao 2003–2004* [Blue Book of China].

John, P. 2001. *Local Governance in Western Europe.* London: Sage.

Johnson, C., and S. P. Osborne. 2003. "Local Strategic Partnerships, Neighbourhood Renewal, and the Limits to Co-Governance." *Public Money and Management* 23, no. 3: 147–54.

Jones, B. D., ed. 1989. *Leadership and Politics.* Lawrence: University Press of Kansas.

Jones, P. S. 2003. "Urban Regeneration's Poisoned Chalice: Is There an Impasse in Community Participation-Based Policy?" *Urban Studies* 40, no. 3: 581–601.

Jones-Correa, M. 1998. *Between Two Nations: The Political Predicament of Latinos in New York City.* Ithaca, NY: Cornell University Press.

Jouve, B., and C. Lefevre. 2002. "Metropolitan Governance and Institutional Dynamics." In *Globalism and Local Democracy. Challenge and Change in Europe and North America,* edited by R. Hambleton, H. V. Savitch, and M. Stewart. Basingstoke, UK: Palgrave Macmillan.

Judd, D. 2000. "Strong Leadership." *Urban Studies* 37, no. 5–6: 951–61.

Judd, D., and M. Parkinson. 1989. *Leadership and Urban Regeneration: Cities in North America and Europe.* Thousand Oaks, CA: Sage.

Jun, J. S., and D. S. Wright. 1996. *Globalization and Decentralization: Institutional Contexts, Policy Issues, and Intergovernmental Relations in Japan and the Unites States.* Washington, D.C.: Georgetown University Press.

Kamo, T. 2000. "An Aftermath of Globalization? East Asian Economic Turmoil and Japanese Cities Adrift." *Urban Studies* 37: 2145–65.

Kandeva, E., ed. 2001. *Stabilisation of Local Governments.* Budapest: LGI-OSI.

Kantor, P. 1988. *The Dependent City: The Changing Political Economy of Urban America.* Glenview, IL: Scott Foresman.

Keating, M. 2001 "Governing Cities and Regions: Territorial Restructuring in a Global Age." In *Global City-Regions,* edited by A. J. Scott. Oxford: Oxford University Press.

Keating, M., J. Loughlin, and K. Deschouwer. 2003. *Culture, Institutions and Economic Development: A Study of Eight European Regions.* Cheltenham, UK: Edward Elgar.

Keil, R. 1998. *Los Angeles: Globalization, Urbanization and Social Struggles.* Chichester, UK: John Wiley.

———. 2000. "Governance Restructuring in Los Angeles and Toronto: Amalgamation or Secession?" *International Journal of Urban and Regional Research* 24: 758–81.

Keil, R., and P. Lieser. 1992. "Frankfurt: Global City—Local Politics." In *After Modernism: Global Restructuring and the Changing Boundaries of City Life,* edited by M. P. Smith. New Brunswick, NJ: Transaction.

Keil, R., and K. Ronneberger. 1994. "Going Up the Country: Internationalization and Urbanization on Frankfurt's Northern Edge." *Environment and Planning D* 12: 137–66.

———. 2000. "The Globalization of Frankfurt am Main: Core, Periphery and Social Conflict." In *Globalizing Cities: A New Spatial Order?* edited by P. Marcuse and R. V. Kempen. Oxford: Blackwell.

Kelly, S. 2004. *Driving Change: Housing Policy and Urban Renewal in Dublin's Inner City.* Paper to the Housing Studies Association Annual Conference, Belfast.

Kelly, S., and A. MacLaran. 2004. "The Residential Transformation of Inner Dublin." In *Dublin Economic and Social Trends,* Vol. 4, edited by P. J. Drudy and A. MacLaran, pp. 36–59. Dublin: Centre for Urban and Regional Studies, Trinity College .

Kersting, N., and A. Vetter, eds. 2003. *Reforming Local Government in Europe.* Opladen, Germany: Leske and Budrich.

Kesteloot, C. 2000. "Brussels: Post-Fordist Polarization." In *Globalizing Cities: A New Spatial Order?* edited by P. Marcuse and R. V. Kempen. Oxford: Blackwell.

Kettl, D. F. 2000a. *The Global Public Management Revolution: A Report on the Transformation of Governance.* Washington, D.C.: Brookings Institution.

————. 2000b. "The Transformation of Governance: Globalization, Devolution, and the Role of Government." *Public Administration Review* 60, no. 6: 488–97.

————. 2002a. "Managing Indirect Government." In *The Tools of Government: A Guide to the New Governance,* edited by L. M. Salamon, pp. 490–510. New York: Oxford University Press.

————. 2002b. *The Transformation of Governance.* Baltimore: Johns Hopkins Press.

Khan, S., and A. Piracha. 2003. *Planfirst and Thereafter: The Process of Reforming the Planning System in Neo-Liberal Climate.* Paper presented at the first State of Australian Cities Conference, University of Western Sydney, Sydney.

Kim, J., and S. Choe. 1997. *Seoul: The Making of a Metropolis.* Chichester, UK: John Wiley.

Kim, W. B. 1999. "National Competitiveness and Governance of Seoul, Korea." In *Urban and Regional Governance in the Asia Pacific,* edited by J. Friedmann. Vancouver: Institute of Asian Research.

————. 2000. "Repositioning of City-Regions: Korea after the Crisis." In *Global City-Regions: Trends, Theory, Policy,* edited by A. J. Scott. Oxford: Oxford University Press.

Kincaid, J. 1999. "De Facto Devolution and Urban Defunding: The Priority of Persons Over Places." *Journal of Urban Affairs* 21: 135–67.

King, A. D. 1990. *Global Cities: Post-Imperialism and the Internationalization of London.* London: Routledge.

Kirby, P. 2002. *The Celtic Tiger in Distress: Growth With Inequality in Ireland.* Basingstoke, UK: Palgrave Macmillan.

Kirlin, J. J., and M. K. Kirlin. 2002. "Strengthening Effective Government—Citizen Connections through Greater Civic Engagement." Special issue. *Public Administration Review* 62: 80–5.

Klijn, E. H., and J. Koppenjan. 1999. *Network Management and Decision Making in Networks: A Multi-Actor Approach to Governance.* Working Paper. University of Twente, The Netherlands. NIG Working Paper 99–2.

Kloosterman, R., and D. Broeders. 2002. "Urban Policies in the Netherlands: From 'Social Renewal' to 'Big Cities Policy.'" In *Globalism and Local Democracy: Challenge and Change in Europe and North America,* edited by R. Hambleton, H. V. Savitch, and M. Stewart. New York: Palgrave Macmillan.

Knox, P. L. 1995. "World Cities in a World-System." In *World Cities in a World-System,* edited by P. L. Knox and P. J. Taylor. Cambridge: Cambridge University Press.

————. 1997. "Globalization and Urban Economic Change." *Annals of the American Academy of Political and Social Science* 551: 17–27.

Kobenhavn Commune. 2006. Integration. http://www3.kk.dk/Integration2.

Kohn, M. 2000. "Language, Power and Persuasion. Toward a Critique of Deliberative Democracy." *Constellations* 7, no. 3: 408–29.

Kong, Y. 2001. *Jiedu Shanghai* [Understanding Shanghai]. Shanghai: People's Publishing.

Kotter, J. P. 1988. *The Leadership Factor.* New York: Free Press.

Krasner, S. D. 1984. "Approaches to the State: Alternative Conceptions and Historical Dynamics." *Comparative Politics* 16, no. 2: 223–46.

Krummacher, M., R. Kulbach, V. Waltz, and N. Wohlfahrt. 2003. *Soziale Stadt—Sozialraumentwicklung—Quartiersmanagement: Herausforderungen für Politik, Raumplanung und soziale Arbeit.* Opladen, Germany: Leske and Budrich.

Kuhlmann, S. 2004a. "Trajectories and Driving Factors of Local Government Reform in Big Cities: The Case of Paris." Paper to the European Group of Public Administration Conference, Ljubljana, Slovenia.

Kuhlmann, S. 2004b. "From 'Napoleonic Centralism' to 'Democratie de Proximite': The Metropolis of Paris between Global and Local Challenges." Paper to the European Commission for Political Research Joint Session Workshop 23, Uppsala, Sweden.

Ladner, A., and H. Milner. 1999. "Do Voters Turn Out More under Proportional than Majoritarian Systems? The Evidence from Swiss Communal Elections." *Electoral Studies* 18, no. 2: 235–50.

Landry, C. 2000. *The Creative City. A Toolkit for Urban Innovators.* London: Earthscan.

———. 2006. *The Art of City Making.* London: Earthscan.

Larsen, H. 2002. "Directly Elected Mayors: Democratic Renewal or Constitutional Confusion?" In *Local Government at the Millenium,* edited by J. Caulfield and H. Larsen, pp. 111–35. Opladen, Germany: Leske and Budrich.

Lauria, M. ed. 1997. *Reconstructing Regime Theory.* Thousand Oaks, CA: Sage.

Lawless, P. 2004. "Locating and Explaining Area-Based Urban Initiatives: New Deal for Communities in England." *Environment and Planning C: Policy and Politics* 22, no. 3: 383–99.

Leach, S., and D. Wilson. 2000. *Local Political Leadership.* Bristol, UK: Policy Press.

Lee, R. 2002. "Nice Maps, Shame about the Theory? Thinking Geographically About the Economic." *Progress in Human Geography* 26, no. 3: 333–55.

Lefèvre, C. 2003. "Paris-Ile-de-France Region." In *Metropolitan Governance and Spatial Planning,* edited by W. Salet, A. Thornley, and A. Kruekels. London: Spon.

Le Figaro. 2006. "Les Annales Des Scrutin." http://www.lefigaro.fr/dossiers/dossiers_redaction/popup_base_scrutins/une.html.

Le Gales, P. 2002. *European Cities. Social Conflicts and Governance.* Oxford: Oxford University Press.

Leigland, J. 1990. "The Census Bureau"s Role in Research on Special Districts: A Critique. The Western Political Quarterly 43, no, 2: 367–80.

———. 1995. "Public Infrastructure and Special Purposed Governments: Who Pays and How?" In *Building the Public City: The Politics, Governance, and Finance of Public Infrastructure,* edited by D. C. Perry. Thousands Oaks, CA: Sage.

Leimdorfer, F. 2003. "L'espace publique urbain à Abidjan: Individus, associations, État." In *L'Afrique des citadins. Sociétés civiles en chantier,* edited by D. Abidjan. Paris: Karthala.

Lelieveldt, H. 2004. "Helping Citizens Help Themselves: Neighborhood Programs and the Impact of Social Networks, Trust, and Norms on Neighborhood-Oriented Forms of Participation." *Urban Affairs Review* 39, no. 5: 531–51.

Lepofsky, J., and J. Fraser. 2003. "Building Community Citizens: Claiming the Right to Place-Making in the City." *Urban Studies* 40, no. 1: 127–42.

Lever, W. F., and I. Turok. 1999. "Competitive Cities: Introduction to the Review." *Urban Studies* 36, no. 5–6: 791–3.

Levin, J., and G. Rabrenovic. 2004. *Why We Hate.* Amherst, NY: Prometheus Books.

Levine, M. A. 1994. "The Transformation of Urban Politics in France: The Roots of Growth Politics and Urban Regime." *Urban Affairs Quarterly* 29: 383–410.

Lichtenberger, E. 1976. "The Changing Nature of European Urbanization." In *Urbanization and Counterurbanization,* edited by Brian J. L. Berry (Hrsg.). Beverly Hills and London: Sage.

Lijphart, A. 1997. "Unequal Participation: Democracy's Unresolved Dilemma: Presidential Address, American Political Science Association, 1996." *American Political Science Review* 91 (March 1997): 1–14.

Lijphart, A., R. Rogowski, and R. K. Weaver. 1993. "Separation of Powers and Cleavage Management." In *Do Insitutions Matter?* edited by R. K. Weaver and B. A. Rockman. Washington, D.C.: Brookings Institution.

Lin, G. C. S. 1999. "State Policy and Spatial Restructuring in Post-Reform China." *International Journal of Urban and Regional Research* 1978–95, no. 23: 670–96.

Linder, W., and A. Vatter. 2001. "Institutions and Outcomes of Swiss Federalism: The Role of the Cantons in Swiss Politics." *West European Politics* 24: 95–122.

Local Finance in the Ten Countries Joining the European Union in 2004. 2004. Paris: Dexia.

Logan, J., and H. Molotch. 1987. *Urban Fortunes: The Political Economy of Place.* Berkeley: University of California Press.

López, H. 1991. "Salario Mínimo o Salario Medio: ¿Cuál es el Objetivo?" *Revista de Economía Colombiana* 232 (January/February).

———. 1996. *Ensayos Sobre Economía Laboral Colombiana.* Bogotá: Fonade / Carlos Valencia Editores.

Loughlin, J. 2001. *Subnational Democracy in the European Union.* Oxford: Oxford University Press.

Lovering, J. 1995 "Creating Discourses Rather than Jobs; the Crisis in the City and the Transition Fantasies of the Intellectuals and Policy-Makers." In *Managing Cities: The New Urban Context,* edited by P. Healey, S. Cameron, S. Davoudi, S. Graham, and A. Madani. Chichester, UK: John Wiley.

Lowndes V. 2001. "Rescuing Aunt Sally: Taking Institutional Theory Seriously in Urban Politics." *Urban Studies* 38, no. 11: 1953–71.

Lukensmeyer, C. J., and S. Brigham. 2002. "Taking Democracy to Scale: Creating a Town Hall Meeting for the Twenty-First Century." *National Civic Review* 91, no. 2: 351–66.

Lynn, L. E., Jr. 1998. "The New Public Management: How to Transform a Theme into a Legacy." *Public Administration Review* 58, no. 3: 231–38.

Mabileau, A. 1996. *Kommunalpolitik und -verwaltung in Frankreich.* Basel, Switzerland: Birkhäuser.

Machule, D., Buero d*Ing Planung, D. Danne, and J. Usadel. 2003. *Mitwirken in Wilhelmsburg 2002. Teil I.* Hamburg: Mitwirken in Wilhelmsburg.

MacLaran, A. 1993. *Dublin: The Shaping of a Capital.* London and New York: Belhaven.

MacLaran, A., and B. Williams. 2003. "Dublin: Property Development and Planning in an Entrepreneurial City." In *Making Space: Property Development and Urban Planning,* edited by A. MacLaran. London: Arnold.

MacLean, M. J. 2004. *Decentralization, Mobilization, and Democracy in Mature Neo-Liberalism: The Bolivian Case.* Unpublished PhD thesis, Department of Political Science, University of Toronto.

MacLeod, G., and M. Goodwin. 1999. "Space, Scale and State Strategy: Rethinking Urban and Regional Governance." *Progress in Human Geography* 23: 503–27.

MacPherson, K. 1999. Rights to the City: Urban Land Reform and Municipal Power in China. Paper presented at the 1999 ACSP Annual Conference, Chicago.

Maldonado, J. L. 2003. "Metropolitan Government and Development Strategies in Madrid." In *Metropolitan Governance and Spatial Planning,* edited by W. Salet, A. Thornley, and A. Kruekels, pp. 359–74. London: Spon.

Manor, J. 1999. *The Political Economy of Democratic Decentralization.* Washington: World Bank.

Mansilla, H. C. F. 1992. "Economía Informal e Ilegitimidad en Bolivia." *Nueva Sociedad* (Caracas), 119 (May/June): 36–44.

March, J. G., and J. P. Olson. 1983. "Organizing Political Life: What Administrative Reorganization Tells Us about Government." *American Political Science Review* 77, no. 2: 281–96.

Marinetto, M. 2003. "Governing Beyond the Centre: A Critique of the Anglo-Governance School." *Political Studies* 51, no. 3: 592–608.

Marquand, D. 2004. *The Decline of the Public.* Cambridge: Polity Press.

Marshall, T. H. 1950. *Citizenship and Social Class.* Cambridge: Cambridge University Press.

Massey, D. 1993. "Power-Geometry and a Progressive Sense of Place." In *Mapping the Futures: Local Cultures, Global Change,* edited by J. Bird, B. Curtis, T. Putnam, G. Robertson, and L. Tickner. London: Routledge.

———. 1995. *Spatial Divisions of Labour: Social Structures and the Geography of Production.* London: Macmillan.

Mathur, O. P. 2003. "Fiscal Innovations and Urban Governance." In *Governance on the Ground. Innovations and Discontinuities in Cities of the Developing World,* edited by P. McCarney and R. Stren. Baltimore: Johns Hopkins.

Mau, B. 2004. *Massive Change.* London: Phaidon.

Maxwell, R. 2005. "Integrated Yet Alienated: Ethnic Minority Political Participation in Britain and France." Paper to POLIS Conferences, Paris, June.

Mayer, M. 2003 "The Onward Sweep of Social Capital: Causes and Consequences for Understanding Cities, Communities and Urban Movements." *International Journal of Urban and Regional Research* 27, no.1: 108–30.

Mayo, S. K., and D. J. Gross. 1989. "Sites and Services—and Subsidies: The Economics of Low-Cost Housing." In *Government Policy and the Poor in Developing Countries,* edited by R. M. Bird and S. Horton. Toronto: University of Toronto Press.

Mayr, K. 2003. "Immigration: Economic Effects and Political Participation—An Overview and Assessment of the Literature." Working Paper, Centre for the Study of Globalisation and Regionalisation. Warwick, UK: University of Warwick.

McCarney, P. L. 2003. "Confronting Critical Disjunctures in the Governance of Cities." In *Governance on the Ground. Innovations and Discontinuities in Cities of the Developing World,* edited by P. L. McCarney and R. E. Stren. Baltimore: Johns Hopkins University Press.

McDonough, J. E. 2000. *Experiencing Politics: A Legislator's Stories of Government and Health Care.* Berkeley: University of California Press.

McGuirk, P. 1994. "Economic Restructuring and the Realignment of the Urban Planning System: The Case of Dublin." *Urban Studies* 31, no. 2: 287–308.

———. 1995. "Power and Influence in Urban Planning: Community and Property Interests Participation in Dublin's Planning System." *Irish Geography* 28, no. 1: 64–75.

———. 2000. "Power and Policy Networks in Urban Governance: Local Government and Property-Led Regeneration in Dublin." *Urban Studies* 37, no. 4: 651–72.

———. 2003. "Producing the Capacity to Govern in Global Sydney: A Multiscaled Account." *Journal Of Urban Affairs* 25, no. 2: 201–23.

———. 2005. "Neoliberalist Planning? Re-Thinking and Re-Casting Sydney's Metropolitan Planning." *Geographical Research* 43, no. 1: 59–70.

McGuirk, P., and A. MacLaran. 2001. "Changing Approaches to Urban Planning in an 'Entrepreneurial City': The Case of Dublin." *European Planning Studies* 9, no. 4: 437–57.

McLeod, G., M. Raco, and K. Ward. 2003. "Negotiating the Contemporary City." *Urban Studies* 40, no. 9: 1655–71.

McNeil, J. 1997. "Local Government in the Australian Federal System." In *Australian Local Government. Reform and Renewal,* edited by B. Dollery and N. Marshall. Melbourne: Macmillan.

McPhail, I. 1978. "Local Government." In *Federal Power in Australia's Cities,* edited by P. Troy. Sydney: Hale & Iremonger.

Medearis, J. 2005. "Social Movements and Deliberative Democratic Theory." *British Journal of Political Science* 35, no. 1: 53–75.

Milburn, A. 2006. "We Can't Let the Right Be the Voice of the 'Me Generation,'" *The Guardian,* London, February 21.

Miller, G. 2000. "Above Politics: Credible Commitment and Efficiency in the Design of Public Agencies." *Journal of Public Administration Research and Theory* 10, no. 2: 289–327.

Milward, H. B., and K. G. Provan. 2002. "How Networks are Governed." In *Governance and Performance: New Perspectives,* edited by C. J. Heinrich and L. E. Lynn, pp. 238–62. Washington, D.C.: Georgetown University Press.

Mitchell, J. 1992. "Policy Functions and Issues for Public Authorities." In *Public Authorities and Public Policy: The Business of Government,* edited by J. Mitchell. Westport, CT: Greenwood.

———. 1999. *The American Experiment with Government Corporations.* Armonk, NY: M. E. Sharpe.

Montero, A. P. 2001a. "Decentralizing Democracy: Spain and Brazil in Comparative Perspective." *Comparative Politics* 33: 149–69.

———. 2001b. "After Decentralization: Patterns of Intergovernmental Conflict in Argentina, Brazil, Spain and Mexico." *Publius* 31: 43–64.

Montgomery, M. R., R. Stren, B. Cohen, and H. E. Reed. 2003. *Cities Transformed. Demographic Change and its Implications in the Developing World.* Washington: National Academies Press; London: Earthscan.

Mouritzen, P. E., and J. J. Svara. 2002. *Leadership at the Apex: Politicians and Administrators in Western Local Governments.* Pittsburgh, PA: University of Pittsburgh Press.

Muramatsu, M., F. Iqbal, and I. Kume. 2001. *Local Government Development in Post-War Japan.* Oxford: Oxford University Press.

Murphy, P., and C. Wu. 2001. "Globalization and the Sustainability of Cities in the Asia Pacific Region: The Case of Sydney." In *Globalization and the Sustainability of Cities in the Asia Pacific Region,* edited by F. Lo and M. P. Marcotullio. Tokyo: United Nations University Press.

Musso, J., C. Weare, K. Jun, and A. Kitsuse. 2004. "Representing Diversity in Community Governance: Neighborhood Concils in Los Angeles." Urban Initiative Policy Brief. Los Angeles: University of Southern California Urban Initiative.

Myrvold, T. M., and H. S. Osttveiten. 2000. "Look to Oslo? The Work of Parliamentarian Models of Government in Local Politics." Paper to the IPSA World Congress, Quebec, Canada, August 1–5.

Nalbandian, J. 1990. "Tenets of Contemporary Professionalism in Local Government." *Public Administration Review* 50, no. 6: 654–62.

———. 1991. *Professionalism in Local Government: Roles, Responsibilities, and Values of City Managers.* San Francisco: Jossey-Bass.

———. 1994. "Reflections of a 'Pracademic' on the Logic of Politics and Administration." *Public Administration Review* 54, no. 6: 531–6.

———. 1999. "Facilitating Community, Enabling Democracy: New Roles for Local Government Managers." *Public Administration Review* 59, no. 3: 187–97.

———. 2000a. Conversation with John Arnold, former city administrator, Topeka, Kansas.

———. 2000b. "The City Manager as Political Leader." *Public Management* 82, no. 3: 7–12.

Nalbandian, J., and C. Nalbandian. 2002. "Contemporary Challenges in Local Government." *Public Management* 84, no. 12: 6–11.

———. 2003. "Meeting Today's Challenges: Competencies for the Contemporary Local Government Professional." *Public Management* 85, no. 4: 11–16.

Naschold, F., and G. Daley. 1999a. "Learning from the Pioneers: Modernizing Local Government. Part One." *International Public Management Journal* 2, no. 1: 25–51.

———. 1999b. "The Strategic Management Challenge: Modernizing Local Government. Part Two." *International Public Management Journal.* 2, no. 1: 52–67.

———. 1999c. "The Interface Management Frontier: Modernizing Local Government. Part Three." *International Public Management Journal* 2, no. 1: 68–89.

Naughton, B. 1995. "Urban Space: Introduction." In *Urban Spaces in Contemporary China: The Potential for Autonomy and Community in Post-Mao China,* edited by D. Davis, R. Kraus, B. Naughton, and E. Perry. New York: Cambridge University Press.

Navia, P., and M. Zimmerman. 2004. *Las Ciudades Latinoamericanas en el Nuevo [Des] Orden Mundial.* Mexico, DF, and Buenos Aires: Siglo XXI Editores.

NBSC (National Bureau of Statistics of China). 2005. *China Statistical Yearbook 2005.* Beijing: China Statistical Publishing House.

———. 2006. News release. http://www.stats.gov.cn.

Neuwirth, R. 2005. *Shadow Cities. A Billion Squatters, A New Urban World.* London: Routledge.

Newman, P., and A. Thornley. 1996. *Urban Planning in Europe: International Competition, National Systems and Planning Projects.* London: Routledge.

———. 2005. *Planning World Cities. Globalization and Urban Politics.* Busingstoke, UK: Palgrave Macmillan.

———. 1997. "Fragmentation and Centralisation in the Governance of London: Influencing the Urban Policy and Planning Agenda." *Urban Studies* 34: 967–88.

New York Times. 2000. "Rich Brazilians Rise Above Rush-Hour Jams," February 15.

Ng, M. K., and W. Tang. 1999. "Land-Use Planning in One County, Two Systems: Hong Kong, Guangzhou and Shenzhen." *International Planning Studies* 4: 7–27.

Noblit, G. W., and R. D. Hare. 1988. *Meta-Ethnography: Synthesizing Qualitative Studies.* Newbury Park, UK: Sage.

Norquist, J. 1998. *The Wealth of Cities: Revitalizing the Centers of American Life.* Reading, MA: Addison-Wesley.

Norris, D. F. 2003. "If We Build It, They Will Come! Tourism-Based Economic Development in Baltimore." In *The Infrastructure of Play,* edited by D. R. Judd. Armonk, NY: M. E. Sharpe.

NSW Department of Planning. 2005. *City Of Cities. A Plan for Sydney's Future.* Sydney: NSW Government.

O'Hearn, D. 2001. *The Atlantic Economy: Britain, the US and Ireland.* Manchester: Manchester University Press.

———. 1992. *Putting Ireland in a Global Context.* Cork, Ireland: University College Cork.

O'Leary, B. 1987a. "British Farce, French Drama and Tales of Two Cities. Reorganisations of Paris and London Governments 1957–1986." *Public Administration* 65, no. 4: 369–89.

———. 1987b. "Why Was the GLC Abolished." *International Journal of Urban and Regional Research* 11, no. 2: 193–216.

O'Toole, L. J., Jr. 1997. "Treating Networks Seriously: Practical and Research-Based Agendas in Public Administration." *Public Administration Review* 57, no. 1: 45–52.

Ocampo, J. A., ed. 1987. *Historia Económica de Colombia.* Bogotá: Siglo XXI Editores.

O'Cleireacain, C. 1997. "The Private Economy and the Public Budget." In *The City and the World: New York's Global Future,* edited by M. E. Crahan and A. Vourvoulias-Bush. New York: Council on Foreign Relations Press.

ODPM (Office of the Deputy Prime Minister). 2005a. *Sustainable Communities: People, Places and Prosperity.* London: Stationery Office.

———. 2005b. *Vibrant Local Leadership.* London: Office of the Deputy Prime Minister.

OEIS/MA (Observatorio para la Equidad y la Integración Social en Medellín and Antioquia). 2002. *Observar* 8 (December).

Oriente Virtual. 2005. "Servicios el Sector más Estratégico."

Osborn, D., and P. Hutchison. 2004. *The Price of Government.* New York: Basic Books.

Osborne, D., and T. Gaebler. 1993. *Reinventing Government. How the Entrepreneurial Spirit is Transforming the Public Sector.* New York: Plume.

Özcan, E. 1992. *Türkische Immigrantenorganisationen in der Bundesrepublik Deutschland.* Berlin: Hitit Verlag.

Pagonis, T., and A. Thornley. 2000. "Urban Development Projects in Moscow: Market/State Relations in the New Russia." *European Planning Studies* 8: 751–66.

Panafrican News Agency. 2001. "Municipal Elections Generally Calm." Abidjan, March 26, 2001.

Papademetriou, D. G. 2001. "International Migration and Cities." In *Democracy at the Local Level. The International IDEA Handbook on Participation, Representation, Conflict Management and Governance,* edited by T. D. Sisk. Stockholm: International Institute for Democracy and Electoral Assistance.

Papillon, M. 2002. Immigration, Diversity and Social Inclusion in Canada's Cities. Ottawa: Canadian Policy Network.

Parnreiter, C. 2002. "Mexico: The Making of a Global City." In *Global Networks, Linked Cities,* edited by S. Sassen. New York: Routledge.

Parry, G., G. Moyser, and N. Day. 1992. *Political Participation and Democracy in Britain.* Cambridge: Cambridge University Press.

Paus, E. 1983. *Stagnation between Export Promotion and a Protected Internal Market. The Colombian Textile Industry.* PhD dissertation, University of Pittsburg, Pittsburg, Pennsylvania.

Peck, J., and A. Tickell. 1994. "Searching for a New Institutional Fix: The *After*-Fordist Crisis and the Global-local Disorder." In *Post-Fordism: A Reader,* edited by A. Amin. Oxford: Blackwell.

Pei, M. 1998. "Chinese Civic Association: An Empirical Analysis." *Modern China* 24, no. 3: 285–318.

Perlman, J. 1976. *The Myth of Marginality. Urban Poverty and Politics in Rio de Janeiro.* Berkeley and Los Angeles: University of California Press.

Perrons, D. 2004. *Globalization and Social Change: People and Places in a Divided World.* London: Routledge.

Perrons, D., and S. Skyers. 2003. "Empowerment through Participation? Conceptual Explorations and a Case Study." *International Journal of Urban and Regional Research* 27, no. 2: 265–85.

Perry, D. C. 2003. "Urban Tourism and the Privatizing Discourses of Public Infrastructure." In *The Infrastructure of Play*, edited by D. R. Judd. Armonk, NY: M. E. Sharpe.

Peteri, G., and V. Zentai. 2002. "Lessons on Successful Reform Management." In *Mastering Decentralization and Public Administration Reforms in Central and Eastern Europe*, edited by G. Peteri, pp. 13–31. Budapest: LGI-OSI.

Peters, B. G. 1995. *The Politics of Bureaucracy.* White Plains, NY: Longman.

Peterson, P. E. 1981. *City Limits.* Chicago: University of Chicago Press.

Petersson, Susie, and Kasper Nizam. 2001. "Do Integration Councils Matter?" *Administrative Theory & Praxis* 23, no. 2: 269–278.

Pickvance, C., and E. Preteceille. 1991. "Introduction: The Significance of Local Power in Theory and Practice." In *State Restructuring and Local Power*, edited by C. Pickvance and E. Preteceille. London: Pinter.

Pierre, J. 2005. "Comparative Urban Governance: Uncovering Complex Causalities." *Urban Affairs Review* 40, no. 4: 446–62.

Pierre, J., and B. G. Peters. 2000. *Governance, Politics and the State.* London: Macmillan.

Pierre, J., and G. Stoker. 2002. "Toward Multi-Level Governance." In *Developments in British Politics*, edited by P. Dunleavy, A. Gamble, R. Heffernan, I. Holliday, and G. Peele. Basingstoke, UK: Palgrave Macmillan.

Pimlott, B., and N. Rao. 2002. *Governing London.* Oxford: Oxford University Press.

Polanyi, K. 1957. *The Great Transformation: The Political and Economic Origins of Our Time.* Boston: Beacon Paperback.

Polèse, M., and R. Stren, eds. 2000. *The Social Sustainability of Cities. Diversity and the Management of Change.* Toronto: University of Toronto Press.

Pollitt, C., and G. Bouckaert. 2000. *Public Management Reform. A Comparative Analysis.* Oxford: Oxford University Press.

Pont, R. 2001. "A Conversation with Raul Pont, Mayor of Porto Alegre." In *The Challenge of Urban Government. Policies and Practices*, edited by M. Freire and R. Stren. Washington: World Bank.

Porter, D. R., B. C. Lin, S. Jakubiak, and R. B. Peiser. 1992. *Special Districts: A Useful Technique for Financing Infrastructure.* 2nd edition. Washington, D.C.: Urban Land Institute.

Porter, M. E. 2002. "Regions and the New Economics of Competition." In *Global City-Regions. Trends, Theory, Policy*, edited by A. J. Scott. Oxford: Oxford University Press.

Pozzobon, R. M. 1998. *Os Desafios da Gestão Municipal Democrática. Porto Alegre.* Sao Paulo: Instituto Polis.

Procacci, F., and C. Rossignolo. 2006. "New Urban Leaders and Community Involvement. The Italian Case Studies." In *Legitimacy and Urban Governance. A Cross-National Comparative Study*, edited by H. Heinelt, D. Sweeting, and P. Getimis. Abingdon, UK: Routledge.

Puig-Farrás, J., and B. Hartz-Son. 1999. *La Negociación de la Flexibilidad del Trabajo.* Medellín: Fondo Editorial Escuela Nacional Sindical/Editorial Alas Libres.

Punch, M. 2000. *Uneven Development and the Third Space in the Urban System: Evidence from Dublin.* Unpublished PhD thesis, Trinity College, Dublin.

———. 2001. "Inner-City Transformation and Renewal: The View from the Grassroots." In *Dublin: Economic and Social Trends*, edited by P. J. Drudy and A. MacLaran. Dublin: Centre for Urban and Regional Studies, Trinity College.

———. 2002a. "Local Development Issues on the Urban Periphery: Tallaght from the Bottom Up." *Journal of Irish Urban Studies* 1, no. 2: 61–78.

———. 2002b "Economic Geographies of the Urban System: Top Down/Bottom Up Trajectories of Development and Change in Dublin's Inner City." *Journal of Irish Urban Studies* 1, no. 2: 31–54.

———. 2004. "Economic Restructuring in Dublin: Global Connections, Local Variations." Edited by P. J. Drudy and A. MacLaran. *Dublin Economic and Social Trends* 4: 17–35.

———. 2005. "Problem Drug Use and the Political Economy of Urban Restructuring: Heroin, Class and Governance in Dublin." *Antipode* 37, no. 4: 754–74.

Punch, M., D. Redmond, and S. Kelly. 2003a. "Mapping the Uneven City: Urban Restructuring, Entrepreneurial Governance and Social Conflict in Dublin." Paper to the Royal Geographical Society and Institute of British Geographers' Conference, London.

———. 2003b. "Taking Liberties: Access to Housing in Dublin's Inner City." Paper to Conference "Towards Environmental Citizenship," Urban Institute Ireland, University College Dublin.

———. 2003c. "Restructuring the Divided City: Gated Communities and Socio-Economic Change in Dublin's Inner City." Paper to the Gated Communities Conference, "Building Social Division or Safer Communities," University of Glasgow.

Purdue, D., K. Razzaque, R. Hambleton, and M. Stewart. 2000. *Community Leadership in Area Regeneration.* Bristol: Policy Press.

Putnam, R. 1993. *Making Democracy Work: Civic Traditions in Modern Italy.* Princeton, NJ: Princeton University Press.

———. 1995. "Bowling Alone." *Journal of Democracy* 6, no. 1: 65–78.

———. 1996. "The Strange Disappearance of Civic America." *American Prospect* 7, no. 24.

Putnam, R. D. 2000. *Bowling Alone: The Collapse and Revival of American Community.* New York: Simon and Schuster.

Radford, G. 2003. "From Municipal Socialism to Public Authorities: Institutional Factors in the Shaping of American Public Enterprise." *Journal of American History* 90, no. 3: 863–90.

Rakowski, C. A. 1994. "Convergence and Divergence in the Informal Economy Debate: A Focus on Latin America, 1984–92." *World Development* 22, no. 4: 501–16.

Randolph, B. 2004. "The Changing Australian City: New Patterns, New Policies and New Research Needs." *Urban Policy and Research* 22: 481–93.

Randolph, B., and D. Holloway. 2005. "Social Disadvantage, Tenure and Location: An Analysis of Sydney and Melbourne." *Urban Policy and Research* 22: 481–93.

Randolph, B., L. Pang, and J. Hall. 2001. *Who Cares About Western Sydney?* Western Sydney Regional Organisation of Councils and the Urban Frontiers Program, University of Western Sydney.

Ranney, D. 2003. *Global Decisions, Local Collisions. Urban Life in the New World Order.* Philadelphia: Temple University Press.

Rast, J. 1999. *Remaking Chicago: The Political Origins of Urban Industrial Chicago.* DeKalb, IL: Northern Illinois University Press.

Ray, B. 2003. "The Role of Cities in Immigrant Integration." http://www.migrationinformation.org/issue_oct03.cfm.

Redmond, D. 2001. "Social Housing Policy in Ireland: Under New Management?" *European Journal of Housing Policy* 1, no. 2: 291–306.

———. 2002. "Policy and Practice in Tenant Participation: Empowering Tenants?" *Journal of Irish Urban Studies* 1, no. 2: 1–18.

Reid, M. 2002. "Rapid Transformation in Post-Socialist Cities: Towards an Uncertain Future." In *Globalism and Local Democracy,* edited by R. Hambleton, H. V. Savitch, and M. Stewart, pp. 95–107. Basingstoke, UK: Palgrave.

Resina, J. R. 2001. "Madrid's Palimpsest: Reading the Capital against the Grain." In *Iberian Cities,* edited by J. R. Resina. New York: Routledge.

Revista Dinero. 2000 "Nuevo Aire a los Grupos." *Revista Dinero* 103.

Rhodes, R. A. W. 1996. "The New Governance: Governing without Government." *Political Studies* 44, no. 4: 652–67.

———. 1997. *Understanding Governance.* Buckingham: Open University Press.

Ridley, N. 1988. "The Local Right: Enabling not Producing." *Policy Study,* no. 92. London: Centre for Policy Studies.

Rivlin, G. 1992. *Fire on the Prairie.* New York: Henry Holt.

Röber, M. 2002. "Vom Zweckverband zur dezentralisierten Einheitsgemeinde: die Entwicklung der Berliner Verwaltungsorganisation im 20. Jahrhundert." In *Moderne Verwaltung für moderne Metropolen: Berlin und London im Vergleich. Stadtforschung aktuell,* edited by M. Röber, E. Schröter, and H. Wollmann. Opladen, Germany: Leske and Budrich.

Röber, M., and E. Schröter. 2002. "Berliner Politik-und Verwaltungsstrukturen: Neue Zeiten und alte Probleme." In *Moderne Verwaltung für moderne Metropolen: Berlin und London im Vergleich. Stadtforschung aktuell,* edited by M. Röber, E. Schröter, and H. Wollmann. Opladen, Germany: Leske and Budrich.

Rodriguez-Pose, A., and J. Tomaney. 1999. "Industrial Crisis in the Centre of the Periphery: Stabilisation, Economic Restructuring and Policy Responses in the Sao Paulo Metropolitan Region." *Urban Studies* 36: 479–98.

Rohr, J. A. 1978. *Ethics for Bureaucrats.* New York: Marcel Dekker.

Rolnick, R. 1999. "Territorial Exclusion and Violence: The Case of São Paulo, Brazil." *Comparative Urban Studies Occasional Papers Series,* no. 26. Washington: Woodrow Wilson International Center for Scholars.

Romzek, B. S., and M. J. Dubnick. 1987. "Accountability in the Public Sector: Lessons from the Challenger Tragedy." *Public Administration Review* 47, no. 3: 227–38.

Rose R. (2005) *Learning from Comparative Public Policy. A Practical Guide.* Abingdon, UK: Routledge.

Rosenbloom, D. H. 1983. *Public Administration and Law: Bench v. Bureau in the United States.* New York: Marcel Dekker.

Rosentraub, M., D. Swindell, M. Przybylski, and D. R. Mullins. 1994. "Sports and Downtown Development Strategy: If You Build It, Will Jobs Come?" *Journal of Urban Affairs* 16: 211–39.

Ross, J. 2001. "Management Philosophy of the Greater London Authority." In *Public Money & Management* 21, no. 4: 35–41.

Ross, R. J. S., and K. C. Trachte. 1990. *Global Capitalism: The New Leviathan.* Albany, NY: State University of New York Press.

Ross, S. A. 1973. "The Economic Theory of Agency: The Principal's Problem." In *American Economic Review* 63, no. 2: 134–9.

Roubaud, F. 2003. "La Crise Vue d'en Das à Abidjan: Ethnicité, Gouvernance et Démocratie." *Afrique Contemporaine,* no. 206 (Summer): 57–86.

Rueda, Bedoya R. 1998. "Desplazamiento Forzado por la Violencia Política en Colombia: Problemas de Legitimidad y Gobernabilidad del Estado." Unpublished master's thesis, Universidad Nacional de Colombia, Law School, Medellín.

Sacks, J. 2002. *The Dignity of Difference: How to Avoid the Clash of Civilizations.* London: Continuum.

Saegert, S. 2006. "Building Civic Capacity in Urban Neighbourhoods: An Empirically Grounded Anatomy." *Journal of Urban Affairs* 28, no. 3: 275–94.

Saito, A. 2003. "Global City Formation in a Capitalist Developmental State: Tokyo and the Waterfront Sub-Centre Project." *Urban Studies* 40: 283–308.

Saito, A. and A. Thornley. 2003. "Shifts in Tokyo's World City Status and the Urban Planning Response." *Urban Studies* 40: 665–85.

Salamon, L. M. 2002a. "The Tools Approach and the New Governance: Conclusion and Implications." In *The Tools of Government,* edited by L. M. Salamon, pp. 600–610. New York: Oxford University Press.

Salamon, L. M., ed. 2002b. *The Tools of Government.* New York: Oxford University Press.

Salet, W., A. Thornley, and A. Kreukels. 2002. *Metropolitan Governance and Spatial Planning.* London: Spon.

Sanders, H. 1992. "Building the Convention City: Politics, Finance, and Public Investment in Urban America." *Journal of Urban Affairs* 14, no. 2: 135–60.

———. 1999. *Flawed Forecasts: A Critical Look at Convention Center Feasibility Studies.* White Paper Number 9, Pioneer Institute for Public Policy Research, Boston.

Sanford, M. 2002. "What Place for England in an Asymmetrically Devolved UK?" *Regional Studies* 36: 789–96.

Santos, M. 1996. "Sao Paulo: A Growth Process Full of Contradictions." In *The Mega-City in Latin America,* edited by A. Gilbert. Tokyo: United Nations University Press.

Sarmiento, Placencia E. 2000. *Como Construir una Nueva Organización Económica.* Bogotá: Editorial Oveja Negra.

Sashkin, M., and M. G. Sashkin. 2003. *Leadership that Matters*. San Francisco: Berrett-Koehler.

Sassen, S. 1994. *Cities in a World Economy*. Thousand Oaks, CA: Pine Forge.

———. 1998. "Swirling That Old Wine Around in the Wrong Bottle: A Comment on White." *Urban Affairs Review* 33: 478–81.

———. 2001a. *The Global City. New York, London, Tokyo*. 2nd edition. Princeton, NJ, and Oxford: Princeton University Press.

———. 2001b. "Global Cities and Developmentalist States: How to Derail What Could Be an Interesting Debate: A Response to Hill and Kim." *Urban Studies* 38: 2537–40.

———. 2004. "Globalization Theory and Cities." Presentation to the Workshop on Globalization and Cities, Chicago.

———. 2006. *Cities in a World Economy*. 3rd ed. Thousand Oaks, CA: Pine Forge.

———, ed. 2002. *Global Networks. Linked Cities*. New York: Routledge.

Saunders, P. J. 2001. "Why 'Globalization' Didn't Rescue Russia," *Policy Review*, February and March, 27–39.

Savitch, H., and R. Vogel. 2000. "Paths to New Regionalism." *State and Local Government Review* 32, no. 3: 158–68.

Savitch, H. V. 1998. "Global Challenge and Institutional Capacity: Or, How We Can Refit Local Administration for the Next Century." *Administration and Society* 30: 248–73.

———. 2002. "The Globalisation Process." In *Globalism and Local Democracy: Challenge and Change in Europe and North America*, edited by R. Hambleton, H. V. Savitch, and M. Stewart. Basingstoke, UK: Palgrave.

Savitch, H. V., and P. Kantor. 2002. *Cities in the International Marketplace: The Political Economy of Urban Development in North America and Western Europe*. Princeton, NJ: Princeton University Press.

———. 2003. "Urban Strategies for a Global Era." *American Behavioral Scientist* 46: 1002–33.

Savitch, H. V., and R. K. Vogel. 1996. "Introduction: Regional Patterns in a Post-City Age." In *Regional Politics: America in a Post-City Age*, edited by H. V. Savitch and R. K. Vogel. Thousand Oaks, CA: Sage.

———. 2005. "The United States: Executive Centred Politics." In *Comparing Local Governance: Trends and Developments*, edited by B. Denters and L. E. Rose. Basingstoke, UK: Palgrave Macmillan.

Sayre, W.S., and H. Kaufman. 1960. *Governing New York City: Politics in the Metropolis*. New York: W. W. Norton.

Schiffer, S. R. 2002. "Sao Paulo: Articulating a Cross-Border Region." In *Global Networks, Linked Cities*, edited by S. Sassen. New York: Routledge.

Schon, D. A. 1983. *The Reflective Practitioner: How Professionals Think in Action*. New York: Basic Books.

Schröter, E. 1998. "Ein Bürgermeister für London: Neue Pläne und alte Probleme der Metropolenverwaltung." *Verwaltungsarchiv* 98, no. 4: 505–25.

Schubert, D. 2002. "Wirklich ein Paradigmenwechsel? Das Programm und seine Vorläufer." In *Sociale Stadt: Ein politisches Programm in der Diskussion*, edited by C. Holl. Stuttgart: Deutsche Verlags-Anstalt.

Scott, A. J. 2002. "Industrial Urbanism in Late-Twentieth-Century Southern California." In *From Chicago to L.A.: Making Sense of Urban Theory*, edited by M. J. Dear. Thousand Oaks, CA: Sage.

Scott, A. J., J. Agnew, E. W. Soja, and M. Storper. 2001. "Global City-Regions." In *Global City-Regions: Trends, Theory, Policy*, edited by A. J. Scott. Oxford: Oxford University Press.

Scottish Executive. 2002. *Better Communities in Scotland: Closing the Gap*. Edinburgh: Scottish Executive.

Searle, G. H. 1996. *Sydney as a Global City*. Sydney: NSW Department of Urban Affairs and Planning.

———. 2002. "The Demise of Place Equity in Sydney's Economic Development Planning." *Australian Geographer* 33: 317–36.

Searle, G. H., and M. Bounds. 1999. "State Powers, State Land and Competition for Global Entertainment: The Case of Sydney." *International Journal of Urban and Regional Research* 23: 165–72.

Sellers, J. M. 2002. *Governing from Below: Urban Regions and the Global Economy.* Cambridge: Cambridge University Press.

Selznick, P. 1992. *The Moral Commonwealth.* Berkeley: University of California Press.

Senatsverwaltung für Arbeit, Soziales und Frauen. 2002. *Die Ausländerbeauftragte des Senats von Berlin, "Repräsentativumfrage zur Lebenssituation türkischer Berlinerinnen und Berliner."* Berlin: Senatsverwaltung für Arbeit, Soziales und Frauen.

Senatsverwaltung für Stadtentwicklung. 2004. *Quartiersmanagementgebiet.*

Sergiovanni, T. J. 2000. *The Lifeworld of Leadership.* San Francisco: Jossey-Bass.

Sharpe, L. J. 1995. *The Government of World Cities: The Future of the Metro-Model.* Chichester, UK: John Wiley.

Shaw, K., and G. Davidson. 2002. "Community Elections for Regeneration Partnerships: A New Deal for Local Democracy?" *Local Government Studies* 28, no. 2: 1–15.

Short, J. R., and Y. Kim. 1999. *Globalization and the City.* Essex, UK: Longman.

Short, J. R., C. Breitbach, S. Buckman, and J. Essex. 2000. "From World Cities to Gateway Cities: Extending the Boundaries of Globalization Theory." *City* 4: 317–40.

Siemiatycki, Myer. 2006. "The Multicipal Franchise and Social Inclusion in Toronto: Policy and Practice." Community Social Planning Council of Toronto and Inclusive Cities Canada. October.

Siemiatycki, M., and E. Isin. 1997. "Immigration, Diversity and Urban Citizenship in Toronto." *Canadian Journal of Regional Science,* Spring and Summer, no. 1, 2, 73–102.

Silverman, R. M. 2003a. "Progressive Reform, Gender and Institutional Structure: A Critical Analysis of Citizen Participation in Detroit's Community Development Corporations (CDCs)." *Urban Studies* 40, no. 13: 2731–50.

———. 2003b. "Citizens' District Councils in Detroit: The Promise and Limits of Using Planning Advisory Boards to Promote Citizen Participation." *National Civic Review,* Winter, 3–13.

Simmie, J., ed. 1994. *Planning London.* London : UCL Press.

Simpson, D. 2004. "The New Machine: Mayor Richard M. Daley of Chicago." In *Inside Urban Politics: Voices from America's Cities and Suburbs,* edited by D. Simpson. New York: Pearson Longman.

Sisk, T., ed. 2001. *Democracy at the Local Level.* Stockholm: International IDEA.

Sit, V. F. S. 2001. "Increasing Globalization and the Growth of the Hong Kong Extended Metropolitan Region." In *Globalization and the Sustainability of Cities in the Asia Pacific Region,* edited by F. Lo and P. J. Marcotullio. Tokyo: United Nations University Press.

Skelcher, C. 2005. "Jurisdictional Integrity, Polycentrism, and the Design of Democratic Governance." *Governance* 18, no. 1: 89–110.

Skelcher, C., N. Mathur, and M. Smith. 2005. "The Public Governance of Collaborative Spaces: Discourse, Design and Democracy." *Public Administration* 83, no. 3: 573–96.

Smart, A. 2002. "The Hong Kong/Pearl River Delta Urban Region: An Emerging Transnational Mode of Regulation or Just Muddling Through?" In *The New Chinese City: Globalization and Market Reform,* edited by J. R. Logan. Oxford: Blackwell.

Smith, D. A., and M. Timberlake. 1995. "Conceptualising and Mapping the Structure of the World System's City System." *Urban Studies* 32: 287–302.

Smith, G. E., and C. A. Huntsman. 1997. "Reframing the Metaphor of the Citizen-Government Relationship: A Value-Centered Perspective." *Public Administration Review* 57, no. 4: 309–18.

Smith, M. J. 1993. *Pressure Power and Policy: State Autonomy and Policy Networks in Britain and the United States.* Pittsburgh, PA: University of Pittsburgh Press.

Smith, M. P. 2001. *Transnational Urbanism: Locating Globalization.* Malden, MA: Blackwell.

Smith, M. P., and J. R. Feagin. 1987. *The Capitalist City: Global Restructuring and Community Politics.* Oxford: Basil Blackwell.

Smith, N. 1984. *Uneven Development.* Oxford: Basil Blackwell.

———. 1996. *The New Urban Frontier: Gentrification and the Revanchist City.* London: Routledge.

———. 2002. "New Globalism, New Urbanism: Gentrification as Global Urban Strategy." *Antipode* 34, no. 3: 427–50.

Smitha, K. S. 2006. "Urban Governance and Bangalore Water Supply & Sewerage Board (BWSSB)". Unpublished paper, Institute of Social and Economic Change, Bangalore.

SMSB (Shanghai Municipal Statistics Bureau). 2003, 2004, 2005. Shanghai statistical yearbooks. Beijing: China Statistical Publishing House.

Soos, G. (2006) "Introduction." In *The State of Local Democracy and Central Europe*, edited by G. Soos. Budapest: LGI-OSI.

Sorensen, E., and J. Torfing. 2005. "The Democratic Anchorage of Governance Networks." *Scandinavian Political Studies* 28, no. 3: 195–218.

South West Inner City Community Network (SWICN). 1999. *The South West Inner City Network Action Plan 1999–2006: Critical Perspectives. An Agenda for Action.* Dublin: SWICN.

———. 2002. *Liberties/Coombe Integrated Area Plan: Minority Report.* Dublin: SWICN.

Souza, C. 2001. "Participatory Budgeting in Brazilian Cities: Limits and Possibilities in Building Democratic Institutions." Working Paper No. 28, University of Birmingham Project in Urban Governance, Partnership and Poverty, Birmingham, UK.

Soysal, Y. N. 1994. *Limits of Citizenship: Migrants and Postnational Membership in Europe.* Chicago: Chicago University Press.

Spearrit, P. 2000. *Sydney's Century.* Sydney: UNSW Press.

Spearrit, P., and C. De Marco. 1988. *Planning Sydney's Future.* Sydney: Allen & Unwin.

Sposati, A. 1996. *Social Exclusion/Inclusion Map of the City of São Paulo.* Unpublished document. São Paulo.

Sproats, K., and P. May. 2004. *Struggles for Town Hall: Local Government Reforms in Sydney.* Unpublished manuscript, University of Western Sydney, Sydney.

Stadt Dortmund, Statistik und Wahlen. 1999 *Dortmunder Statistik: Die Dortmunder.*

Stadt Planungsamt Dortmund. 2003. *Urban II: Zukunftsinitiative für die Dortmunder Nordstadt.* Unsigned government publication, Dortmund, July.

State of Illinois. 1998, 1999. *Compliance Audit Report.*

Statistisches Landesamt. 2003. *Hamburg Regionale Stadtteil-Profile.* Unpublished government document. Hamburg: Behörde fuer Inneres.

Statistics Canada. 2001. Census of Canada. http://ww12.statcan.ca.

Staubach, R. 1995. *Lokale Partnerschaften: Zur Erneuerung benachteiligter Quartiere in deutschen Städten.* Werkbericht No. 35 der Arbeitsgruppe Bestandverbesserung.

Steinmo, S., K. Thelen, and F. Longstreth, eds. 1992. *Structuring Politics: Historical Institutionalism in Comparative Analysis.* Cambridge: Cambridge University Press.

Stewart, M. 2003. "Towards Collaborative Capacity." In *Urban Transformation and Urban Governance. Shaping the Competitive City of the Future,* edited by M. Boddy. Bristol: Policy Press.

Steyvers, K., M. Breuillard, and H. Reynaert. 2003. "Elected Mayor Reforms and Local Leadership in Belgium, Britain and ." Paper to the ECPR conference, Marburg, September 18–21.

Stilwell, F., and P. Troy. 2000. "Multilevel Governance and Urban Development in Australia." *Urban Studies* 37, no. 5–6: 909–30.

Stivers, C. 1994. "The Listening Bureaucrat: Responsiveness in Public Administration." *Public Administration Review* 54, no. 4: 364–9.

Stoecker, R. 2003. "Understanding the Development-Organizing Dialectic." *Journal of Urban Affairs* 25, no. 4: 493–512.

Stone, C. 1980. "Systematic Power in Community Decision Making." *American Political Science Review* 74: 978–90.

———. 1989. *Regime Politics: Governing Atlanta, 1946–1988.* Lawrence: University Press of Kansas.

———. 1995. "Political leadership in Urban Politics." In *Theories of Urban Politics,* edited by D. Judge, G. Stoker, and H. Wolman. Thousand Oaks, CA: Sage.

———. 1989. *Regime Politics: Governing Atlanta 1946–1988.* Lawrence: University of Kansas Press.

———. 1993. "Urban Regimes and the Capacity to Govern: A Political Economy Approach." *Journal of Urban Affairs* 15: 1–28.

———. 2004. "Its About More than the Economy After All: Continuing the Debate about Urban Regimes." *Journal of Urban Affairs* 26, no. 1: 1–19.

————. (Forthcoming). "Who is Governed? Reconsidering How Local Citizens Fit into the Political Order of Cities." In *Theories of Urban Politics*, edited by J. S. Davies and D. L. Imbroscio. London: Sage.

Stren, R. 1978. *Housing the Urban Poor in Africa. Politics, Policy and Bureaucracy in Mombasa, Kenya.* Berkeley: Center for International Studies, University of California.

————. 2003a. "Decentralization and Development: Rhetoric or Reality?" Paper presented to the Canadian Political Science Association, Halifax, Nova Scotia.

————. 2003b. "Introduction: Toward the Comparative Study of Urban Governance." In *Governance on the Ground. Innovations and Discontinuities in Cities of the Developing World*, edited by P. L. McCarney and R. Stren. Baltimore: John Hopkins University Press.

Sundberg, J. 1991. *Participation in Local Government: A Source of Social Deradicalization in Scandinavia.* Bergen, Norway: LOS.

Svara, J. 1999. "The Shifting Boundaries between Elected Officials and City Managers in Large Council-Manager Cities." *Public Administration Review* 59, no. 1: 44–53.

Svara, J. H. 2001. "The Myth of the Dichotomy: Complementarity of Politics and Administration in the Past and Future of Public Administration." *Public Administration Review* 61, no. 2: 176–83.

————, ed. 1994. *Facilitative Leadership in Local government. Lessons From Successful Mayors and Chairpersons.* San Francisco: Jossey-Bass.

Sweeting, D. 2002. "Leadership in Urban Governance: The Mayor of London." *Local Government Studies* 28, no. 1: 3–20.

Sweeting, D., R. Hambleton, C. Huxham, M. Stewart, and S. Vangen. 2004. "Leadership and Partnership in Urban Governance: Evidence from London, Bristol and Glasgow." In *City Matters. Competitiveness, Cohesion and Urban Governance*, edited by M. Boddy and M. Parkinson. Bristol: Policy Press.

Swianiewicz, P. 2005a. "Cities in Transition: From Statism to Democracy." In *Urban Governance and Democracy: Leadership and Community Involvement*, edited by M. Haus, H. Heinelt, and M. Stewart, pp. 102–29. London and New York: Routledge.

————. 2005b. "Poland: A Time of Transition." In *Comparing Local Governance: Trends and Developments*, edited by B. Denters and L. E. Rose, pp. 100–18. Basingstoke, UK: Palgrave Macmillan.

————. 2006. "Innowacyjność w zarządzaniu samorządami gminnymi województwa warmińsko-mazurskiego." In *Konkurencyjnoś i innowacyjność Warmii i Mazur*, edited by W. Dziemianowicz, M. Juchniewicz, W. Samulowski, and K. Szmigiel. Olsztyn, Poland: Urząd Marszałkowski.

————, ed. 2001. *Public Perception of Local Governments.* Budapest: LGI-OSI.

————, ed. 2002. *Consolidation or Fragmentation? The Size of Local Governments in Central and Eastern Europe.* Budapest: LGI-OSI.

Swianiewicz, P., and A. Mielczarek. 2005. "Parties and Political Culture in Central and Eastern European Local Governments." In *Faces of Local Democracy*, edited by G. Soos and V. Zentai, pp. 13–79. Budapest: LGI-OSI

Swianiewicz, P., A. Mielczarek, and U. Klimska. 2006. "Uneven Partnerships: Polish City Leaders in Search of Local Governance." In *Legitimacy and Urban Governance*, edited by H. Heinelt, D. Sweeting, and P. Getimis, pp. 114–30. London and New York: Routledge.

Swyngedouw, E. 1997. "Neither Global nor Local: 'Glocalization' and the Politics of Scale." In *Spaces of Globalization*, edited by K. R. Cox. New York: Guilford.

————. 2000. "Authoritarian Governance, Power, and the Politics of Rescaling." *Environment and Planning D: Society and Space* 18: 63–76.

Swyngedouw, E., and G. Baeten. 2001. "Scaling the City: The Political Economy of 'Glocal' Development—Brussels' Conundrum." *European Planning Studies* 9: 827–49.

Tardanico, R., and L. R. Menjívar, eds. 1987. *Global Restructuring, Employment and Social Inequality in Urban Latin America.* Coral Gables, FL: North-South Center Press.

Taylor, M. 2003. *Public Policy in the Community.* Basingstoke, UK: Palgrave Macmillan.

Taylor, P. J. 1994. "The State as Container: Territoriality in the Modern World-System." *Progress in Human Geography* 18: 151–62.

———. 1995. "Would Cities and Territorial States: The Rise and Fall of their Mutuality." In *World Cities in a World-System,* edited by P. L. Knox and P. J. Taylor. Cambridge: Cambridge University Press.

———. 1996. "On the Nation-State, the Global, and Social Science." *Environment and Planning A* 28:1917–28.

———. 2004. *World City Network: A Global Urban Analysis.* London: Routledge.

TCC (Toronto City Clerk). 2003. *City of Toronto Plan of Action for the Elimination of Racism and Discrimination.* Toronto: City Council.

TCF (Toronto Community Foundation). 2001a. *Vital Signs 2001.* Toronto: TCF.

———. 2001b. *Municipal Voter Turnout.* Toronto: TCF.

———. 2004. *Vital Signs 2004.* Toronto, Canada: TCF.

Teaford, J. 1984. *The Unheralded Triumph: City Government in America, 1870–1900.* Baltimore: Johns Hopkins University Press.

———. 1990. *Rough Road to Renaissance: Urban Revitalization in America, 1940–1985.* Baltimore: Johns Hopkins University Press.

Tedros, A., and F. Johansson. 2006. "The Interplay of Central and Local. Social Inclusion Policy from Above in Swedish Cities." In *Legitimacy and Urban Governance. A Cross-National Comparative Study,* edited by H. Heinelt, D. Sweeting, and P. Getimis. Abingdon, UK: Routledge.

Téllez Ardila, A. M. 1995. *Las Milicias Populares Otra Expresión de la Violencia Social en Colombia.* Bogotá: Rodríguez Quito Editores.

Terry, L. D. 1998. "Administrative Leadership, Neo-Managerialism, and the Public Management Movement." *Public Administration Review* 58, no. 3: 194–201.

Thake, S. 2001. "Regeneration Professionals." *Regeneration,* June 8.

Thornley, A. 2003. "London: Institutional Turbulence but Enduring Nation-State Control." In *Metropolitan Governance and Spatial Planning,* edited by W. Salet, A. Thornley, and A. Kreukels. London: Spon.

Thurmaier, K., and C. Wood. 2002. "Interlocal Agreements as Overlapping Social Networks: Pick-Fence Regional Agreements as Overlapping Social Networks." *Public Administration Review* 62, no. 5: 585–98.

Tiebout, C. M. 1956. "A Pure Theory of Local Expenditures." *Journal of Political Economy* 44: 416–24.

Togeby, L. 1999. "Migrants at the Polls: An Analysis of Immigrant and Refugee Participation in Local Elections." *Journal of Ethnic and Migration Studies* 25, no. 4: 665–94.

Toki, H. 2003. *Tokyo Mondai no Seijigaku* [The Politics of Tokyo Problem]. 2nd edition. Tokyo: Nihonhyoron-sha.

Tolbert, P. S., and L. G. Zucker. 1996. "The Institutionalization of Institutional Theory." In *Handbook of Organization Studies,* edited by S. Clegg, C. Hardy, and W. R. Nord. London and Thousand Oaks, CA: Sage.

Toro-Vanegas, J. I., J. A. Bernal-Medina, A. E. Pérez-Florez, and W. Gómez-Agudelo. 1993. *La Tercera Pata de la Mesa: Historia y Cultura de los Trabajadores de Sofasa.* Medellín: Sintrauto.

Townsend, J. G., G. Porter, and E. Mawdsley. 2002. "The Role of the Transnational Community of Non-Government Organisations: Governance or Poverty Reduction?" *Journal of International Development* 14, no. 6: 829–39.

Townshend, J. V. 1984. "A Mayor for Paris: An Early Example of Decentralisation." *Public Administration* 62, no. 4: 455–72.

Travers, T. 2004. *The Politics of London. Governing an Ungovernable City.* Houndmills, UK: Palgrave Macmillan.

Uitermark, J. 2003. "'Social Mixing' and the Management of Disadvantaged Neighbourhoods: The Dutch Policy of Urban Restructuring Revisited." *Urban Studies* 40, no. 3: 531–49.

UN (United Nations). 2002. *Report of the World Summit on Sustainable Development.* New York: UN.

———. (2004) *World Urbanization Prospects. The 2003 Revision. Data Tables and Highlights.* New York: UN Department of Economic and Social Affairs.

UNCHS. (United Nations Centre for Human Settlements). 1996. *An Urbanizing World. Global Report on Human Settlements 1996.* New York: Oxford University Press for UNCHS.

———. 1999. *Global Urban Indicators Database.*

———. 2001. *Cities in a Globalizing World: Global Report on Human Settlements 2001.* London: Earthscan Publications.

UNDP (United Nations Development Programme). 1994. *Governance for Sustainable Human Development,* Washington, D.C.: UNDP. UN-HABITAT. 2003. *The Challenge of Slums. Global Report on Human Settlements 2003.* London: Earthscan.

———. 2006. *State of the World's Cities, 2006/7.* London: Earthscan.

Uprimny-Yepes, R. 2001. "Violence, Power and Collective Action: A Comparison between Bolivia and Colombia." In *Violence in Colombia 1990–2000: Waging War and Negotiating Peace,* edited by C. Bergquist, R. Peñaranda, and G. Sánchez. Wilmington, . DE: Scholarly Resources Books.

Van den Berg, L., J. van der Meer, and P. M. J. Po. 2003. "Organizing Capacity and Social Policies in European Cities." *Urban Studies* 40, no. 10: 1959–78.

Verba, S., K. Schlozman, and H. Brady. 1995. *Voice and Equality: Civic Voluntarism in American Politics.* Cambridge, MA: Harvard University Press.

Vidal, A., and D. Keating. 2004. "Community Development: Current Issues and Emerging." *Journal of Urban Affairs* 26, no.2: 125–137.

Vogel, R. K. 2000. "Decentralization and Urban Governance: Reforming Tokyo Metropolitan Government." In *Urban Government Governance Around the World,* edited by B. A. Ruble, R. E. Stren, J. S. Tulchin, and D. H. Varat. Washington, D.C.: Woodrow Wilson International Center for Scholars.

Wainwright, H. 2003. *Reclaim the State. Experiments in Popular Democracy.* London: Verso.

Walker, R. 1996. "Another Round of Globalization in San Francisco." *Urban Geography* 17: 60–93.

Walsh, K. 1995. *Public Services and Market Mechanisms. Competition, Contracting and the New Public Management.* London: Macmillan.

Walton, J. 1977. *Elites and Economic Development: Comparative Studies on the Political Economy of Latin America.* Austin: University of Texas Press.

Wang, Z. 2004. *2010 World Expo: Innovation and Development- Shanghai Development Report 2003–2004.* Shanghai: Shanghai Finance University Press.

Ward, K. 2003. "Entrepreneurial Urbanism, State Restructuring and Civilising 'New' East Manchester." *Area* 35, no. 20: 116–27.

———. 2005. "Geography and Public Policy: A Recent History of 'Policy Relevance.'" *Progress in Human Geography* 29, no. 3: 310–19.

Ward, P. M. 1995. "The Successful Management and Administration of World Cities: Mission Impossible?" In *World Cities in a World-System,* edited by P. L. Knox and P. J. Taylor. Cambridge: Cambridge University Press.

———. 1998. *Mexico City.* Chichester, UK, and New York: John Wiley.

Weber, R. 2003. "Equity and Entrepreneurialism: The Impact of Tax Increment Financing on School Finance." *Urban Affairs Review* 38, no. 5: 619–44.

Wegener, A. 2002. *City of Toronto: A Case Study on Strategy in Development.* Toronto: City of Toronto.

Whitaker, G. P., L. Altman-Sauer, and M. Henderson. 2004. "Mutual Accountability between Governments and Nonprofits: Moving Beyond 'Surveillance' to 'Service.'" *American Review of Public Administration* 34, no. 2: 115–33.

White, J. W. 1998. "Old Wine, Cracked Bottle? Tokyo, Paris, and the Global City Hypothesis." *Urban Affairs Review* 33: 451–77.

Wickware, D. 1999. "Mas Allá de la Economía Formal." *La Era Urbana* (Otoño), pp. 5–9.

Wilks-Heeg, S. 1996. "Urban Experiments Limited Revisited: Urban Policy Comes Full Circle." *Urban Studies* 22: 1263–79.

Williams, R. 1973. *The Country and the City.* London: Chatto and Windus.

———. 1977. *Marxism and Literature.* Oxford: Oxford University Press.

Williamson, O. E. 1981. "The Economics of Organization: The Transaction Cost Approach." *American Journal of Sociology* 87, no. 3: 548–77.

———. 1985. *The Economic Institutions of Capitalism.* New York: Free Press.

Wilson, D. 1998. "From Local Government to Local Governance: Recasting British Local Democracy." *Democratisation* 5, no.1: 90–115.

Winston, D. 1957. *Sydney's Great Experiment: The Progress of the County of Cumberland Plan.* Sydney: Angus and Robertson.

Wolf, F. M. 1986. *Meta-Analysis: Quantitative Methods for Research Synthesis.* Beverly Hills: Sage.

Wolfson, J., and F. Frisken. 2000. "Local Response to the Global Challenge: Comparing Local Economic Development Policies in a Regional Context." *Journal of Urban Affairs* 22: 361–84.

Wollmann H. 1999. "La décentralisation en Angleterre, en France et en Allemagne. De la divergence historique à la convergence?" *Revue francaise d'administration public,* no. 90 (April–June): 313–28.

———. 2000. "Local Government Systems: From Historic Divergence Towards Convergence? Great Britain, France and Germany as (Comparative) Cases in Point." *Environment and Planning C: Government and Policy* 18, no. 1: 33–55.

———. 2003. "Public Sector Reforms and Evaluation: Patterns and Trends in an International Perspective." In *Evaluating Public Sector Reforms,* edited by H. Wollman. Aldershot, UK: Elgar.

World Bank. 1992. *Governance and Development.* Washington, D.C.: World Bank.

———. 2000. *Entering the 21st Century. World Development Report 1999/2000.* Washington: World Bank.

———. 2002. *The Little Data Book.* Washington: World Bank.

———. 2005. *A Better Investment Climate for Everyone. World Development Report 2005.* Washington: World Bank.

World Urban Forum. 2006. "Participatory Budgeting: Building Participatory Democracy and/or Improving Municipal Finance." Networking event, Vancouver, June 21.

WSROC (Western Sydney Regional Organisation of Councils). 2005. *Futurewest Greater Western Sydney Regional Planning and Management Framework: Final Report.* Blacktown: Western Sydney Regional Organisation of Councils.

Yahagi, H. 2002. "Tokyo no Risutorakucharingu to 'Sekai-toshi' no Yume Futatabi [Restructuring of Tokyo and the dream of world city again]. In *Daitoshiken eno Kousou* [New Strategy for Metropolitan Restructuring], edited by T. Kodama. Tokyo: University of Tokyo Press.

Yeh, A., and F. Wu. 1996. "The New Land Development Process and Urban Development in Chinese Cities." *International Journal of Urban and Regional Research* 20, no. 2: 330–54.

Yeoh, B. S. A., and T. C. Chang. 2001. "Globalising Singapore: Debating Transnational Flows in the City." *Urban Studies* 38: 1025–44.

Yergin, D., and J. Stanislaw. 1999. *The Commanding Heights: The Battle between Government and the Marketplace That Is Remaking the Modern World.* New York: Simon and Schuster.

Yeung, H. W. 2000a. "State Invervention and Neoliberalism in the Globalizing World Economy: Lessons from Singapore's Regionalization Programme." *Pacific Reivew* 13: 133–62.

———. 2000b. "Neoliberalism, Laissez-Faire Capitalism and Economic Crisis: The Political Economy of Deindustrialisation in Hong Kong." *Competition and Change* 4: 121–69.

Young K., and L. Grayson. 1988. "Abolition: The Reform of Metropolitan Government in England 1983–1986." Birmingham and London: Universities of Birmingham and London.

Yue, C. S. 2001. "Singapore: Global City and Service Hub." In *Globalization and the Sustainability of Cities in the Asia Pacific Region,* edited by F. Lo and P. J. Marcotullio. Tokyo: United Nations University Press.

Zachary, G. P. 2000. *The Global Me. New Cosmopolitans and the Competitive Edge.* New York: Public Affairs.

Zakaria, F. 2003. *The Future of Freedom: Liberal Democracy at Home and Abroad.* New York: W. W. Norton.

Zeigler, D. J., and S. D. Brunn. 1980. "Geopolitical Fragmentation and the Pattern of Growth and Need." In *The American Metropolitan System: Present And Future,* edited by S. D. Brunn and J. O. Wheeler. New York: John Wiley.

Zhang, T. 2000. "Public Participation in China's Urban Development." In *Handbook of Global Public Policy,* edited by S. Nagel. New York: Marcel Dekker.

———. 2002. "Urban Development and a Socialist Pro-Growth Coalition in Shanghai." *Urban Affairs Review* 37, no. 4: 475–99.

Zhu, J. 1999. "Local Growth Coalition: The Context and Implementation of China's Gradualist Urban Land Reforms." *International Journal of Urban and Regional Research* 23, no. 4: 534–48.

Zimmerman, J. F. 2003. "The Greater London Authority: Devolution or Administrative Decentralization?" Paper presented to the Annual Meeting of the American Political Science Association, August.

Zivier, E. R. 1998. *Verfassung und Verwaltung von Berlin.* Berlin: Verlag Arno Spitz.

Index

Lightning Source UK Ltd.
Milton Keynes UK
UKOW050324030212

186568UK00001B/16/P